Gospel
of
John

Gospel
of
John

The Life and Light of Man
Love to the Uttermost

F. B. Meyer

CHRISTIAN LITERATURE CRUSADE
Fort Washington, Pennsylvania 19034

CHRISTIAN LITERATURE CRUSADE

U.S.A.
Box 1449, Fort Washington, PA 19034

CANADA
Box 189, Elgin, Ontario KOG 1EO

First Lakeland edition 1970
This Printing 1988

ISBN 0-87508-346-3

PRINTED IN THE UNITED STATES OF AMERICA

PREFACE

THIS IS the Gospel of the Divine Life of Jesus. The eagle has always been its recognised emblem, as denoting its sublime and heavenly character. And, clearly, in its diction, its insight into the deepest truths, its repeated testimony to the Glory and Deity of our Lord, it holds a unique place among the records of His life.

It soars. It holds fellowship with the Throne. Its eyrie is in the Heart of God. And yet, in one of its aspects, this Gospel is as much the record of the Man Christ Jesus, as of the Only-begotten Son; and for this it is of inestimable worth to all who desire to follow in His steps.

There is no part of Scripture more conducive to the culture of the inner life; and it is under this aspect that it is considered in the following pages.

This attempt to present some of the unsearchable wealth of this Gospel may be compared to a shell-full of water dipped up by a child from a vast fresh-water lake; but such as it is, it is commended to the people of God with the desire that it may be used by the Divine Spirit to bring them into a deeper knowledge of Life, Light, and Love, as they are in Jesus Christ our Lord.

F. B. MEYER.

THIS BOOK

ON

THE UTTERMOST LOVE OF CHRIST

IS DEDICATED

TO

MY DEAR WIFE,

WHOSE PATIENT CARE OF OUR HOME HAS ENABLED ME
TO WRITE SO MUCH AND TRAVEL SO FAR
IN HIS SERVICE.

CONTENTS

10 CONTENTS

1

THE WORD

"In the beginning was the Word, and the Word was with God, and the Word was God."—JOHN i. 1.

HOW AMAZING is the opening of this Gospel! The writer does not stay to introduce himself, to mention his name, or give proofs of his trustworthiness. With singular abruptness, with no attempt to substantiate his own claims or the claims of this marvellous treatise, he casts it into the teeming world of human thought and life, as Jochebed launched the cradle on the bosom of the Nile.

Did he feel that the matter of the book would sufficiently vindicate its truthfulness; and that it would authenticate itself as bread, and light, and water, and spring flowers do? Did he feel that the Spirit who inspired it might be left to care for it? To ask such questions is to suggest the answer. But is there not a marvellous audacity in the casting forth of this Gospel, unannounced, unauthenticated by the recommendations of great names? Yet the result has vindicated the Evangelist. For, as the experience of the Church grows—nay, as our own experience grows—new depths of beauty and truthfulness reveal themselves in its pages, and compel belief in all whose hearts are pure enough to recognise the Divine.

Our writer does not name the gross errors of his time, which were beginning to obscure the dawn of our holy faith, as clouds steal up upon a too radiant sunrise. Why should he preserve these flies in amber? It is enough for him to announce, positively and dogmatically, the Truth; sure that the conscience of man would not fail to recognise her face and the accents of her voice, and eventually turn from all others to cleave to her alone.

Nor can we wonder that the fisherman of Galilee was able thus to write for all the world to hear. Truths of universal importance are perceived less by the intellect than by the heart. Things which are hidden from the wise and prudent are revealed to babes. An intense religious conviction will stimulate the action of all the faculties; as a jar of oxygen quickens into brilliant coruscations the burning phosphorus. But how much must we not attribute to the teaching of that blessed Spirit, who found congenial work in glorifying the Lord through the pen of his dearest friend and aptest pupil! Very majestic are the opening words, and this designation of our Lord:—

THE WORD. We need not ask whence this term came. It may have been a pebble from the brook of Old Testament Scripture, or a phrase borrowed, as Neander suggests, from the current talk of Ephesus, where this Gospel was written about the year A.D. 97. But, whencesoever it came, it is here re-minted by the Spirit of God, and is most significant.

As words utter thought, so does Christ utter God.—A man, newly arrived from the busy outer world, sits among his family, absorbed and rapt in thought. Wife and child are hushed into a great stillness as they look upon his face, which tells a tale of inner conflict; as the foam-flecked surface of a mountain stream reveals the agony of its boulder-broken career. They cannot even guess what oppresses him until he opens his lips and speaks. The friends who gathered to the consecration of the angel-heralded boy had no idea by what name the aged priest would call him, till the trembling hand indented the wax of the writing-tablet with the Divinely-appointed name of Christ's forerunner.

So man had not known God, unless Christ had uttered Him. An Egyptian temple bore this inscription on its portico: "I am He that is, and was, and shall be; and no mortal has ever lifted my veil." A profound Eastern thinker, in the very dawn of the world's life, cried: "Oh that I knew where I might find Him! . . . Behold, I go forward, but He is not there; and backward, but I cannot perceive Him." An altar in Athens, the brain of the world, was erected to "the unknown God." But Christ uttered God. "No man hath seen God at any time; the only-begotten Son, which is in the bosom of the Father, He hath declared Him."

There are three ways in which Christ has uttered God, as these introductory verses prove: in Creation; in his Teaching; and in his Incarnation.

God is Life.—Not simply living, in contrast to dead idols; but life-giving. The fountain of life ever rises from the depths of the abysmal Godhead. Yet that life had been an unknown quantity, had not the Word uttered it in creation, which his hands have wrought; so that the universe is a poem (in the strict meaning of that word) wrought out of the majestic substance of God's underived and eternal Being.

God is Light.—But the light had been undiscovered, because insufferable, unless the Word had shed it forth on created vision, revealing yet tempering its beauty, passing it through the luminous and yet shrouding veil of his words.

God is Love.—Love is the essence of his being, and all love everywhere is the far-travelled beam and ray of his heart (Eph. iii. 15, R.V. *mar.*). But that love had never been realised, unless the Word had embodied it in a human life, with caresses for little children, tears for broken hearts, tender pity for the lost, agony unto death for mankind. Lift up your eyes and hearts, and behold with devout rapture your glorious Lord, uttering the depths, the hidden depths of God (1 Cor. ii. 10, 16). He has not only done so, but He will continue to do so through all ages, as we are able to bear it (John xvii. 26). We have only yet, at his feet, commenced to learn the alphabet, the first broken syllables of the Divine Science; but it is probable that the ages of eternity are to witness an eternal progression in this sublime theology. Our knowledge ever increasing our capacity to know; our capacity ever leading to fresh hunger; our hunger ever appropriating the blessedness of the fourth Beatitude. Remember the majestic Apocalyptic vision, in which the seer beheld Christ riding forth on his snow-white steed, his eyes as flame, his head girt with many crowns, his vesture dipped in blood; but this is the name by which He was known —a name symbolic of his eternal ministry—*his name is called the Word of God* (Rev. xix. 13).

Before illustrating in detail our Lord's three-fold utterance of the Father, there are one or two thoughts suggested by the sublime opening sentences of this Gospel which we do well to notice.

I. THE ETERNITY OF THE BEING OF THE LORD JESUS.—"In the beginning was the Word." Is there not here an evident reference to the opening of the Book of Genesis, "In the beginning God created the heaven and the earth." But what a contrast! At that moment, described as the beginning, and which may be pushed back far enough to include all the demands of modern geologists, you do not find the heavens and the earth, which as yet are not; but you do find the Word already in existence. The words in the one case expressly exclude the eternity of matter; but in the other they expressly include the eternity of the Word. Moses strikes the chord to descend the stream of Time; John strikes it to look out on the expanse of Eternity lying beyond created things, but in which the Word was already existing.

It is not so difficult to wend one's way slowly back into the past, or to imagine the successive ages during which the world was being prepared for man's habitation. But when we reach the place where the links of the time-chain stop, and we stand at the first moment of the creation of time and matter, and look out into the void on the other side—it is then that thought staggers and gives way.

There is no light to guide us—sun, moon, and stars are not created. No spirit to lead us; cherubim have not begun to love, or seraphim to burn. No stepping-stone for our feet; for space is unoccupied save by the all-pervasive presence of God. No sufficient unit of measurement; since, when arithmetic has reached its uttermost, the mighty aggregate is but a mote floating in the sunshine of the Being of God. What shall we do then, as we learn the pre-existence of the Word, but worship Him?

That mind must indeed be slow to perceive which does not recognise that what is eternal must be Divine. If it be true that before the mountains were brought forth, or the earth was formed, the Word was, then, from everlasting to everlasting He must be God. Wherefore "unto the King eternal, immortal, invisible, the only wise God, be honour and glory for ever and ever."

II. THE PERSONALITY OF THE LORD JESUS.—"He was with God." We may not at first perceive the significance of this clause, any more than the casual tourist sees the importance of an embrasure in the fortifications where sheep browse, and soldiers stand at ease. But if ever there should come again days of conflict, like those which swept across the early Church, in which men should assert that the Word was but a momentary and impersonal manifestation of God, we should instantly revert to this significant clause, and cry, It cannot be—*The Word was* WITH *God. The same was in the beginning* WITH *God.*

The preposition selected by the Evangelist is very significant. It means communion with and movement towards. It denotes the intimate fellowship subsisting between two, and well befits the intercourse of the distinct Persons of the one and ever-blessed God. "The face of the everlasting Word was ever directed towards the face of the everlasting Father." He was in the bosom of the Father. "He makes the Divine glory shine outwardly because He is filled inwardly. He contemplates before He reflects. He receives before He gives."

We are not then surprised to hear the Divine colloquy: "Let *us* make man"; or to learn that Jesus knew the Father (x. 15). How could He do other, when, "trailing clouds of glory behind him," He proceeded and came forth from God?

Let us never forget that our Saviour, who lived, and died, and rose, and is our familiar Friend, is a distinct personality, who was before all worlds, and will be unchanged for evermore. This is what we want. It is not enough to give us an abstraction, an ideal, a word. Our hearts crave One, and, blessed be God, they may have One who may be a living, bright reality.

> *More present to faith's vision keen*
> *Than any earthly object seen;*
> *More dear, more intimately nigh,*
> *Than e'en the dearest earthly tie.*

III. THE DEITY OF OUR LORD JESUS.—"The Word was God." He is not said to be *the* God; for that assertion would ascribe to the Son the totality of the Divine Being, and contradict the doctrine of the Holy Trinity. And He is not said to be *Divine*, which would lessen the emphasis. But He is said, distinctly and emphatically, to be God. "God manifest in the flesh."

He was born of a woman; yet He made woman. He ate and hungered, drank and thirsted; yet He made corn to grow on the mountains, and poured the rivers from his crystal chalices. He needed sleep; yet He slumbers not, and needs not to repair his wasted energy. He wept; yet He created the lachrymal duct. He died; yet He is the ever-living Jehovah, and made the tree of his cross. He inherited all things by death; yet they were his before by inherent right.

And what is the Word to us?—In his first Epistle, the holy Apostle tells us his intention in declaring that which he had seen and heard and handled of the Word: it was that others might share with him his fellowship with the Father and the Son. And fellowship means partnership, a common participation in a common stock; and, in this case, a blessed share in the very life and light and love of God.

But how many such things become ours? There is a sense in which the orator, the thinker, the friend, is able to infuse himself into us by his fervid and quickening words. And is there not also a deep sense in which Jesus is the Word of God, because through Him God is ever pouring Himself into our hearts and lives? As a man puts himself into his words, and by them communicates himself to others, so has God embodied Himself in Jesus, and those who receive the Son receive the Father, who has sent Him (Matt. x. 40).

As the Father has put Himself into the Word, so has the Word put Himself into his words. "The words that I speak unto you, they are spirit, and they are life." Live then in meditation on the *words* of Jesus; so that his being may become infused into yours, and through the Word the eternal Father may come and make his abode within you (John xiv. 23).

So shall you be inspired by the very life and indwelling of God, and be lifted increasingly out of the time-sphere into the eternal; into fellowship with all noble souls, with all saints and angels, with all who, through all worlds, live on Him, who is the Eternal and Divine Word, ever-blessed, ever to be adored.

2

THE WORD IN CREATION

"The same was in the beginning with God. All things were made by Him; and without Him was not any thing made that was made."
JOHN i. 2, 3.

IT IS A distinct loss to many of us, whose lives are spent in the heart of great towns, that we miss those enlarged conceptions of Nature which are suggested by the far horizon of the sea; the outlines of distant hills; the snowy summits of the Alps; or the outspread panorama of woods, rivers, and pasture lands. And the privation affects us principally in this, that contracted views of Nature sometimes carry with them more limited views of God's being and glory than if we dwelt in habitual contemplation of the vastness and splendour of his Creation.

One of the first thoughts which occur to the devout mind, on emerging from the straitened conditions of city life into the larger world of Nature, is to reproach itself that it has entertained such dwarfed ideas of God. And whilst it does not abate one note of the tender strain, *Our Father*, it adds to it the deep bass of the Psalmist's awe, "Great is the Lord, and greatly to be praised, and his greatness is unsearchable."

Such thoughts open straight on the passage before us. We look, and rightly, on the Lord Jesus, as Brother, Saviour, Friend; but do we always conceive of Him as invested with the awful glory of Godhead? We cannot be too intimate and tender in our relations to Him; but we do well sometimes to go outside to see what He has done, that we may know how great He is, who is so near and dear.

"THE SAME WAS IN THE BEGINNING WITH GOD."—At first this seems merely to sum up and repeat the previous verse. But it does more. It tells us that He who was before the beginning was also at the beginning; and that face-to-face fellowship, which had subsisted before all worlds, was in active exercise at the august moment when the ever-blessed Trinity proceeded to create. "Let *us* make man."

"ALL THINGS MADE BY HIM."—The Greek is very significant: *All things became, i.e.,* came into being, *through Him.* This *became* is in striking contrast to the *was* of the previous verse, and indicates the passage from nothingness to being. *Became, i.e.,* all things emerged out of nothing at the creative fiat. There is a beautiful parallel in another passage of this Gospel, in which our Lord affirms, "Before Abraham *became*, I am" (viii. 58).

The preposition "through" is always used of the office of our blessed Lord in the work of creation (I Cor. viii. 6; Col. i. 16; Heb. i. 2) and is full of meaning. It leaves God the Father as the origin and source of all things, so that the elders are justified in their perpetual ascription of worship before his throne (Rev. iv. 11); but God the Son, our Lord, is the organ through which the creative purpose moves. Through Him the infinite God utters Himself in his works.

In the ancient record of creation with which the Bible opens, two phrases are to be noticed—*created* (Gen. i. 1, 21, 27) and *God said* (which occurs ten times). Into each of these we must now read the announcement of this text. Note those three acts of creation. Whatever else we may concede to men of science, we must insist on retaining these for God, and ascribing them to our Lord. And whenever God is said to speak, we must listen for the well-known accents of a voice we love.

It was the voice of Jesus that said, "Let there be light"; and the new ethereal substance spread like a haze of glory through space. It was the hand of Jesus that made the expanse between cloud and sea, in which the birds fly (Gen. i. 20). It was the bidding of Jesus that drove the turbulent waters from the land into the ocean-bed which He had scooped. It was the thought of Jesus to splinter the mountain peaks; to thrust the frozen glacier down into the valley by inches; to pour forth the rivers; and to shake down over the hills the falling foam of the cataract. It was Jesus that carpeted the earth with flowers, and devised the innumerable sorts of plants, and planted the noble forest-trees. It was Jesus that rolled the stars on their orbits, to tell forth the glory of God, and to keep time on Nature's dial. It was Jesus that made the fish to flash in the deep; the reptile to creep in the brake; the firefly to glance through the forest; the birds to sing in the woods; flocks to browse on the hills; and herds to traverse the prairies.

It was Jesus who created the human nature which, in after years, He was to assume. He made man in the image and after the likeness of what He was Himself to be in the fullness of time. What strange emotions must have filled his heart as He built up that first man from the red earth!

"WITHOUT HIM WAS NOT ANYTHING MADE THAT WAS MADE."—This is added to make exceptions impossible. The Greek is very emphatic. *not one single thing.* You must not except angels because too great, nor emmets because too small; not worlds because too ponderous, nor dust-atoms because too insignificant; not electricity, nor light, nor heat, because too ethereal, nor the ichthyosaurus, nor the toad because too ungainly. The hand of inspiration writes the name of Jesus where artists put theirs, beneath all things in heaven and on earth, visible or invisible, whether they be thrones, or dominions, or principalities, or powers.

> *"Not a flower*
> *But shows some touch, in freckle, streak, or stain,*
> *Of his unrivalled pencil."*

"IN HIM WAS LIFE."—We must light up these words by his own: "As the Father hath life in Himself," the source and fountain of all being, "so hath He given to the Son" that is, in the subordinate position which He voluntarily assumed for the purposes of creation and redemption—"to have life in Himself." All life is of God in its original reservoir; and all life is in the Lord Jesus, as a cistern of supply, from which all demands for life of every sort are met.

All life—natural and physical, animal and intellectual, spiritual and religious—is in Him. The whole universe of living things was not simply brought into being by Christ; but it is kept in existence and sustained in living beauty by the constant communications of his fullness —as a vale is kept in fertile beauty, luxuriant with vegetation, by the spray of a perennial waterfall. As the Word, He creates; as the Life, He sustains. As the Word, He declares God; as the Life, He communicates his essence. "As the Word, He is God without us; as the Life, He is God within us."

Apart from Christ, you may exist; but you have no life in you. "He that hath not the Son of God, hath not life." You may have many attractive and amiable qualities, much that is correct in behaviour, and beautiful in appearance; but you have no *life*.

But if you are in Christ, opening all your being to Him, door behind door, back into the most sacred chambers of your being, so that He has free and unhindered entrance into your entire nature; then, as the Nile, descending through the channels cut by the Egyptian peasantry, bears life and fertility into their gardens and cornfields, so will He bring his own life, the life of God, "life indeed," into you, and though you were dead, yet shall you live (John xi. 25).

(1) *Say "No" to your Self-life.*—It is in proportion as we curtail the self-life that we increase the Christ-life. Michael Angelo was wont to say of the chippings that fell thick on the floor of his studio, "While the marble wastes, the image grows"; and as we chip away ourselves by daily watchfulness and self-denial, the life of Jesus becomes more manifest in our mortal body (2 Cor. iv. 10, 11). A rosebud may be grafted into a briar; but the briar must never be allowed to put forth its own shoots beneath it, or they will drain away its strength: therefore the gardener must ever mercilessly bud them off. After the same manner must we deal with every assertion of self. "I have been, and am, crucified with Christ . . . Christ liveth in me."

THE WORD IN CREATION

(2) *Yield to the Christ-life.*—This is the law of all natural forces; if you want them to help you, you must yield them obedience. In using them, you are less their master, and more their slave, than you suppose. They are willing to toil for you day and night; but on the one condition that you should study and obey the laws of their operation. And it is so with respect to that greatest of all forces, the life of the Son of God. It is throbbing in every believer's heart. And the difference between Christians consists in this, that some ignore its presence, or, at least, are very careless of its promptings, whilst others are ever on the alert to translate into instant obedience, the tiniest impressions. As you yield to the Spirit of life which is in Christ Jesus, you become more conscious of his blessed strivings within, they increase in number and power, and bear you upward, as when the ocean pours its tides up an estuary or river, and reverses the direction of its flow.

(3) *Replenish waste by going again to the source.*—There is so much leakage in us that we speedily exhaust what we have received. The oxygen absorbed by the blood is soon exhausted by its contact with the waste of our tissues, and needs to be drawn back through the veins to be soaked again in the air of our lungs; so does the freshness of the Divine life within us need to be daily renewed, and we must go back to Him in whom it is ever brimming, that out of his fullness we may receive, and grace for grace. It is in the reading of his Word, in prayer, and in waiting upon his ordinances, especially in the Lord's Supper, that the inner life becomes thus replenished and "fulfilled with his grace and heavenly benediction."

"THE LIFE WAS THE LIGHT OF MEN."—All true life is luminous. The lowest forms of physical life are light; as when the keel of the vessel ploughs up the wave, and leaves long lines of phosphorescent glory in its wake. And who does not know of some community which has been lit up by the glow of some noble life! During his life in our mortal body, Jesus could not be hid; no bushel of obscurity sufficed to conceal Him. And now, when He enters into contact with any soul or life, that soul begins to glow, that life to shine.

We are like so many unlit candles, some of coarser and some of more refined material, clustered together in a darkened chamber, but not one of us able to dispel its gloom, or cope with its dense obscurity; but just so soon as we touch Jesus Christ, or are touched by Him, we begin to sparkle and shine. His Life is Light. "Arise, shine! for thy light is come." "Awake thou that sleepest, and arise from the dead, and Christ shall give thee light."

These then are our closing reflections:

(1) How great must He be, through whom this great universe was made, who was one with God the Father in its inception, and one in its execution! He could not have been less than divine, or the infinite God

could not have found adequate expression through his means. Only the Infinite can be the channel for the Infinite.

(2) We may learn something of the beauty of his mind. The beauty sleeping in a seed reveals itself by the colours of the flower as they unfurl to the sun, and the fragrance that fills the air. The beauty in the unexplored heart of a friend reveals itself in the verses we suddenly light upon, or the books which bear his name. The beauty of the artist's mind is discovered in the pictures or statues which he has produced. And what revelations are made to us of the beauty of the conceptions of our Lord, as we arm our eyes with telescope or microscope, and study the infinite above or the infinite beneath!

(3) We can trace some lingering remnants of the grandeur of our original nature, in that we ourselves, sinful and fallen though we be, are able to admire the works of his hands, and to repeat his "very good" of all that we behold of his power and skill. Devils seem devoid of this power; for they are pictured as haunting uninhabited and desolate places, roaming through desert places, and infesting the ruined heaps of the past.

(4) We can understand the miracles and parables better. In the one, our Lord was simply re-asserting his original power over nature; as when Ulysses returned after years of wandering, and bent with ease the bow which had defied the efforts of all who had essayed to use it in his absence. And in the other, He simply read out the meaning which He had hidden in vines, and seeds, and natural processes; for all things around us are made after the pattern and type of spiritual realities.

(5) We may be sure that He who made can and must redeem. It is impossible to suppose that He through whom all things were made could stand by and see them vitiated and spoilt by sin, without making a single effort to arrest the progress of the devastator, and to restore the universe to its pristine beauty and order. We are not then surprised to learn that the same paragraph which tells us that all things were created by Him, also tells us that it pleased the Father by Him to reconcile all things to Himself, whether they be things in earth or things in heaven (Col. i. 16–20).

He who is the Alpha must also be the Omega; He who created by a word must redeem by his blood; He who originated must see that He is not robbed of the fruits of his toil; He who said, "Behold, I make," must also say, "Behold I make all things new."

3

The Word as Light

"That was the true Light, which lighteth every man that cometh into the world."—John i. 9.

It is not for us to attempt to celebrate the Praise of Light. What a wonderful conception it was of the mind of God! How delicate the loom of that creative skill on which it is constructed day by day! And how complete an argument for the divine workmanship is afforded by the adaptation between the element of Light and the crystalline gate of the eye by which it enters man's soul! (Luke xi. 34–36.)

Themes like these rather become such as our great epic bard, whose blindness made him more sensible to the value of that which he had lost, and whose lofty genius could alone find terms to describe its worth. Or, better still, Light might well be the subject of a sonnet by that angel minstrel who composed the majestic Psalm of Creation which is perpetually sung before the throne (Rev. iv. 11). But neither could proceed long with his task without rising from the material substance—for ethereal as light seems to be to our dull sense, it is still material—to that glorious Being who made it as a parable and emblem of his Divine nature. "God is Light, and in Him is no darkness at all" (1 John i. 5).

But the glory of the Father's nature is of such insupportable splendour that it would be impossible for any creature that He has made to behold and enjoy it; and it is very consolatory to be told in the opening verses of the Epistle to the Hebrews that our Lord Jesus is "the effulgence of his glory" (Heb. i. 3, R.V.). The human eye could not bear the full splendour of the sun's heart or surface of golden cloud, but it can bear the far-travelled and diluted ray; so, though we could not behold the nature of God in its direct and original manifestation, we can behold his glory in the face of Jesus Christ (2 Cor. iv. 6). And for this reason we hail thankfully and adoringly the announcement that the Word is the Light.

I. The Characteristics of the Light.—*Light is pure.*—It is so pure that evil cannot stain or impurity defile it. It will pass through a fœtid and poisonous atmosphere without contracting taint, or carrying a germ of poison with it, as it issues forth to pursue its ministries of mercy beyond. So pure was our blessed Lord. Evil fled abashed before Him. He gauged the power of temptation, not by yielding in a hair's breadth, but by resisting and overcoming it. When He died, after thirty-three years' close contact with men, his spirit was as absolutely stainless as when He came into the world. And the instant effect of his life within our hearts will be to kindle a purity as sweet and chaste and unearthly as his own.

Light is gentle.—With each dawn its tides revisit us after having traversed the abyss with inconceivable speed; but its wavelets break so gently that they fail to shake the dewdrop from its blade of grass or the trembling petal from the overblown rose. Even the gossamer of the spider's web does not quiver as the sunbeams strike it. And how apt a symbol is here of that gentle goodness which made the shepherd-boy great, which leads the flock into the pastures of tender grass, and fans with anxious care the dull sparkle of smoking flax! And when His love is shed abroad in our hearts, it begets a corresponding gentleness in judgment, speech, and behaviour. All true Christians are *gentle folk.* "The wisdom that is from above is first pure, then peaceable, *gentle,* easy to be entreated, full of mercy" (James iii. 17).

Light is all-pervasive.—It kindles a line of watch-fires on the pinnacles of an Alpine range; but it does not neglect the hill-slopes up which the plovers follow its last retreating beams. It gilds the golden roofs of the palace; but it glides through prison-bars to sparkle in the tear-drops of the repentant prodigal. It lights the good man to his work, and the bad man to his home after the unholy revels of the night. Nor is it otherwise with the loving-kindness of Christ, which misses none in its daily ministry, however poor, and sad, and lonely; which includes the evil and the good, the just and the unjust; which "lighteth every man that cometh into the world." And it is thus with those in whom his life repeats itself. They, too, are said to be "without partiality." Their lives resemble the sun and the rain (Matt. v. 45).

Light reveals.—It revealed to Jacob the deception practised on him by Laban under the cover of darkness. It revealed to the host of Midian the meagre force before which it had fled panic-stricken, misled by the noise of the crashing pitchers and the flashing of three hundred lights. In darkness the traveller lies down to spend the night beneath the open sky, in terror lest he may stray to the brink of the ravine; but the morning, with rosy finger, reveals that he has been sleeping within a stone's cast of his home. So does Christ reveal. He is the light of all our seeing. He not only lights up our inner sight, but He casts a light on God, and providence, and truth, and the mysteries of redemption, which, apart from Him, notwithstanding all our intelligence, had been obscure and unknown. In his light we see light. Light is whatsoever doth make manifest. Let us lift up our souls unto Him who is light, so that we may be filled and saturated with his nature and being, and made to glow with it in this dark world; as I have seen a certain kind of diamond, which, after having been held up for some short period in sunlight, has continued to sparkle like a star when carried thence into a darkened chamber. "We all, with unveiled face beholding as in a mirror the glory of the Lord, are transformed (*i.e.*, transfigured, it is the same Greek word as in Matt. xvii. 2) into the same image from glory to glory, even as from the Lord the Spirit" (2 Cor. iii. 18).

I. THE MINISTRY OF THE LIGHT.—*The Word was the Light of unfallen man in Paradise.*—In the glades of Eden two trees were planted; the one the tree of life, the other of the knowledge of good and evil. It is impossible not to see in these a lively representation of Him who is Life and Light, and who, from the first, must have been the organ and channel of Divine communication to mankind.

It was in the person of the Son that the ever-blessed God walked with our first parents in the cool of the day; conversed with them; uttered the memorable prohibition; sought them in their fall; and, with sad prevision of all that it must cost, foretold the ultimate triumph of the woman's Seed. Even then He rejoiced in the habitable part of the earth, and his delights were with the sons of men. Even then He was the Light of man's moral nature, teaching him all he knew, and prepared to lead him on to know the deep things which lay concealed as a landscape under a morning haze. Even then the Son had commenced his favourite ministry of manifesting the Name of his Father (Matt. xi. 27; John xvii. 26).

The Word was Light in the World amid the long dark ages which preceded the Incarnation.—"The Light shineth in darkness, and the darkness comprehended it not." There are two methods by which darkness is produced. The one by absence of light; the other by loss of sight. It is dark when the sun sets, and primæval darkness resumes for a brief parenthesis its ancient sway; but it is also dark when the eye is blind. And the darkness mentioned here is not the first, but the second.

There has never been an age in which the Divine Light has not shone over our world. Not Gospel light, not the light of revelation, not the light as we have it; but still, Light. And whatever light existed was due to the presence and working of the Lord Jesus. *He shone* in the good He did; giving rain from heaven, and fruitful seasons, and in the food and gladness with which He filled men's hearts, so that He left not Himself without witness (Acts xiv. 17). *He shone* in the clear testimony given since the creation, through the works of nature, to the everlasting power and divinity of God (Rom. i. 20). *He shone* in the intuitions of truth, which we call conscience, and which are his voice in the human breast, and are so evidently referred to here as the true light, lightening every man coming into the world (Rom. ii. 14, 15). *He shone* also in those great movements towards righteousness, which

seem to have swept from time to time over the heathen world. Whatever of truth there was in any of these must have been due to Him. It
was of the heathen that the Apostle spoke when he said: "That which
may be known of God is manifest in them; for God manifested it
unto them" (Rom. i. 19, R.V.).

But the light shone amid blind and darkened hearts, which could
not comprehend it. Though men knew God, they glorified Him not as
God, neither were thankful; and, as the result, "they became vain in
their reasonings, and their senseless heart was *darkened*" (Rom. i. 21).
Since they would not believe, the god of this world was permitted to
blind their eyes.

It is characteristic of this Gospel, and it well befits its theme, that so
much space is given to the story of the man born blind (ix.), for such
is really the condition of the race; and it is significant that that story
is prefaced by the announcement so constantly reiterated by the Lord,
"I am the Light of the world" (ix. 5; see also viii. 12; xii. 35, 46). A
family born blind; a race stricken with blindness, as Saul was, and
groping for someone to lead it by the hand; a vault, like that in which
the dead are buried, around which the sunlight plays, whilst not one
beam can enter—such is a picture of our race. "The Light shineth in
darkness."

The Word was the Light of the chosen people.—Throughout their
history God sent them prophets, rising up early and sending them,
that they might bear witness to the coming Light. They were not that
Light, but they came to bear witness to it (John i. 8); just as the moon
and planets bear witness to the sun while he is absent, though every
moment is bringing him nearer to close their reign. Of these John the
Baptist is here cited as the greatest and last.

We need not recapitulate their names—the evangelical Isaiah; the
plaintive Jeremiah; the seraphic Ezekiel; the abrupt Habakkuk; Amos
the herdman; and Haggai the priest. They are not all mentioned here;
but are summed up in the greatest of all, John the Baptist, of whom
Christ Himself said: "Verily I say unto you, among them that are born
of women there hath not risen a greater." All these were lights; John
was "a burning and shining lamp"; but their light was not their own,
it was derived from Him to whom they all bore witness. They spake
of Him. The testimony of Jesus was the spirit of prophecy. Overtop-
ping other men in the grandeur of their personal character, and by the
gift of the Spirit of Inspiration, they saw the day of Jesus, as mountain-
peaks first catch sight of the rising sun; and they declared to the world
of men below what glory was on the way.

What a new interest would come into our reading of the Old Testament Scriptures, if we always remembered that they testify of Jesus,
and glisten with light caught by anticipation from his life; and if we
sought to discover what the Master meant when, beginning at Moses

and all the prophets, "He expounded unto them in all the Scriptures the things concerning Himself."

As every dewdrop on the morning meadow glistens with the sunlight, each of them reflecting the whole sun, so do the paragraphs of the prophets flash with the presence of Jesus. They are beautiful in his beauty; strong in his strength; true in his truth. The lips may be those of man, the voice that of a prophet; but through all, the Word of God speaks, and the true Light shines. In the pages of the prophets the quick ear of love detects the accents of Him who spake as never man spake. Indeed, we are told expressly that the Spirit of Christ was in the prophets announcing that Gospel which is now preached throughout the world (1 Pet. i. 11, 12).

Finally, the Light became incarnate.—Too bright to be beheld, the Light of God curtained Himself in human flesh, as the face of Moses beneath his veil, or the Shekinah beneath the folds of the tabernacle. Such is the direct force of the word translated *dwelt* in verse 14. It might be better rendered *tabernacled*. But of this more afterwards.

And it is not possible to do more than take one brief glance at that bright world which awaits us, when, *in the ages of eternity, our blessed Lord will be still the Everlasting Light*. For it is written that the heavenly city will not need sun nor moon to shine in it, because the Lamb is the light thereof (Rev. xxi. 23). And so, from the first creation of man till the new creation; from the garden of innocence to the city of matured and tested holiness; from the origin of the race in its lonely and single representative to the untold myriads of his progeny who shall stand in the unsullied purity of robes washed white—always and everywhere, the Word of God is the Light of men, the *true* light, that is the archetypal light, of which all other lights are types and illustrations.

III. THE RECEPTION OF THE LIGHT.—(1) *Before his Incarnation* "He was in the world." In every spring, in every sunbeam, in every God-breathed thought, in every providence; walking up and down the aisles of his own temple; brooding over the teeming myriads of mankind. In Him they lived and moved and had their being. He was not an absentee from his own creation. In Him all things consisted and were maintained (Acts xvii. 28; Col. i. 17).

"And the world was made by Him." Mark this touching repetition of *the world*; we shall often meet with it again. It is used repeatedly, as when a bereaved parent, brooding over the sin or misfortune of some beloved child, repeats his name again and again. "O my son Absalom! my son, my son Absalom! O Absalom, my son, my son!" And see how the Holy Spirit emphasises the fact that our Lord was the organ through whom creation was wrought.

"And the world knew Him not." As though a man might build a splendid mansion—with frescoes on its walls, fountains splashing in marble wells, luxuriant furniture, exquisitely-planned grounds—put it in trust for the sick or destitute, go away for years, and on returning be denied admittance, or watched as an intruder; until, touching some secret spring, he showed such knowledge and power as to compel recognition of his claims.

It was a sorrowful confession, extorted from our Lord, by all his experiences, both before and after his Incarnation—"the world hath not known Thee." And it is confirmed by the Holy Ghost when He says, in the wisdom of God, "the world by wisdom knew not God." Alas for the poor world, vaunting its science and its pride, but not knowing that glorious Being who was in it from the first!

(2) *At his Incarnation.*—"He came unto his own, and his own received Him not." Throughout the Old Testament the Jews are spoken of as God's peculiar treasure; but here they are described as Christ's, because Christ is God. They were his by the calling of Abram; by the covenant of circumcision; by the passage of the Red Sea; by the desert discipline; by the education of history: but when He came to them, they cried, "We will not have this Man to reign over us."

"They received Him not." This is a note which we shall hear again; but in the meanwhile, the word seems carefully chosen to suggest that it was not a case of ignorance, but of wilfulness. They knew, or might have known, who He was; but they deliberately refused to enquire into his credentials, and they shut the door resolutely in his face. This is why they are a nation of weary-footed wanderers, bronzed by the sun of every clime, having everywhere a recognition, but nowhere a home.

(3) *Since the Incarnation.*—There has been no longer a dealing with nations, but with individuals. Many have received Him, rising above the general indifference around. Mary in the highlands of Nazareth; Elisabeth in the hill-country of Judæa; Simeon in the temple; Huldah the prophetess; and Zachariah the priest, are representatives of untold multitudes beside. And to as many as have thus received Him He has given the right to become the sons of God.

Stepping across the humble threshold of their hearts, He has suddenly thrown aside the garments of his great humility, which He had worn as a disguise and test. Then, rising in the full stature of his Divine Manhood, He has taken from out his skirts a parchment patent of sonship and heirship, and, handing it to the recipient and astonished spirit, has declared that from henceforth it may dare to reckon itself, without presumption, a child of God, and an inheritor of the Kingdom of Heaven.

And for lineage, it is revealed that all such may trace their descent past earthly parentage—"not of blood"; past natural instinct or desire —"not of the will of the flesh"; past human volition—"not of the will of man": to the thought, and purpose, and grace of the Eternal Father, to whom be glory for ever and ever.

4

THE WORD MADE FLESH

"The Word was made flesh, and dwelt among us (and we beheld his glory, the glory as of the only-begotten of the Father), full of grace and truth."—JOHN i. 14.

"THE WORD *became* flesh," thus the Revised Version better renders the original. But what a profound mystery these words cover!

Open the golden compasses of thought to measure, if it be possible, the distance between these two extremes, *the Word*, and *flesh*. The Word, the eternal and ever blessed Son of God; the fellow of Jehovah; able to utter God because Himself God; through whom all things were made. Flesh, a frail and transitory fabric woven from the dust, and destined to return to dust; limited to time and space; comprehending, as it does so evidently, not only the human body, but the entire human nature of which the flesh is the outward and visible embodiment. What verb shall unite extremes so infinitely removed? What link is there for these two?

The Word *made* flesh? It is true, but not enough.

The Word *was wrath with* flesh! So it might have been; but this is not the knot of union.

The Word *pitied* flesh! That had been marvellous, but also insufficient.

The Word *clothed* Himself with flesh! Even that were inadequate; for in that case He would only have borrowed a temporary disguise, which He might as easily have thrown off, and there had been no entire oneness.

No. THE WORD BECAME FLESH! He was the same Divine Being as before. He kept his place in the bosom of the Father during his earthly life (iii. 13). Though confined to time and space, He kept his identity with Him whose Being is beyond either. There was no break or cessation in the essential Oneness of his personality, even when He stooped to be born of the virgin mother. But, as far as we can understand it, though in the essence of his Being He underwent no change, yet He voluntarily gave up the Divine mode of existence, that He might assume the human, and might bear it with Him through death and resurrection to invest it ultimately with the Divine glory that He had with the Father before the worlds were made (xvii. 5).

Note, for a moment longer, that word *flesh.*—It seems to have been carefully selected, to show that the nature of the Lord Jesus sums up in itself all the different traits and attributes of our many-sided nature, sin excepted. If we had been told that the Word became a man, it would have seemed as if men only could have perfect sympathy with Him, or that his nature contained only the elements of manhood. But, since the word *flesh* is used, we feel that not one sex but both, not one age but all, not one race but the entire human family, may find its characteristic properties in his lovely glorious Being. No one form of human life has an exclusive right to Him. All forms of life find their counterpart in Him. All rays of colour blend their hues in the white light of his nature. All sides of love, like the double optics of a stereoscope, do but set forth that one infinite love which fills his heart.

"Christ gathers up in Himself the ideal virtues of man and woman, of boyhood and girlhood, of age and middle life," of European and Asiatic. All that is most noble and strong in men, all that is most graceful and tender in women, all that is most winsome and engaging in little children, all that is lovely in anyone, is to be found in our dear Lord in whom is neither Jew nor Greek, neither bond nor free, neither male nor female, since Christ is all and in all (Gal. iii. 28; Col. iii. 11).

This distinguishes Christianity from all religions beside. They are tribal, topical, limited in their range to the people among whom they have originated. Take Mohammedanism, for instance. It no doubt has some grains of precious truth, as, for instance, the unity of God; but it can never become a world-wide religion, because there are large portions of our common human nature which can find no response or representation in the character or teachings of Mohammed. To use the expression of another, "the mosaic of humanity is not totalized in him."

But Christ touches man at every point, man as man, through every grade and variety of manhood. There is no note in the great organ of our humanity, with the exception of the jarring discord of sin, which does not, when it is struck, awaken a sympathetic vibration in the mighty range and scope of the being of Christ.

This is the secret of that wonderful fascination which Jesus has for men. We feel that He can understand us. "He is touched with the feeling of our infirmities." "He is made in all things like unto his brethren." And as, we shall see in a moment, every man can find in Christ the complement of his nature, the supply of his deficiencies, the fullness for his need.

DWELT AMONG US.—*Tabernacled* is the better word. What is there here but an allusion to the wanderings of the desert, during which Jehovah dwelt in a tent or tabernacle, a pilgrim like the rest! Listen to his own words: "I have not dwelt in any house since the time that I brought up the children of Israel out of Egypt, even to this day; but have walked in a tent and in a tabernacle" (2 Sam. vii. 6).

All that was a symbol of eternal realities. The Tabernacle was a material representation of the great truth of the Incarnation. It was made after the pattern of the nature of our Lord, which, as the sublime

THE WORD MADE FLESH

antitype, was eternally present to the mind and thought of God. Well then might Jesus speak in the same breath of the temple and of his body (ii. 21). And well may the Holy Ghost here use the same comparison.

We are the pilgrim host. Our bodies are but frail, shifting tabernacles, to be as easily dissolved as a tent is struck (2 Cor. v. 1), and amidst us has been reared the true Tabernacle, which God has pitched and not man; and through which the Shekinah has shone, kindling the frail curtains of mortal flesh with dazzling radiance on its passage through their folds in waves of glowing glory.

There were times when the light that shone in the most holy place could not be confined there; but issued forth, and flooded the entire structure so that the multitudes without could discern its splendour. And so in the earthly life of our blessed Lord there were moments when the glory of the Only-Begotten of the Father broke through the limitations which He had assumed, and bathed his mortal body in transcendent light and beauty. Such a season was the Transfiguration, when even his garments became white as the light. Then were the Apostles "eye-witnesses of his majesty." Then did they behold his glory, "the glory as of the Only-Begotten of the Father."

WE BEHELD HIS GLORY.—It is as if the writer said, "There can be no mistake. The Lord was no mere appearance, or phantom, or vision of the imagination. My eyes are dimming now; but once they were bright and keen, and could not have been deceived. My head is white with the snows of many winters; but it often lay on his bosom. I can easily recall the accents of his voice; often have I felt the clasp of his hand. And if there is one day I remember above others, it is that in which He challenged us to behold his hands and his feet, and assure ourselves that it was not a spirit, but Himself. 'We have not followed cunningly devised fables'; and we could not have been mistaken as to the glory, which refused to be hid, but inevitably betrayed his divine power and Godhead."

FULL OF GRACE AND TRUTH.—Grace is mentioned three times in this paragraph; and it is the fitting climax to the golden series of revelations. The keynote of Nature was Order; of History, was Justice; of Conscience, was Righteousness; of Jewish revelation, as summed up in the name of Moses, was Law. But the keynote of the Incarnation was Grace—the unmerited love of God—which made itself of no reputation and took up the nature of man.

God's glory is his grace When Moses desired to behold his glory, this was the reply wafted back into his soul: "I will make all my goodness pass before thee, and I will proclaim the name of the Lord before thee; and will be gracious."

But it is grace allied with truth.—He is a just God and a Saviour. There is a bridal between his righteousness and his mercy. Deep down in the solid granite of everlasting truth are laid the foundations of the Temple, of which the doors stand ever open to welcome the *whosoever* of mankind. Who would wish it otherwise? Who would care for a love which contravened the most elementary conceptions of justice in our hearts, and which might one day have to yield to disturbing scruple and compunction?

OF HIS FULLNESS HAVE ALL WE RECEIVED.—The *all we* cannot only mean the writer himself and his fellow apostles who had seen the Lord, but all the believers of that early age, to whom he wrote, scattered in different places, and removed by sixty years from the death of Christ; and not them alone, but all who have become one with Him by a living faith.

The Apostle sheds an exquisite light on these words when he says, "It pleased the Father that in Him should all fullness dwell. In Him dwelleth all the fullness of the Godhead bodily. And in Him ye are made full" (Col. i. 19; ii. 9, 10, R.V.).

God longs for us to live full lives; and that we may, He has stored all his glorious resources into the nature of the Man Christ Jesus, so making them accessible and putting them within the reach of the weakest and most sinful of his children. Thus does the channel of the Nile bring water which is generated in the mountains of Central Africa, within reach of the Egyptian peasants, whose gardens are situated on the edge of the burning sands. Why then are we so content with poverty and emptiness? Let us receive out of his fullness. It is continually throbbing like an ocean against the walls of our hearts; it is for us to open and let it in, that it may cover the long unsightly reaches of ooze and sand.

Let us ask the Holy Spirit to teach us the blessed habit of taking what we need from hour to hour. The uplifted eye of faith will at any moment cause a tide of his fullness to enter, enriching, strengthening, and blessing the soul.

GRACE FOR GRACE.—Wave on wave. It is a mistake to rest on past or present experiences, eking them out with jealous care, lest they should run short. The best means of getting more grace is to use the grace we already have. It is the law of all life, especially of spiritual life: "To him that hath shall more be given, and he shall have abundantly."

We may not always perceive the flow of the golden oil of grace from its Divine reservoir. We may not be always sensible of the Divine communications. But if we claim them by a naked faith, and if we live up to the limits of what we have got, so as to become spendthrifts of our spiritual revenues, there will be no stint in the blessed stores with which we shall be enriched for ever.

5

THE WORD DECLARING THE UNSEEN GOD

"No man hath seen God at any time; the only-begotten Son, which is in the bosom of the Father, He hath declared Him."- -JOHN i. 18.

WITH THIS marvellous verse, the Evangelist brings to a close his sublime prologue. It is a befitting introduction to all that follows. Like some noble portal to a temple of transcendent size and beauty, it admits the reverent soul into this Divine Gospel, thrilling the heart, quickening the imagination, and preparing the thought for things which have not entered into the heart of man to conceive. Here is the seed-plot of the Gospel. Here is the standpoint from which the nature and ministry of the Lord are to be viewed. Here are struck those three keynotes —Life, Light, and Love—which, in different combinations, vibrate through the entire range of the writings of the Apostle John.

We believe in the Being of God. Vast as this universe is with depths and heights, and its immeasurable expanse, we believe that it is filled throughout with his mighty Spirit. He is everywhere. He knows everything. He can do all things. But the human heart pines to know what He is. Man seeks after God, groping in the dark, if haply he may feel after Him and find Him, and read the secret of his inner being. "What is God? What does He think and feel? What will He be to me?"

You send me to study Nature. But I find there nothing but his power and Godhead, his deeds, not his heart. And sometimes I am baffled by the apparent working of a malign power by which the creature is brought into subjection.

You send me to study Providence. But the march of God through the ages is so vast, and his footsteps so far apart, that they seem to be hidden in the sea, and his path in the dark waters; so that it is hard to understand the true trend and character of his dealings with the children of men.

You send me to decipher the Names of God. *El-Shaddai*, the God of Might, on whom difficulties which threaten to overwhelm us break harmlessly, as storms on the brow of the Matterhorn. *Jehovah*, the Unchangeable, who knows no shadow of turning; whose word is inviolable, and his covenant sure. *Jehovah Sabaoth*, the Lord of hosts, on whose bidding legions of bright spirits wait. But, after all, these names rather disclose the might and splendour of a sovereign, and do but increase my dread of Him as my sins come back to memory.

Is there nothing more? May I not see Him? Is there no open door of vision where I may stand and satisfy the hunger of my soul; no spot in all the wilderness where I may shelter behind a rock and catch a glimpse of his majesty as He passes by, escorted by the serried ranks of angel armies? "Oh that I knew where I might find Him, that I might come even to his seat!"

But it may not be! NO MAN HATH SEEN GOD AT ANY TIME. *Never yet.* Not Moses; for he was hidden under the hand of God, and saw not his face. Not Elijah; for God was not in the earthquake or fire. Not the favoured three; for the cloud of glory dazzled them with its splendour. And even in the Apocalyptic vision, the rapt gaze of the seer beheld only the circumambient halo as of the jasper and sardonyx stone. And if we were to search the annals of any other nation, we should receive from every quarter the reply, addressed by a grey-haired Indian to Sir John Franklin during one of the expeditions of that renowned explorer: "I am an old man now, but I have never seen God."

And the explanation is given in those memorable words of a later Scripture: "He only hath immortality, dwelling in the light which no man can approach unto, whom no man hath seen, nor can see." "The King eternal, immortal, invisible, the only wise God." If the vision of the glory of God as it was veiled by the human nature of our Lord was so awful, in its dimmed radiance of glory, that the beloved disciple fell at his feet as dead, what would not be the effect of its insufferable splendour on the nature of any created being! It is of God's mercy that there are as many dense curtains between Him and us as covered the tabernacle of old, and veiled the unearthly glory of the Light that shone there.

But, surely, there must be some satisfaction for this hunger of the soul to know God, and of that other hunger, more eager still and harder to bear, for love. Our hearts pine for God and for love. What will we not give to appease our yearning for love! This makes us seek so eagerly for human friendships; mourn so bitterly if they are withdrawn; feel so lonely if they come not within our reach. Oh that this great and invisible God were Love! But how can we know? Hush! the Word hath declared Him; hath told the secrets of his inner being; yea, more, hath let those inner secrets reveal themselves through his words and life.

I. THE QUALIFICATIONS OF THE WORD FOR DECLARING THE UNSEEN GOD.—(1) *His Eternity.*—This was indicated by John the Baptist (15). Our Lord was his cousin, younger by six months, and John had already been for eighteen months before the people when Jesus came from Nazareth to be baptized. Thus, in a very true sense, "our Lord came after him." But when the greatest of woman-born saw him approaching, he who had never quailed before the face of man, whether royal or priestly, lowered his erect bearing to a deep humility, and cried: "This one must take precedence of me; it is his by right, for He was before me." And so speaking, he is the spokesman of the entire prophetic band, whom he represents.

Ask Isaiah, the evangelic; or Abraham, the ancestor of the Jewish race; or Noah, standing on the green-sward of a new world; or Adam, the first man; or the oldest star that first glimmered on the bosom of the night; or the most ancient elder who stands at the foot of the eternal throne; and from each the reply comes back dimmer and fainter from ever further distances, *He was before me*.

Jesus is the Alpha; the beginning; the first. He was before time, as we have seen. As Isaiah tells us, He is the Father of Eternity. And therefore He is well qualified to declare God.

(2) *His Nature.*—"The only-begotten Son." Many ancient manuscripts give this phrase as *God only begotten*. God has many sons, but only one Son. Angels are sons by their creation. Penitent sinners are sons by regeneration and adoption. But our Lord Jesus is Son in an altogether unique and unrivalled sense. He is Son by generation. "Thou art my Son, this day have I begotten Thee" (Psa. ii. 7; Acts xiii. 33). And He is the *only* Son thus begotten.

It is a profound depth, for which our thought has no fathoming-line. But clearly this phrase indicates that our Lord Jesus shares in its fullness the very Nature of God. "He is a partaker of that incommunicable and imperishable essence which is sundered from all created life by an impassable chasm."[1] He is the object of such love as an Abraham might have felt to his son, his only son, Isaac; but multiplied by the difference which must ever part the finite from the infinite. He used the expression of Himself, because it constituted in Jewish speech the very strongest method of claiming equality with God. It was well understood in that sense by the Jews, who instantly charged Him with blasphemy, and sought to avenge so daring an assumption of Deity (v. 18).

Is it not significant that the humblest and meekest Being that ever trod on our world—the pattern of perfect holiness, whose perceptions as to the truth of his own being could not have been mistaken dared not withdraw a single iota of his claim, but died, rather than evade its entire force? (xix. 7). He could not abate those claims, because He thought it not robbery to be equal with God. He was ever conscious of his Divine oneness with God (x. 30). He knew whence He was (viii. 14). He lived in constant fellowship with God (x. 15). And therefore He was well qualified to declare Him.

(3) *His Intimacy with the Heart of God.*—"Which is in the bosom of the Father." At a Jewish table the guests reclined on couches in

[1] The late Canon Liddon.

such a way that one might easily lean back his head on another's breast. Of this privilege the beloved Apostle availed himself at the last opportunity which offered. The breast is near the heart. By this tender and sacred clue he helped himself, and has helped myriads in succeeding ages, to realize the deep love, the close intimacy, the perfect acquaintance, subsisting between the Word and the unseen God; so that He is well able to declare Him. "I know Him" (viii. 55). The preposition "in" might be rendered "into," as if there was an ever deeper and closer approximation.

(4) *His Human Nature.*—"The Word was made flesh." He was the Son of God; but throughout this Gospel He speaks of Himself repeatedly as the Son of Man. *Not* A Son of Man. *Not* the Son of A Man. But, as if He were the child, offspring, and representative of the entire human family—*the* Son of Man (iii. 14). Whilst, therefore, as the Son of God, He was able to know God perfectly, as the Son of Man He was able perfectly to express, unfold, and reveal Him; so that all might understand the deepest thought and being of the ever-blessed One.

II. THE MODE OF DECLARATION.—This is very wonderful. He spoke about God; corrected men's false conceptions; confirmed their vague and visionary hopes; and poured floods of light upon the mysteries of God's nature, which had been hidden from ages and generations.

His choicest revelations were made to the little inner group that gathered closest around Him. He gave them God's word. He manifested the name of God to the men who had been given Him out of the world. In tender, glowing words He made known to them all that was concealed from other eyes in that ever-blessed word, which the Jews dared not pronounce, Jehovah (xvii. 6, 14, 26). All that language could convey was conveyed in the words of the Word.

But He did more; He so emptied Himself, He became as to his human nature so utterly dependent on his Invisible Companion that the life of God declared itself through his. He did nothing of Himself, but what He saw the Father do. He lived by the Father. He spoke only what his Father said to Him. He made known only what He heard from his Father. His words were not his, but the Father's that sent Him. The very works He did were disclaimed by Him. Remember his emphatic declaration: "The Father which dwelleth in Me, He doeth the works" (v. 19; vi. 57; xii. 50; xiv. 10).

And thus, when Philip said to Him on one occasion, "Show us the Father," the demand elicited a sad and heart-weary reply, "Have I been so long time with you, and yet hast thou not known Me, Philip? He that hath seen Me hath seen the Father. Believest thou not that I am in the Father, and the Father in Me?"

This then was our Lord's way of declaring God. God wrought and spoke through his human life, that as men beheld its grace and truth, they were able to study as through a veil, or from a reflecting mirror, the very nature of the unseen God. In blessing little children; in welcoming the lost and desolate; in lessening human pain; in weeping true tears of sympathy; in bearing our griefs and carrying our sorrows; in dying for our sins; in seeking and restoring an erring disciple, as a gardener might lift up a flower bent downwards by the storm—in all these things, Jesus declared God, just letting the God that was in Him live through Him in each lovely act and tender word.

III. THE DECLARATION.—"The Father." From his first talk with the woman by the well to that other talk with women at the sepulchre, the one choice word with which he designated God was—Father (iv. 23; xx. 17). In that name He came. Of that name He spoke. By that name He taught us to commence our daily prayer. Into that name we must be baptized. Within that precious name, as a rampart of sure defence, we are to live. He is the Father's gift. Heaven is the Father's home. True worshippers are the objects of the Father's search. Humble hearts are the chosen dwellings of the Father's love. All who belong to Him are dear to the Father's heart. God is his Father, and the Father of all those who have received Him, and in doing so have obtained the right to become sons of God. Other men, as Paul said, may be his offspring; but they are sons.

Not orphans or desolate are we! Never lonely again! Never pining for a love which mocks our yearnings and evades our reach! Never roaming the universe to escape God, or dreading Him as unknown and unknowable! Never again shrinking from life for its solitudes, or from death for its mystery, or the hereafter for its terrors! But nestling ever in the strong, tender arms of a Father who pities us, and whose love is as much more sensitive than that of any earthly father—as his nature, thoughts, and ways are higher and better than ours; or as the fire is greater than the straw which is lit at its blaze (Eph. iii. 15).

What a blessed lot is this! Let us bathe our tried, fearful hearts in these rays of sunshine, with which Jesus has lit up life and death, earth and heaven; and, as the little child, in the dark tunnel or on the turbulent waves, forgets its alarm with its father's voice in its ear, its father's heart as pillow, its father's arms as encircling walls, so, amid the problems and perplexities of life and death, let us trust the Fatherhood of God, soft as a summer zephyr, deep as ocean depths, and be at peace.

6

THREE MEMORABLE DAYS

"I am the voice of one crying in the wilderness, Make straight the way of the Lord."—JOHN i. 23.

"Behold the Lamb of God, which taketh away the sin of the world."
JOHN i. 29.

"The two disciples heard him speak, and they followed Jesus."
JOHN i. 37.

BETHABARA lay beyond the Jordan from Jerusalem. The river there has a breadth of one hundred feet, and, except at the time of the winter floods, a depth of three to seven feet. It would, therefore, exactly suit the purposes of the great preacher, with his baptism of repentance. The almost tropical luxuriance of the valley is in striking contrast to the wilderness of sand and hill around.

The attention of the nation was as much arrested by his look as by his words. The spare form attenuated by fasting and austerity; the flashing eye, full of living energy; the unshorn Nazarite locks; the rough haircloth garment; the independence of much that other men hold needful; the thrilling herald voice, piercing like a two-edged sword to divide and discern soul and spirit. It is no matter for wonder, then, that the whole community was stirred; and that crowds poured forth to him from the neighbouring metropolis, as well as from the towns and villages clustering at the foot of the Lebanon.

This time of success and fame lasted for, perhaps, twelve or eighteen months. And then there happened the memorable events described in this paragraph, and which transpired on three following days (29, 35).

The greater number of those that flocked to hear the Baptist returned to their homes to discuss his words or to live out their new vows; but several of the flower of Israel attached themselves to Jesus permanently. Amongst them was the writer of this Gospel; and he was, without doubt, a witness of the events which he describes, the crisis of his own life, and the culminating point of the ministry of his earliest teacher.

I. THE FIRST DAY: SELF-ABNEGATION (19–28).—As the influence of John's preaching spread, it became impossible for the religious authorities to ignore it. The Sanhedrin especially, which is constantly referred to in this Gospel as *the Jews,* and which held itself entrusted with the religious interests of the nation, was compelled to take action. A deputation of Priests and Levites, principally derived from the Pharisee

36

party (24), was therefore arranged to go to the Jordan, make inquiries, and report. Their inquiries were to be twofold: first, who he was; secondly, why he baptized. The former question interested the whole council; the latter, the Pharisees, who were the ritualists of their day.

Imagine a vast circle. On the one side stands the herald of the new age, surrounded by the chivalry of a noble youth; on the other the greybeards, representing an order of things old and ready to vanish away. How breathless was the silence which followed the first inquiry! "Who art thou? Art thou the Christ?"

Thousands would have been glad to believe he was, and at a word would have unfurled the old standard of the Maccabees, and rallied to rid the land of the usurper. They had not, however, long to wait. Without a moment's vacillation he confessed, and denied not, but confessed:

"I am not the Christ."

"Who art thou, then? Malachi told us in his closing words, which have lit our path through the gloom of four hundred years, that the great prophet of Horeb should announce the Messianic day. Art thou Elijah?"

Had they asked if he preceded the Messiah in the spirit and power of Elijah, he must have answered in the affirmative; but to the question as they put it, there was only one reply:

"I am not."

There was yet another suggestion. "Moses said that God would raise up a Prophet like unto himself. The Prophet art thou?" "The abruptness of the question," says Bishop Westcott, "is remarkable."

And again, amid the hushed suspense, the Baptist, with increasing brevity, answered "No."

Each response must have been followed by the murmur of many voices discussing it. And the ardent disciples of the great preacher would have felt some little disappointment and chagrin. It seemed as if he were deliberately spurning the nation's homage, and missing the greatest opportunity of his career.

The suppositions furnished by the generally received Messianic programme were now exhausted; and it only remained to put some general question which should force the Baptist to define his own position. "Then said they unto him, Who art thou? that we may give an answer to them that sent us. What sayest thou of thyself?"

Then came an utterance, sublime in its humility: "I am only a voice crying amid the uninhabited places of the wilderness, Prepare a way for the King."

And this humility was characteristic of John, though he was the greatest of woman-born. He knew that he was *not* the Light, but sent to bear witness of it; *not* the Sun, but the star that announces the dawn, and wanes in the growing light; *not* the Bridegroom, but the Bridegroom's friend; *not* the Shepherd, but the porter to open the door into the fold (iii. 27-30; x. 3).

This humility is as rare as it is fascinating. We are all so apt to use our relationship to Christ as a means of enhancing our own importance, and attracting attention. Though we formally ascribe the supremacy to our Lord, we are elated when our name is on every lip, and our work in every thought, even though we should never have been heard of had it not been for Him. But there was nothing of this in John. He had the lowest possible conception of himself. Whilst all men mused in their hearts whether he were the Christ, he was ever heralding the Coming One. As they magnified the worth of his baptism, he declared that it was inferior to the Messiah's, as water is to fire in cleansing properties. When they trembled before his searching words, he spoke of the great Husbandman, who, fan in hand, was about thoroughly to purge his floor. The motto of his inner life seems to have been, "I must decrease." Repeatedly he avowed himself unfit even to loose the sandal-thong of Him whose herald he was.

Two things led him to this blessed condition.—In the first place, he realized that a man can receive nothing, except it be given him from heaven; and that therefore all popularity, gifts, and influence, are precious talents to be administered with the best possible stewardship (iii. 27). And in the second place, he had seen the Lord, as was clear from the answer he gave to the further inquiry of the deputation concerning his right to baptize.

"It is quite true," said he, in effect, "that I am not the Christ, nor Elijah, nor that Prophet; but listen! Though ye know it not, the Messiah is already come, and I have seen Him. He has stood on these banks. He has mingled with these crowds. He has descended into these waters. He is standing amongst you now. The new era has dawned. And therefore I administer baptism, the sign and initiation of that long-expected time."

What awe must have settled down on the people! How they must have looked at each other, wondering of whom he spake! Could it be that at last the day had come of which kings and prophets and righteous men had spoken, but died without seeing! And can we wonder at the humility of the speaker?

We need to cultivate more of this lovely spirit, content to stand in the shade and cast a light on the blessed Lord; to be voices witnessing for Him, whilst the speaker's form is draped in gloom. But probably nothing but close friendship with the Bridegroom of souls will ever bring this about. We must live nearer to Him, catching the glow of his love, baptized into its furnace heat. Oh, to love Him, to listen for his footfall with a lover's hushed spirit, to find our heaven only in his love, and in the thought that He is loved! Then we shall be timid of attracting a single thought to ourselves which might have found its way to

Him. Then we shall be eager to hoard up all the love and devotion which men give us, that we may cast them as crowns at his feet. Then we shall be willing to be pedestals from which his beams shine the farther; as the slender, graceful curves of the lighthouse tower are unseen, whilst from its lantern the reflectors flash beams of light far out to sea. It is only to those thus humble as little children that God reveals the true character of his Son. Thus it was with John the Baptist.

II. THE SECOND DAY; CHRIST-DESIGNATION (29-34).—"The next day John seeth Jesus coming to him." He was probably coming straight from the scene of the temptation. For forty days He had been alone, with no companionship save that of wild beasts, amid the sterile hills which stretch for miles on either side of the Dead Sea. Directly John saw Him, he knew Him. "This is He of whom I said, He that cometh after me is become before me, for He was before me." How did John know Him?

It is probable that, though cousins, they had not met till some six weeks before. John had spent his years in the seclusion of the deserts, Jesus in the highlands of Galilee. Therefore John said, "I knew Him not." Was it one of the providential arrangements of the only wise God, that the Christ and his forerunner never met until Jesus came to Jordan to be baptized of John, lest it should be said they were acting in collusion? Or even if John may have known Him as his cousin (i.e., after the flesh), yet he knew Him not as the Baptizer with the Holy Ghost, or the Son of God. But He who sent him to baptize with water had revealed to him a sacred sign by which he should recognize the Lord whom he announced. For that sign he had watched and waited patiently for a long time. Thousands passed through his hands; but as yet he had not beheld it, and the months seemed long, as they slowly passed away.

At last Jesus presented Himself at the Jordan. John would have hindered Him, indeed "was hindering Him". He, doubtless, knew of the events which had preceded His birth; had heard of "that Holy Thing" which had been born; was familiar with his blameless, holy life; and desired, therefore, to debar Him from a rite which implied confession of sin. He felt that he had himself more need to be baptized as a sinner, than to administer the baptism of repentance for the remission of sins to Him, who was, so far as observation went, sinless.

His objections were, however, silenced by the appeal to him to do his part in bringing in the everlasting righteousness, which Daniel identified with the mission of the Messiah. "Thus it becometh us to fulfil all righteousness."

It was probably the custom that the candidate for John's baptism, either audibly or silently, should confess his sins ere he submitted to the sacred rite. But in this case, having no sins of his own, our Lord would probably make a vicarious confession, confessing the sins of the nation, with which, there and then, as the sacrificed lamb He identified Himself. It was the Jewish custom to set apart four days before the lamb was to be sacrificed in the Passover; and thus there may have been an anticipation of this solemn act of our Lord's baptism in the river Jordan, the river of judgment.

As He emerged from its waters, the long-expected sign was given. The Spirit descended on Him from heaven like a dove. We cannot but recall the ancient record of the deluge, and the ark, and the dove which found no place for her rest. Here at last there was a home in which the dove-like Spirit might take up an abode. Here, at least, was one heart in which He, who had been long an exile, might settle. From the waste of waters He came to the sacred Ark.

Twice over we are told that "He abode on Him." No fitful enduement this! No transient baptism! No ephemeral experience! For us, too, as for Him, there is an abiding experience to be enjoyed—an experience of spiritual grace to break on us; not to wane, as in the case of some of the Old Testament heroes, but to increase in ever-growing power from year to year, until we are filled unto all the fullness of God.

We may not stay to note the energy with which the Spirit drove Him into the wilderness to be tempted. How marvellous that union of brooding gentleness and irresistible driving force! As if the blessed Spirit—who had waited with the patience of God for four thousand years, while, in one dispensation after another, man was continually overcome by the tempter—now that the Second Man was come, impelled Him to the victory which He foreknew. It was from this conflict that He returned on the second of these memorable days.

For six weary weeks the Baptist had eagerly scanned the faces of the crowds to discover that face. But hitherto in vain. At last he descried it—worn with conflict and fasting, but radiant with victory; and as he saw it, he announced the Christ: "This is He of whom I spake. The same is He which baptizeth with the Holy Ghost. Behold the Lamb of God, which beareth away the sin of the world."

Dean Milman suggests that when John, beholding Jesus as He came to him, said, "Behold the Lamb of God, which taketh away the sin of the world!" he alluded to flocks of lambs, intended for the forthcoming Passover, then passing from the rich pastures of Perea to Jerusalem by the ford near the scene of the Baptist's labours. But surely there is a deeper thought. John was clearly a deep student of Isaiah's prophecies. He cannot but have been quite familiar with that chapter which reads like a fifth Gospel, as it foretells how the servant of the Lord would be led as a lamb to the slaughter, an allusion which, of course, was based on the offering of the morning and evening lamb, and on the great Paschal Feast, which lay at the foundation of the national history.

We cannot stay to trace the complete analogy between the lambs and the Lamb, between the Passover and the supreme event of our Redemption. The points of likeness and contrast are deeply interesting. But we must let that witness of the Holy Ghost, through those human lips, have its due weight with us. Evidently the main aspect in which we are to view our Divine Lord, is in his sacrificial character. "The Lamb as it had been slain" must be *beheld* both here and hereafter, in this world and in all worlds. Not his character, however fair; not his words, however much light they cast on the mysteries of life and death; not his miracles, however strong their testimony to his Divine mission: but his appointment to bear the sin of the world, *this* is the primary aspect in which we are to behold Him.

Look into these words; the Gospel glistens in them, as the whole sun in a single dewdrop. They tell us that the sacrifice of the cross is the outcome of the thought and preparation of the infinite God. Jesus is the Lamb of God. They remind us that his propitiation for sin is not for ours only, but for *the whole world.* They give a clue to the cause of that mysterious anguish which at times overwhelmed Him. They describe the attitude which we should ever adopt of beholding Him—an attitude by which we are able to appropriate the nutriment of his flesh and blood, of which the paschal supper was a type. O blessed Lamb! what shall we say *of* Thee or *to* Thee? Words fail us. Thou wast made sin for us. Thou hast washed us from our sins in thy blood. Thou has put away sin by the sacrifice of Thyself. Thou art longing that every soul of man should know and rejoice in thy yearning love, thy glorious work. We praise, and adore, and worship Thee. Worthy is the Lamb that was slain!

But remember ever to unite the double burden of John's preaching. We need not only blood, but fire. It is much to be justified, but we need to be sanctified; much to know of the atoning death, but we need union with the Lamb in his resurrection life; much to have the blood sprinkled on the inner shrine, but we need that the Shekinah fire should burn there with quenchless power; much to have the baptism of water, but at the best that is negative, and we need something positive, searching, quickening, and God-like.

After all, John was right. Christ is the greater Baptizer. Beyond death and the grave He received the Spirit, that He might shed Him forth. And now He stands among us whom He has redeemed, eager that, having washed us in his blood, He may complete what He has begun with that holy baptism of which John spake, and which is as much our privilege as the cleansing of the blood. Ah! brethren and sisters, *we have need to be baptized of Him.* Not the blood without the fire; not the fire apart from the blood. Not the Christ of Calvary only, but the Christ of the throne. Not pardon alone, but deliverance and salvation.

But let us remember that just as Jesus could not be manifested to Israel, until John had come baptizing in water (31); so it is still. John the Baptist must still do his work in the soul. And only when there has been repentance and confession of sin, which submission to John's baptism signified, is a sinner prepared to receive the Saviour. There is profound truth in that saying of McCheyne, "Only a broken-hearted sinner can receive a crucified Christ."

This suggests a very serious question to many who have no clear consciousness of Christ, no glad realization of his presence, no rejoicing with joy unspeakable and full of glory. May not this lack arise from their not having entered into the meaning of those preliminary conditions which were represented by the Baptist? Only as we know the sinfulness of sin, and the preciousness of the atoning blood of Christ, can we apprehend the power of his resurrection and rejoice in the hope of his coming and his kingdom. May God the Holy Spirit make us a people prepared for the Lord (Luke i. 17).

III. THE THIRD DAY; DISCIPLE-DESERTION (35–37).—On the third day John again looked wistfully and eagerly on Jesus as He walked. It was perhaps the last time those eyes were to behold Him. Again he designated Jesus as the Lamb of God; but there was a significance in his words which was instantly detected by the two disciples who stood beside him. He meant by those words to transfer their allegiance from him to his Lord. Henceforth they were to behold *Him*. So at least they seem to have understood him. "They followed Jesus."

As the preacher looked on their retreating forms, and realised that his work was done, and that henceforth all the crowds would follow them and ebb away, did he have a feeling of jealousy or regret? Evidently not. Or if there were a momentary sense of desolation and loneliness, it must have been instantly wiped out by a great sense of joy. To quote his own matchless words, "This my joy therefore is fulfilled" (iii. 29).

It is sad to see the crowds depart; to note the drying of the brook whose waters were so sweet, the ebbing of the tide, the waning of the day, the falling of the leaves; but, where the soul has learnt to live in Jesus and for Him, it is not so hard to die to all these things, because the Lord has become its light and its salvation, the strength of its life and its everlasting joy.

7

THE SON OF MAN

"Verily, verily, I say unto you, hereafter ye shall see heaven open, and the angels of God ascending and descending upon the Son of Man."
                                                            JOHN i. 51.

THIS CHAPTER abounds in striking names and titles for our Lord. They are a study in themselves. The Word; the Light; the Life of Men; the Only-begotten of the Father; the Christ; the Lamb of God; the Master; Son of God; and King of Israel. But the climax, with which this marvellous enumeration closes, is as wonderful as any: *The Son of Man.* It occurs eighty times in the Gospels, and is always applied by our Lord to Himself.

It is a glorious word, brimful of hope to every member of the family of mankind. To be Son of David, or Son of Abraham, would limit Him to a family or race; but to be Son of Man is equivalent to being the second Adam, and to have a relationship to every man. He was the epitome of humanity, sin excepted. All can find a response in his nature. The one Man, the Man of men, the supreme flower and glory of the human family, the Divine Man—such was the Son of Man, who as such stands now amid the supernal glory of his Father's throne (Acts vii. 56).

The nature of our Lord Jesus is infinite in its extent. On the one hand it touches the heights of Godhead, on the other the depths of manhood. To use his own comparison (51), it resembles the mystic ladder, which in the dream of the wanderer, linked the far distant depths of sky—where, more brilliant than sun or moon, the light of the Shekinah shone—with the moorland, strewn with huge boulders of stone, on which he lay. At one end is the title, Son of God; at the other, Son of Man. And there is not one of the human family too frail or sinful to pass upward through the blessed Lord, his birth and death, his resurrection and ascension, from the lowest depths of degradation to the furthest heights of blessedness.

Here, probably for the first time, our Lord used this title of Himself. It is possible that its full meaning will only be disclosed long ages after we have entered the meridian light of eternity.

I. THE SON OF MAN ATTRACTING MEN.—He had just come victorious from his encounter with the devil. With an imperative of spiritual energy, which human lips had never addressed to the tempter before,

He had made the prince of this world slink behind Him. The next step was to lay the foundation of a society, through which He might carry forward his victories, opposing the kingdom of darkness with a kingdom of light, until that has been realized for the race which He realized on the mountain brow for Himself.

In the Apocalypse, John beheld the completed city, New Jerusalem, descending out of heaven; and was able to study its foundations, as he could not have done had it been earthborn. They seemed like the breastplate of the high priest in colour, though greatly multiplied in extent. There were the blue sapphire; the green emerald; the dark-red sardonyx; the brilliant topaz; the hyacinth; and the amethyst. And on each the name of an Apostle. In this chapter we find the Master-builder quarrying the stones, which seem common enough in their origin, but which, under his touch, shall glisten as slabs of jewels in the foundations of his Church. There is no forecasting what will be the outcome for the simplest believer who once is willing to let Christ have his way with him.

Christ attracted men largely from the lower ranks.—Macaulay tells the story of the famous cathedral window, constructed by the apprentice from materials which his master threw away, and which was so much more beautiful than his that he made away with his life in jealousy. And it was out of those orders of society which the great men of the time held in contempt that Jesus began to construct the society against which the gates of hell cannot prevail. "The common people heard Him gladly." "Then drew near the publicans and sinners for to hear Him." The true David recruited his army from the lapsed and lost, and chose his officers from the ranks of publicans, and fishermen, and artisans (1 Sam. xxii. 2).

Christ attracted men of very different make.—In the Apostolic band there were at least three groups, besides minor varieties. The *Boanergic*, comprising those of largest gift and strength of character—Peter and Andrew, James and John. The *Reflective*, who were apt at questioning and slow to believe—Philip and Thomas, Nathanael (or Bartholomew) and Matthew. The *Practical*, who superintended the business arrangements of catering for the rest. All these varieties were attracted to Jesus. He needed them, and they Him.

Christ attracted men to Himself.—He published no manifesto; elaborated no system of doctrine; insisted on no theological examination. His person was his theology. He appealed to the craving of the human heart for love, and offered Himself to supply its needs, pledging Himself to lead his disciples from the "Come and see" of the first interview, to the vision of "those greater things," which include the Sermon on the Mount; the Sacrificial Death; the Resurrection and Ascension; the Descent of the Holy Ghost; and which extend also to those marvellous discoveries of Divine truth which fill the Epistles.

"Not the Man through the doctrine; but the doctrine through the Man." Not first the head and then the heart; but first the heart and then the head. The trust of the soul in One who gathers up our intellectual assent as He bears us forward into all the truth.

Men were attracted to Christ in very different ways.—Some by preaching, as when the Baptist proclaimed Him on the Jordan bank to the disciples standing beside him. Though that sermon failed on the first occasion, on the second it was the means of converting his entire audience: "And they followed Jesus."

Others are brought through human relationships. God has bound us together in families, that these human relationships may become a very network of communicating wires, through which to send the sparks and impulses of his own love. The Bible does not say how many souls Andrew brought afterwards to Jesus; but it does say, he *first* found his own brother Simon. As boys they had played on the silver sands; as youths they had sailed the long night through in their father's yawl; as young men they had left their homes drawn by a common impulse to the Jordan. And when Andrew found Christ, he had an irresistible influence over Peter and won him. The little taper lit up the great light. Have we all used our home ties enough for the winning of souls to our Lord?

Others were brought by the Master's direct influence. "He findeth Philip, and saith unto him, Follow Me." I love to think of the thousands who owe their all to the direct touch of the love of Christ, falling on them as the light of an infinitely distant star through the tube of the telescope, photographing itself for ever on the prepared paper. Far from the sound of the church-going bell, amid the deep silence of the night watch in the bush or on the prairie, or tossing on the bosom of the deep, the Love of God still finds men.

Others are brought to Christ by the call of friendship, following on long courses of previous preparation. Often must Philip have left the shores of his native lake, and crossed the hills for Cana, where Nathanael dwelt; and the two would earnestly discuss the signs of the times, the desperate straits of their country, the preaching of the Baptist, the advent of the King. And for long periods the guileless Israelite would be lost in deep reverie as he sat beneath his favourite fig-tree, pondering the things which Moses in the Law, and the Prophets, did write, and engaged in earnest prayer. It was not difficult to win such a one, when Philip broke in on his retirement with the news of his discovery.

Jesus Christ is God's magnet put down amongst men to attract them to Himself.

II.—THE SON OF MAN READING AND REVEALING MEN.—The Spirit had been given to Him without measure; and by his indwelling He knew what was in man, read men as we read books, and interpreted them to themselves that they might know themselves and Him.

He knew the yearning for love that dwelt in the heart of John, who clearly was one of the two who first followed Him with timid footsteps, longing to know some of the secrets of his inner life: "Master, where dwellest Thou?"

He knew how timid and weak was the soul that lay beneath the burly form and impetuous self-assertion of Andrew's brother, and He called him by a name which well became him—Simon Bar-Jona, the son of a timid dove.

He knew where to find Philip; the qualities which were worth finding in him; and the magnetic sentence which would bind him for ever to his side: "Follow Me."

He knew the guileless simplicity and purity with which Nathanael's soul was filled, untainted by the luxurious tastes with which the Romans were enervating his native land; and had seen the devout thoughts passing through his heart, before Philip called him. The tree has never grown which could conceal a soul from the eye of Jesus.

So He reads us still. He knows our downsitting and our uprising, and understands our thoughts afar off. We lie before Him naked and opened, as the sacrificial victim before the priest. What though the sharp two-edged sword be in his hand, yet He is not a High-priest who cannot be touched with the feeling of our infirmities!

The Lord who dwells on high
Knows all, and loves us better than He knows.

III. THE SON OF MAN COMPLETING MEN.—Whatever we need most, we can find in Him. He is the all-sufficiency for all human need; the supply of every lack; the answer to every inquiry. Not his gifts, but Himself. Do we need purity? He does not simply give us purity, but He is in us "that Holy Thing." Do we want life? He does not merely impart it, but He is Himself our life. Do we require strength? The Lord is the strength of our life. As the rest of a circle is the complement of a segment, however small, so is Jesus the complement of all who believe.

Andrew is always ranked with Peter, James, and John; yet he was excluded, not arbitrarily, of course, from three memorable scenes, where the others witnessed the glory of their Lord. He reminds us of men of large gift, who yet fall short of the first rank by some defect in ardour, dash, enthusiasm. O ye Andrews of the Church, come to the Son of Man! that He may supply that missing link; breathe into you that lacking power; baptize you in his sacred fire: "so that ye come behind in no gift," waiting for his coming.

A very different man was *Peter*. Liking to gird himself; foremost to speak, to act, to deny; the born leader and spokesman of the rest; ardent in love, but sadly needing stability; essaying to walk the waves, and sinking; meeting with God-given answer the Master's challenge as to His nature, and within a few moments becoming an offence; flashing his sword in the moonbeams with terrible execution, and denying with oaths; plunging into the lake for the shore, where in the grey dawn the beloved form was standing, but presently silenced by "What is that to thee?" A strange mixture of strength and weakness, of ardour and inconstancy! Such are some of us. But when men like Peter come to the Son of Man, He completes them, and impregnates them with the strength of his own rock-like character; so that they become rock-men in their degree, as mossy nests are turned to stone beneath the drip of the limestone caves.

John's nature reminds us of the lakes, which, like his own Galilee, lie among the hills. On calm days the placid and pellucid waters mirror the curtains of the heavens, whether blue, or dark, or star-bespangled. But when the wild winds rush down on them, they are lashed into fury, and no boat can live. John was filled with an almost divine power of loving. This won the love of Jesus; led him to lean on that sacred breast; secured the trusteeship of the beloved mother; and enabled him to read the secrets of the Redeemer's character hidden from the rest. But, withal, he would sit on the right or left of the throne, and call for fire from heaven on offending villagers. Evidently, such a nature needed to be softened and toned, and taught how long-suffering, and forbearing, and pitiful, Divine love could be. Some of us also need to take our love to Jesus that it may be rid of earthly elements, and attempered to his own.

Nathanael made use of such fragmentary hints as were within his reach, and arrived at one of the sublimest of conclusions; but there were great gaps which needed to be filled up, like the blanks in the maps of Africa some twenty years ago. He saw something; but he was capable of seeing more, and he was told that he should see greater things than any that had come within his ken. He recognised in Jesus the Son of God, the King of Israel: but he had yet to learn that Jacob's ladder was a sign of blessing beyond the limits of his own children; that it was a type of Jesus the Son of God, who was not only King of Israel, the nation, but Son of Man, the race.

This is Christ's invariable mode. There is always more to follow. On every blessing which He puts into our hands He writes this inscription, "Thou shalt see greater things than these." If conversion, adoption; if adoption, heirship; if heirship, the throne; if grace, glory.

I know not how many maimed and incomplete hearts may be reached by these words. But it may be that hundreds who will read them have been wearily conscious of heart-ache and heart-need; waiting for someone who never comes; watching for a light which never

8

The First Miracle

*"This beginning of miracles did Jesus in Cana of Galilee, and mani-
fested forth his glory; and his disciples believed on Him."*—JOHN ii. 11.

THIS IS one of those precious memories which the mother of our Lord
pondered in her heart, and doubtless often recited in that home to
which this Evangelist led her from the cross. Several incidents in this
Gospel may be traced to that fellowship in love and sorrow which,
until her death, must have linked his mother and the disciple whom
Jesus loved.

Is it not wonderful that this was our Lord's first miracle! Had we
been asked to select the one which seemed most appropriate to stand
as the frontispiece of his earthly ministry, we should have selected the
raising of Lazarus, the calming of the storm, or the feeding of the
hungry crowds; but who would have chosen this? The inventive
genius of man would have conceived an introductory scene which
combined the chief features of the Transfiguration and of the giving
of the law. How different is the simplicity of this incident!

In the previous chapter we are told that the Apostles beheld in Jesus
Christ the glory of the Only-begotten of the Father; and when we ask
one of those eye-witnesses to give a sample of its choicest manifestations, we are conducted to a little village in the highlands of Galilee,
at the distance of an afternoon's walk from Nazareth, where the Master
sits at a simple marriage feast amongst his friends, and makes wine
out of water to supply their lack.

The miracles of this Gospel are signs (xx. 30), carefully selected as
bearing upon the special characteristics of our Lord's person and work,
which the Evangelist had set himself to portray. There was a distinct
purpose in his performing this miracle as his first, and in its being set
so prominently at the front of this narrative. We are told that He
manifested forth his glory; and we reverently ask, How? As we strive
to answer that question, may we again sit at his table, and hear
Him speak!

I. IT WAS HIS GLORY TO SHOW THAT TRUE RELIGION IS CONSISTENT
WITH ORDINARY LIFE.—There is a common tendency to associate the
highest type of religion with rigorous austerity of life, as if the human
were too common to be divine. We fancy that he whose thoughts
commune most deeply with the Eternal must be a stern, silent, and

solitary man. This type of the religious life was exemplified in the old
prophets, who dwelt in the solitudes of unfrequented deserts and hills,
withdrawn from the common joys and engagements and ties of human
existence; only emerging now and again to pour on the ears of awestruck crowds the burning words of the living God. Such had been
John the Baptist. The deserts, his home; the locust and wild honey,
his fare; the camel's cloth, his dress. And we might have expected to
find the Son of God more rigorous still in his isolation; rearing Himself
in severe and solitary grandeur, like the Jungfrau among the Alps.

But no. His early years are spent, not in a desert, but a home. He
comes eating and drinking. He moves freely amongst men as one of
themselves. He interweaves his life with the life of the home, the
market-place, and the street. And in pursuance of this purpose He
wrought his first miracle at a peasant's wedding.

Travelling by easy stages from the Jordan valley, He had reached
Galilee. Finding his mother gone from Nazareth, He followed her over
the hills to Cana, and for her sake was invited with his six new-made
followers to the simple feast. It was a time of simple-hearted enjoyment. "The bridegroom crowned with flowers with which his mother
had crowned him in the day of his espousals; the bride adorned with
her jewels, sitting apart among the women." And though He was the
Son of God, no cloud would veil his face or cast a restraining spell
upon the guests.

This is the harder type.—Easier, like the anchorite, to be separated
from the world, than, like the Saviour, to be in it and not of it. Easier
to decline an invitation to the house of the great than to go there and
behave as the Son of God. Easier to refuse the things of sense than to
use them without abuse. Easier to maintain a life of prayer far from
the haunts of men, than to enter them maintaining constant fellowship
with God in the unruffled depths of the soul. Nothing but the grace of
the Holy Spirit can suffice for this. But this is sufficient if daily and
believingly sought.

It is most honouring to God.—The idea of the ascetic life is that
every human feeling is a weakness, and every natural instinct a sin.
No woman's caress, no childish voice, no tender love, none of the
jewels or flowers of existence, may soften the rigours of that lot. But
is not all this a libel on God's original creation? Has He made so
great a mistake in creating us that we must thwart his ideal at every
step, ere we can rise to our true manhood? Must we make ourselves
other than men before we can be saints? Surely, to reason thus is to
dishonour the wisdom and love of God in our original creation. And
the Incarnation teaches us, as does this miracle, that God does not
require an emasculated, but a fulfilled and purified humanity.

It is most useful to the world.—Of what use is salt, except in contact
with the corrupting carcase? The holiness which builds three taber-

nacles amid almost inaccessible rocks is of little help to the breaking hearts of devil-possessed men in the valley below. This, at least, is not our Saviour's message. "Go," says He, "to Jerusalem and Samaria, to the crowded cities and homes of men. Live amongst them, kindling them with the passion of your holiness. Suffer little children to come to you; publicans and sinners to draw near to you; crowds to follow you. All I ask is that whether ye eat or drink, or whatsoever ye do, ye should do all to the glory of God."

II. IT WAS HIS GLORY TO TEACH THE BEAUTY OF WAITING MEEKLY FOR GOD.—If ever there was a being who might have claimed to act on the prompting of his own spirit, it was surely our blessed Lord. But there never was one who lived in more absolute and entire dependence on the Father from the first. It comes out very clearly here.

His advent with his friends threatened the whole family with a disgrace which to the hospitable mind of the Jew would be irreparable. The wine ran short. Mary, who seems to have had considerable influence in the house, was made aware of the fact, and quickly guessed its cause. She could not endure the thought of inflicting, however unconsciously, so great a mortification on that kindly circle; and she suddenly conceived the hope of helping them through Him whom she had been wont to count her obedient son. Why should He not now assume the position which had been predicted from his birth? She could not have been deceived in all that had been told her; but it had been long and hard to wait. Yet surely the salutation of the Baptist and gathering of disciples were omens of an approaching change. Why should He not now blossom out into all that splendid glory with which Jewish anticipation invested the Messiah?

Her implied request must have appealed closely to the tender heart of Christ. All that she felt, He felt also. But He could not take his commands from her entreaty, or even from the warmth of his own emotions. He addressed her with a title consistent with the most perfect tenderness—indeed, He used it from his cross; but, waiving her suggestion with a common Aramaic expression, went on to announce that henceforth his eye would be, if possible, more closely fixed on the dial-plate of his Father's will, following the index-finger of his purpose, waiting till it should reach the hour, and the alarum for action should ring out. "Mine hour is not yet come."

It was so that He waited or acted throughout his life. The Gospels abound in references to his hour. Before it struck He was calm and peaceful, however pressing might be the apparent need for action. When it struck He acted instantly and decisively. Afterwards, He returned unto his rest. This is almost the hardest lesson in Christian living. We listen to the advice of friend; the threatening of foe; the pressure of circumstance. We think we must do something. Like King Saul, we force ourselves and offer the sacrifice. We pray hurriedly and throw ourselves into the breach, to discover, when too late, that we have run without being sent, and have defeated our own object by too much haste. "My soul, wait thou," might often be addressed to ourselves by ourselves. Not a moment behind God; but not a moment before Him. Ready for his hour to strike.

III. IT WAS HIS GLORY TO SHOW THE INWARDNESS OF TRUE RELIGION.—In the entrance-hall six stone waterpots were standing, "after the manner of the purifying of the Jews." Their superstitious dread of uncleanness made it necessary to have large supplies of water ever at hand. Without washing no one ate (Mark vii. 3). The feet of each guest were washed on arrival (Luke vii. 44). The washing of cups and jugs and bottles, says the Talmud, went on all day. And in this we have a symbol of that religion which consists in external rites, and is content if only these are maintained.

But the Master turned the water of outward ceremonial washing into wine for inward drinking. Surely there is deep symbolical meaning here, in illustration of which we recall two sentences, the one from the Old Testament, the other from the New. "Thy love is better than wine"; and "Whoso . . . drinketh my blood hath eternal life."

The most spiritual men in the old Jewish system were constantly emphasising the impotence of mere ritual to save and sanctify the soul. David felt it (Psa. li. 16). Isaiah felt it (Isa. i. 13). Micah brings it out in clear relief (Micah vi. 7). And here our Lord in this striking miracle seems to say, "The days of ceremonialism are past; the system which was sent to teach spiritual ideas by material substances and external rites is at an end; the tedious routine of outward ablutions, which has diverted men's attention from the inner life and the befitting garb of the soul, must be laid aside; I am come to teach men to love, to live by faith, to array themselves in robes washed white in my blood, and to rise through close participation in my death to a life of stainless purity and flawless beauty. Not water, but blood. Not washing, but drinking. Not the outward cleanliness, however fair and right; but the purity of the heart, the deliverance of the spirit from the polluting taint of evil." We are not surprised to learn next that He cleansed the Temple, and that He told Nicodemus that even he must be born again.

IV. IT WAS HIS GLORY TO AWAKEN US TO SEE THE DIVINE POWER IN THE ORDINARY PROCESSES OF NATURE.—The world is full of miracles; but they are so gradual and quiet that we are often blinded to their wonderfulness, till the flash of a sudden "sign" awakens us from our strange neglect.

It seems doubtful whether the Lord changed all the contents of the six stone jars, or only that which was drawn from them. The latter would more resemble his way, who gives us, not granaries of grain, but daily bread; and who deals out supplies of daily strength. But, even if He had turned all the water into wine, there would be no obstacle to our faith. The sin of drunkenness was not the sin of Palestine, as it is of London; and therefore did not require the special methods of prevention which the principles of his Gospel now lead us to adopt. And we must remember that the light wines of the Galilean vintage were very different to the brandied intoxicants with which we are too familiar.

But this is the interesting point: that we see compressed into a single flash the same power that works throughout the wine-lands every summer, transforming the dew and rain into the juices that redden the drooping clusters of the vines. The superficial man looks at this miracle and cries, "Oh, wondrous day that beheld so great a deed!" The spiritual man looks at it, and, whilst not underrating its marvel, walks the world with a new reverence, because he knows that the same Divine power is throbbing all around. The power revealed in feeding the five thousand is required to cover the autumn fields with grain. The power needed to raise the dead shows how much is constantly demanded to keep us living. The power that quells the storm indicates how much is being exercised to maintain the stable equilibrium of the world.

This is the glory of the miracles of Jesus, that they have taught us to look on the world around us with new and opened eyes. We hear his voice in the summer wind, and amid the roar of the pitiless storm. We catch sight of his form awakening Nature from her wintry sleep by his touch, as once the daughter of Jairus from her couch. We stand spellbound before his power, as once they did who saw the wonderful works of his hands. He is the same yesterday, to-day, and for ever. In Him all things consist. And as for this world, it teems with the miraculous:

> And every common bush afire with God;
> But only he who sees takes off his shoes.

V. IT WAS HIS GLORY TO SHOW THE ASCENDING SCALE OF GOD'S GIFTS.—The devil ever gives his best first; and when the appetite is somewhat palled, he puts on his worse, even to the worst. Gold at the crown, clay at the foot. Feasting with harlots, then famine with swine. Goshen with its pastures, followed by Egypt with its fetters. Ah! you who read this page, and are living a heartless, worldly life, make the most of it, it is the best you will ever have. After you have "well drunk," there will come coarser tastes, more depraved appetites. That which has satisfied will fail to satisfy; and in its stead will come forms of sin and temptation from which at the first you would have started back, crying, "Do you take me for a dog, that I should ever come to this!"

The Lord Jesus, on the other hand, is always giving something better. As the taste is being constantly refined, it is provided with more delicate and ravishing delights. That which you know of Him to-day is certainly better than that you tasted when first you sat down at his board. And so it will ever be. The angels, as his servants, have orders to bring in and set before the heirs of glory things which eye hath not seen, and man's heart has not conceived, but which are all prepared. The best of earth will be below the simplest fare of heaven. But what will heaven's best be! If wine in the peasant's house is so luscious, what will be the new wine in the Father's kingdom! What may we not expect from the vintages of the celestial hills! What will it be to sit at the marriage supper of the Lamb, not as guests, but as the Bride! Oh, hasten on, ye slow-moving days; be quick to depart, that we may taste that ravishment of bliss! But for ever and ever, as fresh revelations break on our glad souls, we shall look up to the Master of the feast and cry, *"Thou hast kept the best until now."*

9

THE TEMPLE OF THE BODY

"He spake of the temple of his body."—JOHN ii. 21.

WHAT IS your body? An inn, thronged with busy traffic! A library, whose shelves are being gradually filled with the gathering stores of knowledge! A counting-house, dedicated to money-making, in which the amassing of wealth, or the maintenance of a competence is the one and all-important object! A playhouse, used for no higher purpose than pleasure-seeking! A stye, where swinish passions revel! "But He spake *of the temple* of his Body."

The conception was full of beauty.—As the temple at Jerusalem, with its marble pavements, its pillared cloisters, its terraced courts, its rich adornment, was one of the fairest spectacles under the sun, so is the human body, designed and built by the Divine skill, worthy of its Creator. Consider those ivory pillars of bone; those alabaster walls of flesh; that many-toned organ of speech; those long corridors of brain and nerve, through which thought and emotion move; those storied archives where memory resides as the custodian of the records of the past: and tell me if you do not see an exquisite beauty and delicacy in the Lord's comparison, as "He spake of the temple of his Body."

The conception was as new as it was beautiful.—Men had been wont to consider the body as the seat of evil, and the principal impediment to a saintly life. The Epicurean, like the "fleshly school" of the present day, gave himself up to obey its wildest impulses, as though a rider should throw the reins on the neck of a fiery steed. The Stoic sought to crush out and starve all natural instincts. And this has been the motive of asceticism in all ages. "I fear that I have ill-treated my brother the ass," said St. Francis of Assisi, a few hours before his death, as he looked with a kindly and half-humorous pity on his worn and emaciated body, prematurely exhausted by vigil, fasting and maceration.

At the most, men were prepared to give to God a part of their being, one room out of many to be his shrine, the organ of veneration, the attitude of worship, the hour of morning prayer. But the Son of Man said that the body was not in itself evil, and that it might be the shrine and home of God; the temple of Him who dwells in the high and holy place; whose Being fills the immensity of the universe, but who makes his dwelling-place with loving and contrite hearts. He said, moreover, that not one organ but every organ; not one attitude but all; not one engagement but each—should be pervaded by the thought of worship and dedication, cleansed in the blood of atonement, made fragrant with the perfume of incense, and included in priestly ministry and service.

And the conception became characteristic of Christianity.—Wherever the religion of Jesus went, men conceived a new idea of the sacredness of the body. Had He not worn it? Had He not carried it through death into the light of Easter, and the glory of the throne? Had He not spoken of it as a temple? The natural instincts could be neither common nor unclean. And it must be possible so to order and rule them as that they should be the willing servants of a holy will and consecrated purpose; not impeding the symmetrical beauty of the loftiest characters, but promoting it; and doing the will of God on earth as it is done in heaven.

From this source the Apostle derived the motive-power with which to nerve his converts in their conflict with the evils of their time. Writing to those at Corinth, one of the fairest in the sisterhood of fair cities with which Greece had adorned herself, the beauty of whose temples was only equalled by the voluptuousness and impurity of the worship which defiled the loveliest achievements of human art, he said emphatically, "Know ye not that ye are the temple of God, and that the Spirit of God dwelleth in you? If any man defile the temple of God, him shall God destroy; for the temple of God is holy, which temple ye are." (1 Cor. iii. 16, 17; vi. 19; 2 Cor. vi. 16.)

Is it not significant that, in his first miracle, our Lord hastened to put honour on marriage at the wedding feast; and in his second public act, by a single word, reinstated the body in its rightful place as the help-meet and shrine of the consecrated soul, a thing which may be presented as a sacrifice unto God, holy, and acceptable, and reasonable (Rom. xii. 1)? Surely thus it became Him as Son of Man! "He spake of the temple of his Body."

I. THE TIME OF HIS SPEAKING.—It was the month of April. The land was green with pastures, and carpeted with myriads of flowers; the air vocal with the singing of birds, and laden with sweet scent; the thoroughfares thronged with pilgrims for the Passover, and with flocks for the Paschal Feast. Jerusalem was in her glory. And at such a time there seemed nothing extravagant in the panegyric of the patriot Psalmist, when he sang, "Beautiful for situation, the joy of the whole earth is Mount Zion, the city of the great King."

After the miracle at Cana, our Lord went down to Capernaum, with which most of his disciples were associated, and which thenceforward became his home. But He did not stay there "many days," as the time had come for Him to inaugurate his public ministry in the metropolis of his people, and at the very heart of their religious system.

II. THE PLACE OF HIS SPEAKING.—It was in the temple that He who was Himself the temple of God, spake of the body as a temple. And there was a special fitness in the coincidence. The temple had three divisions. The outer, which lay beneath the gaze of Israel; the inner, or Holy Place, where the white-robed priests went to and fro on their sacred ministries, awed by the sense of the nearness of God's manifested presence; and the innermost, or Most Holy Place, where the Shekinah, in Solomon's temple, shone between the bending forms of the cherubim.

Similarly tripartite is the nature of man. The body is its outer court. Next to that is the soul, the seat of consciousness, of thought and will, of emotion and imagination, a family of priests meant to minister to God, in robes of stainless purity, under the sense of his presence, their every movement music, their every act worship. But beyond this wondrous play of soul-life is the spirit; that in which man is most like God, and by which he is capable of becoming God-filled and God-possessed. For it is through the spirit that man's nature opens out into the world of spirit, of the infinite and eternal, and becomes the residence and shrine of God (1 Thess. v. 23; Heb. iv. 12).

The nature of man is a trinity in unity. Three constituent portions make up each individual unit of the human family. All are not temples, but all may be. In many, alas, the most sacred chamber, with its marvellous capacities for God, is untenanted and unexplored, given over to darkness and neglect. At regeneration the Divine residence is inaugurated. The Holy Ghost is distinctly described as dwelling within the believer; not therefore always patent to our consciousness, because deeper than the sphere of motion, and in the spirit.

In our second birth marvellous possibilities present themselves. Almost immediately the soul, which is the seat of consciousness and choice, must elect whether it will permit itself to be most largely influenced by the body or the spirit. If it choose the former, saved though it be, it will inevitably become carnal, and unable to digest God's deep and secret teaching (1 Cor. iii. 2); but, if it choose the latter, it will become increasingly spiritual—the light of the Most Holy will stream with growing intensity into the holy place of thought and feeling, until the whole tenor of the inner life is ennobled and purified. And thence the waves of blessed life will pass outwards to the body, till every member experiences the sacred influence, and begins to sparkle and glow; as when the light of the Shekinah brake through all curtaining restraints, and bathed in glory the entire fabric, standing in its earliest completeness. How perfectly this was illustrated in the Transfiguration, in which the body of the blessed Lord shone as the sun, and even his clothes were white as the light!

You will never be able to govern the body by the unaided power of the soul. Go deeper than the soul-life, however fervid its love or strenuous its resolves. Avail yourselves of the indwelling grace of the Holy Ghost. Let the parting veil be rent and withdrawn. And then, through the recipient soul, the life and light and love of God will stream forth to ennoble and irradiate the entire nature.

III. THE OCCASION OF HIS SPEAKING.—The hills of Moab were hardly purple with the dawn before the highways were crowded with throngs hurrying to the temple. But the tortuous streets were rendered almost impassable on account of the traffic and business caused by the vast concourse of people. There were sellers of trinkets and souvenirs; drovers of sheep and oxen with their charge; exchangers of the coins of all the world for the half-shekel, which must be paid by every Jew in temple currency. Had all this hubbub been confined to the adjacent streets, it had been sufficiently objectionable; but, for purposes of gain, it had been permitted to intrude into the lower temple court, that of the Gentiles. There, steaming with heat, and filling the sacred edifice with stench and filth, were penned whole flocks of sheep and herds of oxen; while drovers and pilgrims stood around in eager contention as to price. There, too, were men with cages of doves, the offerings of the poor. And beneath the shadow of the arcades, sat the money-changers, each behind his little table, covered with piles of coin. A very shambles, with the noise of an Eastern bazaar!

An apt symbol this, not only of the intrusion of the world-spirit into the Church, but of the harbouring of darker and sadder evils in the heart. Not alone amid the ruins of heathen fanes, but in the secrets of our hearts, do vultures build their filthy nests, and unclean creatures make their lair. Traffic in the forbidden; the forms of brutelike passions; the rattle of unhallowed gain; the sweltering press of care and worry and rush—have crowded God out of our life. Mammon, Beelzebub, and Satan, have usurped his place. With us, as in Ezekiel's vision, the walls of the chambers of imagery are covered with delineations of obscene creatures, before which we offer incense. With us, as with Job, our increasing knowledge of God is gauged by a deeper abhorrence of of ourselves: "Behold, I am vile."

But when the Lord Jesus enters, He cleanses.—Hastily knotting together a number of small cords, gathered from the litter at his feet, He advanced to the traffickers, and bade them begone. They looked at Him aghast. Who was He, that He should issue such a decree? But they quailed beneath the glance of that flashing eye and the commanding attitude of that spare form. Sin is weakness. The evil-doer cannot stand before the servant of God armed with no weapon save the force of a blameless character and the energy of a quenchless zeal. So, moved by a sudden and irresistible impulse, they slowly and sullenly began to retire, driving their charge before them, and uttering the deepest maledictions against an authority they dared neither dispute nor resist.

The dove-sellers followed them, carrying their wicker cages; whilst the money-changers, after a scramble to collect what coins they might amid the ruthless overthrow of their tables, and the pouring forth of their stores, also hastened away. And the temple-court was clear.

Would you be rid of darkness? Let in the light! Would you cleanse the stable? Let in the river! Would you be delivered from impurity of heart and life? Let in the Saviour! He will cleanse the temple. This action was deeply significant of what He will effect in us.

Many would meet Him at the threshold and make terms; but this will never do. You may wish Him to pass into the upper courts without noticing the lower. You may desire to know before admitting Him what He will consider wrong and contraband, and to enter upon a discussion of the whole matter. You may seek to bribe Him into inaction or acquiescence. But it may not be. Jesus must be Lord or nothing. He will have his way, or not enter. He will only take from us what we would be the first to renounce, did we know all that He knows. He will do it gently, if we will let Him, taking away the evil desire, giving us something better, extracting the cancer under chloroform. But He must be free to act.

Sometimes, when He cannot attain his end by gentleness, He uses *a scourge of small cords*. Very small things aid Him in his work of purification. A child's remark; a case in a newspaper; a sentence in talk, or from a book; a disappointment; an illness; a loss; a sarcastic rejoinder; any one of these may be a strand in the cord, or a cord in the scourge, employed to drive out evil. But better these than hornets (Exodus xxiii. 28).

There always will be remonstrance.—The Pharisees challenged his right to act thus, and demanded a sign. His answer foreshadowed his violent death and the perfecting of his body through resurrection. These allusions were dark sayings even to his disciples, till after they were fulfilled. His words were angrily referred by the Jews to the fabric of the temple, and were never forgotten. At his trial, and at his cross, they were repeatedly flung against Him as a taunt. But they have been abundantly verified. In destroying his body so far as death could do it, they in effect destroyed their temple, and struck the death-knell of their system, whilst his risen body is now seated on the right hand of the throne of God.

But over all remonstrances the zeal of Christ must triumph.—Ah, that blessed zeal, which ate up his life in three short years; which quailed not at its task, and shrank not back though the path it trod led straight to the cross; which set against the opposition and malice of men the vision of the accomplished purpose of God; and which conquered by the fire of its own pure passion! It cleansed the temple courts, not once only, but again. And will it do less for us? We too are the house of God; and the zeal that led our Saviour to cleanse the

10

A PSALM OF LIFE

"That which is born of the flesh is flesh; and that which is born of the
*Spirit is spirit."—*JOHN iii. 6.

BORN! That is true of us all. We were not asked if we would be born,
or of whom we would be born. But we awoke gradually from months
of almost unconsciousness to find that we had been born. And birth
was the gate into life. Through birth we entered the blessed kingdom
of life.

But what life? There are many kingdoms of life, rising one above
another. Into which of these were we born? The lowest is the kingdom *of vegetable life,* with fungus and palm, with lichen and oak,
with hyssop and cedar. But our kingdom is higher than this. The
next is the kingdom *of animal life,* separated by an impassable gulf
from that beneath it, embracing all living things, from the microscopic
organisms of deep-sea dredgings, or the invisible kingdoms that exist
in drops of water, to the noblest forms of creature-life around the
throne of God. But our kingdom was higher than this. The next is the
kingdom *of mind and soul*: in which there are the faculty of reason;
the rudiments of conscience; the sparkle of wit; the aurora-glory of the
fancy; memory as librarian; poetry as minstrel; hope, as fresco-painter;
love (to use Spenser's exquisite simile) as mother of all. Into this kingdom we were born, when in our first birth we passed into the light of
life. If we were to adopt the phraseology of the New Testament, we
might call this *the kingdom of the flesh*; for the flesh is employed in a
very wide and special sense, and includes the whole drift of human life,
even to its thoughts, "That which is born of the flesh is flesh" (Rom.
viii. 6, 7).

But above this kingdom there is another—the kingdom of *the spiri-*
tual and eternal. This is the supreme realm of life, the element and
home of God. Our Lord alludes to it twice in the same breath as "the
kingdom of God" (3, 5). The kingdom into which we are born as babes
is filled with bright and beautiful things; but it is shut off from this by
a gulf as vast as that which severs the vegetable from the animal, or the
animal from the moral nature of man. As easily might the water-lily
become the spaniel that dived for it, or the spaniel the poet Cowper,
who sings his exploit, as that which is born flesh become spirit. As
there is no entrance into the kingdom of the flesh-life save by natural
birth; so there is no entrance into the kingdom of the spirit-life, save

by spiritual birth. Only that which is born of the Spirit is spirit. And this made our Lord so emphatic in repeating his announcement, "Ye must be born again."

Nicodemus was an admirable type of the world of men outside the kingdom of the spirit-life. He believed in God, having no sympathy with the cold infidelity of the Sadducees. He was, probably, like another of the same school, blameless in all the righteousness of the law, and irreproachable in moral character. He would be classed among the high-churchmen of his time. Courtly, thoughtful, inquisitive; willing to consider the claims of any new system; prepared to acknowledge Christ as a teacher; perplexed at spiritual truth; thinking that it was only needful to know in order to be—how apt a type is he of the children of the flesh!

See him as he muffles his face in his cloak, and steals along in the shadows cast by the full Passover moon, startled by his own footfall, fearful lest the watchman on his beat should recognize the magnate of the Jewish Sanhedrin in the suppliant for entrance at the door of the humble lodging of Jesus of Nazareth. A nervous, timid old man this, defending his friends on general principles; not liking to identify himself too publicly with a dead enthusiast; fonder of asking questions than of arguing points (John iii. 4. 9; vii. 50, 51; xix 38, 39).

To such a man Christ said, "Ye must be born again." When Christ says *must*, it is time for us to wake up. He is so gentle, winsome, tender. He is always persuading, inviting, entreating. He so seldom uses the imperative mood. When, therefore, He speaks thus, it becomes us to inquire into the matter on which He insists so earnestly.

I. THE NATURE OF THIS LIFE.—It is "eternal life." This is the epithet perpetually applied to it throughout this chapter and the writings of the beloved Evangelist. Our Lord was the first so to describe it (15). The Holy Ghost repeats the words as though to stamp them on our minds (16, 36; iv. 14, 36; vi. 54; x. 28; xii. 25; 1 John v. 13). Surely they cannot simply mean everlastingness, the duration of a never-ending existence. To have that alone were to gain nothing by our second birth. Nay, it would repeat the mistake of the old Greek myth, in which the goddess obtained for her lover immortal life, but forgot to claim also immortal youth, so that his years became an insupportable anguish. "Eternal" refers rather to the quality than the quantity of that life, and tells us that it is altogether removed from the conditions of space and time, and partakes of the blessed, timeless, glorious, spiritual, nature of God.

This life is never shadowed by dread of condemnation (18); it suns itself in the very light of God's face (20); it does the truth (21); it finds its true nest and home in the very heart of God (13).

II. THE SOURCE OF THIS LIFE—GOD. "The Father hath life in Himself" (v. 26). To use the sublime language of the Psalmist, "In Thee is the fountain of life." All life finds its source and origin in the nature of God; as the verdure of an oasis in the desert, or of a valley among the hills, is entirely due to the presence of a perennial fountain, which makes music through the years. Drain away the fountain, and the glade slowly fades into the desert. Blot out God, and the universe becomes as devoid of life as the moon.

From the firefly that flashes through the forest glade to the firstborn sons of light—the seraphs, who burn in ceaseless adoration before the throne—all the life that exists throughout the universe is due, if I may say so, to the spray of the Divine fountain of life. And this is specially true of spiritual life. Underived, independent of supply, original and ever-flowing, all spirit-life has its centre, home, and fountain-head in God.

III. THE STORAGE OF THIS LIFE.—If we may use the words, the Father stored his life in the human nature of our Lord. It dwelt in Him in its fullness, and it pleased the Father that it should be so. By a deliberate act, He gave to the Son to have life in Himself. And so at last that life was manifested, and men saw it, and bore witness of that eternal life, which was with the Father, and was manifested to them (Col. ii. 9; John v. 26; 1 John i. 2).

Of course we know that, as the second person of the ever-blessed Trinity, our Lord Jesus shared from before all worlds in the inherent life of God; but when He became the Son of Man, it was the Father's special bestowment that stored up in his human nature all the marvellous life of which we speak. It was as if our God yearned to make us partakers of his Divine nature; but, since the fountain-head was in his own being, and He knew that it would be inaccessible to us, therefore, in tender pity and condescension, He brought it within our reach in the human nature of our blessed Lord. Who need be afraid of Jesus? What little child may not venture to his arms? What penitent not kiss his feet? What trembling one not lose all terror in his presence? Thank God that He has put his best gift on so low a shelf that the weakest and smallest of his children may go and take it for themselves!

But it was not enough simply to store the life in Jesus. It had to be made accessible to us through his death, resurrection, and ascension. There is, therefore, special significance in the repeated references of this chapter to the Son of Man being lifted up on the cross (14, 16). That precious death was the full, perfect, and sufficient sacrifice and satisfaction for the sin of the whole world, through which alone our sins can be pardoned, or we accounted worthy to stand in the presence of the holy God. But, at the same time, it made Him able to pass on to others that life which was in Himself; and, as He passed through death into resurrection, He became the author of eternal life to all who are united to Him by faith.

He was filled, that out of his fullness we might be filled. He died that we might live. Having overcome the sharpness of death, He opened the kingdom of heaven to all believers.

IV. THE COMMUNICATION OF THIS LIFE.—"Born of water and of the Spirit." All the world of Judæa was ringing with talk of John's baptism. At this very time he was baptizing in Ænon, because there was much water there. This then was our Lord's point, when He spoke of *water*. He clearly referred to the work of his Forerunner, and all that it meant of repentance and confession of sin. It was through John that men were to come to Himself. The porter must open the gate of the true fold. And the Lord Jesus would not for a moment allow this man, ruler though he were, to escape the wholesome ordeal of taking his place with every other sinner on the Jordan banks, and of thus becoming one of the people prepared for the coming of the Lord. In every soul there has to be a process analogous to that signified by the baptism of John. First the baptism of water, then the baptism of fire. First repentance, then remission of sins. Born of water and of the Spirit.

But at the most this is only part, and, though necessary, the less part, of the process. We need not only to turn from the old life, but to become possessed of the new. And this is the express function of the Holy Spirit. He is significantly called "the Spirit of life in Christ Jesus" (Rom. viii. 2).

Faith is receptiveness. Those that believe are those that receive (i. 12). Now the one spot in all the universe where faith is most easily and constantly called into operation is at the cross of Jesus. When the soul beholds that mystery of love, the Son of Man dying for its sins, uplifted on the cross, as the serpent on the pole, it yearns after Him with a passion which is God-begotten; it cannot refrain from faith; it opens towards Him the deepest recesses of its being: and *that* is the blessed moment of the impartation of the germ of the new life through the agency of the Holy Spirit. We may not say which precedes the other. They are simultaneous, as the simultaneous movement of the spokes of a wheel, or as a child's first cry with its first bath.

We may not have been conscious of this gracious overshadowing of the Holy Spirit, our hearts may have been too much occupied with love and penitence and ecstasy to think of aught else than of the death which atoned for sin and made us nigh to God; but in after years we must look back to that moment as the birthday of our eternal life, the hour when we passed from death unto life, and became alive unto God through Jesus Christ our Lord. Ah, august and glorious experience, never to be forgotten, never to be excelled in all that may transpire through untrodden ages, by which we were translated from death into life, from the power of darkness into the kingdom of God's dear Son!

V. THE LAWS OF THAT LIFE.—(1) *Mystery*. As the wind (8). Whilst our Lord was speaking with this inquirer, "trusting Himself to him," as He did not to the majority of those who sought Him (ii. 24), the night-breeze may have passed over the city, stirring the vine-leaves as they drooped over the casement, and breathing through the open window. "Mark this wind," said our Lord; "how mysterious it is! You cannot see it, though you can feel it. You know not from what scenes it comes, or to what it hurries; its laws and ministries; why it is now a hurricane, and again a zephyr, now laden with the softness of the western sea, and again hot and feverish with the fire of the desert waste—of all this you are ignorant; and do you think that you will be more able to understand the nature or laws of that new life of which I speak?"

It must be always so. No kingdom can understand another kingdom. You must be born into life to know life. It is only by what you experience of life in yourself that you can judge of it in others. This is the contention which the Apostle enforces in words that burn with undimming flame, though almost two thousand years have elapsed since they were first penned: "The things of God knoweth no man, but the Spirit of God" (1 Cor. ii. 11–16).

Those, therefore, who hear us talk of the new birth may well marvel, as did Nicodemus; and it is almost useless to try to make these mysteries plain. As well ride on the wind, or follow the rush of the tide as it drives its foaming steeds up the estuary. But we who have it know it. We are conscious of its throb, its pulse, its ecstasy. We have traced its parentage to the nature of God. We hear its music as it rises up like a fountain towards eternity.

Thank God that, with all its mystery, the wind is all-pervasive. No lung so consumptive, no mine so deep, no orifice so small, no court so foetid, but it will enter to purify and heal. So, unless we seal ourselves hermetically against Him, the Divine Spirit will enter our natures, ridding them of the miasma which has gathered there, sowing the germs of life, and inspiring us with the very nature of God.

(2) *Knowledge*. Though we do not come to the Lord Jesus primarily as Teacher, yet we cannot receive the new life without turning naturally to Him as its Teacher and Guide. Come to Him as Teacher, and you only marvel. Come to Him as Saviour, and, being saved, you learn, whilst sitting at his feet, not earthly things only, but heavenly (12).

It is passing wonderful how soon the new-born babe begins to understand things which baffle the wise and prudent. That which the intellect cannot receive is welcomed by the loving humble spirit. We receive the Spirit of God, and we come to know the things that are freely given to

c

us of God. They are revealed by the Spirit, who searches the deep things of the Divine nature. Oh for more time to spend bending over these translucent but infinite depths, beneath the teaching of such a Master!

(3) *Growth.*—As the Baptist said of the Lord, using the third *must* of this chapter, "He must increase, I must decrease." This also is true of the Christ-life within. It is destined to grow and increase, from strength to strength, from grace to grace, till Christ is perfectly formed within us.

The growth of the Divine life is in exact proportion to the denial of the self-life. Bear about in the body the dying of the Lord Jesus. Learn what it means to be crucified with Christ in daily acts of unselfish love and pity. Mortify the deeds of the body in the power of the Eternal Spirit; and as the mould is broken, the true ideal will emerge in the perfect beauty of eternal life.

11

THE SHADOW OF THE CROSS

"As Moses lifted up the serpent in the wilderness, even so must the Son of Man be lifted up."—JOHN iii. 14.

IN A WELL-KNOWN picture, a modern painter has given us an imaginary incident in the youth of our Lord. It is the carpenter's shop. Boards sawn for use are propped against the walls, the floor is strewn with chips and curls of wood and heaps of sawdust, various tools mingle in the confusion, or are placed in the rack ready for use. Mary is kneeling close beside the Christ, the level rays of the setting sun strike through the casement, and as the young carpenter draws Himself to his full height and extends his arms, a shadow as of one crucified is thrown on the opposite wall. Mary, at least, sees that shadow of the cross, and it recalls the prediction of the venerable Simeon, which had for the moment chilled her motherly rapture, whilst he foretold the sword which should pierce her soul.

This, of course, is fancy; and yet it is without doubt that, to Mary, at least, the anticipation of crushing sorrow, in connection with that wondrous Being with whom her own life was so mysteriously entwined, was an ever-present source of grief.

When did the first realization of his death break on the human consciousness of our blessed Lord? Of course, as the Son of God, He must always have anticipated it. From eternity it had been present to his mind. Before the mountains were brought forth, or the foundations of the earth were laid, in purpose and intention, He was the Lamb slain. He emptied Himself with the express purpose of becoming obedient to the death of the cross. But there was perhaps a moment when it first broke on his soul as the Son of Man. Whenever that moment was, it lay far back before the day when He took up his public ministry; for from his earliest words and onward to his latest it is evident that He was living in the anticipation of Calvary.

The shadow of the cross rests on all the incidents and words of his public life. Nowhere does the sun of his life shine in a clear sky. The darkness is denser here and thinner there, but it is everywhere; "as the twilight creeps noiselessly into evening's sunniest nooks, and quietly masters all the land without the winnowing of its silken wing being heard or seen." Let us for a moment trace it. Calvary is a low hill; but it casts a long shadow.

In his first appeal to his fellow-countrymen from the court of the cleansed Temple, He spoke clearly of the destruction of his body, in which the destruction of their own Temple was foreshadowed (ii. 19).

In his first recorded conversation He said positively and unmistakably that He must be lifted up, not simply to the right hand of the Father, but as Moses lifted up the serpent in the wilderness (iii. 14). Between Him and the bright Home whither He was going lay the blackness of the midnight of the cross.

He spoke of his flesh as given for the life of the world (vi. 51). He broke the full horror of his death to the inner circle of his adherents on the eve of his transfiguration, exciting their vigorous remonstrance (Matt. xvi. 21); He set his face to go to Jerusalem, knowing full well that the predicted hour had nearly struck (Luke ix. 51); He described the Good Shepherd as giving his life for the sheep (John x. 11); He accepted the gift of Mary's love for his burying (xii. 7); his last utterances were full of similar references (xv. 13); He went to meet the band which Judas led, knowing the while to what He went (xviii. 4).

And perhaps there is no scene in all his life more touching than when the question of certain Greeks, at the close of his public ministry, plunges Him into deep and heart-rending meditation; from the midst of which come the cries of his human soul in agony, and He uses again these very words about the Son of Man being lifted up, adding to them a marvellous forecast of the effect that it should have on the minds and hearts of men throughout all lands and all coming years (xii. 32, 33).

I. The Heroism of the Son of Man.—He evidently foresaw all. The bodily torture—the shame and spitting; the racked muscle and quivering flesh; the slow agony of death—these were present to Him, and the bitterness of the soul, and the God-forsakenness of the spirit. He to some extent must have gauged the weight of the world's sin, which He was to bear away. And his soul was troubled beyond what words can tell, as He came within the penumbra of that eclipse. No eye would pity, no hand would save; lover and friend must stand afar off; the disciples would forsake Him and flee; the very heavens would veil their blessed light. He must be accounted as "sin", and go forth alone as the scapegoat. In front of Him He saw the winepress which He must tread alone. And yet He was not rebellious, neither turned away. He gave his back to the smiters, and his cheeks to them that plucked off the hair; He hid not his face from shame and spitting (Isa. L. 6).

Who does not know the pain of anticipating some awful agony—a separation from some twin soul, an operation, an inevitable break-up of some blessed abode of human bliss? Under circumstances like these, the life drags on its weary length in almost unsupportable anguish, which gnaws it away, as the fret of the sea-billow does the base of the cliffs. At such times the very event we dread is almost a welcome relief from the agony of anticipation. And it is conceivable that the outward tumult of Calvary was positively this to the human nature of Jesus.

And yet He never faltered. Is there not a side light here on the heroic tenacity of his purpose, on the strength of his will! Gentle as a woman, He is mightier than the mightiest of men. Simple as a child, He is strong as God. Lamb though He be, He is Lion too. "For the joy set before Him, He endured the cross, despising the shame." What wonder, then, that having overcome the natural instinctive dread of the pain of death in which all men, more or less, participate, He has been able to overcome the world, and its prince, and the power of darkness, and to save with a great salvation!

This Saviour of ours, my brothers, is no effeminate weakling, no creature of circumstances, no hysterical enthusiast; but a Man who knew what it was to endure the long strain of anticipated agony; who could suffer silently, locking up the secret in his heart; who could face without blanching the direst anguish that man ever bore. It may be that you, too, have some kind of prevision of the cross and shame which await you; but be strong, yea, be strong, because He has gone this way before you, and can make you more than conquerors. You can go through no darker rooms than He has traversed; and you may have what He could not have, the company of One who is touched with the feeling of your infirmities, because He has been tempted in each point like you. Let those especially who, through fear of death, are all their lifetime subject to bondage, understand how completely the blessed Lord can sympathise with them; and let them claim his heroism, and that He Himself should be in them that strength and confidence which they need.

II. THE NATURE OF HIS DEATH.—*Evidently it was not a martyrdom,* —A martyr is wholly at the discretion of his foes. His main object, as the name denotes, is to give a witness to certain neglected and unpopular truths. He is engrossed with this, and does not specially address himself to the question of his fate. If he prove a hindrance and reproof to the men of his time, he must probably suffer the direst penalty they can inflict. But it is no part of his primary purpose to incur that fate; and he has not thought of expiating the sin of those who hound him to his death.

Far different was the main purpose of the Lord Jesus. True, He came as a witness to the truth; but most of all He came to be the sin-offering of our race, and to pass through death into resurrection on behalf of a company which no man can number. Other men die because they have been born; our Lord was born that He might die.

His death was voluntary.—The Father sent the Son; but the Son came. He was not forced suddenly and unexpectedly into the scenes of death. He deliberately walked directly into them, fore-knowing and choosing all. Never for a moment did He admit that his life was taken from Him. He said that He laid it down of Himself, and that He had received this power from his Father. Never for a single moment did He swerve from the acquiescence of his will with his Father's. And can we doubt the voluntary character of his death, as we remark how safe He was until his hour had come, and whilst He remained among the hills of Galilee, or as we behold the marvellous display of his power which flung his captors to the ground on their backs?

No unwilling victim He! Not dragged to the slaughter! "Led!" From the depths of his steadfast soul the words rang out, "I delight to do thy will, O my God." He trod the path to the brow of Mount Moriah as willingly as Isaac had done in his innocence before Him; though He knew, as the lad did not know, that He was to be God's Lamb.

But if all were voluntary, how splendid the tribute to his love! A love that never faltered; that counted the gain more than the pain; that was prepared to bear all to win his Bride. Oh, love of the heart of Jesus, the more we think of thee, the more thou passest knowledge, whilst we stand baffled before thy depths and heights! A love that gave itself under the spell of some sudden impulse were much; but a love that could steadily face years of soul-gnawing agony, this is love indeed! Blessed is the spirit which will resign itself to the inevitable; but more blessed far the spirit which, for very love, will resign itself to the inevitable, and stand at a stake, or hang on a cross, constrained, not by chains or nails, but by its own devotion.

His death was necessary.—The corn of wheat must fall into the ground and die, if it were not to live alone. I love that word *must.* If there had been another way it would have been selected; but there was no other way. In no other way could the love of God have free course and be glorified. In no other way could the curse of Adam's sin be removed from the race. In no other way could our sins be borne, or our salvation achieved. In no other way could we obtain the life of God stored up in the human nature of Jesus. In no other way could He pass to his great reward. *Must*—God Himself had considered all other possible alternatives in vain, and this was the verdict of Deity. *Must*—in the very nature of things, it was peremptory. *Must*—it could not have been otherwise, if He would become the Saviour, Priest, King, Brother, and Life-giver of men. Oh, sad yet blessed necessity! *Sad,* because it cost Him so much; *blessed,* because it has brought us so much.

III. THE JOY OF THE SON OF MAN.—Throughout all the long travail of his soul He was sustained and animated by one delightful anticipation. For the joy set before Him (Heb. xii. 2), He looked through the shadow towards the sun-glints on the horizon to which He went. The joy of doing his Father's will, of rolling away all imputation from his Father's character. The joy of undoing the work of the first Adam, and of becoming, as the second Man, the Head of a redeemed race. The joy of drawing all men to Himself, and of winning for Himself the Church as his Bride. The joys of marriage, and victory, and deliverance, all crowded into one long ecstasy. This sustained and nerved his spirit.

We may just now be near despair. The days are dark. There is much to depress in the slow progress of the Church. The angels must weary as they stand at the twelve open gates of heaven counting the driblets that pass in, while the multitudes reject the invitation of God's love. Iniquity abounds, and the love of many waxes cold. But why should we falter or despair? *He* never did.

Let us keep our eye on the streaks of the breaking day. Let us keep our ears attentive for the first peal of the marriage bells. Let us cultivate his patience and his joy. "If we suffer with Him, we shall be glorified together." "O death, where is thy sting! O grave, where is thy victory! The sting of death is sin; and the strength of sin is the law. But thanks be to God, which giveth us the victory through our Lord Jesus Christ." Wherefore lift up your heads and rejoice, for your redemption draweth nigh.

Ah, what will not that day of redemption bring!—when the regions of the air will no longer be infested by wicked spirits, which rule the darkness of this world; when creation herself shall be delivered from the bondage of corruption, which was, perhaps, flung upon her by the sin and fall of Satan and his hosts; when the Bride of Christ, built up as Eve of old from her Bridegroom's wounded side, shall be brought to Him to share his authority and glory; when from our position beside Him we shall rule angels, and reign on the earth; when God shall have vindicated his wisdom and love in the permission of moral evil! Oh, day of surpassing blessedness; of light too dazzling for mortal eye; of rapture too intense for mortal hearts, we long for thee even as our Lord does! And for love of thee, will be content to wait till the mystery of iniquity has fulfilled its destined course, and we hear the voice that shall welcome us who have shared his sorrow to be partakers of his joy. "Everlasting joy shall be upon their heads. They shall obtain joy and gladness; and sorrow and sighing shall flee away."

12

"SENT"

*"For He whom God hath sent speaketh the words of God: for God
giveth not the Spirit by measure unto Him."*—JOHN iii. 34.

WE PASS but slowly over these earlier chapters of this marvellous
Gospel, because they are so thickly strewn with treasures. And we
need not grudge the time or labour; because they are the seed-plot of
the whole. To understand them is to have a key to the inner life of
our blessed Lord, and to gain the true standpoint for understanding
not only this Evangel, but the other writings of the beloved Apostle.

The word which stands at the head of this chapter is full of the
music rung out by the Christmas chimes. It was one of the watchwords
of Jesus; and, with the exception of the word Father, oftener on his
lips than almost any other; occurring twice in this chapter and more
than forty times in this book, it challenges our attention. What does it
mean? "The Father sent the Son to be the Saviour of the world." This
is an inquiry which is shrouded in deep and impenetrable mystery,
dark with excessive light, before which angels are speechless; and yet
it becomes us to know all we may, for employing one of his expressive
parallels, on the evening of his first resurrection day, our Master said,
"As my Father hath sent Me, even so send I you" (xx. 21). In so far,
then, as we can understand the true meaning of the Father's mission
of the Son, we shall be able to understand also the Son's mission of that
little band which included not the Apostles only, but the two who had
arrived from Emmaus, together with several others not formally included in the Apostolic circle (Luke xxiv. 33); and which thus represents the entire Church, of which we are part.

I. THE ORIGIN OF OUR LORD'S MISSION.—In his Divine nature our
Lord was one with the Father and the Spirit in conceiving the marvellous scheme of man's redemption. In the essence of his being, the
Lord our God is one God; and in the very depths of that absolute oneness, the plan of our redemption was conceived and planned, and its
purpose executed. But it is also true that the whole Godhead was one
with Christ in every act of his incarnation. "God was in Christ, reconciling the world unto Himself." "God was manifest in the flesh."

It is a mistake to describe the work of Jesus as if He stepped in
between an offended God and a race of sinners, averting the thunder-
bolts which were being launched upon them, and interposing by his

own action to appease an otherwise implacable wrath. It is undeniable that the holy nature of God is absolutely set against the wilful disobedience and ungodliness of sinful men. But, nevertheless, the loving nature of God yearns, with all the love that ever breathed through the being of our Saviour, over the fallen and erring children of our race.

The Roman Catholic errs in attributing more tender love and sympathy to the mother of Jesus than to her Son; and in calling upon her to intercede with Him for sinners, reminding Him of her motherhood. This we condemn, and rightly. We turn away, in spite of their consummate art, from the pictures in which the mother pleads with her enthroned Son, as from his throne He meditates vengeance upon the race that crucified Him. But let us take care lest we fall into a similar error, and suppose that the Son is more merciful than the Father; when, in point of fact, they are one in an indissoluble unity. Just as you may analyse the ocean brine in the creek that runs far up into the land, so you may analyse the nature of the Godhead in that marvellous inlet of Deity into the life of men, which we know as the Holy Incarnation. "He that hath seen Me hath seen the Father."

All this lies embedded in these most precious words: "He *gave* his only-begotten Son." "The Father *sent* the Son." At certain times, it may be desirable to accentuate the willinghood on the part of our dear Lord, which made his incarnation and death his own act and deed of unparalleled love. But just now it is befitting to emphasize the other side of the wondrous mystery, and to insist that the love of the Giver is not less than the love of the Given; and that the compassion of the Sender was every whit as tender as that of the Sent. And in saying this, we surely gratify the heart of the Son, who repeatedly turned the thoughts of men from Himself to Him who had sent Him, as if He would attribute to Him any credit or praise which was due for so marvellous an interposition. "Neither came I of Myself, but He sent Me" (viii. 42). Just as the Holy Spirit deprecates the concentration of attention on Himself, lest aught should be diverted from the ever-blessed Son who sent Him (xvi. 14); so does the Son pass on our love and trust which gather around Him so fondly, to the Father whose commissions it was his meat and drink, as the Son of Man, to fulfil. To use his own words, He sought the glory of Him that sent Him (vii. 18).

We often meet with those who concentrate all their thought and love on the Lord Jesus, but who have not yet learnt towards the Father that love which casteth out fear. To Jesus they pray. On Jesus they lean. In Jesus they rest. This is natural in the earlier stages of the Christian life. But it should not be ever so, or we shall become stunted and one-sided in our growth. As the Spirit reveals the Son, so we must ask the Son to reveal the Father, as He has promised to do to the weary and heavy-laden who come to Him; and ultimately the

Father will reveal Himself to the loving and obedient heart (Matt. xi. 27, 28; John xiv. 23).

II. OUR LORD'S CONCEPTION OF HIS MISSION.—We cannot tell what was in his thought when our Lord spoke so constantly of having been sent. Was there present to Him some parting scene in which the Father gave Him up to the work of our redemption? Is there an allusion in his words to a wrench, a surrender, a sacrifice, like that which rends our hearts when we give up to some necessary but distant and painful expedition, the one who is dearer to us than life? When the mother gives up her boy to the service of his country; when the newly-married bride waves her heart-breaking farewell to the husband who sails on some distant and perilous enterprise, and the chords of nature are strained to breaking: is there not some faint shadow of the yet more stupendous giving up on the part of the Infinite God? Gifts are only worth the love that makes them; an infinite gift means infinite love; and such love is capable of infinite pain (x. 36).

But whatever it was that the Lord looked back upon, it is clear that the consciousness of his mission was one of the strongest and most formative factors in his human life. He realized that the Father had sent Him, not to condemn but to save the world (iii. 17); to be its Life, and Light, and Love; to reveal to men the hidden nature of the invisible God; to put down all rule, authority, and power; and to deliver back the kingdom to God the Father, so that God might be all in all.

He was utterly absorbed in this commission.—He had no thought of Himself, of his own glory, or of the esteem of men. To be about his Father's business; to do the works which his Father had given Him to finish (v. 36); to speak the words which He had heard from the Father (viii. 26); to fulfil the commandment enjoined on Him by the Father (xii. 49)—these constituted the programme and object of his life. Dear as was the salvation of the world, and the winning of the Bride of his choice, all was subordinated to a higher purpose, and included in the sweep of a wider plan, by the accomplishment of the purpose of his Father's will. Hence his judgment was unbiased and just, because his motive was absolutely pure (v. 30).

Surely it would be well if we were animated by the same ardent passion. We set ourselves too low an aim, hence so much of the disappointment that comes in Christian endeavour. We set ourselves to seek the conversion of the unsaved, the building up of believers, the extension of the kingdom of our Lord; and are depressed unless the special aim on which we have set our hearts is realized. But if only we could labour in the spirit of our Master, and understand that we are co-workers with Himself in his devotion to his Father's purpose, we should feel that, if only we were true to that, we were fulfilling our life-plan, even though some pet ambition remained unrealized and unfulfilled. "Though Israel be not gathered, yet shall I be glorious in the eyes of the Lord, and my God shall be my strength." The sun includes, in his march through space, the motions of his satellites; and to live to do the will of God includes all those other motives which enter into the life of men.

Our Lord believed that the Father's supplies were adequate to the needs of his commission.—God never sends us to do a work for which He does not equip and enable us. And in doing his work, it is wise constantly to be falling back on his resources. The one thing of which we need to be assured, and the only thing concerning which we should be at all anxious, is the assurance that we are where God would have us be, and engaged on his work. Where this is clear, we need have no care for anything beside. God is pledged to find the stuff for every tabernacle which He commissions us to build. He expects no soldier to conduct a campaign at his own charges. If we go down the mine, He will hold the rope, and send down all supplies.

This was our Lord's attitude. As Son of Man He had emptied Himself of those inherent attributes which were his as the equal and Fellow of God; they were always within his reach, but He forbore to use them; and elected to live a life of complete dependence, yielding up his holy will, and receiving by faith, as we should, all the reinforcements and supplies required in the execution of his commission.

He lived by the Father (vi. 57); He was ever conscious of his Father's companionship, robbing life of its loneliness (viii. 29); He expressly denied that his works or words were his own, and insisted that they were all given, as He needed them, by Him who had sent Him forth (xiv. 10–24). Remember how He said, "My doctrine is not mine, but his that sent Me" (vii. 16); and how He hastened, amid the gathering shadows, to work the works of Him that had sent Him (ix. 4). It was his sufficient justification to the accusation of his foes, that He was only working out what the Father had wrought within Him, up to that very moment of time, Sabbath though it were (v. 17).

It is a lesson which we need in this busy life to ponder deeply. There are three stages in the dying of self. First, we must die to self as being able to achieve our justification; then as being able to effect our sanctification; and lastly, as being able to accomplish any efficient spiritual work. We must learn to die to the energy of the self-life in our Christian activities. He who sent us must give us the plan, and supply us with the power. The doctrine we teach, the words we speak, the works we do, must be received by us from Him who has sent us, as his were received from the Father who sent Him. Then a great peace would settle down upon us, born of a great faith; and we should be able to say, with the saints of a former age, "Thou wilt ordain peace *for* us; for Thou hast wrought all our works in us." He whom God hath sent has only to speak the words of God.

Difficulties are absolutely nothing to the man who knows that he is on the mission on which God has sent him. They are only opportunities for him to show his power; problems to manifest his skill in their solution; thunder-clouds on which to paint the frescoes of his unrealized tenderness. Oh to live as Jesus did, putting Him in that place in our lives, which his Father occupied in his own life; so as to say, The living Saviour hath sent me, and I live by Him, eating of his flesh, and drinking of his blood, depending on his help! (vi. 57).

III. THE HIDDEN POWER OF OUR LORD'S MISSION.—"God giveth not the Spirit by measure." What a word is this! It is said that Solomon gave up the task of enumerating the wealth of treasure that he put into the house of the Lord; and our Father puts no limit on the supply of his Spirit to those whom He sends forth.

As the Son was sent forth to do a work unparalleled in its scope, its sufferings, and its results, the blessed Spirit was bestowed on Him to a commensurate extent. Conceived of the Holy Ghost in the virgin; anointed by the Holy Ghost at his baptism; driven by the Spirit into the wilderness nerved empowered, sustained by the Eternal Spirit in his sacrifice on the cross; raised by the Spirit of Holiness from the dead; and ever receiving from the Father new supplies of the Spirit in his ascension and mediatorial reign: let us be glad and rejoice, for if such measureless supplies came down on the head of our Aaron, we may gladly anticipate some droppings for ourselves as they run down to the fringe of his skirts.

That Spirit which rested on Him is ours. And we may have all of Him that our exigencies demand or our faith can take. There is absolutely no limit save that which we ourselves impose. The oil will go on running so long as we can bring vessels, and will only stay when there is not a vessel more. "He is able to do exceedingly abundantly above all that we ask or think."

On the one hand is our life mission to do the will of Jesus, who has sent us, and who waits to show us what He wants us to do; on the other hand is the unmeasured supply of the measureless Spirit that empowered his earthly life. He is our life-blood, our inspiration, our bond of connection with our Head; nothing shall daunt, nothing overmaster us; the works that He did we will do, yea, greater works than these, because He is gone to the Father, and with added power shall do through us by his Spirit what even He, in his earthly life, could not effect.

13

LIFE AS A FOUNTAIN

"Whosoever drinketh of the water that I shall give him shall never thirst; but the water that I shall give him shall be in him a well of water springing up into everlasting life."—JOHN iv. 14.

HIS NINE months' tour in Judæa was too successful to please the Pharisees; and it became necessary for our Lord to transfer the scene of his ministrations to Galilee, where the authority of the Sanhedrin was less rigorous, and the people were liberalized by the larger admixture of Gentile residents. There were two roads thither from Jerusalem, the circuitous one along the Jordan valley, and the more direct one through Samaria. Jesus selected the latter for reasons which dated from the council-chamber of eternity.

It was the month of January. The weather bright and warm; the copses vocal with sweet-voiced birds; the brooks murmuring along their beds; the pasture-lands bright with flowers; and all the land astir with the sounds of industrious toil. After a morning's walk, about noon, the little band reached the neck of a narrow valley that lay between the mountains of Ebal and Gerizim. And there the embrasure of an ancient well lent a ready resting-place for the Master; whilst his disciples went forward to the town of Sychar, lying some mile and a half further up the valley, to purchase food.

He sat there, deeply musing on the beauties of the scenery and the historic associations of the place, and in fellowship with his Father. Few came to the well at that hour, though later it was thronged with women, bringing their pitchers to obtain a supply of water for their homes. But, presently, the solitude was broken by a woman of Samaria, who, avoiding her sex, came at an hour when she would be unobserved, and escape the taunt, the sneer, the averted look, of those who had not fallen, perhaps because they had never been tempted, as she had. To this woman, on that spot, our Lord spake words which are immortal.

That well-head is, indeed, a pulpit from which He addresses all who wearily seek after life and joy and blessedness, bidding them to come to Himself.

I. THE CONTRASTS OF THIS CHAPTER.—He is evidently under constraint, for the word *must* (4) is applied to Him; yet He speaks with the accent of unlimited prerogative.

He is weary; yet He proposes to give rest from heavy burdens and wearisome pilgrimages (15).

He asks for a drink of water; yet He offers to set flowing wells and fountains of water (10).

He is a suppliant for the gifts of another; yet He talks of being able to give with unlimited munificence (14).

He is an obscure stranger; yet He is greater than the venerable patriarch whose name had lingered for long centuries round that spot (12).

He hungers; yet He eats of meat of which no one knows, and finds sustenance in the act of doing the will of his Father (34).

He is surrounded by the signs of sowing time; yet He proclaims that He is amid the joys of harvest (35).

But chief among these contrasts is the one drawn by Himself between the cool, deep, dark depths of Jacob's well, about a hundred and fifty feet below, and the springs or fountains which He was prepared to open up in the heart of this woman, and of whomsoever else He could induce to accept them.

The "living water" should be a fountain.—At the best the water in Jacob's well was stagnant; but *this* should rise up with all the spontaneity and freshness of a spring, whose sources lie far up among the hills, and which is ever flashing up with graceful beauty from the surface of the ground.

It should be within.—The inhabitants of Sychar, like us, had to go out to get their supplies. Like the woman, they all went *thither* to draw; they have thus become types of all the world (for it is the universal habit of men to go outside themselves for their delights and pleasures); but *this* should be within, like those springs of water in the castles of Edinburgh and Dover, which are beyond the reach of the invader, and flow with perennial blessing for the beleaguered garrisons (14).

It should be eternal.—Jacob's well would dwindle in its supplies, choked with stones and *débris*; but *this* would rise up in the hearts where it was opened, unaltered by the flight of years, unstanched by summer's heat or winter's frost, descending from the timeless life, and returning to it again, eternal as the nature of God (14).

It should be satisfying.—"Whosoever drinketh of this water.shall thirst again," is a legend that might be engraved on the low stone wall of Jacob's well; and equally on every theatre, and other place of worldly amusement or sin, the votaries of which get sips, not draughts: but this would satisfy. In the failure of human love, in the absence of blessed friendships and companionships, in the subsidence of every Cherith brook, those who received what He longed to bestow should never thirst.

Oh, brother-men, have ye received this blessed gift, with its fresh spontaneousness, its inner hidden blessedness, its eternal timeless essence, its power of entire satisfaction? If not, why not seek forthwith from Him by faith a boon so inexpressibly precious, to have

which were to make wildernesses flower and deserts sing? How foolish
to barter this for jewels, pearls, or gold; for earthly delights; for
worldly success!

And if you ask me what it is which He describes under this charming imagery, I reply, It is true religion; nay, better, it is the love of
God in the soul; nay, best of all, it is Himself. Jesus in the heart—
living there by the power of the Holy Spirit; descending thither in
great humility; and rising up in us ever fresh, ever refreshing, ever
fertilising, amid the droughts and desolations and wildernesses of our
mortal life.

II. THE INDEPENDENCE OF CHRIST.—(1) *He is independent of race.*—
It was of no consequence to Him that this woman was a Samaritan,
He being a Jew. At one bound He overleaped the barriers of national
prejudice, and offered his most precious wares to an alien. He is the
Son of Man, and deals with that one human heart which beats under
all breasts alike. In Him is neither Jew nor Gentile. His Gospel, like
bread, water, spring flowers, love, is independent of race.

(2) *He is independent of religious bigotry.*—In the days of Ezra and
Nehemiah, these mongrel Samaritans had sought to be included with
the Jewish people; a proposal which met with strong rebuffs. They
resented the affront; built a temple of their own at Gerizim to rival
that at Jerusalem; claimed for their mountain a superior holiness to
that of Zion; favoured the Romans because the Jews hated them; and
even defiled the Jewish temple by scattering bones there at the time of
the Passover. The Jews therefore had no dealings with the Samaritans,
and held that salvation was only from themselves.

But the Lord Jesus brushed all this aside, as a man might a cob-
web swinging across a garden pathway. What were these distinctions
to Him, so long as those who sought the Father did so in spirit and in
truth? (24) The flock was more to Him than the folds; the army than
the device on the banner of any single regiment. And so it will be with
us, in proportion as we partake of his spirit. Surely the time is coming
when we shall see Christians of all schools drawing into an outward
unity, and viewing with comparative indifference the various names
by which they have been tarred.

(3) *He is independent of character.*—The people who possess a
character of which they are proud, who can produce first-rate testi-
monials as to their flawless conduct, and who can trace back a long
pedigree of religious ancestry, do not stand so good a chance with Him
as this woman did; because, though hitherto she had been abandoned
and fallen, yet of late there had been gleams of desire for better things,
which proved her capacity for the richest bestowments that He could
make. It is to the worthless, and sick, and hopeless, that our Lord is
primarily sent.

(4) *He is independent of payment.*—"The water that I shall *give.*" The white-robed company clustering around the throne cannot give it, nor the morning stars that rejoiced over the birthday of the young world; nor the venerable elders; nor the living creatures with their ceaseless chant. But the Lamb who is in the midst of the throne pours forth its ceaseless floods from the very heart of that throne. And He can give, because He gave Himself up to the death of the cross. By the agony that issued in the cry, "I thirst," He was enabled to open fountains adequate to banish thirst from the universe of God.

(5) *He is independent of apparatus.*—"Thou hast nothing to draw with, and the well is deep." Yes, it is deep—deep as the nature of God; as his deep things; as the excellent height of glory; as the bottomless pit of human need; but He needs nothing with which to draw the waters. He speaks, and it is done. He utters his voice, and the earth melts. He breathes a wish, and life pours into the sea of death, and sweeps it away for ever.

III. THE PROBING OF THE SINNER'S HEART.—"Go, call thy husband!" What a train of memory that word evoked! Beneath its spell, she was back long years; again an innocent girl, courted by him in the sunny vineyards of Gerizim; going with him to his home as his loving wife. Then perhaps there came a growing coldness, leading to alienation and dislike, ending in infidelity. That husband might have died of a broken heart. She had tried to banish his memory and his face, though they would haunt her. What a spasm of remorse and fear seized her, as she remembered that grave within her heart, where her first love lay buried, trampled down by the unholy crew of wilder later passions!

But why awake such memories? Why open the cupboard-door and bid that skeleton step down? Why unsod that grave? Why lay bare that life-secret? It could not be otherwise. The wound must be probed to the bottom and cleansed, ere it could be healed. There must be confession before forgiveness. The sin had to be called to remembrance, ere the son could be raised from death by the prophet's hand. This woman must judge her past sins in the light of those pure eyes, ere she could know the bliss of the fountain opened within the soul.

So it must be with us, if we would have the living water. Go, call thy husband; pay back those dishonest gains; make up that long-standing feud; recall those violent, uncharitable words; summon husband, wife, child, that bright-eyed boy whom you misled, that pure fame you tarnished, that nature, like virgin snow, which you trampled under foot. Call them I say. Will they not come? Then call them louder and louder yet. Ah, they cannot come; they will never come till summoned by the archangel's voice! But, though *they* come not,

Jesus says to thee, "Come hither." At his feet there is forgiveness and plenteous redemption. His hands can scatter benediction. His lips are laden with messages of comfort and peace.

But there must be complete confession.—"The woman said, I have no husband." It was quite true; but there was a further truth. She was living in illicit union with one not her husband, having had five husbands. Ah these fatal secrets which no man has the right to pry into! —shame bids us hide them; but in dealing with the great High Priest we must not hide or cloak one of them.

If we will not do this of our own accord, He will do it for us, extracting the whole black story from our lips by questions; or Himself telling us, as He did this woman, the naked story of the past. Nothing that has ever occurred in our lives has escaped the keen notice of Christ, or been forgotten by Him; and here or hereafter we must hear every detail told with circumstantial clearness by his lips. But it is a thousand times better to hear it now, when the dread recital may be followed by the loving announcement: "Thy sins, which were many, are all forgiven thee."

How we wince when our Lord comes into such close quarters with us!—as the bloodshot eye dreads the light, or the broken limb evades the touch, or the bankrupt hides his ledgers. Like this woman, we start some old worn-out theological controversy, to put Him off the scent (20). There are plenty of people who spend their lives in theological disputes and refinements, because in this way they dexterously manage to pass muster as religious people; though, all the while, they dread anything like definite appeals to their hearts.

But when the ordeal has been borne, and the confession made, the soul receives the blessed inrush of the living water; and, unable to contain itself, speeds to tell the wondrous story to those who have been most familiar with its former life; and, as it narrates the marvellous experience of what it has discovered Christ to be, a whole cityful of people are stirred with the throb of genuine revival, and hasten to the feet of Him who is Priest and Prophet both—Prophet to tell us of all things that ever we did, and Priest to absolve.

14

DARING TO ACT IN FAITH

"Jesus saith unto him, Go thy way, thy son liveth. And the man believed the word that Jesus had spoken unto him."—JOHN iv. 50.

SPEAKING after the manner of men, our Evangelist is very particular in his selection of the incidents in the life and ministry of our Lord which he records. For the most part, he avoids those given by the Synoptists; and chooses fresh and unique illustrations of the outflowing of that fullness which it pleased the Father should dwell in Him.

But, in addition to this, he selects those that suggested conversations and discourses which he desired to record. In nearly every case there is an evident object in the recital of any given incident, because of the deep and blessed spiritual lessons to which it gave rise; the kernel in the shell; the apple of gold in the picture of silver.

It has often, therefore, been a matter for question, what specific purpose was served by the introduction here of the story of this pious nobleman. It is an exquisite incident; and no doubt chronologically it belongs to this period of our Saviour's ministry. It may have been one of those stories which the mother pondered in her breast, from the day when she first heard it fresh from the lips of those who were immediately concerned. But is there no further reason for its insertion here? Surely there is. And we can but adore the grace of the Holy Spirit who arranged that there should be placed on record so graphic and touching an illustration of what faith is, and how it takes and appropriates God's best gifts.

We all know what it is to ask for blessings which the heart craves, as flowers do sunshine, and children love. For some of these we are able to quote a definite promise, in which God has pledged Himself to give what we need. When this is the case, it is not enough to plead for an answer in a perfunctory, careless way on the one hand, or in a half-despairing tone on the other. But to *claim* the answer, and take it from the open hand of God, not always feeling a sensible communication pass between Him and us, but sure that it has done so, and that we have the petitions we desired of Him; the basis of our confidence being our certainty that He will keep his word. At such times, though there may be no single sign of an answer to our prayer, no cloud, small as a man's hand, presaging the great rain, yet we are able to go down the mountain slopes, thanking God in anticipation for the blessing which we have received from his fatherly bounty.

There are other cases in our inner history in which we are unable to cite a specific promise, or an analogous case, from God's Word; but a conviction is wrought into our hearts by the Spirit of God. It cannot be accounted for by natural or constitutional causes; it thrives amid the most searching self-scrutiny, and gathers strength as we pray about it through the years; it is corroborated by the trend of spiritual principles, and the circumstances of daily providence. Concerning any such matter, it is also possible, not only to beseech and pray, but to reckon with an assured faith—a faith based on the character of God— that He will do according to the Word on which He has caused us to hope. The cases of the conversion of beloved friends, and of restoration to health, amongst many others, may be included in this second class of claiming prayers.

It is obvious that many of our prayers do not come under either of these two headings. They are not based on promise; they cannot stand the tests which have been just suggested. And, as a consequence, we cannot exercise faith concerning them; or reckon on the answer being forthcoming; or give thanks as those who are sure that the blessing has been consigned, even if not delivered. Such prayers after awhile will fade and die away on the lips which once uttered them most passionately. The man who lives near God cannot exercise faith for, and will soon leave off praying for, or desiring, the things which it is not God's will to grant.

Dismissing, then, these latter prayers, which are born in the unreclaimed wastes of our inner life—as the *ignis fatuus* in the swampy morass, and which vanish before the increasing light of the perfect day—we have to deal with those prayers concerning which we are authorized to exercise a faith that cannot be misled. And in all such cases it is clear that we are called upon, not only to offer up prayers and supplications, with strong cryings and tears, unto Him that is able to save and help, but *to take deliverance,* and go on our way sure and glad; not looking for our warrant to any set of emotions, but to the unchangeable word and character of the Eternal God.

This is precisely what this nobleman did. News travelled fast through the crowded populations of Galilee. With lightning speed the tidings spread that He whose boyhood and manhood had been spent among their hills, whose first miracle had been wrought in one of their village homes, and who had already attracted the notice and hatred of the leading dignitaries of the metropolis, was again among them, and at Cana. The Galileans received Him with open arms, "for they had seen all things that He did at Jerusalem at the feast."

Amongst others, the tidings reached this nobleman, perhaps Chuza, Herod's steward, or Manaen, his foster-brother. It was a sad time with him; for his son was at the point of death. But there was suggested a sudden hope; and he started at once to use every endeavour to bring this wondrous Miracle-worker to his home. He never supposed that the Master could as easily heal from a distance; or that He could, if need were, raise the dead; but he had faith to believe that where He came disease must flee.

Our Lord, with unerring accuracy, detected the weak point of his faith: it needed so many outward signs and encouragements; it must have the assurance of the outstretched hand, the audible voice, the physical presence; it craved the assurance which the outward and physical, the sensuous and emotional, supply. And in the absence of these it was in danger of expiring. But faith like this hardly merits the name, though, alas! it is too common with us all. We are brave at swimming so long as we are in our depth. We are grand soldiers so long as we stay within the castle enclosure. We believe so long as we can see or feel.

But wherever our Lord finds faith He sets Himself to mature and foster it. There was a germ of it in this suppliant's heart, capable of expansion into a noble growth; and He beheld it with eager joy, and immediately sought to develop it by the only means through which faith can ever grow—namely, by trial. "Jesus said unto him, thy son liveth." That was all. No sign, no renewed assurance, no appeal to emotion or sense; just the assurance of those majestic lips, and it was enough. Without another word, and apparently without hesitation, "the man believed the word that Jesus had spoken unto him, and went his way."

Comparing the length of time occupied on his homeward journey with the distance between Cana and Capernaum, the conviction forces itself home on our minds that he made no particular haste back. Why should he? The boy was living, doing well. The home was already astir with glad surprise. He was sure of it, probably had thanked God for it, and could not be more sure though he were to see the bright smile of his darling. And it is quite likely that he stayed for the night at some wayside inn to sleep off, in a long, deep, child-like sleep, the effects of long watching, intense anxiety, and the swift journey to Cana. There was nothing extraordinary in this. Faith, when it is as it should be, is as restful and glad for a promise as for some evident deliverance. Could there be a better illustration of the simple faith which believes the promise of God, and acts upon it, reckoning on the accomplished purpose of its prayer? We may apply this in several directions.

(1) *For forgiveness.*—Suppose you come, as a penitent, to the great High Priest, conscious of a very heavy load of sin. It may be for the first time or the thousandth. You tell the sad, dark story, not hiding or extenuating aught; not excusing or palliating; not trying to shift the blame on others; not lumping all sins together, but naming each alone, as brought to mind by the Holy Spirit. And when the confession is complete, you naturally look up and ask for forgiveness. But you have

a perfect right to go a step further, and claim it; yes, and be thankful for it, even though as yet you have not caught a glint of light from his face.

He who said to the nobleman, "Thy son liveth," says that "if we confess our sins, He is faithful and just to forgive us our sins, and to cleanse us from all unrighteousness." Oh that we would believe this word which Jesus speaks, and go our way, restful and satisfied that so it is! Instead of this, we try to *feel* forgiven. Now, suppose that the nobleman had tried to feel that his son lived before he started home. In all probability he would never have started. But the question of what he felt does not seem to have entered his mind. It was enough to him to have heard the voice of Jesus, and he started with buoyant assurance.

It is a mistake to wait for feelings. Believe the word of God. Will to believe it. Take forgiveness. Thank the Lord for it. Reckon that it is so because He has said it, even if you do not experience a thrill of emotion. And if you dare to step out in faith, you will discover how blessed are they that believe; for there is always a performance of those things spoken by the Lord.

(2) *For victory over sin.*—How many fail because they are always praying for deliverance, without claiming and giving thanks for it! They go to the Lord Jesus each night with the same story of defeat, and each morning utter the same almost despairing cry for help—a cry that seems to strike against the irresponsive heaven, for it brings no deliverance. Yet the Lord has promised to save his people from their sins, and to keep them from falling. It is not enough, then, to ask Him to do it. We may, and should go further, and say, "Do as Thou hast said."

Claim victory, take victory, thank for victory before even you go into the fight, in the assurance that Jesus will be around you as a wall of fire, an invisible but real defence. He said, "I give you power to tread on all the power of the enemy, and nothing shall by any means hurt you." There it is waiting for you; appropriate it, and go your way, saying like David as he entered on his conflict with Goliath, "The Lord saveth, for the battle is the Lord's."

(3) *For all the priceless gifts of the Christian life.*—How shall we take that gift of living water of which our Lord speaks, which quenches all thirst and pacifies all desire, and makes the inner life like a garden of the Lord, and even issues forth to water and refresh others? We cannot feel it enter. There is no flow of purling streams in liquid music. But we can take the priceless boon by faith.

The heart, for instance, may be aching for "the touch of a vanished hand, and the sound of a voice that is still." It thirsts. But it goes to Christ, and lays open its need, and claims the all-satisfying draught. Instantly Christ meets the claim, and fills the longing soul with goodness. "My peace, my rest, my satisfying joy I give thee, dear heart," says He; "be comforted." And the soul believes the word which the Master has spoken, and goes its way, not feeling any strong surge of emotion, but assured that it has received great spiritual bestowment; and as the days go by, in its power to endure, its patience, its calm joy, it knows that it was not a vain thing to wait on God.

And so it is with all God's promised gifts, and especially that of the Holy Spirit. If we wait to feel them, we shall miss them. But if we dare to claim them, taking them by faith, and uttering words of thanks, it shall be to us according to our faith.

It is not always possible to exercise this faith which claims. At such times it is useless to fix our attention on the faith, for faith is the result of other things. And if it is deficient, it will be wise on our part to turn our thought on these, and question where we are wrong.

Of course, God will never allow us to believe for anything which is outside his purpose to give. Very often we lack faith, not because the object we seek is outside God's purpose, but because our spiritual life is at so low an ebb. The thing is there on the shelf; but our faith cannot reach high enough to lift it down. Let us not rebuke ourselves merely as deficient in faith; but let us adopt that regimen on which alone faith can wax strong.

There are three conditions for the faith that can claim all that God is ready to give.

It must be associated with a good conscience (1 Tim. i. 5-19). So long as the conscience is uneasy and perplexed, conscious of evil not judged, and of a perpetual struggle to pacify itself, faith is as impossible as a mirror of the heavens on the sea when it is being swept by violent winds.

It must feed on the promises of God. Abraham is said not to have considered the physical difficulties in the way of the accomplishment of the Divine promise, but to have looked steadfastly towards, and reckoned absolutely upon, the word of his Almighty Friend. So must it be with us all. We cannot live by bread alone, but by every word of God.

It must dare to act in the absence of emotion, stepping out as bidden on the yielding water, in sheer faith, and finding that it becomes a sheet of rock beneath the feet. To such a faith nothing is impossible.

15

The Divine Master Workman

"My Father worketh hitherto, and I work."—JOHN v. 17.

AN INTERVAL of some months lies between the previous chapter and this, in which many of the incidents in our Lord's crowded Galilean life took place. Our evangelist does not touch on them—first, perhaps, because they had already been fully described by the other three; and secondly, because he wanted to concentrate all his force on the great contest which his Master waged in the very stronghold of Jewish prejudice, and which led, step by step, to the terrible final catastrophe of his death.

This visit to Jerusalem was, without doubt, crowded with incidents, of which a single specimen only is given here, because it introduced one of those startling disclosures of our Lord's inner being which roused undying opposition among his foes, but constitutes for ever a mine of spiritual wealth to those who love Him.

We must pass over the touching pathos of the incident itself, in order to fix on the salient feature, that our Lord not only healed the sufferer after thirty-eight years' deferred hope, but did so on the Sabbath, and bade him carry his bed home. This bidding clashed with Jewish custom and Pharisaic ritual; but the man rightly inferred that He who could work so great a miracle was supreme in the spiritual sphere, and could set aside the petty and vexatious exactions of the religious leaders of the time.

It was impossible, however, that the Pharisees and others could silently acquiesce in this assumption of a superior authority to their own; and they seem to have cited Jesus before the authorities on the formal charge of Sabbath-breaking. But his judges were little prepared for the line of his defence, which convulsed the assembly in paroxysms of religious fury, and revealed some of the deepest facts in our Lord's life and consciousness. His opening words contain the text and pith of all that followed: "My Father worketh hitherto, and I work."

I. OUR LORD'S CONSCIOUSNESS OF DEITY.—"He said that God was his Father," or, as the Greek might be rendered, "His own Father" (18). When He spoke thus, they felt that He claimed God as Father in a unique sense, and they sought the more to kill Him; not only because He had broken the Sabbath, but because, in saying this, *He had made Himself equal with God.*

It is most important that we should not read our western notions into our Lord's references to his Sonship. We must understand them as they were understood by those to whom they were first addressed. In their judgment they conveyed the assertion of equality. And He who uttered them knew that it would be so, and carefully picked these very words because they meant so much. "He thought it not robbery to be equal with God."

To my mind that is almost the strongest proof of the Deity of our blessed Lord. Not primarily that He wrought marvellous works, or rose from the dead; but that his holy, humble spirit thrilled with the consciousness of his Deity. On these grounds I would be prepared to argue the whole question of our Lord's Divinity. By friend and foe alike, He is held to have been the holiest that ever trod our earth. *But the holiest must be the humblest.* He will not strive, nor cry, nor lift up, nor cause his voice to be heard in the streets; He will not assume anything which He is not; He will curtain, so far as He can, the intrinsic splendour of his nature. And yet, for all that, see how this meekest and lowliest of men accentuates his oneness and equality with God. This, indeed, was the charge on which He was condemned to die. Silent in reference to all other charges, when He was solemnly challenged as to *this,* He saw no incongruity between his desolate, suffering, rejected condition, and the claim to be, in a unique (and, to the Jewish mind, a blasphemous) sense, the fellow and equal of the Eternal (Matt. xxvi. 63, 64; John xix. 7).

But the Holiest must also be the clearest and most certain in all spiritual insight. Could it be otherwise? Our perception of the truth of things is dimmed and obscured by the grossness of our flesh, the earthwardness of our dispositions, the evil of our hearts. But when these are removed, we no longer see through a glass darkly, but face to face. "Blessed are the pure in heart, for they shall see God." It is a commonplace of moral philosophy that character means vision, insight, knowledge. We cannot but believe, therefore, that, even apart from his divine self-consciousness, our Lord could not have been deceived when He announced Himself as his Father's equal. To his perfect human soul all truth lay revealed as a summer landscape beneath the eye of the sun; and especially this truth, rearing itself prominently from among all the rest.

All other holy beings refuse in horror ascriptions of Divine homage and worship. Apostles and angels join in crying, "See thou do it not." Consider, then, how great this Man was who, though holiest and humblest of men, forbade none who would prostrate themselves before Him, falling on the ground and praying to Him as God.

Clearly, then, the Son of Man is competent to fulfil all the functions of God. Is untiring energy working ceaselessly through the ages characteristic of the living God? So it is of the Son of Man: "My

Father worketh hitherto, and I work" (17). Is it the prerogative of the Father to raise the dead, and quicken them? So it is of the Lord Jesus; listen to the majestic words: "The Son quickeneth whom He will" (21). Is it the peculiar right of the Creator to be the Judge of men, because He understands the mechanism of their inner being and weighs their opportunities? This is also the Redeemer's right: "The Father hath committed all judgment unto the Son," and his voice shall summon the dead from their graves to his bar (22). Is it the peculiar attribute of God to be the fountain of life, so that life, inherent, underived, perennial, is ever rising up in his mighty being, maintaining here an angel and there a humming-bird? This is also an attribute of our blessed Lord. The glorious possession of inherent life is his also; it has been given Him to have life in Himself (26). The entire sum and totality of the attributes of Deity are resident in the nature of the Son of Man.

Obviously, then, men should honour the Son as they honour the Father (23). Nor has this been lacking. When He ascended to his throne, there followed Him from the heart of the Church a tide of adoration, which has only become deeper and wider with the lapse of time. In the first days of the Church, believers were known as those who called on the name of the Lord Jesus. To Him, the ascended and glorified Master, were addressed the prayers of the infant Church about to select an Apostle; of the first martyr, in the moment of his mortal agony—a moment which must ever test the habitual practice of the soul; of Ananias, who talked with a holy familiarity, which gives a glimpse into his prayer-closet: and these are but specimens of myriads. The records of early Church history teem with hymns, and prayers, and dying words, and fervent ejaculations, written on parchment, or scrawled in rude hieroglyphics on the walls of catacombs and prisons, all to the same effect.

The instincts of the Christian heart are not then hopelessly at fault when they prompt prayer to our ascended Lord. He does not scruple to ask for such honour as men give to God. He insists that they who do not honour Him withhold honour from the Father. He claims that every knee should bow to Him, and every tongue acknowledge that He is Lord. He does not chide the threefold circle of adoration, by which his throne is ceaselessly surrounded, as elders, saints, and angels fall down and worship the Lamb with the same adoration with which they adore the Supreme.

II. THE FELLOWSHIP BETWEEN THE SON AND THE FATHER DURING OUR LORD'S HUMAN LIFE.—And as we study it, let us remember that golden key to the unlocking of the treasures of this precious Gospel, that we are to be to the Lord Jesus all that He was to his Father, and that He is willing to be to us all that his Father was to Him. And as we con these wondrous statements of that inner fellowship between

Father and Son, we shall see that the after parable of the vine was founded on a union which already subsisted; and shall learn how close, and intimate, and all-embracing our Lord would fain have our union with Himself to become.

"He did nothing of Himself," i.e., He originated nothing, did nothing at the prompting of his own will; but always leant on his Father for direction and inspiration (19). No vine ever clung to its trellis-work, and no child to its mother, as He to his Father. Though all his Divine attributes were within his reach, and might at any moment have been called into operation, He forebore to use them, that He might learn the life of dependence and faith, the life which was to be ours towards Himself. This is why the sacred writers speak of the faith of our Lord Jesus (Gal. ii. 20; Heb. xii. 2).

He was ever conscious of his Father's love and presence.—He lived in the present tense of his Father's love, which was so real as to rob his life of all sense of loneliness (20; viii. 29). He knew that his Father heard Him always, as his spirit rose in perpetual fellowship and communion, unhindered by the densest clouds of human unbelief (xi. 42). Yea, there was something deeper still in his habitual realization that the Father dwelt in Him; so that his words, and works, and influence, and plan of life were the perpetual working out of what his Father was working in (17; xiv. 10). And why should not we live in a fellowship equally hallowed and close? It was his one desire that his relationship with his Father should be the model of our relationship with Himself (xvii. 21, 23). And thus it shall be by the grace of the Holy Spirit who, Himself God, is (if I may use the term) the all-pervasive medium between the Father and the Son, and who links all whom He fills into that same sacred oneness.

He was perpetually engaged in reading the open book of his Father's will.—He had no will of his own to seek, no object of his own to serve (30). He had come, in his Father's name, to do his Father's will, and to glorify his Father's name (30, 43; xvii. 4). It was the passion of his being to do God's work on God's plan. And his eye was thus ever kept on the movement of the cloud of his Father's unfolding purpose. The Father showed the Son what He was doing. And the Son, having seen it, translated it into the language of daily human life (20). But what a model for ourselves! If He whom we worship as Lord took on Himself so absolutely the form of a servant, how fair would our life be if we more deeply received of his spirit; and, through obedience here, prepared ourselves to sit by his side in the glory, and reign with Him!

These are glimpses of what our life may become. There will be pain to suffer, a conflict to maintain, a work to do, in face of opposition which may grow ever more violent; but, amidst it all, there may be unbroken fellowship with the ascended Lord by the grace of the Holy Spirit, through whom alone it can be originated and maintained. Ah, that clear heaven of azure blue, unflecked by cloud—what a reflection it casts on the face of the quiet, upturned heart! This is the spiritual equivalent of the land that drinketh water of the rain of Heaven!

III. THE PLAN OF OUR MASTER'S WORK.—Our Lord was as careful of the promptings of his Father as a jeweller of gold leaf. If the Father wrought within Him up to any given moment of time, He never hesitated to give free play to the holy impulse, though it should bring Him into collision with the religion of his time. "See," said He, "Sabbath or no Sabbath, my Father moved Me to this miracle. I could do no other than yield. Ye must reckon with Him" (17).

He waited for the Father to show Him what next He would have Him do. The pattern of his life was gradually outspread before Him, as that of the tabernacle was unfolded before the great lawgiver, shut up with God. He seemed ever a learner in his Father's workshop, making all things on the pattern shown Him from hour to hour. This made Him so still, so calm, unmoved by difficulty, unperturbed amid a hail of murderous stones (viii. 59; ix. 4). And it would bring rest, and unity, and power, into our own lives, if it were the one purpose of our being to discover and do only the good works which God hath before ordained that we should walk in them. Better do less that we may do more. Better stand still than run without being sent. Better withdraw oftener from the valley to the brow of the Transfiguration mount, than, by fussy activity, miss the radiant vision, and the bitter need which waits for us at the mountain foot.

And thus our Lord's life-work was ever on an ascending scale. From making water wine, to making blood the ransom price of souls; from raising the daughter of Jairus, to the calling of Lazarus from a three days' death-sleep; from cleansing the temple, to works of redemption, resurrection, and judgment. God was ever showing Him yet greater things. The plan of his life was ever becoming fuller; its stream deeper, its current swifter. Nor will it be otherwise with ourselves. Be true to the power you have, and it will increase. The limb becomes defter by use. And he who yields his 'prentice hand to be nerved and used by the great Master Workman, shall find, as the years pass by, that he will be able to accomplish results, the mere dreams of which had never visited him in the most ecstatic moments of his youth.

O glorious Servant of God, and worker for men, breathe into us thine own spirit; that following in thy steps we may at last participate in thy rest and reward!

16

THE WILL OF GOD

"I seek not mine own will, but the will of the Father which hath sent Me."—JOHN v. 30.

THE PASSIONATE desire of the heart of the Lord Jesus was to do the Will of God. As He stepped down into our world, He appropriated David's words, with a significance that David could never have put into them, "Lo, I come; in the volume of the book it is written of Me; I delight to do thy will, O my God." And He clung to it as a handrail down the steep dark staircase by which He went to his death, saying, as He descended into the gloom, "O my Father, thy will be done!"

It is evident, though we cannot penetrate the mystery in which the whole subject is enshrouded, that our Lord, as far as his human nature was concerned, had a will, which could be denied and subordinated to the will of his Father. We cannot fathom or explain, but we cannot ignore his repeated references to *his own will*. It was the perfect expression of his holy, glorious nature; but it was a distinct and special force in the mechanism of his inner life. "I seek not mine own will, but the will of the Father"; "I came down from heaven, not to do mine own will, but the will of Him that sent Me"; "Not *my* will, but thine be done" (John v. 30; vi. 38; Luke xxii. 42). He subordinated his own will to God's; and so came, as all do who begin by choosing it, to delight in it as altogether lovely.

To do God's will meant, in the experience of our Great High Priest, obedience to death, even the death of the cross; it meant shame and spitting, a breaking heart, a soul exceeding heavy, as laurels bending low under a weight of rain; it meant the cry of forsakenness. But He was ever nerved and sustained by the thought that it was the will of his Father. He did not look at the Fatherhood through the cross; but at the cross through the Fatherhood. Never for one moment did He lose faith in the infinite love which was leading Him through darkness into light, through death to life.

There are many thoughts given us in our Lord's acceptance of his Father's will.

I. IT IS THE SUFFICIENT PURPOSE OF LIFE TO DO THE WILL OF GOD.—Among the aims of our Saviour's life we may enumerate his desire to save the lost; to put away sin; to purchase for Himself a people; to win for Himself a bride; to destroy the works of the devil. But all these were included in the sweep of a wider, grander purpose than any, as the orbits of the planets are included in the march of suns; viz., the sublime aim of doing his Father's will.

Nor is there anything loftier or more inclusive throughout all worlds than this; for the will of God is the perfect expression of his character, which is infinite love, strength, and wisdom, woven in perfect unity. But do we not often sink below this level, and, missing this high purpose, involve ourselves in disappointment?

Not infrequently do I receive letters from discouraged Christian workers in which they complain sorrowfully of the lack of conversions in their ministry, and questioning whether it would not be better for them to abandon their positions for some other calling. Now, it is right and Christlike to yearn with soul-travail over the lost, and to track them in their wanderings through the wild; and, if there is a cessation of salvation work in our service, it should lead to solemn questionings and searchings of heart. But neither this, nor the ebbing away of people, nor the appearance of failure, is a true indication that we should forsake our post. We cannot explore the Divine purpose, or know the special function which God is fulfilling by our means. The one question for us is, Are we where God would have us be? We may be pawns standing for hours on the same square of the chessboard; or sentries at outpost duty far from the camp: but if it is the will of God for us to be there, it is enough. We can laugh at what the world deems failure; we can exist without the fulfilment of our chosen gauges of success, if only we are in the current of our Father's will.

The ground is hard; the outlook unpromising; helpers few; success rare as a gleam across the sea on a stormy day. But God has put us where we are; and it is enough, abundantly enough.

We know God's will by several unmistakeable signs; by the sure impression of his Spirit on our heart; by the teaching of his holy Word; by the unerring indication of the circumstances in which we are placed, and by which we may be bound or tied or nailed to a certain post. We may suffer keenly; heart and flesh may threaten to fail; our life-blood may seem to be ebbing drop by drop from our heart: but, if God shows us no way of escape, and no path of retirement, we must take it as his will that we should keep just where we are. It is his will, and it is enough. His blessed will! His lovely will! The will of our Father! Hush, my heart, there can be no mistake! He has not forgotten thee. And some day it will be a sufficient reward to know that He was satisfied.

II. THE BLESSED RESULTS OF DOING THE WILL OF GOD.

(1) *It feeds the spirit.*—An hour before, the Master had sent his disciples to buy food, and He, too exhausted to accompany them,

awaited their return beside the well; but now that they have hastened back, He seems indifferent to the bread they bring. "Hath any man brought Him aught to eat?" No. But He has been fed in doing. "My meat is to do the will of Him that sent Me, and to finish his work" (iv. 34).

So is it ever. Not only in the devout study of the Word, or in attendance on some public ministry, but in doing the will of God, though it may only lead to a wayside talk with a wayfarer, the soul is nourished and fed. Obedience to God's will can never take the place of communion with Him; but it is a valuable adjunct. Do what lies to your hand, not because you must, but because you discern God's will in it; and you will discover that to expend is to expand; that to give out is to increase; that to feed crowds is to accumulate baskets of provision; and that to water others is to be watered.

(2) *It clears the judgment.*—How often are we perplexed about our course! We stand where many roads meet, not sure which to take. We waver and vacillate, and finally run to this friend or the other, or adopt some questionable method of ascertaining our path. Why all this difficulty? Much of it arises from the intrusion of self-will, which deflects our judgment, as the masses of iron on a steamship deflect the needle from the pole. Our eye is not single, and therefore our body is not full of light. "My judgment," said our Lord, on the other hand, "is just, because I seek not mine own will, but the will of the Father which hath sent Me."

Our God must have a purpose for each of his children, and in everything. In his mind there must be an ideal of what we should do under all circumstances of daily living. And He is not unwilling to show it to us; it is there held out for us to see; and if we fail to see it, it is probable that there is some obliquity in our vision. Beware of this; search your heart to see what it may be which prevents you from apprehending God's purpose. It will not be long ere you discover some lurking reluctance to have God's will done completely; and only when this is dragged to light and judged, will you descry the Star of Bethlehem glimmer out in the morning sky to guide you.

There are cases in which the will is unbiased by self-will, and yet it seems impossible to discern God's will: then we must wait; the lesson is evidently patience, and there is no alternative but to stand still, in spite of all remonstrances to the contrary, till a path is cleft through the mighty waters.

(3) *It gives Rest.*—What an agony must they suffer whose life seems at the mercy of some cruel fate, or iron destiny, or implacable, unalterable law! They beat their breasts against the bars of their cage till they fall panting, dying to the floor. Many an imperturbable face hides a broken heart, or one eaten through with unrest. But as soon as the soul has learnt to recognise God's will in all the events of life—

in the falling of a sparrow to the ground, and of a hair from the head; in what God permits as well as in what He appoints: in the coming of a Judas to betray, as much as in the advent of an angel to strengthen —then there is rest. The current of the life which had dissipated itself in many side channels settles down to an even and steady flow towards the sea, which draws it to itself.

If you would look up, though with tear-blinded eyes, and recognise that it is your Father's will for you to be fixed in that difficult position; to be separated from that twin soul; to drink that bitter cup; to be exposed to calumny and hate; to do that uncongenial task; that it is the will of One who loves you infinitely, and is making all things work together for good—then you would find rest to your soul. This was Christ's way. The doing of the Father's will was the yoke He took and bore, and has consecrated for ever. So take your side by Him in the long, difficult furrow, yoked with Him. "Take my yoke upon you, and learn of Me," said He, "for I am meek and lowly in heart: and ye shall find rest to your souls" (Matt. xi. 29).

(4) *It is the key to certain knowledge.*—We want to know. All around us stretches the great unexplored continent of God's nature, in which we have appropriated but a few acres of clearing. To know God would surely bring into our lives deeper draughts of that eternal life to drink of which quenches the inner thirst. But how shall we know Him, and how be sure of aught we think we know? There is no hesitation in our Lord's majestic answer: "If any man will do his will, he shall know of the doctrine, whether it be of God, or whether I speak of Myself" (vii. 17).

The cause of much of the ignorance of men is traceable to the will. They are not willing to know or to retain God in their knowledge. But when they renounce their prejudices, and put their wills on God's side, and become as little children, content to be taught, the true knowledge begins to steal into their being, and grows unto the perfect day. Then they no longer need books of evidences or arguments to prove the truth of Christ; they have seen Him for themselves, and know that the Son of God is come, and has given them an understanding, that they may know Him that is true.

In dealing with professed sceptics or seekers, or those who seem unable to believe, it is of the highest importance, therefore, to probe their will, and see if they are holding to anything which is inconsistent with this attitude of entire acquiescence with the will and ways of God; until this is the case, neither conversion nor regeneration is possible.

(5) *It introduces to a large family.*—Our Master knew what loneliness was in his family life; for, with the exception of his mother, his nearest refused to believe in Him. What ecstasy, then, must He have felt on that day when, after his friends had endeavoured to stay Him from getting into deeper collision with the Jewish leaders, "He stretched

forth his hand toward his disciples and said, Whosoever shall do the will of my Father which is in heaven, the same is my brother, and sister, and mother."

And is this really the case, that those who live in the will of God may claim the kinship of all in all worlds that live for the same? Are there bonds, invisible as air, yet firm as adamant, which bind us for evermore in family ties with all holy souls, and which knit us, above all, to Him, the Royal and Divine Man? Then isolation is impossible. Gulfs are bridged. Barriers are pierced. Space is annihilated. Christ and we may be one; and we may be one also with redeemed spirits, and bright angels, and all great souls that have been, are, and shall be, in so far as we and they participate in the fixed resolve to do or suffer in all things the will of God.

III. AN EXHORTATION TO CHOOSE THE WILL OF GOD.—Refuse it, and it will crush you. Take it grudgingly, and it will chafe you into sores. Withhold from it some portion of your life, and you spoil your obedience in all the rest. But why all this reluctance? The will of God must be infinitely lovely and beautiful, because He is that. To put it away is to put Him away. To refuse it is to refuse Him. Stand out no longer, but yield!

So many make the mistake of trying to like the will of God, or of working themselves up into a state of resignation and stoical indifference. This will never do. Begin, not with it, but with Him. Distastefulness passes out of the will of those we love and trust. Choose Him, and you will come to choose his will. Will his will, and you will come to delight in it. Tell Him that you are willing to be made willing, and leave Him to bring every thought into captivity to Himself.

The will of God may lead into the garden of Gethsemane; but the path to the Easter dawn lies there. There is no other way, and there is no danger of being lost (vi. 39); but the certainty of an ever-deepening sense of blessedness, and serenity, and heaven, the law of whose perfect joy is that strong angels do his will, hearkening unto the voice of his Word.

17

The Father's Name

"I am come in my Father's name."—John v. 43.

How much there is in a name! A palace lay wrapt in mysterious slumber. The king asleep on his throne; his counsellors strewn in various attitudes on the highly-polished floors, each grasping tightly the symbols of his office, but all beneath the spell; the maidens twined in various attitudes by fountain and loom, which for many a year had stood unused. And what was needed to awaken all that sleep-bound palace, save the speaking of one word, the right word, the word which should untie the mystic spell? Many essayed to speak it, but in vain. Yea, themselves succumbed to the charm they failed to loose. And all around them crept the briar-rose. Until one came, before whose tread the thorns were changed to myrtles, and the thickset hedge to honey-suckle. He spoke the word which broke the spell of slumber, and again filled the silent palace with the hum of many voices and the stir of life.

It is a parable. And yet it is a truth. It is true, to a limited extent, in the case of individual hearts and lives, wrapt in lethargy until one voice shall speak that single word which shall arouse to animation, and kindle the glow of life and love. But it is a true picture also of the moral condition of the world. The hearts and consciences of the majority of mankind were drugged in fatal stupor, waiting through the ages spell-bound and torpid. Many a philosopher and teacher, reverend and grave, essayed to awaken the ear and heart of men; but all failed, till One came for whom all were waiting, though they knew it not, and He spake the great word which broke the silence of centuries, and shed life on death, light on darkness, love on despair. Do you ask what that word was? I answer: it was the name so constantly applied by our Saviour to God.—Father.

But, after all, a name may mean comparatively little. It may tell us something of the person who bears it, but not much. Call a man Jacob, or Moses, or Peter, and we infer that he is crafty in character; or was drawn out of a watery grave; or has a rock-like nature, in the clefts of which weaker men may hide. Yet, at the best, it is only a spar from a ship; a brick from a house; a flower from a garden. And the man is labelled, but not known.

So the Son of God was not content to speak of God as the Father; that name had been guessed in the previous centuries. Did not David sing that God pitied us, as a father pities his children? Did not Isaiah address God, saying, "Doubtless Thou art our Father, though Abraham be ignorant of us?"? It was not quite a new name, though it was spoken with new force, and reminted as it passed through those gentle holy lips. But our Lord spent his life in showing how much that name "Father" connoted, or meant, when it was applied to God.

To understand this, let us imagine two young men standing together in some gathering of men for the interests of art or science or literature. Presently the attention of all is directed towards one standing to speak, who wins breathless hearing by his face and voice, "Who is that?" whispers one to the other. "He is my father," is the proud reply. But how little do the words mean to his companion! Then, as the two pass out together, the son begins to explain to his friend how much, in this case, lies behind that title, "father." It may mean so little. It may mean nothing more than the progenitor of life. But in this case it means brother, friend, teacher, adviser, all that men love and revere in one. So Jesus Christ was not satisfied to say that God was a Father. He set Himself to show what sort of Father He was; and what heights, and depths, and breadths, and lengths of meaning lay hidden in that one sweet, tender, though common and oft-spoken, word. This is what He meant when He said, "I am come in my Father's name."

Men are apt to speak lightly to one another about the Fatherhood of God, and to ignore the ministry of Jesus in explaining what that phrase involves. But in ignoring Him, they trample under foot the one torch which can illumine the sculptured glories of this wondrous title, Father. "No man knoweth the Father, save the Son, and he to whomsoever the Son will reveal Him" (Matt. xi. 27). We can only know the Fatherhood of God through the teachings of Jesus; just as we only know the Lord Jesus through the teachings of the Holy Ghost, who makes Him real and present and precious. And, in fact, the man who talks of God the Father, and rejects Christ, proves that he knows nothing of the Father. "If God," said He on one occasion, "were your Father, ye would love Me; for I proceeded forth, and came from God" (John viii. 42).

Many will read these words who do not know God as Father. They cannot look up into his face, and say, with a child's lisp, Abba. They are Christians; but they lack the consciousness of this benignant side of the character of God. He is rather the Judge, the Almighty, the Supreme. Such have need to know what Jesus meant when He said, "I am come in my Father's name." They have need to drink in the meaning of those words, with which our Lord summed up his earthly ministry to his own, "I have manifested thy name unto the men which Thou gavest Me out of the world" (xvii. 6). They have need to learn the whole force of that promise with which our Lord forecast his posthumous ministry, and with which He closed his intercessory prayer, "I have declared unto them thy name, and will declare it; that the

love wherewith Thou has loved Me may be in them, and I in them"
(xvii. 26).

I. THE MANNER IN WHICH OUR LORD DECLARED HIS FATHER'S NAME
DURING HIS EARTHLY LIFE.—*Sometimes it was by contrast.*—He would
recall some trivial instance of a father's love and pity in giving bread,
or fish, or eggs, to some suppliant child. And when his audience were
listening with rapt attention, whilst tears glistened in the eyes of some,
He turned quickly on them, and said, "God is just like that, only as
much more delicate, and tender, and responsive, as his ways are higher
than your ways." It seems as if the Lord loves us to rise heavenwards
from the commonplaces of our homes, and as each tiny incident tran-
spires, to say to ourselves, "This is a little snatch of the love of God;
a clue to the labyrinth of his infinite nature; a glimpse through an
aperture, small as a pin-prick, into his very heart. Yea, our heavenly
Father would do much more than this." And the Apostle Paul brings
out the same idea, when he tells us that every fatherhood gets its meaning and value from God, as torches lit from the sun (Eph. iii. 15).

Sometimes it was directly.—He would point to sparrows lying for
sale in the market, of which two were sold for a farthing, and five for
two farthings, one being thrown into the bargain, and He would say,
"You see how little men think of one sparrow; but it cannot fall to the
ground without your Father." Admire, said He, your Father's taste;
He clothed these flowers. Mark, said He, your Father's care; He provides for these birds, winging their flight overhead. Behold, said He,
this little child; its angel beholds my Father's face.

Here are some of the direct statements He made: The Father is
perfect in his forgiving love (Matt. v. 48); He knows what things ye
need (vi. 8); He is merciful, and longs to give you the kingdom (Luke
vi. 36); He sees in secret, and will most certainly reward (Matt. vi. 4);
He is the Husbandman of souls (John xv. 1); his hand is great enough
to hold all his sheep, and to keep them safely (x. 29). Living in the
heart of God, and between the heart of God and man, He was con-
tinually·telling men what He saw there (viii. 38).

It was also by his life.—His life was one long denial of his intrinsic
glory; as we are called upon to deny our fallen evil selves. And why?
Why did He refuse to speak his own words, to do his own deeds, to
follow the promptings of his own will? (xii. 49, 50; v. 19; vi. 38;
viii. 28). The reason is to be found in his intense desire that the Father
should shine through his human life; that the glory of God might be
thrown on the canvas of mortal flesh; that the Deity might be translated into the familiar speech of men. So, when Philip asked Him to
show the Father, He answered him in amazement, "Have I been so
long time with you, and yet hast thou not known Me, Philip? he that
hath seen Me hath seen the Father" (xiv. 9). In his life, and especially

in his death, Jesus showed what meaning was hidden in his Father's name. To understand these things is to see stars invisible to the naked eye, and to drink draughts further up the stream than is granted to others.

And there is here a deep lesson, too; whatever the name Father was to Jesus, that the name Jesus should be to us. It is in that name we pray. Through that name the Comforter descends. By that name we are called. On that name believing we have life. And we are chosen vessels to bear it. We have not only to hold it fast; we are called upon to declare it. By lip and life, by precept and example, by what we say and what we are, we are called upon to lift up treasure after treasure from the unsearchable riches concealed in the sweet name Jesus, until the appetites of men are whetted with a strong zest, and they are attracted to Him; as the Queen of Sheba was to Solomon by the report which reached her in her own land. "The Name" was the common epithet for Christianity in its earliest days (Acts ii., iii., iv., R.V.).

II. THE EFFECT OF CHRIST'S DECLARATION TO HIS FATHER'S NAME.— *It closed his mouth in self-vindication.*—He stood there in that Jewish court charged with Sabbath-breaking. There were many grounds on which He might have based his claim to be exonerated of any heinous crime; but He forbore to use them. He expressly refused to establish his right to act on his own motion, or the prompting of his own will. "If I bear witness of Myself, my witness is not true" (31). It would almost appear that He thought that He would have been false to his mission, if He had spoken a word on his own behalf.

It stayed Him from summoning witnesses.—He could have summoned into that court John from the dungeon, where he was lying; and the Jews would hardly have been able to refuse his testimony (33). He could have summoned the long lines of healed ones, who had been the subjects of his miraculous power (36). He could have summoned page after page, and line after line of the writings of Moses (46). But He only touched on these things very lightly; as if He mentioned the names of his witnesses, and then refused to subpoena them. And this was his dread, that the attention of men should be diverted from his Father to Himself. And as He took every opportunity to reveal his Father, so here, with no thought of Himself, He set Himself to his wonted task. In utter self-oblivion, in distinct refusal to come in his own name, in passionate eagerness that men should understand the great ocean, God, by this creek which had run up into a human life, He said, "I am come in my Father's name."

But in doing this, He has set up the best vindication of Himself. He refused to vindicate Himself; but his vindication of God is the strongest proof that He had been from all eternity in the bosom of the Father. He lived to reveal God; but in doing so He best revealed Himself. He refused honour from all but from God alone; and such honour has come to Him, that heaven rings with the acclaim, "Worthy art Thou to receive . . . honour."

So it is ever. If you love your life, you lose it. If you lose your life for his sake, you find it. We are too careful of our reputation and standing and honour, and what men say and think. Oh for that divine self-forgetfulness, that self-effacement, that self-oblivion, which finds its one all-sufficient aim in making men think better of Christ, without realizing that there is a backward reflex result in the vindication of the faithful servant. Anything which reflects light shows that it is itself polished.

III. CHRIST'S POSTHUMOUS REVELATION OF THE FATHER'S NAME.— Notice these wondrous words: "The time cometh when I shall no more speak unto you in proverbs, but I shall show you plainly of the Father" (xvi. 25). And again, "I will declare it" (xvii. 26). These passages can only point on to his post-resurrection ministry, when, through the Holy Spirit, He continued the teaching which in his earthly life He had commenced (Acts i. 2). It is of this ministry, also, that He speaks by the mouth of his servant, saying: "I will declare thy name unto my brethren; in the midst of the Church will I sing praise unto Thee" (Psa. xxii. 22; Heb. ii. 12).

Whenever in a congregation of the saints, there is an outburst of genuine song, you may detect the voice of Jesus singing with them, and identifying Himself with it. And He still teaches us by mystic influences and infallible tokens the deeper meaning of the Fatherhood of God, leading us, not to anything outside the boards of the Bible, but to a deeper appreciation of what is there. So also He will do for ever.

O souls of men, do ye not long to know the Father, to hear his voice, to feel his touch, to be canopied by his love, so that all life may be a residence in his home? It is gloriously possible, if you are really born again, for only such have the right to call God, Father, after this inner sense (i. 12); and if you are willing to let the Master teach you some of those things which are prepared for the lovers of God, and which he reveals by his Spirit.

And as we know more of the meaning of God's Fatherhood, we shall experience more of the love of God, and of the indwelling of the Lord Jesus. In his own emphatic words He has taught us that the amount of the one will be the measure of the other; *that* "the love wherewith Thou hast loved Me may be in them, and I in them."

18

THE FATHER'S GIFT TO THE SON

"All that the Father giveth Me shall come to Me; and him that cometh to Me I will in no wise cast out."—JOHN vi. 37.

IN THESE chapters we are engaged in catching up some of the favourite thoughts and words of the Redeemer, thinking them over again, and trying, so far as we can, to look at them with his eyes and from his stand-point. And we cannot leave this marvellous chapter without accentuating an expression which comes into prominence here for the first time, but is destined to re-appear more than once or twice—that expression is, *those whom the Father giveth Me*. And may it be that all who read these lines shall be included in that casket of very precious jewels which the Father has given to his Son! There is nothing higher in this world or the next to which any human being can aspire.

I. WHO ARE THEY?—We may not look into the Book of Life, and read the names written there from before the foundation of the world. One only can take that book, and break its seals, and look upon its mysterious pages. The Lamb alone, whose blood purchased each individual mentioned there, may scan its records. But it is not necessary that that book should be opened or read ere we know its contents. There is another method of ascertaining the names it records.

The verse quoted above contains an identical proposition. Its extremes may be reversed in their order, for each is the other's equivalent. And if, on the one hand, it is true that all the given ones shall come; it is also true, on the other hand, that all who come are included among the given ones. Would you know whether you are one of these? Ask yourself if you have truly come to Christ, or believed in Him as Saviour, Friend, and King; for if you have, you may rest assured that you were included in that Divine donation, which dates from the eternity of the far past, and shall be a theme of praise in that which is to come, world without end.

This is Christianity. It does not consist in the acceptance of the Bible as the Word of God; though Christians do accept it to be such, and account it the stable foundation of their hopes. It does not consist in the belief of a creed; though Christians necessarily hold certain definite beliefs. It is not adhesion to any visible church, or body of Christians; though Christians do for the most part associate themselves together. It is *coming to Christ*. And it is evident from comparing the parallel clauses of the thirty-fifth verse, that coming to Him and believing in Him are one and the same thing.

To come to Christ is to lift your heart to Him; if not in prolonged prayer, yet in trustful confidence, in desire and aspiration, in mute expectancy. To come to Christ is to despair of yourself and all others, and to venture all on Him. To come to Christ is to turn your back on the sinful past, and your face towards a glimmering streak of dawn, now visible on the horizon, but destined to grow into a great light. Have you so come to Him, who, though the meekest of men, proposes Himself as the panacea for the world's ills, the bread for its hunger, the satisfaction of its need? If so, then you are certainly amongst the given ones.

Look at that stone, agitated for ages in the depths of primeval oceans, and rounded by the attrition of the currents of unnumbered centuries; or at those hills composed of the remains of infinite myriads of infinitesimal organisms, falling through the still depths of untroubled seas; or at the moon, which bears the evidence of the terrific convulsions to which she has been exposed: and, as you consider any one of these, you are almost overwhelmed by the thought of their antiquity. Yet know, O soul of man, that, before any of these were made, before the silence of eternity was broken by the first angel-voice, in the infinite azure of the immeasurable past, you were named, and passed in deed of gift by the Father to the Son. There was no surprise, therefore, when you came to the Son of Man—this had been anticipated before time began; and it was the answer of your life to the summons of the foreknowledge of God. You have come in time, but you were given in eternity.

Suppose that a geologist, amid his explorations of the traces of earth's earliest life, were suddenly to come across a slab inscribed with his own name and a prediction of the precise date of his coming. With what amazement would he scan that mysterious tablet, and with what awe recognise the Divine omniscience! He did not come because he knew that he was expected, but because of what, as he thought, were the promptings of his own sweet will; but, having come, he discovered that his advent had been long anticipated. So we come to the Saviour under a sense of sin or the stress of sorrow, unaware of any mysterious influence at work: but, having come, we find that we have been the subjects of the drawing grace of the Father (44); that the very grace to come had been given by the Father (65); and that we were included in the Father's gift, so that of us the Son could say, "Thine they were, and Thou gavest them Me, and they have kept thy word."

In dealing with the unconverted, we have only to reiterate the invitation, "Come to Him." This is the one legend that stands over the doorway of the House of Mercy. But, having entered, we learn that all who enter have been given, as a flock of sheep, to the care of the Good Shepherd, whose name is branded on them, defying time and age to erase it (x. 29; Gal. vi. 17, R.V.).

II. THEIR PRIVILEGES.—It is a marvellous list; and, as we write and read, it is through a blinding mist of tears, because we have made so little of our marvellous prerogative—ours by an inalienable right.

(1) *They obtain Eternal Life.*—Outside this charmed circle there is existence, but no life (53). Men may live in pleasure, but they are dead while they live (1 Tim. v. 6). Eternal life is as much above the ordinary life of men as that in turn is above the brute's. It partakes of the nature of that world which awaits us, unseen and eternal, in those glorious ages which we are nearing with every heart-beat. So that of the regenerate it may be said that they are already the children of eternity.

Christ gives eternal life. He not only has life in Himself, but He has received from the Father authority over all flesh, that He should give eternal life to those whom He has given Him (xvii. 2). The life which man forfeited in Eden is given back in the second Man, the Lord from heaven. He is the tree of life, to eat of whom is to become impervious to death; and no sword now turns every way to hinder us from taking and living for ever.

We cannot explain the mystery of the imparting of this eternal life; and we know as little of the life itself. We are sure that it cannot be acquired, but must be given. We are sure that life is not the result of knowledge, but knowledge the result of life. "This is life eternal, that they might know Thee, the only true God, and Jesus Christ whom Thou hast sent" (xvii. 3). We are sure that to have it is to drink draughts of blessedness with which no earthly joy can compare. And we know that by this the religion of the Bible is distinguished from all other religions whatsover, that it provides for the communication of this life to all who believe. Whatever a man professes and knows, without this life he is no Christian; but, with this life, the humblest and weakest believer is a child of God, a member of Christ, and an inheritor of the kingdom of heaven. And this is the life which Jesus gives to all who come to Him, at the first moment of their coming.

(2) *They are safe for ever.*—Notice how He reiterates this, as if to exclude the possibility of mistake. *I will in no wise cast out.* The Greek is very strong, "I will never, never, cast out." So great was the pressure brought to bear on the Patriarch that he was obliged, though against his will, to cast out the slave-girl and her child; and they nearly perished in the desert-wastes. But no pressure shall ever avail with Christ to cast out one who has come to Him. No matter how weak and sinful; though a wreck through sin, with only a fragment of a life to give, He will never, never, cast out. Once inside, there is no putting

out. Again, He says that it is the Father's will that He should lose
nothing of all that He has given (39). In fulfilment of that will, He
stood forth in the garden, accosted the armed band, as their swords
were flashing in the gleaming torchlight, told them that He was the
object of their search, and bade them let the terror-stricken band of
disciples go their way (xviii. 8, 9). An image this of how He stands
between us and all assailants, whether they be the righteous demands
of the Divine law, or the dark and malignant powers of hell. Ever like
this He is inserting Himself between our enemies and ourselves; covering us with his feathers; acting as our shield and buckler; and receiving into his own royal heart the blows meant for our worthless selves.
We cannot be lost, unless we be very Judases, who deliberately open
our hearts to admit the prince of hell (xiii. 26; xvii. 12).

And to make assurance doubly sure, the Lord speaks of those whom
the Father had given Him, as enclosed not only in his own hand, but
also in the grasp of his Father's hand (x. 29). There we lie within the
double safeguard: first of the hand of the Son of Man, and then of
that of the Eternal Father. No member of his body can be amputated.
No sheep of his flock can be torn by the lion of the pit. No Jonah
shall be cast out to lighten the ship of the Church. We are *kept* by
One who neither slumbers nor sleeps, but guards his flock with ceaseless vigilance; exercising his gracious oversight, not by an iron restraint
which we cannot resist, but by a sweet persuasiveness of love from
which we do not wish to escape (xvii. 11, 12).

(3) *They are the subjects of his intimate solicitude.* For these He
gives his flesh and blood to be meat and drink indeed (54). To these
He gives choice revelations of his Father's name (xvii. 6); and passes
on the very words which He receives fresh and living from his Father's
voice (8). These He leads into a certain and settled belief in his Divine
mission (8). For these He specially prays, excluding at times the very
world from his thought, that He may concentrate all his attention on
their interests (9). For these He prognosticates a unity like that between
Himself and the Father. Concerning these He wills that they may be
with Him where He is, so as to behold his glory, and to receive those
further communications concerning the name of God which shall lead
to their fuller reception of the love of God, through the untold ages of
the hereafter (24, 26). Oh, destiny of surpassing wonder! Oh, mystery
of love! Oh, rapture of delight! And does all this hang on our coming
to Jesus? Who then will delay? Ah, purblind race, to hesitate, and
miss privileges so exalted, bliss so supreme!

(4) *They shall be raised up at the last day.*—That expression, *the
last day*, was frequently on his lips (John vi. 39, 40, 44, 54; xi. 24; xii.
48). It is an indefinite expression for those final scenes in which the
history of our race is to be consummated through resurrection and
judgment. Our Lord does not discriminate between the successive

scenes in the last great act; but bulks the whole together, leaving the Holy Spirit to show the various stages through later writers.

It is, however, noticeable how much stress He lays on the Resurrection as essential to the completeness of his work on behalf of those who come to Him. Four times in this discourse He reiterates the assertion (39, 40, 44, 54). It is not enough to impart eternal life. That would bless the spirit, but leave the body untouched. And the Saviour will not rest until the whole of our complex nature shares the emancipation and blessing of his salvation. A transfigured manhood and a glorified body must be the crown of his work for his own; and so, by his mighty power, He will raise us up in the likeness of his glory, and make us sharers of his royal and exalted state (Phil. iii. 21).

It seems incredible, and yet it must be so. Nothing less can explain those mysterious yearnings which thrill within our hearts, and which, unless the structure of our nature is in this single particular abortive, must have their satisfaction. And nothing less will undo the devil's masterpiece of mischief, and bring glory to God out of it all.

But in speaking thus of the given ones, let it not be forgotten that they are given, not for their enjoyment, but for service. The disciples to whom our Lord so often referred under this designation, were the first preachers, teachers, workers, and martyrs of his church. To them, more than to any others, are due the sacred Scriptures of the New Testament, and the structure of the Church. And if we be in the same category, we must never forget, that though we are not of the world as to our calling, yet we are in the world for ministry; and that we have been given to the Saviour to be allied with Him in the service of men, He fulfilling through us the purposes on which He set his heart, and we sharing with Him the travail of his soul, and his ardent, patient, undiscouraged toil.

19

The Bread which Gives and Sustains Life

"As the living Father hath sent Me, and I live by the Father: so he that eateth Me, even he shall live by Me."—JOHN vi. 57.

THIS verse may fairly be said to be the pivot around which our Lord's words about Himself revolve. It certainly gives the secret of his inner life. And it excites our deepest wonder as we read it over and over, trying vainly to explore and understand its wealth of significance. It furnishes a clue also to the interpretation of those other words with which He met the devil, on his first assault, and told him that "Man doth not live by bread alone, but by every word that proceedeth out of the mouth of God." But here He takes a further step, and says that He lives not only by the words of God, but by God Himself.

And there is a further interest in this verse, that it not only affords the clue to the inner life of the Son of Man, but contains an admonition for each one of us to do as He did; exercising towards Himself the same dependence of spirit and attitude as he did towards his Father.

There was a sense, of course, in which, as the Second Person in the Holy Trinity, all power was his in heaven and on earth. But of this, to use the expressive phrase of the Apostle, "He emptied Himself" (Phil. ii. 7, R.V.), and voluntarily took up a life of momentary dependence on his Father; living on his plan, by his strength, for his glory; losing Himself utterly in his all-sufficiency, and appealing to Him in every episode and emergency of his daily life. His spirit was as dependent on Him as his body was on bread; and clung to Him as the vine to the trellis-work on which it is reared. Such is the character of the life which He bids us live towards Himself. "He that eateth Me shall live by Me."

I. OUR LORD AS BREAD.—We might discover many ingenious analogies to please the fancy and delight the mind, but be diverted from the main conception pressed on us, with repeated emphasis, in this discourse.

Bread contains life.—It is made of fine flour, but in the grinding of the flour the life-germs of the wheat are not destroyed, and it is their presence which makes bread the life of our life, the true fuel of our fire. In bread, the life of nature, that living principle which underlies all vegetable growth, and which is due to the direct operation of the living God, is reduced to such a form that it can conveniently become the raw material out of which we weave the texture of our being. And in the human nature of the Lord Jesus there is stored the very life of God. "As the Father hath life in Himself, He gave to the Son to have life in Himself"; so that the Son has brought to our world, incarnated in his wondrous nature, the underived, infinite, and ever-blessed life of the Eternal.

It is the presence of life in bread which causes it to sustain physical life; it is the presence of life in the words of the Bible which renders it a book for all ages and of endless application; it is the presence of life in Jesus Christ which makes Him the food of men. Hearken to his majestic words: "I am the life"; "I am the Resurrection and the Life"; "I am the living One" (xiv. 6; xi. 25; Rev. i. 18).

Bread is all-sufficient for life.—It contains in itself all the elements needed for nutrition. Though a man have an unlimited supply of flesh, he cannot find in such a diet, however plentiful, certain qualities required to build up his frame. But on a bread-diet man will thrive; and he will thrive in proportion to the number of original elements left when the processes of its preparation are complete. Nor is it otherwise with Jesus. In Him there is everything that we need "for life and godliness." He is a hiding-place in a storm of wind; a covert from the tempest; rivers of water in drought; the shadow of a great rock in scorching heat. For the polluted, He is purity; for the irritable, He is patience; for the faint, He is courage; for the weak, He is strength; for the ignorant, He is wisdom. God, who knew the needs of our bodies, stored all nutritive qualities in the corn for us to assimilate as we need. And knowing the needs of our spirits, He stored all the elements required for our spiritual nutrition in our blessed Lord, leaving us to appropriate them as we will.

We cannot understand that wonderful inner mechanism, in virtue of which each part of our nature comes to the bread as soon as eaten, and carries off from it the special particles it requires. But we may all learn the lesson of their participation, and take to ourselves just those things in the blessed Lord which we want most.

Bread must be appropriated ere it becomes life-giving.—However much bread lies around, it avails not to appease hunger, or to do its work of nutrition, unless it is masticated and digested. And what digestion is to food, assimilating it with our bodies, *that* devout and loving meditation on the words and life and work of the Lord Jesus is to our spirits. By the one process there is brought about a union between our bodies and the bread; by the other a union between our spirits and the risen Jesus. In the one we extract the principle of physical life from bread; in the other the principle of spiritual life from the Lord of life.

No figure can unfold the meaning of all this. The only true clue is to be found in the personal experience of believers. They know what is meant, though they cannot tell the art of it to others. But it is a living fact with them, that by turning hearts and thoughts towards Jesus they are able to get strength to suffer and act in ways which, as they look back on them, appear almost past believing. O weak and suffering ones, the greater your need, the more imperative the necessity to eat his flesh! Deliberate eating and mastication are essential to good health; but not less so, after a spiritual sort, to all who would live in soul-health before God.

Yet we may illustrate what feeding on Christ is. A whole family may be fed by the words, and gentleness, and patience, of a single invalid, who thinks herself useless lumber. A generation of young men may be fed by the heroism, or intellect, or example of some chosen leader. An expedition may feed, through long privation and bitter disappointments, on the undaunted courage and inspiring hope of some chivalrous captain. A nation may feed on the deeds or words of a Pitt, a Fox, or a Wellington. And so, in the higher sphere, we may all feed our spirits on Him who offers Himself as the true Bread of man.

The great need for us all is to feed more constantly on Christ. We are so fitful and irregular in our dealings and fellowship with Him. We do not sufficiently "handle the Word of Life." We pray in a kind of despairing way for help, but do not take Him by acts of assimilating, appropriating faith; going forth from fellowship with Him, not gauging by our emotions the amount of benefit received, but by the faith which knows that it cannot look to Christ for aught, without receiving that and more also.

But there are times in every life when, all unexpectedly and un-announced, there steals into our hearts some rich experience of the love and presence of Jesus. It is sent by One who forecasts a coming trial, and prepares us to meet it as He did; who gave his Apostles a rich banquet and an evident token of his power, ere He thrust them forth with his own hand into the very heart of the storm, which was even then gathering about the hills. They had been ill-prepared to meet the toils of that arduous night, had they not been previously so well fed by their Master's royal bounty. And often amid their perils they must have cheered each other by recalling their Master's power. Surely He who brake the loaves into food for thousands could hush the storm into a calm! God sends no crews to sea without first provisioning them. The miracle of the feeding of the multitudes preceded the terror of the storm.

II. THE TEACHING OF THE MANNA.—The manna, of course, contained all the elements of true bread; but there was this peculiarity in it, that it was not produced by any natural process, nor did it grow from the soil of earth: as it is written, "He gave them bread from heaven to eat." How it came, and when, no one knew; but each morning, beneath the hoar frost, round about the camp, lay the small round thing which angels might have made their food, and which heaven had dropped for the sustenance of the chosen hosts.

This is the food to which our Lord specially alludes. For purity and sweetness and sufficiency, the manna was a fitting emblem of Himself; but much more, because it came down, as He had done, from heaven (32, 33, 38, 42, 50, 51, 58).

What a marvellous tribute is here to the heavenly origin of man! His nature is fallen and degraded; but it refuses to be satisfied with anything less than that which comes down from heaven. Men try to content the hunger of their souls by husks from the swine trough and garbage from the dog-kennel, but in vain. And the fact that man, of all the living things on this earth, fails to find his satisfaction in the products of earth, proves that his origin must be sought outside the bounds of the earth-sphere. He whose nature craves heavenly food must himself be of heavenly origin. And God who made him what he is could not fail to provide the nature which He has given with the food of its native sphere.

There was, therefore, special reason why our Lord so repeatedly affirmed that He came down from heaven. He was something more than a son of man. His body might be an earthen vessel, but it held a heavenly treasure. He came down from heaven, and in those words lie the glory of his pre-existence, and the mystery of his incarnation. He came from God, and went to God. Heaven was his home, as, indeed, it had been the creation of his power in ages that lie beyond time's bourne or human vision.

III. LIFE-GIVING THROUGH DEATH.—It is impossible for any one illustration to convey all God's thoughts to us. And though bread is only possible through the death of myriads of corns of wheat, yet this is not the primary thought which bread suggests to us. And, therefore, to emphasize the truth, that the power to communicate life can only be acquired through death, our Lord speaks of the bread which He would give, as *his flesh*, which He would give for the life of the world. Obviously flesh is that which has passed through death.

These are the words that proved so great a stumbling-block to some of his disciples. They said it was a hard saying, and they would not hear it. It was distasteful to them to hear their Master speak of an inevitable death, instead of the thrones of glory on which they had set their hearts. "From that time forth many of his disciples went back, and walked no more with Him." How little did they realize that the crown is only reached by the path of the cross, and that the only life which can be communicated is that which has passed through the grave! There is an evident allusion in these words to that approaching death, which was never far from our Saviour's thoughts, the death of propitiation and atonement. But He did not fail to see that what He was to suffer would be as the breaking of the shrine to let forth the imprisoned spirit of life to bless the world.

Death and resurrection and ascension must precede Pentecost. He must first descend, if He would afterwards ascend to fill all hearts, all lives, all worlds, with the aroma and power of his endless life. The life He had before his death was fair, but not communicable; that which he won in death and its defeat is fairer still, and capable of being given to all who hear and obey his invitation to come.

Doubly precious then is that life which He has given, and gives in unceasing supplies to those who feed on Him in loving lowly trust! It is a life which is death-proof; which has passed through Hades unscathed; which has acquired in the ordeal a virtue that renders it unique; and which, whilst it deals death to all that is of the flesh, enters us to abide, and to lift us to share his glorious life and endless reign.

IV. The Distribution of the Bread.—How significant the lesson of the miracle which served as the text for this discourse! It was the Passover at Jerusalem; but He had kept a royal Passover on those hillsides which teemed with spiritual significance. To do all things decently and in order (10); to begin each meal by giving thanks (11); to expect something more than the bare necessaries of life at the hands of God (11); to guard against waste (12); to learn that giving is the true means of increase (13); these and other lessons were taught, as the wolds and vales were being carpeted with the first sweet green of spring.

But two lessons stood out conspicuously—first, that there was enough for all; and secondly, that the fainting crowds must be fed through the ministry of his disciples. "He distributed to his disciples, and the disciples to them which were set down."

In all our Lord's miracles there is a marvellous economy of power. The servants must fill the water-pots with water before He makes it wine. Jairus and the mother must give their daughter something to eat when the Master has given her back to them. Others must roll away the stone, though only He can throw the life-giving word into the tomb. So here. He used the lad's loaves and fishes as the basis of the miracle; and, instead of distributing the food by miraculous agency, He passed it through the hands of his disciples, giving them a memorable share in the joyous work.

Nor is it otherwise to-day. There is enough in our dear Lord to meet the demands of all that are in heaven and on the earth; no man, or woman, or child, need go unfed. But if the precious Bread of Life, for lack of which men are famishing, is to be brought to them, it can only be by our hands, who stand around the Lord as a kind of inner circle. Oh, shame on us that we are so apt to feed ourselves, neglectful of the cry of the perishing; and that we content ourselves with giving again and again to the same few ranks immediately around us, till they are surfeited, and the rest left without a crumb! What wonder that we cease to enjoy the provisions we misuse; and that they fail before our eyes, leaving no basketfuls of fragments for coming days!

Say not that your knowledge of Christ is too small and fragmentary to be of any avail. Take it to Him; beneath his touch a wondrous transformation will ensue; and, as you give away your all, you will find it grow beneath your hand, because it has passed from his hand to yours, and the slender provision, which threatened to be too little for yourself, shall avail for multitudes.

20

THE WORDS OF JESUS

"Thou hast the words of eternal life."—JOHN vi. 68.

IT WAS a touching question which elicited this reply. Only the night before it had been proposed by some enthusiastic followers that they should take Him by force, and make Him a king. And if our Lord had been the mere enthusiast that some men dare to term Him, and had vacillated for only a moment, the standard of revolt had been erected amid the littered fragments of the supper, and a movement had been started before which the Government of Rome must have trembled.

But our Lord had no ambition to be a literal successor of David and the kings. His kingdom was not of this world. He had told the devil so, at the beginning of His ministry; and now He held steadfastly to his plan. In a few moments the revolt was quelled. His disciples were forcing their little boat towards the other side, beneath frowning skies, and in the teeth of a rising storm. And the crowds suddenly missed Him, as He sped away towards the mountain heights, for a night of fellowship with his Father.

On those lonely heights He perceived the position in which He was placed. He was becoming surrounded by a motley crowd, who came to Him for what they could get, and hoped that He would serve the fierce passions of their revenge. It was needful clearly to undeceive them, and reveal the real character of his mission; and this must be done at once—*to-morrow*, though at the cost of his popularity. Henceforth his way would be as difficult as that of the tiny craft, which, when the moonlight broke out now and again, He could see as a black speck on the turbulent waters beneath.

The following morning, on the further shore, saw a renewal of the excitement of the preceding evening. So our Lord withdrew into the friendly shelter of a synagogue, and spoke the discourse of this chapter, the most deeply spiritual of any of his discourses hitherto; and it changed the whole aspect of his career.

We all know the interest given to the record of a speech by the parentheses, which tell us how it was received. And we are not left without symptoms of the effect of these searching words on the crowds around Him. In the 41st verse, the men who, a few hours before, wished to crown Him, murmured at Him. In the 52nd verse, they strove among themselves. In the 60th verse, many of his disciples, as they listened, said, "This is a hard saying; who can hear it?" In the

66th verse, many of them went back and walked no more with Him. And now, as the shades of evening were beginning to fall, the synagogue was almost empty; and the Lord was left alone with the little company of the twelve, who had been the sorrowful witnesses of the shattering of their Master's popularity, and of the fabric of their own ambitions. He looked round on them, and put the infinitely pathetic question, "Will ye also go away?" And it elicited from Peter, the ready spokesman of the rest, a reply which showed that in those very words, which others had felt so startling and terrible, he at least had found fuel for that inner fire which the Master had kindled by the breath of his lips.

Yes; the words of Jesus are enough to prove that He is the Son of the living God. In their cool depths weary souls bathe; through their pure glow, the dark passages of life are irradiated with heavenly lustre; and by their fascination our wayward hearts are closely bound to Him who spake as never man spake. As He speaks down the long corridors of the ages, his words float towards us with undiminished beauty and force; thrilling, soothing, teaching us, and shedding light on God, and life, and death, and the world to come.

His words are gracious.—So the crowds found them, as they listened in breathless silence to his first sermon in his highland home (Luke iv. 22). And that tender grace has not passed away from them; as the fragrance exhales from flowers after they have long been gathered. They still distil as dew on tender grass, and drop as rain on mown lawns. Disciple as He was in the school of sorrow, He perfectly acquired the art of speaking words in season to them that are weary, words that heal the broken-hearted, and comfort the mourner, and bid the accused go to sin no more. Well may we look up from his words, which are as music issuing from an Æolean harp, into his face and say, "Thou art fairer than the children of men, grace is poured into thy lips; therefore God hath blessed Thee for ever."

His words were authoritative.—So the people said as they broke up into little groups, and went wondering away from the mountain of the Beatitudes, when the spell of the speaker's voice was still fresh upon their memories (Matt. vii. 28, 29). He did not stay to prove the truth of what He said. That was entirely needless, for his words were self-evidencing. They were as incapable of demonstration as the axioms of Euclid; but they were as obviously true. The mind of man might not have been able to elaborate them for itself; but it instantly perceived their truthfulness when presented. Do you try to prove that a coin is genuine gold, when it rings? Do you need to prove that the strain of music which softly steals through Gothic arches is beautiful, when it entrances the listening soul? Do you need to prove that the friend is sincere, when you can detect the rhythm of his heart-throbs? And there is less need to prove the words of Jesus: the soul knows that what He says is true; it has within itself that which assents to every syllable; from its very base there rises a deep Amen, like the boom of the sea-waves in a hollow cavern far below the brink of the cliffs. And this constitutes their authority. Their authority is not in the reason, but in the soul.

His words make the deepest truths current coin.—The world's teachers have hedged themselves about with a narrow circle of disciples, leaving the masses to take their chance. The Pharisee says that the people which does not know the law are cursed (vii. 49). Plato says that it is not easy to find the Father of all existence; and when He is found it is impossible to make Him known to all. Celsus charges this against Christianity, that woollen manufacturers, shoemakers, and curriers had become its zealous supporters. But it is the glory of Jesus that He disembowelled truth's deepest mines of their golden ore, and minted it into common coin, which He threw in lavish handfuls among men. Only when they refused to hear did He hide his meaning in dark sentences; but wherever there was willingness to receive, He was prodigal to bestow. Yea, He set Himself to enwrap his teachings in the fascinating story, the pithy proverb, the sharp antithesis, the methods of speech dear to the crowds of every age, never lowering the truth by its dress, but hallowing the dress, just as common articles are counted heirlooms because once used by the hands of a prince.

All through his ministry, the common people heard Him gladly. The publicans and sinners drew near to hear Him. The officers of the Sanhedrin beneath the power of his words were unable to arrest Him. Thousands would gather in the desert or on the hills, forgetful of all beside, and willing to stand the live-long day to listen to lips which dropped with honey. His words swayed the multitudes as vines swing in the autumn air.

His words are life.—The Master said so Himself, and so did his Apostle (63, 68). They gave life as they were spoken in the ear of death. Those who were in the graves of sensual and sinful indulgence heard Him and came forth; just as those who are in the literal graves of mother earth shall do one day. As the tiny torch of life burns in every seed, so does the life of God Himself tremble in each word of Jesus. "Cast forth thy word," says Carlyle, "into the ever-living, ever-moving universe; it is a seed-germ that can never die; unnoticed to-day, it will be found flourishing, perhaps as a banyan grove, perhaps as an oak-forest, after a thousand years." How true this is of the words of Jesus! Sow them in the scantiest, poorest soil, and leave them; you will be surprised to see the result in the multiform manifestations of holy and useful life.

Those who most ponder Christ's words are most conscious of the life that is in them. They are the best witnesses to verify the repeated references of this chapter to the *living* bread, given for the *life* of the world, of which, if a man eats, he shall *live* for ever. Oh that each reader would acquire the precious habit of feeding on these words, till they become in actual enjoyment both spirit and life!

They are the words of the Father.—It is very beautiful to notice how constantly our dear Lord refused to take credit for his words. He insisted that his doctrine was not his own, but his by whom He had been sent (vii. 16). He spake what He had heard, and had been taught, and had seen with his Father (viii. 26, 28, 38). He said that his Father had given Him a commandment as to what He should say and speak, by which He was absolutely guided. As the Father said unto Him, so He spoke (xii. 49, 50). His word was not his; but the Father who dwelt in Him spoke through his yielded nature (xiv. 24). He simply passed on words as they had been given to Himself (xvii. 8, 14).

What a condemnation and a lesson are here! The one, that we have spoken so many of our own words; the other, that we should henceforth wait more humbly and resolutely on Him, not seeking enticing words of man's wisdom, but waiting for the word from his lips, and warning men from Him.

To whom then shall we go if we leave Him? To Agnosticism with its negations? To Ritualism with its outward pomp? To turn to these would be to leave the fountain of living crystal for the broken cisterns, which, at the best, can hold but a few drops of brackish rain-water. No; we will not go away, but only ask that He would still speak to us the words of eternal life.

21

Rivers of Living Water

"If any man thirst, let him come unto Me and drink. He that believeth on Me, as the Scripture hath said, out of his belly shall flow rivers of living water. But this spake He of the Spirit which they that believe on Him should receive."—JOHN vii. 37–39.

WHAT MUSIC there is in these words! We are transported to the banks of a mighty river, down the bed of which the waters are ever hurrying to the sea. There is very little sound. The great volume of water moves majestically and silently onward, with now and again a musical ripple on its broad and waveless bosom. Flowing from mountain ranges where melting snows feed its springs; replenished from a hundred rills leaping the crags in a veil of mist; purified by being torn and combed in its rush over many a cataract—that river is the perpetual emblem of fertility, freshness, abundance, and sufficiency of supply.

But this is not all. The Lord is not content with speaking of a river. He speaks of rivers. It is as if He bade us add the Missouri to the Mississippi, and to these the Amazon, and to these the Orinoco, and to these the Ganges, and the Danube. River added to river; stream to stream; torrent to torrent; and *all* to set forth the freshness and the abundance of the life that should stream from each thirsty soul, who, having come to Him, the Rock, should in turn become a rock; and, having received out of his fullness, should pass it on to a drought-smitten world.

Do you, my reader, know anything of this? Is your life comparable to a river, nay, to many rivers of holy influence? In the first place, do you know what it is to be satisfied? and in the second place, do you know what it is to communicate to others what you are receiving from the risen Lord? If not, are you not living below your privileges, and would it not be wise to do what the present writer did on one memorable occasion—put your finger on these words, and claim that, in all their heights, and depths, and widths, and lengths of meaning, they should be realized? The world would soon cease to be thirsty if only each believer were to become like one of the ancient rivers of Paradise, which was parted into four heads.

I. THE SPEAKER.—To look at, there was nothing specially remarkable. Very meek and lowly was the King, clad in the simple homespun of the country, perhaps not knowing where He would sleep that very night. Often hungry, because the money was exhausted in the wallet, and thirsty beneath that hot Syrian sun. And yet He speaks of Himself as able to quench the thirst of men, from Himself.

It would seem as if He overleapt the intervening weeks, and thought of Himself as already back in his Father's glory, glorified and sitting on that throne from which the river of the water of life is ever descending to refresh and save. That river is Himself.

Christ is Christianity. In this He differs from all other teachers. They talk about truth, and set themselves to invent vast systems of philosophy which men must master. But our Lord has one panacea for all woes, all needs, all the infinite want of the spirit—and it is Himself. He stood and cried, as if the urgency of his spirit would brook no further restraint, "If any man thirst, let him come unto *Me* and drink. He that believeth on *Me* . . ."

Do we always believe this? We are conscious of almost infinite needs; we thirst and pine for happiness, for rest, for peace, for that indefinable satisfaction which seems so perfectly set forth in the sweet, deep word *love*; we turn from side to side for an answer: for a moment we think we have found it, as we see not far away some rock-hewn cistern, and make for it, only to find that it is broken and will hold no water. Human love fails to quench our thirst, though we drink deeply and widely of its stores. But Jesus is all-sufficient. Rutherford's most rapturous words never told a thousandth part of all his sufficiency and fullness.

He is the Sun; the heart that has learnt the art of basking in His beams may live without human love. He is the Ocean; the life which is open to his fullness is preserved from ebb or fluctuation, and is independent of passing showers, with their pattering raindrops. He is the Man; the Man of men, in whom all the strength of the strong and the sweetness of the lovable dwell in unstinted and infinite abundance: and the nature which has acquired the habit of living in union with Him can exist amid the failure and disappointment of all earthly friendships. All the fullness of God-head is in his vast and multitudinous nature.

Worlds cannot satisfy souls, any more than cart-loads of earth could fill the mouth of the Amazon. Alexander, the conqueror of the world, weeps with discontent, because there is nothing left to conquer. But Christ is always a brimming river; nay, a fountain whose drops are oceans, and whose jets are rivers; and whosoever will bare the soul to Him again and again, not trying to feel satisfied, but trusting for satisfaction, will find longings subside, the ache of disappointment anodyned, the fever-thirst slaked. Try it, O brother man!

II. The Invitation.—"If any thirst." "Any!" Those who are grimed with sin. "Any!" Those who have no claim but their exceeding need. "Any!" Those whom all the world and the Church spurn. "Any!" Publicans and sinners; outcasts and dying malefactors; persecutors and procrastinators. Richard Baxter used to say that, if his name had stood on this page, he would have feared that it referred to some other who bore it; but, since the Lord said *any,* he knew that even he was welcome. The one and only qualification is *thirst.*

Coming to Him is believing on Him. It is the touch of the soul and the Saviour. It is contact; the opening of the inner life to his entrance; the willingness to be possessed; the clinging to Him, as the drowning sailor to the outstretched hand or floating spar. With no emotion, or effort at self-improvement, or endeavour to adjust the circumstances of the outward life, lift your eyes from this page to Him and say, "O Lamb of God, I come!" And instantly you are at the land whither you go. As you come on the earth side, He comes on the heaven side; you go to the utmost bourne of the visible, He comes to the same spot from the bourne of the invisible; and on the borderland you meet Him. Perhaps it were true to say that his arrival there is the attraction which, without your realizing it, draws you to arise and go forth to Him. The sun attracts sparks; the earth, asteroids; the ocean, rivers; and Jesus, souls. To answer that attraction, however feebly, is to come.

III. THE SUPPLY.—"This, spake He of the Spirit, which they that believe on Him should receive." During his earthly life, our Lord supplied so far as possible what each disciple needed by his personal care and oversight. He knew each sheep by name; anticipated by prayerful sympathy the temptations of each; and sought to supply the need of each out of his royal bounty. But even then, as an external presence, He was not able to meet and satisfy the inner restlessness and craving of their hearts. How much less could He do it for them, or for us, when He became invisible and exalted to the right hand of power! But this lack is more than compensated for by the gift of the Holy Spirit.

When Jesus ascended He received of the Father the promise of the Holy Spirit. And then a new era broke on the world. Before the Ascension, the Spirit of God had rested *upon* men, fitting them for service; henceforth He was to be *in them.* This is the glory of our present dispensation, the crown of redemption, the climax of our Saviour's work. "He abideth with you, and *shall be in you*" (John xiv. 16, 17).

In Regeneration the Holy Spirit does literally indwell the believer. His life may be stunted, dwarfed, repressed, as plants in a sickly atmosphere, and as streams choked with the *débris* brought down from the hills; but it can never again be lost. "He abides for ever." But what does He bring, save the life of Jesus? These two are identical. When we are strengthened with might by the Spirit in the inner man, Christ dwells in our hearts by faith. If the Spirit of Christ be in us, Christ Himself is in us. It is a mistake to dissever these two. They are one.

This, then, is the sum of the whole matter. When weary, thirsty souls go to Jesus, He gives them instant relief, by giving them his Holy Spirit; and in that most blessed of all gifts, He Himself glides into the eager nature. He does not strive nor cry; there is no sound as of a rushing storm of wind, no coronet of flame; whilst men are watching at the front door to welcome Him with blare of trumpet, He steals in at the rear, unnoticed; but, in any case, He suddenly comes to his temple, and sits in its inner shrine as a refiner and purifier of the sons of Levi. Jesus Himself is the supply of our spirits, through the Holy Ghost, whom He gives to be within us and with us for ever.

IV. Conditions of Receiving the Holy Spirit.—He was not given to be an indwelling life till Jesus was glorified:—

Because the expiation of sins must precede our reception of the new life.—We must be justified before we can be sanctified. The prodigal must be reconciled with his father before he can sit at the table arrayed in festal robes, and admitted to the highest privileges that the home can yield. The second Adam must undo the results of the sin of the first Adam before He may give to his posterity the most priceless gift of heaven.

Because the power to give the Spirit could only be the reward of accomplished service.—It was only when our Lord had positively regained his Father's throne, standing where He did ere He started forth to the work of our redemption, that He had really finished the work which had been entrusted Him to do. And it was only then, when not only the Atonement of Calvary, but the Resurrection, the teachings of the forty days, and the Ascension leading captivity captive, had been accomplished, that He was able to claim the perfected reward which had glittered before his eyes amid the shame and sorrow of the cross.

Because the glory of the Lord Jesus must be perfected ere it could be communicated.—There is a sense in which, as the Second Person of the Holy Trinity, our Lord had all glory, underived, inexhaustible, and unchanging. But we are speaking of Him now as the wondrous Being who has taken human nature into eternal union with the Divine; who has, so to speak, created in death and resurrection a new unit of being in the universe of God; who has learned obedience by the things that He suffered, that He might be perfectly qualified to be a Priest. And it is surely right and true to affirm that, though, as regards Himself, there was nothing to desire, nothing to add; yet, as regards his office and the communication of his glorified life to others, He could not become all that He needed to be, and is, except through death and resurrection and ascension. But so soon as these were accomplished, He was able, as the perfected second Adam, to bestow his crowned and victorious life on men, and instantly the Spirit was given. The Spirit of Christ came to bring the life of Christ into our hearts; but He could not do it till that life was perfected in ascension glory. This done, the Spirit came.

There are some practical suggestions here for those who are longing for the Holy Spirit's fullness.

(1) *Exercise faith in the Lord Jesus.*—Do not concentrate your thoughts on the Blessed Comforter; but on Him who is exalted to bestow Him, and who constantly says, "I will send Him," "I will give Him to you." To receive the Spirit, we must believe in Jesus; that is, we must open our entire being to Him, expectant and believing.

(2) *Remember that, if you believe, you have received the Spirit.*—"The Spirit which they that believe on Him should receive." You could not believe or call Jesus Lord, but by the Holy Spirit; and ever since you did these things, He has been within you. Do not then ask for a new blessing; but for more of that which you already have. Remove the silt and rubbish which have occupied his place. Put away the sins which have grieved Him. Deny self which has crowded Him out of your life. Keep your soul in an eager believing attitude towards Jesus, and He will flood you with wave on wave of spiritual power.

(3) *Let the Lord Jesus occupy the place where God has set Him— the throne.*—The glory of Jesus is ever connected in Scripture with the reign of Jesus. There must be an ascension and an enthronement within; all things must be put under his feet; principalities and powers must own his sway; and when we glorify Jesus in our hearts and lives, setting Him on the throne, then the Spirit fills us with successive waves of power.

THE PENITENT'S GOSPEL

"And Jesus said unto her, Neither do I condemn thee: go, and sin no more."—JOHN viii. 11.

THIS PASSAGE has been the subject of more eager debate than any other in the Gospels. It is omitted by many ancient MSS.; it is rejected by several of the Fathers; it bears in its fabric, in the original, traces of the tremendous storm through which it has passed. And yet there is no possibility of accounting for its existence, save on the supposition that the incident really took place. It reveals in our Saviour's character a wisdom so profound, a tenderness to sinners so delicate, a hatred of sin so intense, an insight into human hearts so searching, that it is impossible to suppose the mind of man could have conceived, or the hand of man invented, this most pathetic story.

Our Lord, who had spent the night on the Mount of Olives, re-crossed the Kedron, and entered the Temple, probably as one of the first worshippers. When a sufficient number had gathered, He withdrew to a seat against the Treasury wall; and sitting down, began to teach the expectant people.

He had not proceeded far in his discourse, when a band of scribes and Pharisees, adorned with their customary badges of sanctity, and bringing in their midst one who had been guilty of flagrant sin, was seen approaching across the Temple square. Making their way through the opening crowd, they placed their trembling, shrinking prisoner before Him, and intimated that they had come there early for his opinion.

Immorality at that time had reached such a pitch, that the laws of Moses had fallen into disuse, for the very reason that it is impossible to legislate in advance of public opinion. If He confirmed the Mosaic sentence, and insisted on its execution, they would accuse Him to the people as a relentless censor, desirous of reviving the penalties of primitive Judaism. If He refused to confirm it, they could put Him to death, as an assailant of God's law. It seemed impossible for Him to show that tender pity to sinners, which had marked his whole career, and which had placed a publican among his chosen friends, whilst at the same time He maintained the sanctity of the ancient code. It was a shameful plot; and some have thought that He stooped down to write on the ground to conceal the burning shame and holy indignation that leaped to his face.

The accusers stood there unabashed, holding the woman in their midst, and pressing their brutal question. They may have thought, indeed, that his very silence proved Him to be caught in an inextricable dilemma. But their triumph did not last long, for the Saviour raised Himself up, and spake a word which fell in their midst like a bolt from a clear sky: "Let him that is without sin among you cast the first stone at her." In a moment memory and conscience began to work, and at length the oldest man drew back in the crowd and vanished; then the next, and the next, one by one, till the last was gone. And Jesus was left alone with the woman; not alone in the sense of there being no one else present, but that there was no one save the woman left of all who had broken in on his blessed presence. "Woman," said He, turning on her those searching, tender eyes, "hath no man condemned thee?" She said unto Him, "No man, Lord." Then said Jesus, "Neither do I condemn thee; go, and sin no more."

There are three ways of dealing with sin.

I. THE SINNER'S WAY OF TREATING SIN.—It is a terrible thing for a sinner to fall into the hands of his fellow sinners. Sin blinds them to their own faults, but sharpens them to detect the faults of others. They cover themselves beneath the glistening robes of fair excuses, but ruthlessly strip them away from the offenders whom they drag into the light of day.

What a terrible spectacle is here! There is not one of these men who can plead his freedom from this very sin. As they drag this woman forward, each one remembers scenes in the past in which he played a leading part, and which strangely resemble this, with the single exception of not having been found out, or of having been condoned. But they have no burning shame in the presence of their sin; no pity for the sinner; no jealousy for the honour of God; no apparent desire to bring back the wanderer. To them the incident is simply a test-case, suggesting curious speculations, and affording a convenient net for entrapping the steps of Him whom they hated as darkness ever hates the day. They take a prurient pleasure in enumerating all the details—"in the very act." They hold the sinner up as a public spectacle—"setting her in the midst." They leave her to her fate.

There is little hope for the sinner at hands like these. They may send him to the judge and the officer; to the gaol or the reformatory. They may make the case one for light gossip and casuistical distinctions, studying it as an anatomical deformity. They may proudly gather up the robes of their virtuous horror as they sweep past. But there is no attempt to measure the anguish of the sin-stained heart, or the suffering which burns the heart of the Saviour. And the sinner is presently dropped as a curious specimen, when its special peculiarities have been duly examined and entered in a book. Ah, how many there are around us who had never come to what they are, had they not been driven to it by the way in which the religious people around them dealt with their first deviation from the paths of strict integrity! The first wandering steps were eagerly watched, not with the view of following and reclaiming the erring one, but for purposes of gossip or fault-finding. The special features of the sin were eagerly noted and discussed, whilst any palliating excuses were repressed. The sudden silence, the averted looks, the chilling, cutting manner, branded the sin as unpardonable; shut the door upon repentance; and plunged the sinner into deeper and more abundant transgression.

Would that each of us would lock the story of another's guilt in some deep chamber of the heart, until floods of tears had been shed and abundant, prayers offered; and, if mentioned ever to others, only told with the view of securing their co-operation in winning back the stray sheep to the green pastures and still waters of the fold. The world is full of sinners who are plunging into deeper sin, because they have been taught by their more religious fellows that there is no hope for such as they are. But they might be saved if they could only be freed from the religious world and left alone with Jesus.

II. The Law's Way of Treating Sin.—"Moses said that such a one should be stoned." It is with the moral, as with natural law—the least violation of its provisions is immediately and terribly avenged. It may be the first offence, or a very slight one, or one the commission of which was followed by floods of tears and an agony of remorse; but the law at once lifts its heavy arm to smite. Its executioner is commissioned to do his work; and the offender falls beneath its curse and penalty.

The function of the law is twofold. First it has to reveal our need of salvation; to hold up the looking-glass that we may go for soap; to convince us of our disease that we may hasten for the physician; to make us feel the badness of our best till we are shut up to Christ. Next, it has to smite, and scourge, and punish us, when we go aside from the narrow thread-like path of perfect goodness. The sinner, therefore, has no hope as he stands beneath Mount Sinai. He cannot climb those cliffs. Nay, he is smitten down by the pieces of the broken tables as they leap downwards from crag to crag. And Moses, with one blow of his fist, so Bunyan tells us, completes the work.

III. The Saviour's Way of Treating Sin.—In that bowed head and hidden face we get a slight indication of how much it costs Him. Sin cannot change his royal heart, or staunch his pity, or freeze the fountains of his compassion. Nay, it makes Him more careful to show his tender, pitying, pleading love. Was it not to Peter that He sent a special message from the open grave, on the resurrection morning? But though sin cannot alter Him, it makes Him suffer keenly, bitterly.

Have you not seen a woman dying by inches beneath the dissolute conduct of her son? She does not murmur, or chide, or blaze abroad his sins. No other hand than hers shall open that front door to him, as he comes home drunk night after night. And he never hears an upbraiding word from those gentle lips. But God alone can measure what those acts of sin are costing her. Her figure becomes more bent, her hair more white, her steps slower, her heart feebler. And shall woman's love suffer thus, and shall not the Saviour suffer as much more, as his love is more than hers? It is easy for us to come to Him for forgiveness, and to go our ways knowing that the words of complete absolution have been uttered; but do we think enough how much that sin, so soon confessed and put away, cost Him on the cross, costs Him now, and will cost Him, as the scar of it is borne by Him, "crucified afresh"?

The early Church was inclined to suppress this story, lest it might lead to sin. They did not realize how that averted face would make men bow their heads in shame, and beat upon their breasts; not for themselves alone, and not because of any thought of penalty, but because they had torn open his wounds, and woven again thorns for his brow. We go forth from that vision, by his grace, to sin no more.

He sometimes seems to wait ere He utters the words of peace. But this is from no tardiness in his love. He wants those ruthless accusers to drop away, and the soul to have time to realize its sin in his holy presence. And when all hope beside is abandoned, and the hour of self-despair has struck; when He can detect signs of genuine repentance and wistful yearning; when the soul turns from its sin to Him in a very agony of desire—He says, "There is now no condemnation; neither do I condemn thee; go, and sin no more."

Oh, souls conscious of sin, do not wait to be brought into his holy presence! haste thither of your own free will. It is the only place in all the universe where you will be safe. Accusing voices are hushed there, and accusing forms are banished. Wait! He will condemn thy sin, but not thee. And his condemnation will be more in what He looks and is than in his words. Yea, thou wilt accuse thyself a thousand times more than He will. And finally, by right of the propitiation of the cross, He will forgive thee, and send thee forth to tell others the story of a love which fails not, nor is discouraged, in its conflict with human sin; but sets itself to substitute for the reign of sin the reign of grace through righteousness unto eternal life.

23

The Light of Life

"I am the Light of the world: he that followeth Me shall not walk in darkness, but shall have the light of life."—John viii. 12.

On either side of the temple court stood huge golden candelabra. On the first and on each succeeding night of the week of the Feast of Tabernacles, these were lit, and became two immense globes of flame, pouring a brilliant flood of light over temple and city and the deep shadows of Olivet. And it was probably to these that our Lord alluded, when He spoke of Himself as the Light of the world.

Of course it would be quite legitimate to compare Him to the glorious orb of day, "of this great universe the eye and soul." What the sun is to the world of nature, Jesus is in the world of the invisible and spiritual. By Him all things consist in harmonious rhythm and order. From Him come all tides of life and beauty, which go to make us truly blessed. And his influence is exerted so noiselessly and quietly, that we can only compare it to those waves of transparent beauty, which break in their untainted loveliness on the world around; but no ear catches the music of their ripple or the throb of their tides. However, it will be better to turn away from this seductive comparison, in order to apprehend exactly what was in his heart when He said, "I am the Light of the world."

The Feast of Tabernacles commemorated the march of the pilgrim hosts through the desert, fed by manna for their food; supplied with water from the smitten rock for their thirst; guided by a pillar of cloud which had at its heart a torch of fire, though this was only apparent when night had veiled the glaring light of the sun, and it brooded tranquilly over the camp. Our Lord compared Himself to the first of these symbols in the sixth chapter; to the second in the seventh; and to the third in this. He declares that to all the pilgrim hosts of men, He is what the cloud with its heart of fire was to that race of desert wanderers.

Let us form a clear conception of that wondrous symbol, which God took not away from his people; the pillar of cloud, in which He went before them by day to lead them in the way, and the pillar of fire to give them light, to go by day and night (Exod. xiii. 21; Num. ix. 15-23).

I. As to its Nature.—In appearance it was probably like one of those white cumulus clouds which sail majestically and slowly through the blue of a summer sky; like some aerial snow mountain, which is to the heavens what the iceberg is to the seas. We have seen such in the process of being manufactured from the mists that lie low at morning in Alpine valleys; and at night we have watched them as they came to anchor, or were stranded on some rocky peak. The one point of difference lay in the Shekinah fire that shone in the heart of the pillar of cloud. It was always there, though only visible when daylight was gone. But that fire in the heart of the cloud was prophetic of our Lord's Deity, enfolded and enshrined in his humanity. The Word was made flesh and tabernacled among men, who knew not what He was, save when at the time of the Transfiguration the glory that dwelt in Him became evident, bathing his form in waves of light and fire.

And it was his consciousness of this marvellous union of the Divine and human elements, though the Divine was so carefully and constantly veiled from ordinary eyes, that enabled our Lord to speak of Himself as the source of spiritual illumination to all the inhabitants of this million-peopled world. There was no egotism, or self-assumption in his claim. It was the literal truth. He bare record of Himself, because He could say nothing less; and He knew whence He came and whither He went.

And there is a consistency between his claims and his powers which has stopped the mouth of objectors and critics. Though this assertion has stood upon the page of Scripture for very many centuries, in a world quick to detect conceit and expose its hollow pretensions; yet no infidel has ever thought of assailing Him in this, which is the weakest and absurdest assertion ever made, if it be not the deepest, truest, and most sacred. Is there not a secret conviction in the heart of men that Jesus is well able to be this which He professes to be? Does not his universal influence—which is confined to no one type of man, but touches equally European and Asiatic, the shivering Esquimaux, and the enervated South Sea Islander—prove that He is more than man, and that in his human nature there burns the fire of Deity? Nay, as the darkness has grown thicker over the world, and one light after another has died out, leaving Him shining in brilliant and glorious loneliness, has there not been abundant witness borne to the fire which is in the heart of the cloud?

"Yes, Jesus is God: in Him the fullness of the Godhead dwells bodily, and it is because of this that He is able to light and guide the generations of mankind. The Life has ever been the Light of men. Not to believe that degrades the character of Christ below contempt, and leaves us face to face with an insoluble problem of how to account for his influence upon the world.

II. As to its Functions.—The work of the fire-cloud was threefold —to lead, to shield, and to illumine.

It led.—The wilderness was a trackless waste to the hosts of Israel, and they were absolutely dependent on the cloud to show their path, and to find out a resting-place each night. On this point the Divine commands admitted of no doubt or question. When the cloud gathered itself up from the Tabernacle on which it brooded, the hosts must strike their tents and follow. However desirable the site of the camp, they must leave it. However difficult the desert paths, they must traverse them. However uninviting the spot where it stopped, they must halt there, and remain just so long as it tarried.

It might be a Marah, without palms, or wells, or shelter; but thither they must go, and there they must remain, though many days should elapse. It might be an Elim, with palms and wells of water, and everything that could render a residence desirable to the tired travellers; but they must be gone from it when the cloud started, though they had enjoyed it for but a brief spell. The cloud might be taken up by day or by night; but there was no choice, except to follow, or to wander in a trackless waste and die. For the manna fell and the water flowed, and the Divine protection was enjoyed, only where the cloud rested.

It shielded.—For, probably, when the people had pitched their tents on some exposed and scorched plain, it unfolded itself like a vast canopy, its base resting on the Tabernacle which stood in the midst of the camp, whilst its fleecy folds were spread out so as to screen the furthest extremities of the camp from the overpowering heat of the noontide sun.

It gave light.—Whilst the camp was hushed in deep slumber it watched over it like the eye of God. The people had no need of the sun by day, or of the moon by night; for the Lord had become their everlasting Light, and the days of their mourning might have been ended. There was a sense in which there was no night there, and they needed not candle or beacon-fire or torch; for the Lord God gave them light. Following the cloud, they had no need to abide in darkness; they already possessed the light of life.

All this the Lord Jesus is willing to be to us. In Him all the fullness dwells. In his many-sided nature God has made all grace to abound, that we, having all-sufficiency in all things, should be abundantly filled and satisfied out of Him. In days of doubt He will be our Guide; in days of trial our Covert and Shade; in days of darkness our Light. Nay more, as in the Pullman carriage the electric light comes on before the tunnel is entered and lingers after it is left, so special manifestations of the presence of Jesus will precede and follow times of special trial.

The peace and blessedness of our earthly pilgrimage will be in direct proportion as we appropriate Jesus in these various aspects of his character and work. Too many of us reserve Him for special times and purposes, as we keep our capital sacredly sealed from use in the

bank; too few of us use Him as the spending money which we carry
in our pockets and employ for every trifling need.

The needs and trials of life are probably intended by God to compel
us to search for and discover the fullness of Jesus. It is probable that
men would never have discovered the treasures of the natural world
had it not been for the pressure of hunger and want; and it is certain
that many of us had never known what the Lord Jesus can be to the
human soul but for the failure of everything beside, which drove us
to Him. Our Father sometimes gives us a glimpse of perfect bliss
through some earthly channel; and then as suddenly closes it up, that
we may be forced to take the freshly realized thirst to the only fountain which can really appease it.

When we first enter the kingdom, God gives us a whole Christ for the
supply of our infinite requirements; but at first we catch only a glimpse
of the lower shelves of his Divine sufficiency, and perhaps suppose
that they are all. But as we help ourselves to these and grow, the veil
slowly uplifts, and we see other and higher shelves; and gradually our
faith becomes stronger, and taller, and more able to help itself to the
added wealth which it perceives to be its own in Christ Jesus.

There is no need for us then to spend our lives in this world, desolate
and forlorn, lacking the blessedness and power which others so evidently possess, and bemoaning the barrenness of our lot; there, right
before us, is Jesus in all his glorious fullness, waiting to take the shape
of our need, as water of the pitcher that carries it. It is for us to claim
Him, and make ours by faith any special side of his being which our
circumstances specially demand as necessary. When we have learnt
this lesson, we can look with equanimity on frost and thaw, on autumn
and winter, on the dying Cherith and the blighted grain; our sources
of supply lie far away in the nature of God, who is the perennial fountain, the unwaning day, the unending summer of love. The differences
which obtain among Christian men are very largely due to the different
ratio in which they have learnt to appropriate Christ—not by a rush
of emotion, but by a naked faith. Rutherford said truly, "There are
curtains to be drawn aside in Christ that we never saw, of new foldings
of love in Him; I despair that ever I shall win to the far end of that
love, there are so many plies in it."

III. AS TO THE CONDITIONS.—"He that followeth Me. ____" We
must put Christ first. He must hold the position of Leader and Guide,
Primate and King. Our one question must ever be, Which way is He
taking? and we may generally ascertain this as we endeavour to answer
one of the following questions: (1) What is the law of Christ? (2) What
is the will of Christ? (3) What would Christ do under these circumstances? If we are not sure, we must wait till we are; but knowing,
we must follow at all costs. Oh to keep just behind Him—not running

E

on in front, or lagging behind! They say that lambs are taught to follow at the heels of a shepherd, by his dropping for them savoury morsels, such as they like; and we may well follow hard after Him whom we love, and who loves us, upheld by his right hand, because of the inestimable benefits which will accrue.

We cannot follow Jesus except we leave all—our own judgment and wisdom, our schemes and preferences, our predilections and fancies; but if we dare to forsake them, and step right away from the boat, we shall win an abundant compensation. Was Paul a loser, who suffered the loss of all things that he might win Christ?

Follow Jesus, Christian! keep Him always well before thee in every path of duty; in every sphere of service; in every attack, like Jonathan's, on the stronghold of the foe. Tread no track where his footprints do not appear. But when thou descriest them, plant in them thy feet, defying aught to separate thee from Him.

Shall not walk in darkness.—Not in the darkness of ignorance and error; not in the darkness of perplexity and confusion; not in the darkness of joylessness and depression. If any man dares to follow Christ so far as he knows, deliberately sacrificing his own will and way to his, it is simply marvellous how the mists will roll up, the night clouds disperse, and the perplexities which had beset the soul give way as brushwood before the tread of the sportsman. Endeavour to please Christ absolutely; and you will know almost immediately what He wants to be done, and how. You may not be able to see more than a step in advance; but dare to take that step, and you will see the next and the next. "If thine eye be single, thy whole body shall be full of light."

But shall have the light of life.—Light is essential to life. Without light flowers would be colourless, even if they grew; animate and inanimate creation would fail; and the world would hasten back to primeval chaos, out of which light came. And equally necessary is it for the inner life to be sustained and nourished by communion with, and obedience to, the Lord Jesus. Apart from Him it is doomed to wither. In Him, through Him, and by Him alone, can it thrive. There is no doubt about this. Begin even now to believe in and follow Him, though it may involve death and the grave; yet, as surely as the soul follows Him, acting up to all its present convictions of duty, it will emerge into a clearness of vision and a vigour of life which shall vindicate its choice for ever. Let Jesus be your pillar of cloud and fire!

24

CHRIST'S ABSORPTION IN HIS FATHER

*"When ye have lifted up the Son of Man, then shall ye know that I am
He, and that I do nothing of Myself; but as my Father hath taught Me,
I speak these things."*—JOHN viii. 28.

A BELOVED friend of mine told me that on one occasion he met an aged
lady, a member of the Society of Friends, who in earlier life had
known Stephen Grellet; and he asked her if that notable evangelist
were as good and noble as he is depicted in his biography. This was
her reply: "We have many excellent Friends, but no Friend like
Stephen Grellet; when he came into a room you felt that he brought
God in with him."

And is not this the distinguishing characteristic of some men, who
are perhaps notable for nothing else? Of others we say, How splendid!
How noble! How good! Of these we say, How much there is of God
in such a one! That was a great saying of the Apostle, "They magnified God in me." And we should not be content with anything less
than the ideal set before us by our Lord: "Let your light so shine
before men, that they may see your good works, and glorify your
Father which is in heaven."

And this was one of our Lord's most striking characteristics. His
whole being was absorbed in acquiring glory for his Father, and in
pleasing Him. At the age of twelve He started to do his Father's business. At the Jordan He submitted to baptism that He might fulfil his
Father's plan. At the well of Sychar He confessed that to do his
Father's will was both meat and drink. He called all those his kinsfolk
who set themselves to do the will of his Father. The only witness He
cared for was that which his Father bore to Him (v. 32; viii. 18). The
name in which He came was the Father's (v. 43). He professed that all
the attraction wrought by Him upon men was due to his Father's
agency (vi. 44). He was sent by the Father; He lived by the Father;
He could do nothing of Himself; the life He had was given, so also was
the authority with which He executed judgment (v. 26, 27; vi. 57). He
spoke only as the Father taught Him (viii. 28). He could dispense with
all human help, because the Father never left Him alone (viii. 16, 29).
To honour Him, to please Him, to work his works, to live in his love,
to perform his commandments, to show good works from Him, to
glorify his name, to divert the attention of men to Him—such was the
passion of his life (viii. 29, 49; ix. 4; x. 17, 32; xii. 49, 50; xiii. 31). He

ascribed both words and works to the indwelling of the Father (xiv. 10). He avowed his intention to answer prayer that the Father might be glorified (xiv. 13). And, as his hour approached when He must pass through death to glory, from the lowest of the one to the highest of the other, He only wished for glory that He might shed it back again on Him; "Father," said He, "glorify thy Son, that thy Son also may glorify Thee" (John xvii. 1). And in the ages yet to be we are told that He will deliver up the kingdom to God, even the Father, that God may be all in all (1 Cor. xv. 24).

There is much for us to learn here. We choose for ourselves aims and ends too subsidiary, too low. The conversion of the unsaved, the building up of the Church, the extension of the kingdom of God, are in themselves worthy and glorious objects; but they are not the very highest. They do not include it, though it includes them; as the planet does not include the sun, but the sun it. Aim at the planet, you miss the sun; aim at the sun, and you include the planet. There is a purpose, foreshadowed in the life of Jesus, the sweep of which is so wide, the march of which is so majestic, the depth of which is so infinite, as to comprehend all other motives, and to be worthy of an endeavour which, though we approach towards it through infinite ages, must yet for ever be far beyond us. And this is the intention, that God may be pleased and glorified and magnified in our bodies, whether by life or death (Phil. i. 20). There are three steps to this.

I. WE MUST MAKE OURSELVES OF NO REPUTATION.—This is what our Master did. He carefully avoided needless publicity, and never courted notice. Indeed, He chose obscurity for Himself, that men might be compelled to ascribe the marvellous results, which were patent to all eyes, to God.

The leper was to tell no man (Matt. viii. 4); the blind men were straitly charged not to make Him known (ix. 30); whilst the paralysed man was yet feeling the raptures of new-found health, Jesus stole away from the eyes of the crowd (John v. 13); when the people were about to make Him king, He escaped from them, and went away alone (vi. 15). His brethren were well aware of this trait in his character, and urged Him to abandon it; but, in spite of all, He went to the feast, not openly but as it were in secret (vii. 10). It was enough for Him to fall into the ground and die, and to accept any title of opprobrium with which his foes chose to brand Him (Matt. x. 25; Luke vii. 34).

It is a hard lesson; but one well worth our while to set ourselves to acquire. Let us, too, choose rather the shady than the sunny side of the street. Let us be content to be accounted nothing. Let us lay our reputation down beneath his feet, as of old they put their garments beneath the hoofs of the ass that bore Him. So only shall we cease to intercept from Christ any ray of glory which may accrue to Him to garner for his Father.

The last thing that some of us are willing to forgo is our reputation. Not that it is wrong to be anxious to maintain our good name, so far as our doing so may adorn his holy Gospel; but that we are often anxious to maintain it as an end in itself, and altogether apart from the glory of Jesus, and the claims of entire surrender. It is not easy to look up into the face of the Master, and say, "If it be thy dear will, I am willing that my name should be cast out by men as evil, and my reputation trampled in the dust, whilst I am counted as the off-scouring of all things, despised and rejected of men."

But it is men like these who, during their life, were accounted vile and worthless—men like Joseph Alleine, and John Bunyan, and Charles Simeon—who shine now with undimming beauty in the firmament; whilst their persecutors' names have been written in the dust, or are preserved only in connection with the sufferings they inflicted on God's saints.

II. WE MUST TAKE UPON OURSELVES THE FORM OF THE SERVANT.— The household slave who does the most menial service, and washes the feet of the guests, was the chosen type to which our Lord conformed Himself, in the upper chamber on the eve preceding his death. Some are proud of their humility, and will stoop to lowly offices to excite admiration. But there was nothing affected here. The men that beheld the lowly deed felt that it was the natural outcome of the holy heart that throbbed in his breast.

It is probable that none of us can stoop to such a depth as He did. He that has ascended far above all heavens to reign could descend to lower depths than all beside to serve. Still it well becomes us to imitate this lowly office; a task, however, which will be impossible for us to fulfil unless we are so utterly absorbed in our devotion to God in Christ, that we come to feel no office too mean, no service too servile, no ministry too trifling, to render to Him or his. Service like this is a fruit which can only be plucked from trees which have been planted and are tended by the Spirit of God.

III. WE MUST BECOME OBEDIENT UNTO DEATH.—Until our eyes are anointed with the eye-salve of the Holy Spirit, we have no conception of how full the New Testament is of exhortations to death. On three different occasions our Lord insisted on the necessity of a man losing his life. Frequently He spoke of his cross as inevitable for Himself and his disciples; whilst the Apostle of the Gentiles discovered that he must be ever bearing about in his body the dying of Jesus, and filling up that which was behind-hand of the sufferings of the Lord.

It is a searching question for most of us, *Have you died?* Of course we died the death of our Lord, so far as the purpose and intention of God are concerned; but have we, by the eternal Spirit, ever really and practically drunk of his cup, and been baptized with his baptism, had fellowship in his sufferings, and been made conformable unto his death? Death is no child's-play. It is impossible not to be aware of it, when it has become the experience of the soul. There has to be a moment of choice, when one elects to take the hand of Jesus and step down with Him into the valley of the shadow; trembling as to the flesh, but glad in the inmost heart. We then yield to death our intellectual conceptions of truth, our warm and vivid emotions, our keen ambitions, our members that are upon the earth; not making ourselves die, but accepting death wrought in us by the life of the risen Jesus through the grace of the Holy Spirit; not vaunting our death, *but dying*, which is a very different matter; not inventing methods of self-crucifixion, but accepting the stern discipline of his cross in all the providential circumstances of our lot and according to his inworking. So only can we bring glory to God.

What a touching picture is that of the intercourse between John Tauler, the celebrated preacher, and the humble peasant, Nicolas, of Basle. "Know," said the simple-hearted friend of God, "that you must needs walk in the path of which our Lord spake to the young man;— you must take up your cross and follow our Lord Jesus Christ in utter sincerity, humility, and patience; you shall set before you the sufferings of our Lord, and contemplate your own life in the mirror of his. And so doing, without doubt, the eternal Prince will look down on you with the eye of his good pleasure, and will not leave his work undone in you, but will purge you still further as gold in the fire." Is it to be wondered at that after two years of lonely converse with God in this attitude, Tauler entered on a ministry which has never ceased in bringing glory to God?

It is a great mystery, of which each one of us may say, "Not as though I had already attained, or were already perfect, but I follow after to apprehend." May the Lord Jesus Himself teach us what this means, that, as we have been together in his death, we may be together in his resurrection, not only hereafter, but now; that having ventured, not merely to look into his grave, but to tarry there for three days and nights, we may pass through it and upwards into a life which shall be absorbed in no other aim than the glory of God, and shall bring forth abundant fruit to Him whose way is through the sea, and his path in the great waters, and whose footsteps are not known—save by those who dare to follow Him through the dark night, led by his hand down the shelving beach, whilst the waters stand on either side, and thunderstorms roll heavily above. This is the shortest passage to abundant life, and to glory to God in the highest.

25

MADE FREE BY THE SON OF GOD

*"If ye continue in my word, then are ye my disciples indeed: and ye
shall know the truth, and the truth shall make you free. . . . If the Son
therefore shall make you free, ye shall be free indeed."*

JOHN viii. 31, 32, 36.

A NEW invention has lately been announced to the world, by which it
is possible to cleanse the smoke of our great cities, impregnated not
only with carbon, but with other deleterious products. In the shaft of
some great chimney, or in connection with the funnel of a railway
engine, a cistern half full of water is arranged, into which the smoke
is drawn through a narrow valve. The smoke being sucked into the
cistern is compelled to pass through the water, and leaves there not
only the black soot, but also the other products which are destructive
of life. And after the process is complete, it escapes back into the
chimney purified, colourless, odourless, and, to a large extent, innocu-
ous. But the water is almost fetid, charged as it is with ink and poison.
One may dare to imagine how glad the smoke itself must be to be freed
from that which made it harmful to men, to pursue its glad way now
into the upper air. And here surely is an illustration of how sinful souls,
laden with crime and with the deleterious products of evil, may be
made free by the Son of God, "loosed from their sins" (as the R.V. puts
it, Rev. i. 5) "in his blood."

We have nothing to do with the origin of sin. That lies far beyond
our ken. Nor can we tell the ultimate out-working of sin in those ages
which are yet to be; except that we know that its course will be determined by the limits raised by the infinite justice, the infinite holiness,
and the infinite love of God. But we find ourselves and all mankind
tainted, blighted, and condemned; accosted, from our very cradle, with
tears and pain and the sweat of toil, and the certainty of death, which
has passed upon all men, for that all men have sinned. Oh, blessed
announcement that God our Father has taken our part against our
sin, and, in the person of his Son, has come to make us free, that we
may be free indeed!

Sin blinds us.—Never did men utter a more barefaced lie than when
those Jews exclaimed: "We were never in bondage to any man."
Never in bondage! Had they forgotten the long and bitter bondage of
Egypt, commemorated annually by the Passover? Or the dreary captivity of seventy years in Babylon, the memory of which lingered in the

most plaintive odes of the Psalter? From that very Temple court, could they not see the Roman standard floating over the ancient palace of their kings, and hear the bugle-call regulating the movements of the victorious Roman soldiery, whilst Roman officials met them at every turn? They could not have forgotten all this; but, in their pride, they wilfully shut their eyes to distasteful truths. Thus prejudice blinds men. "The eyes of their understanding are darkened." And just as some virulent disease attacks the eyes, by which alone its ravages upon the human frame can be discerned, so does sin rob us of the power of self-knowledge. The ungodly man needs to be convinced of sin. The young Christian permits many things which, in the growing light of coming years, he will be the first to condemn. They who pursue most eagerly the upward path, in proportion as they behold the glory and the purity of God, abhor themselves and repent. But for all that, it is certain that we should never have formed a true conception of what sin is, with our enfeebled vision, and in the murky atmosphere of this world, had it not been that God had shown us its true character in the cross of our Lord Jesus Christ. That agony and bloody sweat, that cross and passion, constitute the only true gauge of the enormity and exceeding sinfulness of sin.

Sin enslaves us.—Here is one of the profoundest sentences ever spoken by our Lord. Men had not been wont to count themselves slaves. They were in the habit of thinking that they could take up sin, or lay it down, at their will—that they were its masters. Christ, however, has shown us that it is not so; but that, every time we yield to sin, we increase its hold over us, and become more deeply enthralled under its tyrannous power, so that we are compelled to obey its behests, however cruel or malignant they may be. "He that committeth sin is the servant of sin."

But sin is not a necessary part of our being.—This comes out so clearly in these remarkable words: "The servant bideth not in the house for ever." This, of course, is an obvious truth. There is a great difference between the relation of your child and your servant. Your child is an integral part of the household. He has been born in it, has become part of it, and, however far he travels, he is one with it by a tie which defies the gnawing tooth of time and the growing distance of long journeying. It is different with a servant. Especially under the provisions of the Levitical law, it was impossible for the servant to abide in the house for ever. His slavery was limited in its duration to the amount of debt he had to work off. The trumpet of jubilee, ringing out its welcome notes, bade the slave go free. In like manner, however long a man may have served sin, and however tightly he may be held in its meshes, yet it has no necessary right over him; he need not abide for ever, he is but a slave in a tyrant's household, who, at any moment, may go free.

How this truth must thrill the hearts of some who read these words! For long they have been sighing under bondage, compared with which that of Egypt was light; they have bitterly cried, "Who shall deliver us?" They have thought that there was no release from their bitter bondage; and their tyrant-master has whispered, mockingly, "Mine for ever!" But let these know that sin is an intruder, a usurper, an alien influence other than God meant in his original making of men. The prison walls need not be perpetual. The chain need not be eternal. The house may be left for ever, never to be darkened again by those who have groaned within its precincts.

Freedom from the tyranny of sin must come to us from without. The slave cannot free himself. He cannot scale those walls, pick those locks, elude that tyrant. Resolutions cannot do it, nor prayers, nor tears. Every struggle only tightens the noose. The slave must be made free. Hence the mission of the Son of God. Himself free, He came into our prison-house, put his Divine Person under the conditions induced by our sins—as Theseus sailed in the ship with the yearly tribute of Athenian youth to the dread monster of Crete whom he was destined to destroy—"and, by death, destroyed him that had the power of death, that is the devil; and delivered them who, through fear of death, have all their life-time been subject to bondage." He shared our lot, though He did not share our sinfulness. Mighty as God, yet weak and frail as man; able, on the one hand, to wield and use infinite power, and, on the other, to suit Himself to the weakest and feeblest of his brethren. "Such a High Priest became us."

I. THE NATURE OF THIS FREEDOM.—It is not freedom to do as we like. That were not liberty, but licence. To be emancipated from all rule and law would be impossible in a well-ordered world, and incompatible with the well-being of others. But the Son sets us free from the unnatural conditions into which sin has brought us; so that we, "being delivered from the fear of our enemies, may serve Him without fear in holiness and righteousness all the days of our life."

We are free from the imputation of Adam's sin; because He as the second Adam has borne it away. Free from the lash of a broken law; because He has paid the penalty, and met its last demands. Free from the weary gnawing of remorse; because He has forgiven us our sins, and blotted them out of his book, and cast them behind his back for ever. Free from the hopeless endeavour to weave for ourselves a robe of stainless righteousness; because He gives us his own, as Jonathan exchanged his apparel with David. Free from the bondage of corruption; the chains of which have been struck off by his mighty hand. Free from the very love of sin; so that its least breath or approach is instantly shrivelled before those habits of woven fibre with which He arrays the soul. Free from the dread of death; because He has died.

Free from the whole entail of evil; except those limitations and failures which must ever weaken the strength of our purpose and lower the temperature of our motives, compelling us to apply constantly for daily cleansing and acceptance through his flawless righteousness.

We do not want more than this. The swallow, with a broken wing, seeks not liberty to feed on carrion; but only to be able to mount again into the sunny air, which is its native sphere. And the soul which is athirst for God and holiness asks for no other freedom than that it should be able to pursue its divine quest unhindered by the restraints of sin.

II. THE MEANS OF THIS FREEDOM.—"The truth shall make you free." The only-begotten Son speaks of truth because He was full of truth, and truth came by Him (John i. 14, 17). And from this point the light of the world repeats often this great word—*truth* (viii. 32, 40, 44, 45, 46; xiv. 6; xvi. 13; xvii. 19; xviii. 37). When He speaks of truth, He means the inner heart of things; their essence and kernel; that panorama of the unseen and eternal which lay before his eye in open vision.

Truth always frees.—The villager will no longer dread to pass some haunted spot when he learns the truth that there are no such things as *fays* or *goblins*. The slave girl will no longer remain in the house of her cruel oppressor when she discovers that he has no longer any claim on her; because some time ago the Act of Emancipation was passed, though the tidings of it have been carefully concealed. The timid soul will no longer question whether it may not have committed the unpardonable sin, when it is taught that that very fear is proof positive that it has never entered this awful state. The dying will be free from all fear, if they realize the truth that the wasp has lost its sting, the viper its fangs, the roaring lion its teeth; and that the iron gate will open of its own accord.

So, when the Lord Jesus reveals the truth of all that He has done for us—that in Him we are accepted and triumphant; that through Him we sit in heavenly places with Satan beneath our feet; that from Him we are equipped with power to tread on serpents, and scorpions, and all the power of the enemy—*then* the whole aspect of our life alters; we see our position, and we take it; we learn our power, and we use it; we realize that we are free, and as such we begin to act. Knowing that we have the right to walk the waves, we step out on them in faith, and find them as rock beneath our tread. Acting by faith in the truth revealed to us, we discover that it is so. Things are not what they seem. We think we are powerless and helpless, and destined to be overcome; but, if we would venture out on Christ's revealed truth, and dare to live by faith, and not by sight, we should discover that all the world is new, and life is ours, with victory and sweetness and power, such as we have never known or dreamt of.

III. THE RESULTS OF THIS FREEDOM.—It is the prerogative of the son; and if you rise up from the chains of the prison to the freedom and joy of the Father's house, if you are no longer entangled with the yoke of bondage, it is a sign that you, too, are no longer a servant, but a son; that, by a blessed act of regeneration, you have passed from the one to the other, from death to life. The moment of soul-emancipation witnesses to the moment of regeneration and adoption. And this again attests that there shall be no going out any more for ever.

"The Son abideth ever in the house"; and the sons abide there for ever, too. Hagar and Ishmael are cast out; but Isaac, the divinely-given Laughter, stays in the home for ever. The child can never cease to be a child. It may sin, and grow cold, and cause pangs of anguish to hearts which would give themselves to save it, but it is a child still, to be brought back through seas of sorrow and fires of pain; it may wander into the far country and waste its years, but it will certainly return home, never to go forth again.

There are many among us who are really in a much better position than they have any conception of. They are children; but they do not know it. They shall never perish; but they fail to realize it. They are in the place of power; but their eyes are blinded and they cannot see it. Oh that such would cry for the heavenly eyesalve, that the eyes of their heart may be enlightened to know "the hope of his calling, the riches of the glory of his inheritance in the saints, and the exceeding greatness of his power toward them that believe"! And, as the Spirit of Truth shall lead them into all the truth, their freedom shall increase with their knowledge in ever-widening circles.

26

THE GLORY OF CHRIST

"I seek not mine own glory."—JOHN viii. 50.

FROM THIS point our Lord begins to speak of his glory, as if He already beheld its dawn, and pressed on with renewed speed to where it beckoned; although the dark ravine of death lay between Him and its sunny heights. The Shekinah that shone within the veil of his human nature was, for the most part, veiled from all besides; except that once on the mount of transfiguration it burst from all restraint, and saturated his human nature with torrents of light, so that the favoured three beheld his glory. But, speaking generally, it was veiled, and the curtains kept close drawn. The time was coming when He should be glorified; and it shall be our task reverently to consider the elements of which that glory was composed, and the conditions on which it rested.

In the olden time, Moses asked to see God's glory. It is difficult to understand what he precisely meant by his request. Did he think that some superb procession would sweep down the mountain rent, in which the loftiest archangels should take a part, as the body-guard of Deity? Did he expect some supernatural unfolding of the mysteries of light, or of fire, or of the spirit-world? We cannot tell. But we eagerly notice that, in his reply, God spake of none of these things; but said, "I will make all my goodness pass before thee." The prayer to behold God's glory was answered by a catalogue of the moral qualities of the Divine nature. In other words, we may accept the affirmation of Professor Drummond, and say that glory means character, or, rather, the revelation of character; so that those who behold it, keen in their appreciation of moral worth, may be constrained to admire and imitate. The glory of Jesus is, surely, the manifested beauty of his matchless character.

In speaking or thinking of the glory of the Lord Jesus, we must ever distinguish, as He did, between the glory which He had with the Father before the worlds were made, and that glory which accrued to Him as the result of his human life. The former was his by inherited right, as the fellow of Jehovah; the other was given to Him by his Father as the reward and guerdon for his obedience to death. The one is incommunicable, the unique property of his Deity; the other is transferable, for He graciously speaks of passing it on to his own. For the first, see xvii. 5; for the second, see xvii. 1, 22, 24.

That He might the better preserve his *incognito* (if we may reverently so term it), and become a merciful and faithful High Priest, by a thorough participation in our human life, He laid aside the evidences of his Divine glory. To use the expressive word of the Holy Ghost, "He emptied Himself." And so He set Himself to win that glory which should result from a perfected character, and from suffering even unto death. It is of this that He speaks, when He says, "I seek not mine own glory." Let it be clearly understood that it is of his glory, as the Son of Man and the obedient servant, that we are now speaking.

I. THE MOTIVE OF CHRIST'S DESIRE FOR GLORY.—That He desired glory is evident. Did He not directly ask for it?—"Father, glorify thy Son." Was there not an accent of satisfaction in his twice-repeated ejaculation—first, when He heard of the inquiry by the Greeks, and again when Judas went out to do the fatal deed of treachery—"Now is the Son of Man glorified!" Are we not warranted in believing that it was the anticipation of the glory into which He must pass through suffering that quickened his pace into the valley of the shadow? (Luke xxiv. 26).

And yet we cannot believe that our Master sought glory for any selfish end. This He could not do. He said explicitly, "I seek not mine own glory." There was not the shadow of personal ambition resting as a cloud over that pure and noble heart. But He desired glory, that He might shed it back again upon his Father.

It was the supreme passion of his being to glorify the Father. As He descended into the dark valley, this was his one cry, "Father, glorify thy name!" Deeper and deeper still He went; and this same entreaty, breaking from his agonized heart, comes back to us yet fainter, and ever fainter. "Now is my soul troubled; and what shall I say? Father, glorify thy name!" Perhaps even the love of the race and the desire to redeem had failed to support his fainting soul, unless his resolution had been empowered and maintained by this all-masterful desire. He was greedy, therefore, of every vestige of glory that He could win by suffering, even though it were unto death; that He might be able, though it were with but a feather-weight additional, to augment the revenue of glory which, through Him, should accrue to God. "Now is the Son of Man glorified, and God is glorified in Him." "Glorify thy Son, that thy Son also may glorify Thee."

What an example He has left us that we should follow in his steps! Human applause, and admiration, and reward, would not hurt us, if we gathered them all only as the vinedressers pluck the produce of the vines for presentation to the owner of the vineyard. It is a high ideal, and yet evidently the Apostle thought it attainable; else he would not have exhorted his converts to seek that glory even in their meals (1 Cor. x. 31). But it is only so that we can come into the deepest fellowship with our Saviour, when we, too, have so drunk of his spirit that we become absorbed in the same supreme object, and seek for the prizes of our high calling that we may cast them at the feet of God. That God may be better understood, and admired, and loved through our life; that men may turn from us to Him as from the jewel to the sunlight in which it sparkles; that more hearts may be brought beneath his sway—be this our aim, at all costs to ourselves.

II. THE DIRECTIONS IN WHICH HIS DESIRE WAS REALIZED.— The Apostle Peter says, "God gave Him glory" (1 Pet. i. 21). In what did that glory consist? (1) *In the indwelling of God in his human nature.*— The glory of the desert acacia-bush was in the fire that burnt there; of the tabernacle in the Shekinah glow; of Zion that God had chosen to dwell there. And the glory of our Lord, as to his human nature, was that in Him the Divine and human blended in perfect union; that the Father dwelt in Him, spake and wrought in Him; and that He was the perfect vehicle for the expression of the incorruptible life, which was, and is, and is to come. This was the glory which the Apostles beheld expressed on the Holy Mount.

(2) *In his perfect endurance of the severest tests.*—The whole brunt of evil broke on Him, as the roll of the Atlantic breaker on some weather-beaten rock. It is impossible to imagine tests more searching and complete than those through which He passed; in journeyings often; in conflicts with the Pharisees and Sadducees; in conflicts with his own brethren; in conflict with the devils that possessed the afflicted; in conflict above all with the prince of this world in that last terrible duel of the cross; in weariness and painfulness; in watchings often; in hunger and thirst; in fastings often; in bloody sweat and nakedness; in the anguish of God-forsakenness and of dissolution. But, so far from being overcome, He rose out of each successive test, having set forth in perfect beauty the appropriate grace which it demanded, and absorbed the whole force of the trial with which He was confronted; so that it passed into Him, and became an addition to his moral strength, as the savage warriors think that the strength of each foe they slay in battle becomes incorporated into themselves.

(3) *In the benefits which He has conferred on men.*—There is no glory so dear to the noble heart as that accruing from helpfulness to others. When it comes we cannot be inflated with pride, because we are already so thankful to know of the blessing which we have been the means of bestowing. And, ah, what glory was it to the blessed Lord, that He has delivered us from the consequences of Adam's sin; that He has borne away the sins of the world; that He has opened the kingdom to all believers; that He has made it possible for sinful creatures to receive and be impelled by the very Spirit of God; that He has obtained for us a life which is death-proof, sin-proof, devil-proof,

the essence and crown of blessedness! To be loved as Saviour, to be trusted as Priest, to be enthroned as King, to receive the unutterable devotion of myriads, and to be able to help them to the uttermost—this surely is one prime element in his glory.

(4) *In the exaltation of his nature.*—"The God of our fathers," said Peter, "hath glorified his Son Jesus." And in his mouth, fresh from the scenes of the Ascension and of Pentecost, these words referred to the glory of his exaltation (Acts ii. 32, 33; iii. 13). We are told that, as a guerdon for his tears and obedience, the Father gave Him a name above every name, and set Him at his own right hand far above all creature life. But this was only possible because his nature was already supreme in its quality. It was no arbitrary act of enthronement; it was the recognition of superlative worth. And as He that descended ascends far above all heavens, that He might fill all things with floods of light, there is given an evidence of the glory of his being, of which the princes of this world were ignorant, but which now shines forth to illuminate all worlds.

These are but the guesses and babblings of a child; yet do they seem tracks that lead our feet towards the heart of this marvellous subject. But who shall tell of the love of the heart of God towards his Son, or of its expression? Here are depths which must be hidden from our scrutiny. As it was the passion of Christ to glorify the Father, so it was the passion of "the Father of glory" to glorify the Son. Yes, and as yet that glorification is only in its beginnings; the first stages alone of of the coronation and enthronement of Jesus "in all his glory" have taken place: the full outburst of his meridian splendour is yet future. Ah, we are yet to behold some wondrous scenes, which will ravish our eyes and fill our hearts with an exceeding weight of glory! "God shall also glorify Him in Himself, and shall straightway glorify Him." And we shall behold his glory, nay, better, share it for ever and ever (John xiii. 31, 32; xvii. 22, 24).

III. THE COST AT WHICH HIS DESIRE WAS REALIZED.—The glory glistens in our view, but we are not always ready to consider its cost. The only path to the glory is that which lies through the tangled thorn-brake of sorrow. The corn of wheat must fall into the ground and die, lying alone and forsaken through the winter with its pitiless blasts and frost. He must descend ere He can ascend. Pain must inflict the wounds in which the pearls of untold glory shall glisten.

Nor can it be otherwise with ourselves. We must be witnesses of the sufferings, if we would be partakers of the glory to be revealed; only as we suffer can we reign with Him; there must be fellowship with his sufferings if there shall be attainment to his resurrection; we must drink of his cup and be baptized with his baptism, if we, would sit right and left of his throne.

27

THE WORKS OF GOD

*"I must work the works of Him that sent Me while it is day: the night
cometh, when no man can work."*—JOHN ix. 4.

THE UTTER restfulness which filled the heart of the Lord Jesus is
beautifully manifested in the introductory verses of this chapter. At
the close of the preceding one He is seen amid the heated altercation
of his foes, enduring the contradiction of sinners against Himself, and
compelled to use some of the severest epithets that ever fell from his
gracious lips. The climax of the argument was reached on his claiming
to have existed before Abraham was. He appropriated the incommunicable name of Jehovah, and said, "Before Abraham was, I AM." And
in a frenzy of indignation the Jews caught up the stones lying about for
the repair of the temple to inflict forthwith the doom of the blasphemer.

But there was a force at work which they little understood, rendering
them powerless to harm him. Was it the spell of his majestic presence?
Was it the aureole of his spotless character? Was it the protecting
power of his Father? Whatever it was, He passed unscathed through
the midst of them; and so left the temple, and began to descend the
great flight of steps, and to pass through the successive courts. On the
way his attention was attracted by a blind beggar, who for years had
been a familiar object as he sat and begged. And albeit that there was
every need to put as far a distance as possible between Himself and the
missiles of his foes, He stopped, made clay, and leisurely healed him.
Is it not evident that He realized his absolute safety until his hour
arrived; and that if there were an opportunity and a prompting to do
God's work, there was the strongest ground also to count upon perfect
immunity till the work was done?

His enemies might chafe and storm around Him; but they could not
hurt Him, or penetrate with word and stone the encasing envelope of
the presence of God. Secure of that protection, He was able to go and
come, fearless and unharmed, serene and quiet, restful and peaceful,
blessing and blessed. Oh for the quiet heart which looks from itself to
God, and considers neither difficulty nor peril, because it is so absorbed
in doing his work! Here the blessed Spirit broods undisturbed, amid
the wild fury of earth's tumult, whispering intimations of God's will,
and nerving the soul with sufficient power to perform.

I. THE CONDITIONS IN WHICH GOD'S WORKS ARE DONE.—The phrase
"works of God," is a familiar one throughout this Gospel. To do them

145

was to feed the Redeemer's soul (iv. 34); they were in an ever-ascending scale (v. 20); they were of a certain definite number, given Him to finish (v. 36); they were the signs and seals of his mission (x. 38); they were not his own, but wrought through Him by the Father (xiv. 10); they were unique in the history of the world (xv. 24); they were definitely finished ere He left (xvii. 4). But it becomes us to learn the conditions under which they were wrought, that we may be able to do those greater works of which He spoke.

(1) *His heart was at rest in God.*—When suddenly aroused amid the tumult of the storm, or pursued by infuriated crowds, or amid the anguish of the grave of Lazarus, or in the garden of his arrest, there was ever the same deep inner calm, which spread an awe on nature, and cast its spell on men. And it is impossible to expect any great thing to be done in the world through a man whose inner life is ever in a state of ferment.

Nature herself teaches the need of repose for the putting forth of her mightiest efforts. It is in the closet, the study, the cave, the woodland retreat, that problems have been solved, resolves formed, and schemes matured. And the river of life itself will lose its most precious properties, if it flows through the muddy and perturbed waters of restless hearts.

It is not possible for us all to have a life of outward calm. In such a world as this, with the opposition of men and the intrusion of sorrow on our most sacred moments, there is perpetual interruption. But beneath all the heart may keep its Sabbath. Trusting in God, resting on Him, rolling off to his charge its anxieties and cares before they have time to soak down poison into its springs, the inner life may thus retain its tranquillity, reflecting God's heaven above, and recipient of the least impulse of God's will.

(2) *He was specially endued with the Holy Spirit.*—Our Lord had his Pentecost before Pentecost. In the same hour He was baptized as to his body with the waters of the Jordan, and as to his spirit with the Holy Ghost. In his address to Cornelius and his friends, the Apostle Peter lays distinct stress on this as the condition on which Jesus of Nazareth went about doing good: "He was anointed with the Holy Ghost and with power" (Acts x. 38).

It should be a serious question with each of us, Have I claimed my share in Pentecost? On his ascension, our Lord received from the Father the promise of the Holy Ghost in its fullest plenitude, that through Him the whole Church might get it. It is ours in Him; we have not to go up to Heaven or down to Hades to win it; we have not to endeavour to merit it, but only to claim it by faith. If on comparing ourselves with the symptoms of Spirit-filling given in the Acts of the Apostles, we are conscious of a grievous deficiency, let us by believing prayer dare to ask for all that is ours in the risen living Saviour.

(3) *He was willing that the Father should work through Him.*—On the day of Pentecost, the preacher clearly emphasized this: "Jesus of Nazareth was approved of God among you by miracles, and wonders, and signs, which God did by Him in the midst of you" (Acts ii. 22). And this statement bears out the affirmation of the Lord Himself, "the Father that dwelleth in Me, He doeth the works" (xiv. 10).

Blessed are we when we learn that secret, no longer to work for God, but to let God work through us; to be brooks of Siloam, pent in given beds, instead of wandering at our own sweet will; to be clay kneaded into any shape; to be earthenware pipes, if needs be, hidden under ground, and trampled beneath the hurrying feet of men, with one end open to the reservoir, and the other to the empty cistern of human need, so that the torrent may come in with even flow on the one side, and pour out on the other with a regularity which escapes notice because it is so unbroken. It was thus that the great Apostle lived who said, "Christ hath wrought through me in word and deed to make the Gentiles obedient" (Rom. xv. 18, literal rendering). So are we bidden to yield ourselves to God, and our members as instruments of righteousness, that He may work in us that which is well pleasing in his sight (Rom. vi. 13; Heb. xiii. 21). "We must work," the R.V. says.

II. THE NEED FOR THESE WORKS.—"A man blind from his birth." We have observed before that the miracles of this Gospel were evidently selected in each case with a special purpose of becoming foils to bring into prominence some characteristic feature in the ministry or teaching of Jesus Christ. Nor is this one an exception to the rule. What emblem could better set forth the condition of mankind than a born-blind beggar? That men are blind, that they are born so, and that they are destitute and bankrupt, needing gold and white linen, and eyesalve, needs no proving. But amid all, He comes who is the Light of the world, and is able to give sight to the blind, and to the poor a share in his measureless wealth.

The Jews had but two hypotheses on which to account for human suffering. "Either this man sinned" (in some previous state of existence), "or his parents, that he was born blind"; with them, special suffering was always the sign of special sin (Luke xiii. 1–4).

There are many who argue thus in the present day. The occurrence of special disaster leads them to search for the sin which must have led to it; forgetting that it does not always follow, and that it has been the problem of the ages that so many of the worst of men have had comparative immunity from suffering—"there have been no bands in their death"—whilst for the godly the waters of a full cup are wrung out. It is true that sin brings suffering; but there is some suffering which is not the evidence of special wrong-doing.

This is therefore a third and broader hypothesis, which our Lord suggests here. "Neither hath this man sinned, nor his parents; but that the works of God may be made manifest in Him." Suffering is permitted for wise and good reasons, which we shall one day comprehend, and amongst them is this: that it may provide a platform on which the grace and power of God may manifest themselves, each new phase of evil leading to some new forth-putting of the heart of God. To how many suffering ones may the Lord Jesus send the message: "This sickness is not unto death; but for the glory of God, that the Son of God may be glorified thereby"!

If only the sufferers who may read these words would bracket together these two texts, this spoken of the blind beggar, and that of the sickness of Lazarus, surely it would be easier to bear the long nights of weariness and the days of pain—not in punishment, not by neglect or mischance, not as the inevitable results of the mistakes or misdeeds of others, but—to give an opportunity for the works and glory of God. What works? What glory? Surely the works of humility, and patience, and gentleness, which his Spirit instils; and the glory of that lovely spirit which his Spirit begets.

But how necessary is it that, as there is the need, we who have the supply be not wanting. If there is need for the works of God to be manifested, we must be at hand, and willing at all costs to manifest them. If there is the opportunity for the glorifying of Christ, we must not be slow to seize it. Make haste!—the night is coming, in which no man can work. Life at the longest is but a day; and before we are aware the shadows have stealthily crept far across the grass, the air has become chill, and the silver crescent of the moon is rocking in the dimming light. What works await us yonder we cannot tell. But the unique work of healing blindness and enriching beggary is confined to earth; and we must hasten to do all of this allotted to us before the nightfall. He lives intensely whose eye is fixed on the fingers of the dial; as the poor sempstress works swiftly whose last small wick of candle is rapidly burning down in its socket.

III. The Subject of these Works.—What a contrast between the opening and the close of the chapter! The blind sees, the beggar is rich. The abject is an apologist. The intruder on the temple steps is a worshipper within the true shrine. The soul ignorant of Christ owns Him as Son of God. And all this because of the individual interest our Lord took in him.

(1) *He detected what was working in his mind.*—Beneath that unpromising exterior were the elements of a noble character. The power which might have run to waste, being dammed up, wrought deeper into his soul. He heard the converse of the crowds as they passed, caught the voices of the Levites chanting their majestic psalms,

detected the benedictions of the priests; and awoke in him indefinable yearnings after God. Unknown to any besides, these arrested the attention of Jesus, who, unconscious of personal danger, bent over him with eager interest, as a child over the first primrose of spring.

(2) *He developed the latent power of faith.*—It was there, but it had nothing to evoke it; and yet it must be evoked ere Christ could give him sight. He could feel, though he could not see. So the Lord put clay on the eye-socket, awaking wonder, hope, expectation; and such was the ladder put down for his faith to climb up into the light. And then in the command to go and wash there was a still further test to his faith, to conform and strengthen it. Is it not thus that the blessed Lord still deals with us; watching the smallest spark of faith, and fanning it into a flame, giving it some very small and obvious thing to do, that it may from a thread become a cable?

(3) *He found him when cast out by all besides.*—His parents disowned him, and the Pharisees cast him out of their synagogue, depriving him of a highly-prized privilege; but Jesus found him. He had been cast out Himself, and knew the weariness and pain of excommunication; and thus acquired the desire and the clue to help another, suffering beneath the intolerance of the religious world. Does not Jesus always steal to our side when we are cast out, or deserted by our friends?

(4) *He answered his hunger for faith.*—"Dost thou believe on the Son of God?" The question startled him; and yet it explained one of the deepest instincts of his nature, though he may have been little conscious of it, and perhaps felt only an utter dissatisfaction with all else, and an insatiable yearning after God. If we live up to what we know, at all costs, we shall most certainly be led into further discoveries of truth. If we dare to go to the pool of Siloam and wash, we shall be gladdened by great revelations and unfoldings of God in Christ. We think we are going to plough a field; and we suddenly come on a box of treasure, struck by our plough, which makes us independent of work for the rest of our lives.

And so obedience passes into worship, and we see that He who has made our life his care, tending us when we knew Him not, is the Christ of God, in whom are hid all the riches of time, all the treasures of eternity: and we worship Him.

28

The Blessed Life of Trust

*"When He putteth forth his own sheep, He goeth before them, and the
sheep follow Him; for they know his voice."*—John x. 4.

Few images could better express the relationship between our Lord
and his people than that of Shepherd and sheep, so often applied to
God in the Old Testament, and appropriated by Christ Himself in the
New. He had already shown that references to Himself underlay the
manna, the water, and the fire-cloud. And now He shows that beneath
the sweet pastoral imagery of the prophets He was ever the glorious
substance and reality.

The Eastern sheepfold is a mere enclosure surrounded by a palisade.
The sheep are brought into it in the evening, several flocks being committed to the care of the common keeper or porter for the night. In
the morning the shepherds return and knock at the closely barred door
of the enclosure, which the porter opens from within. Each separates
his own sheep by calling to them; and the sheep respond, disentangling
themselves from the rest, and when thus collected they follow their
own shepherd, wherever he may lead.

The shepherd alone enters by the door. The robber may break in by
force, the thief by stratagem; but their object is plunder and slaughter,
and the sheep will neither respond to their voice, nor follow them. "A
stranger will they not follow, but will flee from him; for they know not
the voice of strangers." Huddled into a corner of their pen, stricken
with alarm, they dread the rough hand of the intruder.

That sheepfold is the Jewish people. The irruption into the fold of
the sheepstealer represents the audacity and hypocrisy of the Pharisees
and Scribes, who had no purposes but plunder in their heart. They
fleeced the flock for their own advantage (Ezek. xxxiv. 3).

In opposition to them, the Saviour comes as the true Shepherd. He
has no need to scale the wall, or to establish his authority by force or
guile. In Him the porter, who is well represented by John the Baptist,
recognised the true Shepherd of Israel: and He was now prepared to
lead forth his own to green pastures, and beside waters of rest.

I. The Putting Forth of the Sheep.—Up to the end of the last
chapter it might have appeared that the whole of Israel might be included in his flock. But recent events had proved that this could not
be. The Messiah, as Zechariah had foretold, had taken to Himself his

two staves, "Beauty" and "Bands," and had fed the flock for one month, but had finally been compelled to renounce the task as hopeless (Zech. xi. 10–14). The expulsion of the blind man; the decree of excommunication which had struck at Himself and his followers; the violent hostility that dogged his steps—all pointed to the impossibility of gathering the whole nation into his care.

There was but one alternative. He must bring his own from out the Jewish fold—separating them, not by force, but by his gentle voice: calling them by name and leading them out. Is not Jesus always leading us out? He calls the souls of men from the fishing-net and the tollbooth; from scenes of worldly pleasure and haunts of sin; from associations with the flock of slaughter. And the one test of their being his own is that they hear his voice and follow. Not to believe, or obey that voice, or follow it, proves that the soul is none of his.

But a stronger word is used: "He putteth forth his own sheep." The phrase is a very strong one. He casts or thrusts them out; as when He constrained his disciples to get into the ship. So was Israel thrust out of the luxurious fare of Egypt to the simplicities of the desert; so are the young eaglets thrust out by the mother bird when she stirs up her nest, and forces them to learn the joys of flight.

He puts us forth by his providences.—We may have been living in some sheltered home, where love screened us from very contact with a strange and unkindly world; but suddenly the encircling arms are withdrawn, and we are driven forth to stand alone, and to act for ourselves, so far as any human help is concerned. Or we are compelled to leave the dear country village, or the ancestral home, or the land of our birth, to fare forth we hardly know whither. All that is sure is that there is no return; that we have no alternative; that the angel with flaming sword drives us out and keeps the gate behind us.

He puts us forth by the constraints of his Spirit.—We may have been living a self-contained, self-contented life, shut up in some narrow circle of religious thought and life, when suddenly there break on us the voices which summon to another and truer life. We become aware of possibilities of Christian living that had never been suggested to our hearts. From some loftier peak than usual we catch sight of a wider range of truth. We yearn with eager desire for the new power, and joy, and blessedness, which look in at the windows of our soul, and beckon us to go with them; as children who ramble for a long summer day through wood and hill. It is not so much then the outward constraint as the irresistible impulse from within which thrusts us out.

He puts us forth by his direct call.—To how many a young life, all unexpectedly, there has come the summons of the Master, "I am about to evangelize such and such a district, and I want you to accompany Me." To students in the great seminaries of America, to bowed heads and hearts in conventions at home, to souls worshipping in the loneliness of the shrine, there have come voices, bidding them arise and depart, because they are to be sent far hence to the heathen. What heart-searching, what tremour, what mingling of fear and hope, of expectancy and anguish, sweep over the heart when first it hears its name spoken by the Master's lips, and rises up to follow where He leads the way!

If you are his own, it is certain that in some one of these ways you will hear his voice, and feel his crook, putting you forth. The fold is warm and sheltered, and you are accustomed to it, and shrink from the unknown; but it is bare of grass, and lacks the fresh breeze and dew of the mountain-side; there can be no true peace and satisfaction within its walls; beyond its precincts the true life awaits you; and to that the Good Shepherd puts you forth.

II. THE SHEPHERD'S LEAD.—"He goeth before them." This is the place ever assigned to Him in the Old Testament. "He leadeth me by the still waters." "Thou leadest thy people like a flock." He permits none of his own to go along a path which He has not trodden, and in which He has not had previous experience. There is only one exception to this—the experience of sin. With this single exception, "He was tempted in all points like as we are." Take heart, O trembling believer! However strange and hard your path seems to you, if you look closely at it you will detect in its dust the footprints of the Shepherd; and where He has preceded you, you need not fear to follow.

And it is not only true that He passed through all possible experiences of human life during those wonderful years of his sojourn on our earth, drinking every cup, exposing Himself to every grief, tried by every woe, that He might be a merciful and faithful High Priest; but in addition, He accompanies and precedes by only a step each timid child that steps forth from the warm fold to follow Him. To the eye of faith He is always a little in front—removing the stones; selecting the least difficult paths; bending back the briers; driving before Him the wild beasts or robbers that threaten us; and conducting us as safely and quickly as He can to the sweetest, truest life.

It would seem as if the Shepherd is never so real as when we are being put forth from the fold. We could better exist without Him when we are there; but directly we emerge on the life of faith, away from the familiar and friendly, we need Him, and our heart entwines itself around Him with a tenacity which grows stronger as every new trial is met, and mastered, and left behind in the onward journey.

It may be that you cannot discern Him; but this makes no real difference. Dare to believe that if you are in his place—that is, if you are treading a path which is clearly marked out for you by inevitable circumstances and by unmistakable inward promptings, although you cannot see Him, and the way seems lonely, yet—that He is just before you; the darkness veils, but does not obliterate Him; the Lord is going before you, and the Holy One is your rereward.

III. THE FOLLOWING OF THE SHEEP.—"The sheep follow Him." The utter dependence of the sheep on the Eastern shepherd is a beautiful emblem of our attitude towards our Lord. In those vast pasture-lands, rolling over mountain slopes, and dipping into darksome glens, brooded over by a silence that can almost be felt, there arises a very close intimacy between the shepherd and his flock. He forgets the distance between them, and becomes their friend. He is as intimately acquainted with their history, faces, and dispositions, as with those of his own children. He has a name for each, which is sufficient to bring it to his side. And common peril or privation, shared together, but cements the friendship closer.

Nor is the affection only on his side. Stupid as they appear to us, they develop under such conditions an amazing power of attachment, which they manifest in touching trust. They follow the shepherd anywhere.

Let us so trust our Lord. It often grieves the Christian teacher to find souls writing hard things against themselves, because they are attempting to acquire a certain lesson; to reach a certain experience; to attain and keep a certain attitude—altogether apart from Him: as if they had to do all this before they could count on his love and help. They are always trying to know or do something before they get to Him. Whereas the opposite is the only true and safe way; first to keep by his side and at his heel, and then to let Him lead the soul into all it must learn and achieve. Do not attempt the Christian life as a means to closer acquaintance with Jesus; but let your closer acquaintance with Him lead you to pass onward through the land in the length and breadth of it.

If He call you to know some new aspect of truth, throw on Him the responsibility of adding line to line, precept to precept, till it is clear. If He desire you to live a life of daily appropriation and dependence, trust Him to make it possible and congenial. If He bid you separate yourself from some unhallowed alliance, or to quit some unhealthy companionship, or to confess your new-found rapture, let Him understand how absolutely you look to Him to show you just how He would have you act.

Let Jesus Christ stand between you and everything—between you and circumstances; between you and dreaded trials; between you and temptation; between you and your attainments in the blessed life; between you and your projects of Christian usefulness. Follow Him, i.e., let Him go first. If He does not go forward, wait for Him. Every step taken apart from Him, or in front of Him, will have to be retraced with bitter tears.

The attitude of the sheep is *submission*. From the first its attitude is one of utter obedience to the will of another. It has no will of its own; or if it have, it is instantly repressed. So there must be the entire and utter surrender of our will to the will of Christ. This is the hardest lesson we have to learn; but everything of blessedness depends on our coming to a point at which we say, "From this moment and for evermore, in the smallest details, in the routine of daily life as well as in its great crises, I choose the will of God." Never again to do what we wish because we wish it; never again to consult our own preferences or choice; never again to have a way or will of our own; but to follow absolutely and always the path marked out by another: this is the secret of blessedness.

The attitude of the sheep is *dependence*. It would be impossible to *submit*, if we could not also *commit*. But it becomes easy to do the former when we can do the latter. To have an absolute confidence in Him, to lean on Him, to look to Him for direction and help as each moment needs; to trust Him on the rocky mountain path equally as on the green sward; to believe in Him against appearances and our own hearts; to refuse to take a thread or a shoe-latchet from any other hand; to abstain, as David did, from taking advantage even of a means of deliverance, which may seem ready to hand, but which would be inconsistent with his revealed will; to wait only on the Lord till He shall pluck the feet out of the net, and give the heart's desires—this too is the secret of blessedness.

Let us quiet ourselves as weaned babes. The world is unfriendly, and life's paths are perplexing; but He is leading us on who cannot make a mistake, who will give us just as much of a rest and refreshment as we require, and who is more than sufficient to deliver us from the lion and the bear. The memory of his agony and death shall ever be with us, nerving us to believe that He loves us too much, that we have cost Him too much, for it ever to be possible that we should be forsaken or neglected. And so at last we shall be folded with all the flock beside in those sweet pasture lands, in which the Lamb leads his flock unto living fountains of water, and God wipes away all tears from our eyes.

29

THE IDEAL SHEPHERD

"I am the Good Shepherd: the Good Shepherd giveth his life for the sheep."—JOHN x. 2.

THIS CHAPTER is a pastoral idyll, composed and spoken by the Chief Shepherd Himself. It resembles some masterpiece of art, which one visits for days together, only finding on each successive occasion some new beauty. It naturally falls into the three divisions of morning, noon, and evening.

It is morning. The dew lies heavy on the upland wolds; the fresh morning breeze is airing the fevered world; the sun's pavilion glows with gorgeous colours, as he prepares to emerge on his daily pilgrimage; and the shepherds stand knocking at the barred gates of the fold, calling to the porter to let them have their flocks. When the door opens, each calls to his own sheep, and leads them forth, and they follow him to pastures green and waters still. They would flee from a strange voice; but they know their shepherds.

Is not this a true picture of the response which Christ's own give to his voice? Many are the voices which fall on the ears of men in the early morning of their life, summoning them to follow; and in the majority of cases with only too much success. In the hubbub the voice of the true Shepherd is undetected or unheeded, except by a few. But these hear its soft gentle tones, and obey, and follow; and to do so is certain evidence that they are his own. The desire to hear and follow Jesus proves that you are his sheep (4, 8, 27).

Again, *It is noon.* The downs are baking in the scorching glare, and every stone burns like fire; but in that oppressive hour the shepherd remembers a little green glen, where a tranquil lake reflects the azure sky, or a brooklet babbles musically over the pebbles. The grass is green and the boulders cast black shadows. Perhaps an old fold is there, with open doorway, so that the sheep may go in for shelter or out for pasture, till the shadows begin to climb stealthily up the hills.

Thus our Beloved makes his flock rest at noon. He is not Shepherd alone, but fold. In Him as in a safe enclosure we lie down secure. He is the secret place of the Most High, in whom our life is hidden. Nor is He the fold only, He is also the door; there is no ingress to rest, or egress to pasture, except through Him. We can get pasture, abundant life, and salvation only by the Lord Jesus.

Lastly, *It is evening.* The sun is setting, the air is becoming chill, the valleys are deep in gloom. The shepherd hastens downward with his flock to the fold. They are descending together the last dark gorge, densely shadowed by foliage. Suddenly the ominous snarl and scream tell that a wolf has sprung from the thicket, and seized on one of the hindmost ewes or tender lambs; and then the shepherd rushes to the rear, prepared to lay down his life, if needs be, to save. And who can view the struggle which ensues between the shepherd and the wolf, without being reminded of the fourfold allusion of our Lord to the fact that He was about to lay down his life for the sheep (11, 15, 17, 18).

I. THE DOUBLE CONTRAST TO THE GOOD SHEPHERD.—Good does not mean benevolent and kind; but genuine and true. And its significance is pointed by the contrast with the thief and the hireling; by which it appears that the Good Shepherd is One who is imbued with the true spirit of his work, and is an enthusiast in it, not for pay or reward, but by the compulsion of the noble instincts of his soul.

Robbers may turn shepherds, climbing the walls of the fold, or swooping down on the flock and driving it off, as Nabal's were seized on Mount Carmel. But their purpose is for the flesh and fleece, to kill and to destroy. They have no more the true shepherd's heart than a bandit has a soldier's or a pirate a sailor's.

Many such nominal shepherds had the Jews in their national history: kings ruling for their own aggrandisement; teachers who prophesied false and smooth things for place and pelf; Pharisees who lined their nests with what they appropriated wrongfully. Such were the thieves and robbers who came before the Good Shepherd, stealing from God his glory, from men their souls and goods. What a contrast was the Saviour, who expected no reward but hatred and a crown of thorns, a cross and a borrowed tomb, and whose supreme object was to give life, and to give it more abundantly—abundant as the flowers of May; exhaustless as the perennial fountains of his own being; infinite as the nature of God!

The *hireling*, too, may turn shepherd, and, to a certain point, may do his work with credit. He will not desert the flock for frost, or hail, or a thunder shower. His pay will be more than an equivalent for hardship in these respects. But when it comes to the supreme test of sacrificing the life, he breaks down. Love alone can nerve a man voluntarily to lay down his life. Of what use is hire to a dead man? "He that is an hireling, and not the shepherd, whose own the sheep are not, seeth the wolf coming, and leaveth the sheep and fleeth; and the wolf cometh and scattereth them."

There are good men about the world, in the Church and out of it, who have come to sheep-tending as an occupation, because it affords a means of livelihood; men who become pastors because there is a family living to be filled, or the position is an honourable one. Such do their work fairly well, so long as there is no particular danger to be faced. But when the winds of persecution are let loose, and the fires are lit, and the dragoons scour the moors, they renounce their office, and even endeavour to efface the vestiges of their calling (Zec. xiii. 5-7).

Very different to this has been the spirit of the true shepherd, revealed in hundreds of cases of Church history, and above all in our blessed Lord. He has received a great reward, which dazzled his gaze throughout his earthly life. "For the joy set before Him He endured the cross." But there was nothing selfish in it. And it was not for this alone that He fulfilled his self-set task. He loved us. He had taken us to be his own. He had set his heart upon us. And when the question arose of delivering us from peril, He never hesitated to lay down his life. It was his own act and deed. "I lay it down of Myself."

For the most part his life was not his own, but his Father's in Him; yet special power was given Him that He should be able to take individual and personal action in this matter. "He had power to lay it down, and power to take it again." And as the voluntariness of his sacrifice unto death is insisted on, there comes out more evidently the mighty passion of his love for us who hear his voice, and may therefore claim to be his own. Why has He loved us thus? We cannot tell. It is a mystery which will for ever baffle us; but love knows no reason, no law. Surely the Son of God might have discovered, or made, beings more worthy of his attachment. But it was not to be so. He has loved us with the greatest love of all, the love that recks not the cost of life; and there is nothing now of good which He will withhold from his own, his loved, his chosen and purchased flock.

II. THE WORK OF THE GOOD SHEPHERD.

(1) *His knowledge of his sheep.*—The Revised Version brings out the exquisite meaning of verses 14 and 15, which was somewhat obscured in the older version: "I know mine own, and mine own know Me; even as the Father knoweth Me, and I know the Father."

The Eastern shepherd knows all the particulars of each of his sheep; its genealogy, defects, temper, and tastes, and embodies some one of these in the name he gives it. Thus did the Father know all about that one Lamb which stood in so peculiar a relationship to Himself. There was nothing in Jesus hidden from the Father. His eyes beheld his substance, when it was yet imperfect; and in his book were all his members written, when as yet there was none of them, whether of his mystical or of his physical body. Who shall explore or adequately elaborate the perfect knowledge subsisting between the Father and the Son before the worlds were made?

And it is just in this way, with a Divine, comprehensive, and perfect knowledge, that the Lord Jesus knows each of us. He is of a quick understanding to take in our past, with its sad and bitter failures, and our present with its unrealized longings. He knows our downsitting and uprising; our motives so often misunderstood; our anxieties, which cast their shadows over our lives; our dread; our hopes and fears. He intermeddles with the bitterness of our hearts, known only to us and Him. He scrutinizes each guest as it enters, and needs no census to tell Him the inmates of our hearts. "There is not a word on our tongue, but Thou, O Lord, knowest it altogether." It is very blessed to be known thus; so that we do not need to assume a disguise, or enter into laboured explanations. He cannot be surprised, or taken unawares by anything we may tell Him.

Let us, on our part, seek to know Him as He knew the Father; the eyes of our heart being enlightened; the soul illumined by the knowledge which is born of sympathy, fellowship, and purity.

(2) *His seeking love.*—Again the Revised Version, in ver. 16, gives the true intention of our Saviour's words. "Other sheep I have which are not of this fold; them also I must bring (lead), and they shall hear my voice, and they shall become one flock, one Shepherd."

There may be, and there will be, many folds. By the very constitution of our minds we are sure to have different views of truth, of church government, and of the best methods of expressing our love and worship. And there are many who would have us believe that if we do not belong to their special fold, we have no right to assume that we belong to the flock. But it is not so. Our Master never said there would be one fold. There may be many folds, yet one flock; even as there is one Shepherd. The more one climbs up the mountain side, the less one thinks of the hurdles that pen the sheep below in the valley, and the more one rejoices in the essential unity of the flock. Whatever may be your special fold, the one question is: Do you hear and obey the Shepherd's voice? If so, you belong to the one flock, part of which is on that, and part on this side of a narrow parting brook.

These other sheep must be the Gentiles—ourselves. Though He belonged by birth to the most exclusive race that has ever existed, our Lord's sympathies overflowed the narrow limits of national prejudice. He was the Son of Man; and in these words He not only showed that his heart was set on us, but He sketched the work which was to occupy Him through the ages. Ever since that moment He has been bringing in these other sheep, and folding them. Perhaps the work is almost done, and the flock complete; and soon, as He leads his blood-bought ones forth to the pasture-lands of eternity, their unity shall be manifest, and the world shall admire and believe (John xvii. 21).

(3) *His words to his own.*—"He calls them by name." We often speak to the dumb animals of our homes, telling them words they can hardly understand, and to which they can certainly give no response. But there is a dialogue ever in process between the Good Shepherd and his own. He not only calls them by name as He leads them forth, but

He talks to them, encouraging, soothing, communing with them about his purposes, explaining his reasons, indicting his commands.

Holy souls become aware of impressions which are made on them from time to time, promptings, inspirations, largely through the words of Scripture, and sometimes otherwise, which they recognize as the Shepherd's voice. That voice ever calls to self-sacrifice, fellowship, purity, and is different to all other voices. And there grows up a response, the more specially so when the path is lonely, and the sheep keeps close to its Shepherd's heel. Those who follow very nearly behind Him will bear witness to the perpetual converse by which the human friend is able to keep in touch with the Divine.

(4) *His care of his own.*—"I give unto them eternal life, and they shall never perish." Time wears out all things else. It crumbles the mountains, dims the sunshine, loosens the machinery of the universe; but it cannot touch or impair the life of the blessed God, whether it be in Himself, or imparted through Jesus Christ to the hearts of those who love Him. When once that life has come to indwell the believer's heart it must remain. Beneath worldliness, carelessness, and frivolity, burning feebly perhaps, almost quenched in the heavy atmosphere, it is there an incorruptible seed.

Christ's sheep shall never perish. They may wander far from Him, lose all joy and comfort, fall under the rebuke of men, and seem to be living under a cloud; but, if they are really his, his honour is pledged to seek them out in the cloudy and dark day, and bring them back to Himself. His body cannot be dismembered; He cannot forfeit that which it has cost Him so much to purchase. He would rather lose his throne than one of his sheep; for the lion of the pit would glory over Him, and it would be a fatal blemish on his escutcheon that He had attempted but had failed to perform.

You may be a very lame and timid and worthless sheep; but you were purchased by the Shepherd's blood, because He loved you so. There is not a wild beast in all hell that He has not vanquished and put beneath his feet; there is no fear, therefore, of his ability, as there is none of his love. He will deliver you from the lion and the bear, and bring you in triumph to the fold, with all the rest.

30

The Work of an Ungifted Worker

"And He went away again beyond Jordan into the place where John at first baptized: and there He abode. And many resorted unto Him, and said, John did no miracle; but all things that John spake of this man were true. And many believed on Him there."—John x. 40–42.

Beyond the Jordan! To a Jew that was banishment indeed. For that district, called Perea, was comparatively desert. The hills, seamed by impetuous torrents hurling themselves headlong into the Jordan valley, were marked by a few patches of cultivated soil and scattered hamlets; but for the most part they were bleak and cold, and none came there from the country west of the Jordan, except driven by stress of persecution or to escape the arm of the law.

Why, then, did the Son of Man betake Himself thither? At the close of his inimitable parable of the shepherd and his flock, He had gathered all his force to assure his trembling followers that they had nothing to fear from man or devil. On the one hand, they could never perish, because they had within them an indestructible life, identical with his own; and on the other, they were within his hand, whence none should be able to pluck them. But, in case that was not enough to assure timid hearts, He went on to declare that his own hand, with its contents, lay within the strong, all-encompassing hand of his Father; so that there was a double assurance, and none would be able to pluck them out of the Father's hand. How safe are they who hear his voice and follow Him!

But this assertion as to the identification of the Father with Himself in the blessed work of preserving the flock, led Him to affirm the deep underlying truth of the essential oneness of the Father with Himself. He would have us think of the Father and Himself as being one in the deepest and most holy unity. One in essence, in purpose, in operation; so that neither thinks, nor wills, nor acts without the other; and each is altogether present where the other is manifested. The assertion implicated the Deity of the speaker, and startled the Jews to take up stones, so as to inflict at once the doom of the blasphemer.

Nor was this all. He went on to insist that He was the Son of God in a unique sense, and that his life was the outworking of the indwelling of the Father. "The Father is in Me, and I in Him." From all this it is clear that, whatever may be the speculations of modern thinkers, there was no doubt in the human consciousness of Jesus as to his unique relationship with the Father. He used the strongest terms that could set it forth. It is true that He quotes an Old Testament Scripture, which speaks of men who exercise judicial functions as gods, when, by reason of their office, they wield special prerogatives and exercise functions which are Divine in their quality; but He does not for a moment compare these with Himself; and only adduces the passage to show how unreasonable was the attempt to punish Him for a phrase which in the most awful times of Mosaic authority had been allowed to pass without challenge. But their vindictive hate would brook no parley; and, as his hour was not yet come, He deemed it better to go away beyond Jordan, into hiding, until the hand should reach the exact figure on the dial.

There was a special reason why He was attracted to the region beyond Jordan. "It was the place where John at first baptized." Those solemn hills and valleys had been black with the crowds that had gathered from all the land at the cry of that trumpet voice. Those waters had been the scene of countless baptisms. And the people living around had many a story to tell of the grand and fearless prophet who had met with so tragic a death in the dungeon of the neighbouring castle of Machærus. And as the disciples, all of whom had been first moved by the Baptist's influence and preaching, passed over the ground in company with Jesus, what recollections must have been stirred within them; and how sadly must they have contrasted those sunny days with the overcast heavens beneath which at that moment they were passing!

"Many resorted unto Him." Those who had felt the marvellous fascination of the person of Jesus were glad to follow Him anywhere; and as they too came on the familiar scenes, they could not but talk much of the great preacher. "Here he used to sleep. There he used to preach. Yonder he would stand knee deep in the waters to baptize. Do you not remember him calling the Pharisees a set of vipers; and telling the deputation from the Sanhedrim that he was only a voice; and pointing to the Master as the Lamb of God?" "And yet what a contrast was his life to our Master's," might another rejoin; "he did no miracles, there was not a single scintillation of this miraculous Divine power." "No," said a chorus of voices; "John did no miracle, but all things that John spake of this man were true."

John said that this Man should be from heaven, and above all: and it was true.

John said that He should be the Bridegroom of all faithful souls: and it was true.

John said that the Father would not give the Spirit by measure unto Him: and it was true.

John said that his fan would be in his hand, and He would throughly purge his floor: and it was true.

John said that He would bear away the sin of the world: and it was true.

F

And many, as they compared the predictions of the forerunner with their verification in Jesus, "believed in Him there."

I. MIRACLES ARE NOT NECESSARY FOR A GREAT LIFE.—"Among them that are born of women there hath not risen a greater than John the Baptist," said our Lord; but John did no miracle, was the verdict of the crowd. Evidently, then, there may be a great life without miracles.

In the judgment of the world, birth, wealth, genius, deeds of valour, and statesmanship, are deemed essential for the living of a great life; and many a one that can lay claim to none of these has relapsed into apathy and discontent. But how little do such understand the nature of true greatness! The fairest flowers of our race have bloomed from hidden roots. Those who have most enriched the world have said with the Apostles, "Silver and gold have we none." Genius has been overtaken and passed by plodding patience. Great wars have generally been great mistakes and greater crimes. Whereas true greatness consists in doing the appointed work of life from the platform of a great motive; and in nurturing all that is divinest and noblest in the character.

John never thought whether or not he was living a great life. It was his one aim to obey the promptings of the Spirit of God, and to fulfil his course. When all the world was ringing with his fame, in an outburst of genuine humility he said that he was only a voice borne on the desert breeze. It was no care to him that he was unable to work a miracle. He who sent him had not put miracles in the programme of his life; and he was perfectly satisfied with the arrangement. As the herald, it was his business to raise his voice in repeated proclamation of the King; why, then, should he be sad because he had not the special qualificatons of others in his Master's retinue? To fulfil the task for which he had been qualified and sent, and to do it so as to please his King—that was his one ambition and aim; and to do it undaunted by the threats, and unfascinated by the blandishments, of the world —that made him great.

The lesson is for us all. Many who will read these lines are powerless to work miracles. They cannot dazzle or bewilder by the splendour of their intellectual gifts or the brilliance of their endowments. For them, the path in the valley, the monotony of the commonplace, the grey sky of uneventful routine, seem to be the predestined lot. And the very expectation of doing aught worth living for seems to have died out of them. But let such take heart! The real greatness of life is within their reach, if they will only claim it by the grace of God.

Do not try to do a great thing: you may waste all your life waiting for the opportunity which may never come. But since little things are always claiming your attention, do them as they come, from a great motive, for the glory of God, to win his smile of approval, and to do good to men. It is harder to plod in obscurity, acting thus, than to stand on the high places of the field, within the view of all, and to do deeds of valour, at which rival armies stand still to gaze. And no holy act, however trivial, goes without the swift recognition and the ultimate recompense of Christ.

To fulfil faithfully the duties of your station; to use to the uttermost the gifts of your ministry; to bear chafing annoyances and trivial irritations, as the martyr bore the pillory and stake; to find the one noble trait in people who try and molest you; to put the kindest construction on unkind acts and words; to give of your best to the least; to love with the love of God even the unthankful and evil; to be content to be a fountain in the midst of a wild valley of stones, nourishing a few lichens and wild flowers, or now and again a thirsty sheep; and to do this always, not for the praise of man, but for the sake of God—*this* makes a great life.

II. THEME OF OUR MINISTRY.—"John spake of this Man." The Baptist did little else than speak of the coming One. But this was the sufficient object of his ministry. That was all that he was required to do; and to do this well was to fulfil the purpose for which he was sent. And it is not otherwise now. The splendid miracles that shone as jewels on the brow of the first age of the Church have long since passed away; and it may be truly said of her, "She can do no miracles": but her noblest function still remains untouched. She can speak true things of her Lord.

Do it privately.—John spake of Jesus to *two* disciples, as they stood beside Him; and each became a convert and an apostle. It was so that Christianity spread in the first age, until the whole world was penetrated with its power. And probably fewer souls have been won by great preachers than by private individuals, speaking to children, friends, and neighbours, and saying, "Know the Lord."

Do it experimentally.—"I saw and bare record." There is nothing like personal testimony in this age of speculation and doubt. There is no voice so captivating as that which says, "Come and hear, all ye that fear God; and I will declare what He has done for my soul." Who can resist the men, that pointing to their own history as evidence, say, "We know that the Son of God is come, and has given us an understanding that we may know Him that is true; and we are in Him that is true, even in his Son Jesus Christ"? This is an age which asks eagerly for evidence; let us give the evidence of our spiritual senses, which is every bit as good as that of our natural senses, or our intellectual faculties. The spiritual eye is as certain a guide as the physical. "The eyes of our heart have been enlightened, and we have seen the Lord."

Do it unostentatiously.—Let it be as natural as the laughter which bubbles up from the glad heart; or the song of the little child that knows no care, whilst it roams amid the flowers of spring. Do not divert men to yourself. Count yourself to have failed when they speak of you. Be content to be a voice, a messenger, a mirror, flashing the light on to the face of Christ from which it came. And that it may be so, keep the heart full of Jesus. The mouth must speak the things which it has made touching the King, when the heart is bubbling over with good matter.

The one thing which closes the lips of so many is the feeling that critical eyes would detect a flaw between the words and the life of the speaker. But, if there be ground for this fear, why not put the finger of faith on 1 Thess. v. 23, 24, and claim that He who has called to his work, and has inbreathed a yearning for the blameless life, should make it possible, and do exceeding abundantly, far more than He has even taught us to ask or think.

The mouth is one of those members which must be yielded to Jesus for his use; and, if only it is taken away from the service of sin and self to which it has too often been devoted, and handed over to be kept and used by the Master Himself, it is marvellous how all difficulties will disappear, and how easy and blessed it will become to speak of Him. When He wants you to speak, He will show you the audience; He will give you the message; He will supply you with the power.

III. AN ILLUSTRATION OF POSTHUMOUS MINISTRY.—Though John had been dead for two years, his words were fresh in the people's memories; and, as they were compared with their fulfilment, they led many into the faith.

We are doing more good than we know. We are setting streams flowing that shall go on refreshing and blessing men long after we have passed away. We are planting orchards whose shades shall protect, and fruit refresh, generations that shall be born long after our heads are laid low in death. We are giving men thoughts about Christ which now seem utterly wasted and inoperative, but to which they will refer some day as the means of their conversion. And, as they stand over our graves, or meet in the old places where they were wont to gather with us, they will say: "Well! well! he was a good man; he did no miracles, he was not brilliant, he had no genius; but all things he spake of Jesus were true."

What better epitaph could any of us wish? It seems a magnificent recompense for a life of arduous and brilliant service to be buried in the mausoleum of the fatherland, amid the boom of cannon and the peal of muffled bells, whilst the great and good mingle their tears with the lamentations of unknown millions; but for my part I should be satisfied, if I could be sure that, when I am gone, some should gather, in after years, on the simple hillock headed by the stone that records my name, and assent to the truth of this epitaph, as they witness to it from the depths of their own glad experience, "He did no miracle; but all things that he spake of Jesus were true."

31

LOVE'S DELAYS

"When He had heard therefore that Lazarus was sick, He abode two days still in the same place where He was."—JOHN xi. 6.

THE LAPSE of years made it possible for the beloved evangelist to draw aside the veil which curtained the happy intercourse of our Lord with the home at Bethany. We are thus furnished with a conception of the one green oasis in the rugged wilderness through which He passed to his cross; and are able to think of the pure and holy love that broke in upon his loneliness and with true affection softened the bitterness of his last days, so far at least as human love could.

There were marked diversities in that home. Martha, practical, business-like, and thoughtful of all that could affect the comfort and well-being of those she loved; Mary, clinging, spiritual, gifted with all a woman's delicacy of insight and tender sympathy; Lazarus, a man of few words, quiet and unobtrusive. But Jesus loved them each. In the forefront of this marvellous chapter stands the affirmation, "Jesus loved Martha, and her sister, and Lazarus"; as if to teach us that at the very heart and foundation of all God's dealings with us, however dark and mysterious they may be, we must dare to believe in and assert the infinite, unmerited, and unchanging love of God. Whom the Lord loves He rebukes; the sons whom He receives He chastens; the boughs that are capable of bearing fruit are rigorously pruned. This is not joyous, but grievous; nevertheless, in the golden Afterward it yieldeth the peaceable fruit of righteousness to them that are exercised thereby.

I. LOVE PERMITS PAIN.—To that hidden retreat in Perea there came one day a breathless messenger with the tidings of the illness of Christ's friend. The sisters never doubted that He would speed at all hazards to his side, and stay him from death. And if He had done as they expected, He would not only have saved his life, but have spared the sisters the anguish of long suspense, the flickering out of hope, the agony of the death scene, the grave, and the desolate, darkened home. How different were his love and their thoughts of it! "When He had heard *therefore* that he was sick, He abode two days still in the same place where He was."

What a startling *therefore*! He abstained from going, not because He did not love them, but because He did love them. His love alone kept Him back from hasting at once to the dear and stricken home. Anything less than an infinite love must have rushed instantly to the relief of those loved and troubled hearts, to stay their grief, and to have the luxury (which only love can appreciate) of wiping and stanching their tears and causing their sorrow and sighing to flee away. Divine love could alone hold back the impetuosity of the Saviour's tender-heartedness until the Angel of Pain had done her work.

Who can estimate how much we owe to suffering and pain? But for them we should have little scope for many of the chief virtues of the Christian life. Where were faith, without trial to test it; or patience, with nothing to bear; or experience, without tribulation to develop it? These qualities could not be perfected in our Lord without suffering. "He learned obedience by the things that He suffered." And we can only secure the fruit of the autumn by paying the price of wintry frosts and equinoctial hurricanes. Suffering robs us of proud self-reliance, and casts us in an agony at the feet of God. Suffering prunes away the leaves in which we rejoiced, that the sap may find its way into fruit. Suffering isolates the soul, shutting it away from all creature aid, and surrounding it by a wall of fire. The leaves of the aromatic plant must be crushed ere they will emit their fragrance; the ore must be plunged in the furnace ere the gold is set free; the pebble must be polished on the lapidary's wheel ere its brilliant colours are apparent.

> *This leaf, this stone—it is thy heart:*
> *It must be crushed by pain and smart,*
> *It must be cleansed by sorrow's art,*
> *Ere it will yield a fragrance sweet;*
> *Ere it will shine a jewel meet*
> *To lay before the Saviour's feet.*

How soon does pain drive us to the Saviour! Whilst Lazarus was in health, no messenger hasted to bring the Saviour to Bethany. But when death hovered over the little group, they summoned Him with all speed. This is an illustration of how pain, like a surge of the ocean, lifts us up and flings us down at the feet of the Saviour. The dark moaning waters drive the dove to the Ark; the dreary winter sends the swallows south; the sharp pruning knife compels the sap into the leafy crown or ripening branch; tempest roar makes the timid nurslings nestle close to their mother's side. Pain makes God a necessity. It is in the valley that we exchange the word "He" for "Thou." "Thou art with me."

Pain often reveals some unrealized side of our Saviour's character. The sisters had never known Him as the Resurrection and the Life, if Lazarus had not died. David had never known God as his Rock, and Fortress, and Deliverer, if he had not been hunted on the hills of Engedi. Israel had never known God as a Man of War if the nation had not endured the horrors of Egyptian captivity. Thus our very necessities read us lessons of the variety and fullness of the resources of our God. Every stormy wind in its rush whispers some new name for Christ. Every wave that dashes at our feet flings some message from the ocean fullness of his nature. Every crucifixion rends some impenetrable veil that had hung before his heart.

And pain is often suggestive of the noblest acts of sacrifice and self-devotion. It was after Lazarus had suffered that Mary broke her alabaster box over the head of Christ, not only viewing Him as the Resurrection, but preparing his incorruptible body for its brief sojourn in the grave. Many of the masterpieces of literature and art owe their existence to the strange touch of pain, giving a fire, a passion, and an intensity to the brain and heart of genius. If the Master is about to use thee largely in ministering to others, do not be surprised if He puts thee to serve an apprenticeship in the school of pain. Poets learn in suffering what they teach in song. Blood and water flowed from a pierced side. Pearls must be dived for by those whose feet are heavily weighted to make them sink.

And there is this further thought. The Lord permitted those sisters to suffer because of the benefit which would accrue to others. Speaking to his disciples shortly afterwards, He said: "I am glad for your sakes that I was not there." The sisters suffered because their pain offered a platform on which Jesus could erect one of his greatest miracles, to stand as a beacon to weary hearts of all ages. This idea is not foreign to even heathen philosophers. "Accept," says the Emperor Marcus Aurelius, "everything that happens to thee, even if it seem disagreeable, because it leads to the health of the universe; for God would not lay on any man that which he suffers, if it were not useful for the continuance and perfection of the whole." It is probable that no one suffers nobly without in some degree ministering to the glory of God in the well-being of others. Let those who live to suffer, who lie all day in pain, and all night in utter weariness, take heart! In some way that passes our thought they too are fulfilling a useful and blessed office to the entire family of man.

Such are some of the results of Pain; and as we count them over we cannot wonder that God's love allows us to suffer, and is even eager to stand aside to let her do her work. For the time in which Pain can perfect her work is short. She needs to make haste, because the morning cometh in which she will not be able to work.

II. GOD'S LOVE SOMETIMES LEAVES OUR PRAYERS UNANSWERED.— What has become of so many thousands of our prayers? They were not deficient in earnestness; we uttered them with strong crying and tears. They were not deficient in perseverance; we offered them three times a day for years. They were not deficient in faith; for they have originated in hearts that have never for a moment doubted that God was, and that He was the rewarder of them that diligently sought Him. Still no answer has come. The argosies went forth to sea; but, like some ill-fated vessel, have never been heard of since. There was no voice, nor any to answer, nor, apparently, any to regard.

What is the history of these unanswered prayers? Some may say that they sought things which were not good—and this may explain some of the perplexity; but a better clue is given here: this was a prayer touchingly pathetic and earnest, for something which was prompted by natural affection; for something which it was in the scope of God's love to give, for it was given; and yet the prayer was apparently unanswered. The answer was postponed and delayed.

When prayer is unanswered it may be that it has been mistaken in its object, and the mistake will be indicated by inability to continue praying, and by the dying down of the desire in the soul. In other cases, especially when desire and faith remain buoyant and elastic, and still the answer comes not, God's intention is that in the delay the soul may be led to take up a position which it had never assumed before, but from which it will never be again dislodged. No praying breath is ever spent in vain. If you can believe for the blessings you ask, they are certainly yours. The goods are consigned, though not delivered; the blessing is labelled with your name, but not sent. The vision is yet for an appointed time; it will come and will not tarry. The black head may have become white, the bright eye dim, the loving heart impaired in its beating; but the answer must come at length. God will give it at the earliest moment consistent with the true well-being of the one He loves.

III. GOD'S LOVE COMES AT LENGTH.—To the sisters He must have appeared neglectful; but He was not really so. Notice, that after two days, though no fresh message had reached Him, "He said to his disciples, Lazarus is dead." How carefully He must have watched all that transpired in that much-loved home! He saw the messenger's return; the momentary joy his tidings gave; the gradual waning of life; the anguish of the watchers as they beheld the slackening of the silver cords of life. He had followed in thought the funeral train to the rocky tomb. The whole situation was constantly present to Him, till He saw that He could interpose with the best possible result.

So is it ever. His step may linger; but his watchful interest never falters. There is not a sigh, a pang, a tear, that escapes his notice. There is not a fluttering pulse which He does not feel, noticing its tremulous anxiety. He *sits* as a refiner of silver. He knows our sorrows. He is acquainted with our grief. He slumbers not, nor sleeps.

And when He comes He does more than we asked or thought. He raises not the sick, but the dead. He makes the darkness of the tomb the background against which to set forth the lustre of Resurrection glory. He does much more than the wildest fancy could have dreamed. Prayer is seen to be answered in a sweeter, deeper, diviner form than could have been hoped for. The benefit gained by the long delay is evident; and the wisdom of the Divine patience is acknowledged. "Oh the depth of the riches both of the wisdom and knowledge of God; how unsearchable are his judgments, and his ways past finding out!"

In after days the three would not have wished it otherwise. They would review it all, as we shall review things from the hill-summits of glory. And as the whole marvellous story passed before them in after years, they would anticipate the cry with which the Redeemed Church shall hail the unfolding of the Divine purposes in relation to our race, "Amen! Hallelujah! Amen! so be it!"—the reverent assent of the understanding, the acquiescence of the soul. "Hallelujah!"—the glad, long outburst of adoration and praise, of worship and love.

32

ANOINTED FOR HIS BURIAL

"Then took Mary a pound of ointment of spikenard, very costly, and anointed the feet of Jesus, and wiped his feet with her hair: and the house was filled with the odour of the ointment."—JOHN xii. 3.

BETWEEN the last verse of the foregoing chapter and the first of this, an interval of many weeks took place, during which our Lord was in retirement from the hate of the priests, until his hour had come. At first He took refuge in Ephraim, sixteen miles N.E. from Jerusalem, amid the wild, uncultivated hill country which fences middle Palestine from the Jordan valley. Then He crossed to Perea, further from Jerusalem, and more secure. The few weeks spent thus teemed with incidents omitted by our Evangelist but fully recorded by the other three.

At the beginning of the last week of his life our Lord found Himself again in Bethany, and in the beloved home where He desired to spend as much time as possible before He suffered. It was easy to go across to Jerusalem in the early morning, and to return in the cool of the afternoon. On one of the precious evenings a simple entertainment in honour of their Friend was planned by the sisters, and held in the house of Simon the leper, perhaps because it would contain larger numbers.

It is not difficult to imagine the scene. The village in the hollow of Olivet, nestling amid its olive-trees and oleanders. The long-drawn shadows flung by the sun now sinking on the further side of the hill. The rustic, roomy house, perhaps not more than one-storey in height, and covered by creepers. The spacious apartment, with its low tables, surrounded by the couches on which reclined the guests. The simple provision of bread and wine and herbs and freshly-picked fruit. The company, variously composed—Jews from Jerusalem, some reclining, others standing as spectators; while peasants crowd around the door. The Master sits among his apostles. John, with love and fire; Peter, dove and rock; James, the just; Nathanael, the guileless; Judas, the man of Kerioth; Simon, whose flesh had come like that of a little child; Lazarus, fresh from the world of spirits; Martha, intent on hospitable cares; Mary, absorbed with her self-sacrificing love; and above all, the Lord Himself in the place of honour, with the shadow of the cross already gathering over his noble face.

As the meal drew to a close, Mary passed to the back of the Saviour's couch, carrying an alabaster vase of costly ointment; this she poured upon his feet, and then, according to Matthew and Mark, upon his head. Judas scowled as he saw the act of love, and talked of waste; but Jesus smiled, and spoke of everlasting remembrance.

I. MARY.—The love of Christ falling on her heart was reflected back to Him; as the light of the sun shines back on itself from the moon. Not that she ever allowed herself to think about her love to Him; she lived out of sight of what she felt in the all-absorbing thought of what He was. Of this, at least, she was sure, that ever since she had sat at his feet, the Scriptures, the feasts, and the world, were all new to her. And could she ever forget that He had summoned her brother from the grave? There was no doubt the strong pure love of her heart to Jesus, the man; but shining through this, as light through air, was the devout reverence of the believer to the Saviour, of the servant to the Lord.

Twice during his early life our Lord was anointed by a woman. In the first instance, by one who had trodden dark and evil paths; in the second, by this pure saint. How quick of growth is love, whenever it takes root! How ingenious in its inventiveness! How regardless of cost! Such love must show itself. It pines for expression. It must go forth in offices of love for the beloved. Love approves itself by deeds. Not by feelings—they are like bubbles which children blow. Not by words—they are like down which floats away on the wind. But, as the Lord said, "He that hath my commandments, and keepeth them, he it is that loveth Me."

The best love gives its best.—In the words of Jesus, quoted by the evangelist Mark, *it does what it can.* It ransacks the house of its choicest stores, and hastens to bestow them on the object of its attachment. It is not content with giving what it must—the fixed tribute, the specific proportion; it rejoices to give special love-tokens of all that is in possession. And it is on this principle that the Lord accepts our gifts. Whatever is given, He at once turns to what is left, and appraises the offering, rather by what remains behind, than by itself. He hardly notices the munificent gift of gold, because He knows the small proportion it bears to the abundance from which it is taken. He welcomes the farthing, because He knows that it is the widow's all.

I remember once, at the close of an unusually impressive missionary meeting, that I was led to propose to the gathered crowds of Christian people that we should present our Lord with some special article on which we set great store; not with any thought of merit, but altogether as a token of the deep personal love we bore Him. It is the custom of friends to make presents to each other: how much more should we sometimes take the opportunity of giving our Lord that which we prize, and which it will cost us something to renounce; though we forget the sacrifice in the glad love which finds at last an adequate expression. In response to this appeal many there and then gave jewels and ornaments and costly articles, which realized a handsome sum for the Master's cause. We called them alabaster boxes of very precious ointment; and it was sweet to give them. And amongst the letters received afterwards was one from a widow, who said that she had long withheld her assent to her daughter becoming a missionary, because she felt that she could not part with her; but that under the constraint of the love of Christ she would stand out no longer, but gave her to Him as her priceless offering.

Love justifies itself in the eye of love.—Some that sat at table, and one of them especially, thought that Mary would have shown her love better if she had sold the alabaster-box for three-hundred pence, and given the proceeds to the poor. But the Master said it was a good work, good because of the love which prompted it. It is, of course, right to help the poor, to build churches, to subsidise missionary societies. We must compensate for our lack of personal service by giving the results of our labours. But we have no right to criticize a love that expresses itself in some other form—in a psalm, a picture, an act of strange devotion. To our utilitarian brains ours may seem the best method of expressing our love. There is something to show for it. But the love of the other may be deeper and more delicate, because eager to give the beloved one all the rapture of personal enjoyment; and there is an element of unselfish devotion too, purged from the alloy of the desire to see one's gift embodied in some lasting expression.

I have met somewhere with this parable. There were two men, Christians, the one of whom expressed his love for the Master in acts that left little permanent record among men, but which glowed with the fire of enthusiastic devotion. Amongst other things, he built a church in a lonely place in which he spent vast sums on architecture, music, beauty of decoration. But his friend rebuked him. "What," said he, "will you sing psalms when the poor of Christ's flock are perishing and build churches when oppression has to be exposed, evil attacked, foul dwellings cleansed? Will you devote yourself to questions of taste when there is so much to be done amid the squalid quarters of the poor? If you really love Christ do something practical." And the other meekly answered that he did all for the love of Christ; but, feeling rebuked, he went forth to labour amongst the poor; however, he had no gift for it, and failed. And the Master called both to his side, saying to the one that had rebuked his brother, "Rebuke him not; he loves Me not less than thou; and it is sweet to Me to have love expressed in such a way as that it must be meant for Me alone, altogether apart from any benefit it may confer on others."

There are so many mixed motives which enter into our beneficence. We like to feel that we have done something; that we have built a little bit into the fabric of God's kingdom; that we have contributed to the well-being of our fellows. And these are all laudable and worthy aims. But by how much they are prominent in our minds, by so much do they detract from the simplicity and purity of our expressions towards Christ. Let us not leave these undone; but let us supplement them by taking opportunities as they occur of presenting Christ with that which only He knows about, and is the direct personal gift of our affection. It is possible to combine love to Jesus with beneficence to the poor. But if a choice must be made the personal love that does all it can for Him is better than the love that is divided between the Master and the beneficent results of its gifts.

The love of contemplation will sometimes break out in the most heroic acts.—Martha was apt to chide her sister for doing so little in the house. She could not understand a love which seemed so utterly. unpractical. She did not realize that her sister was being led to apprehend truths of which she had no idea; and that probably she was the only one in the world who had really entered into the heart of the Lord's teaching about his approaching death. The busy housewife little dreamt that her younger sister would presently perform a deed of rare and deep significance; which should refresh that beloved heart amid the agonies of crucifixion, even as it left a fragrance on the sacred body, of which all the coarse handling of the next few days could not deprive it.

As she heard the Master speak of his approaching end Mary grasped the whole situation. She saw that she could not be there to perform the last offices of a woman's love. She bethought herself of this ingenious method of anticipating his burying. She resolved that, whatever the indignities offered to that dear form, it should have as royal an anointing as a king's. And Jesus read the meaning of the deed, and put into words the unexpressed eloquence of her soul: "Let her alone; against the day of my burying hath she kept this."

And love kindles love.—Not even Judas would have called this act waste, could he have seen the love it has kindled and the acts to which it has led. It has been spoken of in all the world for a memorial of her. The Lord's prevision has been exactly verified. His Gospel has been preached in all the world, and this woman's deed has been proclaimed with it, stirring the hearts of men and women beneath every sky. No noble act is ever lost. It carries in it the seeds of self-propagation. It sows itself, as wind-wafted seeds will find a lodgment in crannies of the rocks, and interstices of walls. It is found after many days in the heroic purpose and generous act of those who have been inspired by its spirit. Yield yourself to God; let the Spirit of God suggest your method of service: it may be quite different from anything to which others are called; it may even draw down adverse criticism and censure; but if it is for Him, whether it be an act or a gift, it is enough—do it. He will shield you, and reward you with a smile, and put the precious treasure among His choice possessions. Shall an earthly sovereign have a cabinet filled with choice gifts from her subjects, and shall not Christ treasure the love-tokens of his closer friends? The poor you have always with you; do not through familiarity neglect Him, but do Him good.

II. JUDAS.—What a contrast between his face and Mary's! Hers—open, pure, tender, now and again flushed with an exquisite glow from the soul behind. His—dark, hard, forbidding. As the sun draws forth the foetid miasma of the pool, so did this act of Mary's excite his angriest feelings of hatred, though he cleverly cloaked them under solicitude for the poor. That very night, he who now haggled over three-hundred pence, would be selling his Lord for thirty pieces of silver! But his true character was not yet discovered.

We can well imagine that Mary felt an instinctive shudder pass through her whenever Judas came near. Women are shrewd judges of character. The dove knows when the hawk is hovering over her. We can imagine that after Jesus and his disciples had gone forth on any morning from that home, how Mary would say: "I cannot endure that Judas; I do not know what it is, but he never comes near me without making me shudder; and I am sure that he dislikes me in his heart as much as I do him." "Hush," Martha would answer, "you know the Master trusts him with the bag, and he is held in high honour among them for his goodness to the poor." "Well," would the younger sister reply, "it may be so; but I am certain that he is not what he seems."

Ah, how often will a man adopt sanctimonious phraseology to hide his real self, and will talk of the poor, and Christ, and religion, not that he cares for any of these things, but because he desires to add to his own estate or position! *Not that he cares* might be written on the life of many a hypocrite. He comes to church; not that he cares, but to secure admittance to good society. He professes to be a Christian; not that he cares, but to blind people to his deeds. He gives away money; not that he cares, but to win name and fame. And the man who does not care is hardening himself by every act of hypocrisy, until he can sell his Lord.

III. THE MASTER. *He shielded her.*—"Let her alone. Why trouble ye her?" I see her timid look to Him, when those rough words were spoken. Will He sympathize with them? And He cast over her the mantle of his instant protection. Whenever you are molested or assailed, look to Him, shelter in Him, hide in his cleft side; and you will hear Him say, "Touch not mine anointed."

He approved her work.—He called it good. It is very wonderful that He should think of aught which is wrought by human hands as good; but He looks beneath to the love that inspires and prompts. If He shall speak so of any of our poor work, what a heaven it will be! It has been full of failure; the promised crops have failed; our hopes have been dashed with repeated disappointment; and men have either not noticed or turned away with disdain. But if his verdict is *good*, we shall be more repaid.

He interpreted her inner purpose.—No one would have guessed what she meant by that gracious act; but He knew, and vindicated her. Yes, and so it must ever be. He reads our motives; He sees what we put into any act; He understands what we hardly dare to say; and before the universe He will some day give us credit for it all.

What a Master is ours! Oh for crowns for his brow, for alabaster boxes for his person, for tongues to tell his love! Let us anew dedicate ourselves, our lives, our substance, our all to Him; so that the perfume of the sacrifice may fill the homes where we dwell, and the shrines where we worship and work, and the hearts and lives of others.

33

Falling into the Ground to Die

"Verily, verily, I say unto you, Except a corn of wheat fall into the ground and die, it abideth alone; but if it die, it bringeth forth much fruit."—JOHN xii. 24.

THE FAR EAST sent representatives to the cradle of the Son of Man; the far West sent them to his cross. Both hemispheres and all races of men find their centre and meeting-place in Jesus Christ. It is important to bear in mind that these seekers for Christ, whose pathetic entreaty, "Sir, we would see Jesus!" so deeply stirred the Master's heart, were not simply Greek-speaking Jews; but were genuine Greeks, children of the race which, next to the Roman and the Hebrew, has left the deepest impression on our modern life.

They were probably in the habit of frequenting the Jewish feasts; either for purposes of trade, or because they found in the literature and worship of the chosen people some truer satisfaction for the instinctive cravings of their religious natures than could be supplied in the land of their birth. And as the land was ringing with the name and deeds of Jesus, it was natural that they should want to see Him for themselves.

They made their application in the first instance to Philip; perhaps because, as his name indicates, he had Grecian connections, or was even of Grecian origin. Philip called in the counsel and advice of his friend and companion, Andrew; and the two together told the Master of the interesting inquiry, eliciting, in answer, one of the profoundest statements that ever fell from those gracious lips. It is as if the Lord saw in their application a foreshadowing of the advent of a great multitude, which no man could number, of all nations, and kindreds, and people, and tongues, who should be led to seek Him; though He realized also the tremendous cost to Himself, by which alone He would be able to attract them, and hold them, and satisfy the infinite cravings of their hearts. It is of that cost that we are now chiefly to think.

1. DEATH THE WAY TO GLORIFICATION.—"The hour is come that the Son of Man should be glorified." How much this glorification meant to the Master! It was not for Himself; but that He might be the better able to bring a revenue of glory to his Father. Thus He prayed: "Father, glorify thy Son, that thy Son also may glorify Thee."

What majestic stages there are in the glorification of the Holy Trinity! In the first instance, the Father raises the Son from the dead, and gives Him glory; and then raises Him to his own right hand, investing Him in his human nature with the glory He had with Him before the foundation of the world. Then, when Jesus is glorified, the Holy Spirit is given; and He glorifies the Lord by taking of those things which are his, and revealing them to his own. Moreover, in addition to this, He repeats them in their hearts, so that the Lord is glorified in them. And thus, as the Son is glorified—in the first place by the Father, and in the second by the Spirit, and in the third by the unity and spirituality of his Church—He gathers up the triple ray and flashes it, in one strong and direct beam, back on his Father; and thus the passion of his heart is realized (John xvii. 5-10; vii. 39; xvi. 14; xvii. 1).

But at the threshold of all stands the glorification of Jesus through death. It was his constant habit to connect the two. The Christ must suffer ere He could enter into his glory. As Judas went out to do the fatal deed of treachery, the Master said: "The hour is come that the Son of Man should be glorified." And so here the search of the Greeks reminds Him of his approaching end, and this of his glory.

The death of Jesus could not add to his intrinsic glory. What could be added to that character in which Man and God met in perfect balance, as the pure air of the mountains is penetrated and saturated by the clear and blessed light of morning? But the death of Jesus could and did promote his glorification—that is, it opened up to the view of men and angels qualities of his character and attributes of his being which had else remained for ever concealed. The prism cannot add to the glory of the sun by a single ray; but it can glorify each beam of light, which it breaks into a sevenfold band of colour, revealing its hidden glory in a mystery of beauty. The death of the seed in the ground does not add a single property of fruitfulness or beauty which was not there before; but it liberates them, and gives them room to break into manifestation.

And perhaps there is a sense in which each of us must learn to die daily, that the true intrinsic excellence of the character of Jesus may be revealed in us. It is there in germ and essence; but it awaits death to set free its hidden powers. Let us not be surprised, therefore, if we have to pass through death, and in dying are compelled to manifest traits and qualities which else had been hidden and concealed. The death of December must precede the colours of May and the fruits of October.

II. Death the Cure of Loneliness.—"Except a corn of wheat fall into the ground and die, it abideth alone." It would seem as if the very heart of God yearned for society. In perfect blessedness He had been all-sufficient for Himself; but there was within Him a love which could find no expression or satisfaction apart from beings on which it could rest. Love is almost inconceivable unless there be objects on which to expend and for which to sacrifice itself. Did not this underlie that Divine resolve, "Let us make man"?

But it was not enough simply to make objects for love. They must be attached to the Infinite Lover by strong and enduring bands—they must be led to love; there must be reciprocity in affection, and blessedness in mutual tenderness. If a man and woman do not love, there will be unutterable loneliness in the marriage-bond itself. It were not enough, then, for God to create; He must attract, and attach, and bind, to Himself. But to do this involves something more than an act of power; it will demand self-sacrifice, self-giving, self-abandonment, on his part—all that is set forth in the metaphor of falling into the ground to die. God can only cease to be alone when He not only loves, but is loved. And He can only be loved with the one love that can satisfy Him, because it yields all, when He has first given all. Therefore, He gave his only-begotten Son; and in giving Himself Jesus has made it impossible that God should ever be alone again; because self-giving, such as his, will ever excite the love, and gratitude, and devotion, of human hearts through all ages.

There are many lonely people about the world who complain of desolate and solitary lives. They account for their condition by supposing it due to the failure of relatives through death or intervening distance; but, indeed, it is rather attributable to the fact that they have never fallen into the ground to die, that they have always consulted their own ease and well-being, and have never learnt that the cure of loneliness comes through the sowing of oneself in a grave of daily self-sacrifice. The corn of wheat must fall into the ground and die, and it will abide no longer alone.

III. DEATH THE WAY TO FRUITFULNESS.—"But if it die, it beareth much fruit." What vision was that which rose before the mind of Christ when He heard of those Gentiles and spoke of fruit? As to the first man in Paradise the fruit of the tree was pleasant to the eyes, so to the second Man the fruit of the tree of the cross was, above all things, fair and seductive.

It included the bride, his wife; it included the great multitude which no man can number; it included all those deeds of heroism and graces of self-denial to which the story of his cross has given rise as it has sped from land to land; it included harvests of saved souls which shall golden the furrows of eternal ages. All this was possible only because He dared to die. "Without shedding of blood there is no remission." His death was needed to put away sin; to reveal the love of God; to abolish the curse; and to open the kingdom of Heaven to all believers.

There are many who sigh for fruitfulness, that have never yet learnt the deep lesson of the cross of Christ. We can never die in quite the sense in which He died; not by us can there be submission, or sacrifice, or expiation; and yet there is a sense in which we must drink deeply into the meaning of his death if we would be really fruitful. If we would save others, we cannot save ourselves. If we would help men, we must be content to be helpless. If we would receive grafts of the wild olive, we must be content to bear the gash of the pruning knife. If we would fill the world with a sweet savour of the precious ointment, we must be content to be broken boxes. The most fruitful boughs are those from which the foliage and shoots are cut away with unsparing hand, that the sap may accumulate in the swelling clusters.

IV. DEATH THE GATE TO LIFE.—"He that loveth his life shall lose it, and he that hateth his life shall keep it unto life eternal." Our Lord deliberately chose death, because He knew, first, that He could not be holden by it; and, secondly, that it was only through the grave that He could reach the resurrection life and the ascension glory. Therefore it was that He went down into the valley of death, singing as He went, "Thou wilt not leave my soul in Hades, neither wilt Thou suffer thine Holy One to see corruption."

There is also a deep truth for us all in these marvellous words which He repeated on three occasions, as if He would work them into the very texture of our hearts. Not that we are to make death for ourselves, or constantly fling ourselves away into deep, dark furrows at the impulse of our own choice; but that we should be on the alert not to avoid, but to take any opportunity that God gives us, of going into the land of Moriah, to any of the mountains of which He may tell us. Dare to look up into the face of God, O ye who long for the richer, deeper life; and tell Him that you will not choose your path, but that you are willing to follow Him through death, if that is the only portal of life; and then wait for Him to teach you each step that must be taken through the deepening shadows which lie between you and the more abundant life, which is your true heritage!

Death can never be pleasant to the flesh. The knife is sharp, the fire burns, the cup is bitter, heart and flesh fail; and it sometimes seems as if we must relinquish the effort to keep the girded loin and the undaunted attitude. We learn how Abraham felt as for those three weary days he knew that each step was carrying him deeper into the gloom. We cry, "Let this cup pass from me." Falling into the ground to die is no pastime to the little corns of wheat.

But He who has gone through death Himself knows every turn of the valley and every ford in the river. He cannot make a mistake; nor will He take us by a rougher path than needs be. See how his footprints, nail-pierced, have trodden and retrodden the way with the many that He has brought hither and brought through. He would not have brought you by this path unless He had known that you were strong enough to bear it; or that He was strong enough to carry you, if the worst should come to the worst. And so, since He is there, do not fail to say his name a hundred times a day, if need be, repeating it as the antidote to pain: "Jesus! Jesus! Jesus!"

There are times in such experiences when his voice is very distinctly heard, reassuring the soul of a promise. At other times it seems impossible to detect his voice. But then He infuses strength into our nature in a subtler, tenderer way; and instead of strengthening us by his words, He becomes Himself the strength of our heart and our portion for ever.

Our true attitude is the uncompromising surrender of our will to his will; not trying to effect any great changes in our emotional or mental life, but willing his will, completely and always, and asking Him to work in us, to will and to do of his own good pleasure. Let us not court death, or seek to inflict death, or worry as to whether we are dying properly. Let us roll the whole responsibility on Him, and trust Him up to the hilt. His will is our weal.

All along the line of life we must be prepared to erect altars on which we may yield to God in sacrifice, habits, associations, fascinations, which He has revealed as alien to our true well-being. The soul that dares to live this life will find streams flowing from every smitten rock; honey in the carcase of every slain lion; fair winds (as in the old Greek story) following on the offering of every Iphigenia. I saw a beautiful device once—a hollow cross, filled with flowers which fell out as the cross was carried. Shoulder your cross, child of God! After the first step there will be a shower of flowers.

So it must be ever. Day out of night; spring out of winter; flowers out of frost; joy out of sorrow; fruitfulness out of pruning; Olivet out of Gethsemane; the Ascension out of Calvary; life out of death; and the Christ that is to be out of the pangs of a travailing creation.

34

THE TROUBLED SAVIOUR

"Now is my soul troubled; and what shall I say? Father, save Me from this hour: but for this cause came I unto this hour."—JOHN xii. 27.

IN THESE words the Son of Man lays bare his soul. There is no question of the resolute spirit, one with Deity itself in the purpose of redemption; but only a question of the soul, with its sympathetic influence on the flesh. Never for a moment could the blessed Lord swerve from his cherished determination to undo the havoc wrought by Satan in His own fair world. But as He contemplated the awful cost of agony which must first be met by Him, it seemed as if his human nature could never hold out.

In the garden of Gethsemane this awful agony reached its climax. The anguish there anticipated and borne so oppressed his holy, yet weak human nature, that it uttered itself in strong cryings and tears; "and the overflowed soul might have given way to an internal death before the external death of the body, had He not received a strengthening accession of Divine power, in answer to prayer." As Luther says, "A beam may be tested beyond its strength, and may threaten to give way because of the weakness of its nature, not because of anything wanting in itself."

This scene is an anticipation of Gethsemane; the penumbra of the great eclipse. The question of the Greeks had led the Saviour's thoughts to his death and burial, reminding Him that He must fall into the ground to die, before He could bear fruit. He saw, too, the baptism of suffering unto death through which each of his servants must pass, and in which He would die many times again, in sympathy, though not, of course, as Mediator. And as the whole dread aggregate of sorrow arose before his vision, He cried, "Now is my soul troubled."

There is a human side in this scene, which is all that we can understand; but which may help some of us. We cannot launch out into the great deep; but we may wade in the shallows. The humblest Levite in the temple may learn something from the evident anguish of the Great High-Priest, and the way He bore it; though he may not be able to gauge the pressure of that anguish through every part of his wondrous nature, capable to depths equal to its ascents, of downsittings proportionate to its uprisings.

I. THE TROUBLED SOUL.—We cannot be troubled as He was. On us can never rest the weight of the world's sin, nor even of our own.

For us there can never be that lonely resistance to the onset of all the powers of darkness; or the hiding of the Father's face; or the unutterable woe of being made a curse. And yet, who of us does not sometimes taste of trouble beneath which the heart threatens to break down in helpless collapse?

When the love that had filled our life with music is suddenly silenced, or passed on to fill other spheres with its song; when the sun that had flooded our room with light goes off it, and the cold night settles down; when we have to tear out of our lives some evil thing, which had entwined itself about them—as the octopus about the body of the swimmer—and to do it with the anointed head and washed face; when, at the call of duty, which is the call of God, we have to turn our faces away from some radiant rapture, which had long enticed us forward, in order to take a lonelier, rougher path; when we are misunderstood and misinterpreted, by our dearest, misrepresented and maligned; when we see lover and friend stand afar off with veiled faces; when we are perplexed and baffled at God's dealings; when we are called to suffer through the vices and sorrows of those whom we love as ourselves, while we can do nothing to relieve or save them: then we know what it is to say with Jesus, though in thinner tones, "Now is my soul troubled."

Abraham said it as he trod step by step the path which seemed all too short to Mount Moriah, and knew that the hand which had so often rested in the curls of the darling of his old age must presently strike the knife into his heart. Job said it when, pelted by the accusations of his foes, afflicted with a loathsome disease, perplexed at the dealings of God which confounded all his philosophy, he wished that he had never been born. David said it when he awoke to perceive how, by his grievous sin, he had shaken the fabric of his kingdom, and put into the lips of God's foes a reproach which they have never ceased to use. Jeremiah said it, weeping over the disastrous suicide of his nation. The lovers of Jesus said it as they saw Him deliberately court death, and as they cowered together through the day which followed his decease. And these are but samples of myriads more. Indeed, it is questionable if any life reaches it prime, or unfolds all its beauty, unless there have been some dark hours in which cries of pain have borne witness to the troubled soul.

II. THE RESORT OF THE TROUBLED SOUL—"Father!" When the soul is smitten by a huge wave of anguish, it shivers from stem to stern, and for a moment questions with itself as to what it shall say: "Now is my soul troubled, and what shall I say?" At such times let us beware lest we speak inadvisedly. There is a deliberateness about speech which aggravates the inner temper. Repress the utterance, and you will often mitigate the passion of feeling which boils turbulently below. There was no fear of our Lord speaking the wrong word, but there is every fear of our doing so; and when once it is uttered, it stamps itself indelibly not only on ourselves, but on the minds and hearts of others, to go on breeding evil for all coming time.

But there is one word which can never be unfitting: "Father." Once before, our Lord had hidden Himself there, when face to face with the mystery of Divine Providence, which reveals to babes what it hides from the wise and prudent. "Even so, Father!" an expression which might be rendered, "Yes, Father!" Here, again, in this dark hour, He murmurs that dear name over and over, to hush and quiet his troubled soul. And in the garden He repeated it again and again: "O my Father!" "Abba, Father!"

There are times when the soul knows by sure token the presence and love of God. It cannot give reasons why; it is satisfied to know it; as a child lying beneath its mother's smiles knows that she loves it, and as a shivering invalid brought into the sun knows that it is warm. But it is not always so; shadows fling themselves on the landscape. Clouds marshal themselves in the sky. We can no longer live by sight. Then we are tempted to think that we are deserted indeed; and as we yield to this impression, we begin to fall as into a bottomless pit of despondency.

At such times, there is no medicine which will so certainly restore the tone of the soul, as to look up and compel yourself to say "Father." To say it when you do not feel it; to say it in the teeth of every appearance to the contrary; to say it again and again, till presently the bruised heart begins slowly to feel that it is infinitely loved, and is being led each step by a love compared with which the strongest love it ever felt is as a glow-worm's sparkle compared with the sun at noon.

There is no pain which the thought of the Divine Fatherhood will not assuage. But what shall they do who cannot avail themselves of its consolations—or will not? To suffer at the whim of an adverse fate; to be the sport of circumstances and things; to be unable to find a hand reached out in the dark; to miss the Father; to look up and not be able to realize that a Person is shaping the life-course—this must be suffering so acute to test the power of endurance to breaking.

None have the right to call God "Father" after this inner sense, save those who have been born into his family through the regenerating grace of the Holy Spirit. Only to those who believe does He give the right to become sons of God. Only those who are led by the Spirit of God may enjoy that Spirit of adoption, whereby we cry, Abba, Father! But where this right has been conceded, there is the further privilege of counting on the Divine Fatherhood in all time of our tribulation, in all time of our wealth, in the hour of death, and in the Day of Judgment.

But, beside this appeal to and belief in the Father's heart, there is the further solace of willing his will. We may not delight in it; but we can will it. We may not understand it; but we can choose it. It is simply marvellous what rest comes into both heart and life when once the soul dares to look into the Father's face, and cry, I want nothing outside the enclosure of thy choice for me. To walk, as it were, right away from the dear circle of our own preference into the circle of his Fatherly will; to dare to abide in the cleft of that Rock; to do it while the flesh rebels and friendly voices remonstrate—there is nothing like this to cure the heartache. Then the pain begins to assuage; the evil one finding himself discredited ceases to annoy; the judgment is cleared of silt which had spoilt its crystalline beauty; and life begins to assume something of its old buoyancy, enriched and deepened and purified by the ordeal through which it has come.

III. The Petitions of the Troubled Soul.—It is the human nature of Jesus which speaks first. *Save Me from this hour.* There is something here of the same spirit as afterwards cried, "If it be possible, let this cup pass from Me." So terrible was it to become the Substitute for human sin, that it seemed as if all that was merely human in Him could not possibly endure.

It brings our Master very near to us. Often in the process of fitting us for higher service, or in the prosecution of his plans for ourselves and others, God brings us to a point where all our own courage and strength collapse. We feel as if we cannot go on for another inch. Dazzling as the prospect is beyond, we despair of ever wading through the deep waters that lie between. Granted that the welcome shouts to the conqueror are worth a hell of pain, yet how is one to get through that fiery lava-stream which seethes right before the feet? At such times the soul is tempted to say, Save me from this hour; lead me by an easier path; let me forgo the prize, if only I may miss the conflict.

How good and wise it is of our God not to answer such prayers! He hears them, and ponders them, and replies to their spirit. Not for one moment, because He loves us too well, will He allow us to miss the great purpose of blessing that He has in view; but He draws near to our trembling, shrinking nature, and pours in such marvellous strength as we had never dreamed of. We find ourselves calm, self-possessed, restful, almost joyous, in circumstances which, as we had considered them from a distance, had seemed utterly intolerable. Amid a fiery current of pain we are so vividly conscious of the presence of the Son of Man, that we are actually reluctant to leave it. In the deprivation of all that men prize we actually enumerate our unsearchable satisfaction and wealth. And so we bless God for that from which we had asked to be saved. There are thousands of believers who can verify these statements from their own experience.

As we consider these facts we are driven to cancel all thought about ourselves, and to turn to God with the cry, *Father, glorify thy name!*

We have before seen how this desire was ever uppermost with the Son of Man. He would do and suffer anything with that in view. From heaven He engages to answer any prayer which tallies with that supreme ambition of his being. Happy shall we be if it is the supreme ambition of ours also.

"Father, glorify thy name. I will not seek my own comfort or deliverance, I simply dare not; but I am willing, in thy strength, and because I love Thee so, to suffer anything, if only thy glory may be promoted, so that men may think better of Thee, because of what they see in me." What a battle-cry is this—Father, glorify thy name! How it must thrill the hosts of heaven, as they see some dauntless soul descending into death, with these words upon the lips. How it must strike amazement and panic into the hosts of hell! Scævola held his hand in the flame till it was burnt to ashes, to show the stuff of which Romans were made; and here is the spirit of all God's saints. To ignore the shrinking flesh, to trample it in the dust, to nail it to the cross; to follow the path, clearly pointed by the will of God; to charge into the valley of death, whilst destruction is belched from the cannon's mouth, "here is the patience and the faith of the saints."

Then came a voice from the clear April sky. It seemed like thunder to the awestruck crowds who heard the noise but could not detect the sense, as the beasts who hear the noise of our speech, but to whom it is perfectly unintelligible. It well gathered up the results of his life and death: of the former it said, *I have glorified it;* of the second it said, *and will glorify it again.* The revenue of glory accruing to God from this small planet is vastly greater than when Jesus became incarnate; and it is yet to gather till a very storm of hallelujahs breaks in thundering waves of praise around the sapphire throne.

Let us gird up our loins, my brothers, to take the way God leads us, though the brake is thorny, and the path almost impassable; let us never cease to cry, especially when we must speak to vent our anguish, "Father, glorify thy name"; let us call thus out to one another through the darkness, till the gloom becomes vocal with many voices, encouraging the pilgrim host: and then as the morning breaks we shall find ourselves at the margin of the sea of glass, crying, with the redeemed host, "Blessing, and honour, and glory, and power, be unto Him that sitteth on the throne, and to the Lamb for ever and ever!"

35

The World and its Prince

"Now is the judgment of this world: now shall the prince of this world be cast out."—JOHN xii. 31.

THE LORD was still in the current of thought about his approaching death, which had been suggested by the inquiry of the Greeks. He is speaking from the standpoint of his cross, and as if He were already crucified.

What a strange new rendering He gives to the appearances of that day! It would seem as if He were standing at the bar of the world for judgment; receiving its verdict from the lips of Caiaphas, representing its religion; and of Pilate, representing its government: that verdict being registered in the heading of his cross, which was written in Latin, Greek, and Hebrew. And it would seem also as if He were being cast out of the world, as the king's son was cast out of the vineyard and slain by the wicked husbandmen; and that this were the decisive crisis in his existence, and not in his only, but also in that of the few who owned Him as Master.

But none of these things were really so. The world, not He, was being judged. It was standing before Him for his verdict; not He before the world for its judgment. Caiaphas and Pilate, and all the course of this world whom they represented, were passing in long procession before his judgment throne, and were being manifested and judged. And as for the casting out—that was the precise penalty being meted out to the Prince of the World, who wrought beneath those scenes of hate, and treachery, and blood. He, not Christ, was being cast out; cast out potentially, though perhaps the fullness of his sentence has not been meted out to him in actual suffering. Little as they guessed it, the day of Calvary and its cross was the crisis and turning-point of the history of earth and hell, of men and devils; and settled for evermore the question of supremacy between darkness and light, death and life, hate and love.

I. THE WORLD.--The Lord gave a new meaning to this word. We use it of our planet, or of the populations of men that cover its surface. He used it for the spirit of human society; for the course and trend of its thinkings and activities. Take any section, however small, of the great world of men, and carefully study it, and you will discover the presence of an indefinable spirit which sways all hearts, and influences all lives. It is difficult to say what it is. It is something in the air. Men call it fashion, or the spirit of the age. But whatever it is, it determines their pleasures, their opinions, their method of life, and their very dress. This is what our Lord meant when He spoke of the world. And it is probable that the world of one age is as nearly as possible the world of all the ages. There is nothing new under the sun.

The majority of men born into this world are so familiar with this subtle influence that they yield to and grow up in it, from the earliest moments of consciousness; and are unaware of the strength of the current by which they are being carried along. It is only when we are no longer of the world, because chosen out of it, and identified with Christ, that we learn how masterful the spirit of worldliness can be— imperious in compelling obedience; haughty if disobeyed; virulent and deadly in its hate.

This world-spirit met our Lord in full force. At first it sought to fascinate Him with its charm, and by its witchery to beguile Him from the rough path that He had chosen. The crowds thronged his footsteps. The leaders of religious thought were found in his audiences, and invited Him to their homes. The people proposed to make Him king by acclamation. And all the land seemed to lie at his feet.

Then, as its soft fascination failed, the world turned to fight against Him, and oppose his every step. Where flowers had strewn his pathway, jagged stones lay thick. Where pleasant voices had uttered their flatteries, the air was full of murmurs and threats. Where smiles had shed their sunbeams, there frowns and averted faces lined his path downward into the valley of shadows. In his own words we have the results of his experience: "If the world hate you, ye know that it hated Me before it hated you."

But in either case our Lord overcame the world. Its blandishments did not divert Him from his chosen path, and neither did its frowns. It did its utmost and failed; and as He stood at the foot of his cross, whither He had come, notwithstanding all, He raised the shout of victory, "I have overcome the world!" (xvi. 33).

When He died, the world was judged. Its inner motive was unveiled. There could be no longer any doubt as to its true meaning and character. It had come into collision with the Eternal God, representing the life of heaven; and had flung itself against Him in frantic opposition. In condemning Him it had condemned itself; and henceforth none of those who loved Him and the Father that sent Him, could love it or ally themselves with it. The citizens of Edinburgh hooted Mary Queen of Scots, because she wedded Bothwell, the murderer of her first husband, Darnley: and shall not they be convicted of falsehood and treachery who profess to love the Son of God, but in their hearts love the world which cast Him out? Take heart, all ye whom the world knows not! it is fair to presume that you have been chosen out of the world and called to be the sons of God. And as for you, who are entangled in its current and enamoured of its lusts, take heed lest you be proved to have neither part nor lot with Him! (xvii. 14, 15, 16; 1 John ii. 15, 16).

II. THE PRINCE OF THIS WORLD.—There is no doubt as to who is indicated by this significant phrase. Frequently Satan, the arch-enemy of man, is thus referred to by our Lord; as for instance when He said: "The prince of this world cometh, and hath nothing in Me." And when in the Temptation the devil showed Him all the kingdoms of the world in a moment of time, and said: "All this power will I give thee, and the glory of them, for that is delivered unto me," the Lord did not challenge his statement and charge him with falsehood, but by his silence apparently acquiesced in the proud boast.

What does it mean? Are we to believe, as some tell us, that in primeval ages, before sin and death had entered the fair universe, he who is now a fallen spirit, but then a bright archangel, was the appointed ruler and viceregent of our world, which flashed with undimmed beauty in the bright sisterhood of worlds; and that when he lost his first state, he nevertheless retained his supremacy, bringing desolation and evil on all that is connected with the world he rules? It may be so. It is not impossible that the prime object which underlies the divine scheme of redemption is to cast him out of the position which he has usurped, and to bring our world again under the benign sway of heaven. "For this purpose the Son of God was manifested, that He might destroy the works of the devil."

But the task must have been one of tremendous difficulty. Of course the evil one could not be cast out simply by the exercise of such omnipotence as made the worlds; because the sphere of conflict was not the material, but the spiritual. And the conditions of the conflict were greatly aggravated by the fact that Satan had misled our race to love and trust him. Thus it befell that God had not only to dispossess him of a power which he was no longer competent to wield; but to do so in the face of the sworn fealty and allegiance rendered him by the children of the human race.

The world of which we have been speaking is the stratagem by which the devil holds the souls of men in thrall. He does not obtrude himself, as that would alarm them and defeat his purpose; but he conceals himself beneath the course of this world, with which he is identified by the Apostle (Eph. ii. 2). The world is to Satan what the web is to the spider, the bait to the angler, the lure to the fowler. Very specious and attractive were the appearances and the religious professions of the world; but Christ tore the veil from it and revealed its true nature, so that we might be no longer cajoled by its appearances.

But it behoved God to do more than expose the hollowness of the world; it was needful that He should assume our nature, so as to meet and vanquish the devil on his chosen battle-ground, and in the race that he had seduced. This is the clue to the Incarnation. This explains the conflict which raged so fiercely throughout the Lord's brief early ministry. This throws light on the extraordinary way in which the devil was permitted to possess the bodies of men, like so many garrisoned castles. This may cast a light also on much of the agony through which our Lord passed; the evidence of conflict with a hidden foe, as the beach is strewn with wreckage after a night of storm.

Mark the point which had to be decided. I suppose the devil never doubted for a moment that God was stronger than he; but it had to be settled in actual conflict whether God were strong enough to expel him from men who accepted and loved his rule, and whether man could ever be made strong enough to withstand and vanquish him. Was the devil to be for ever supreme over man; or could man ever become supreme over the devil, his hosts, and the world through which he wrought?

Wonderful promises gem the pages of Holy Writ, to the effect that man would some day be more than the devil's match. The earliest promise foreshadowed this; when speaking of the woman's Seed, God said. "It shall bruise thy head." The psalmist celebrated this blessed reversal of what threatened to be perpetual, when he assured the man who dwelt in God's secret place that He should tread on the lion and adder, and trample the young lion and the dragon beneath his feet (Psalm xci. 13). Our Lord foresaw the downfall of Satan as lightning from heaven; and promised to give his disciples power to tread on serpents and scorpions, and over all the power of the enemy (Luke x. 19). The Apostle assured his converts that the God of Peace would shortly bruise Satan under their feet (Rom. xvi. 20).

And all these strange predictions were more than realized in the Cross, the Resurrection, and the Ascension of the Son of God. In his death He destroyed him that had the power of death—that is, the devil. From the grave He came bearing at his girdle the keys of Hades. And at his Ascension his triumph was consummated. Comparing Eph. i. 21 with vi. 12, in the latter of which the same expressions are used of evil spirits that are used in the former of the powers above which Christ was raised, it is fair to infer that his Ascension was resisted by the re-gathering of the broken squadrons of evil for one last assault, but in vain.

It was not wonderful that God should go to God—that the Son should hasten to the Father: and if this had been all, the devil would probably never have sought to stay it. But the matter in dispute then, which was to be laid at rest for ever, was, whether our race should be supreme; whether devils should be put beneath the feet of redeemed men; whether our nature should pass regnant and victorious to the heart of the Throne, into the rare air of which no created thing had ever dared to intrude.

And this is what the Lord's Ascension established for all time. In the grave, the Son of God took human nature into indissoluble union with Himself; more completely, as it appears to me, than even in his Incarnation. In this He took on Him the nature of man; in that He took the nature of man into Himself, and from the brow of Olivet bore it upward to the Throne. If angel-hosts came to greet Him, they were doomed to fall back, as He reached the furthest bounds where their created natures could follow. But as for the human nature which He had made one with Himself, He took that with Him into the very focus of the majesty of God. This, then, is the marvellous result—that our nature is supreme in Him; over all other natures, celestial and terrestrial, whether they be thrones, or dominions, principalities, or powers.

It is very wonderful. We are told that our earth is utterly insignificant amid the myriads of the stars, and our race as the animalculæ, whole kingdoms of which exist in a single drop of water. But bigness is not greatness, nor smallness insignificance. And it has pleased God to select our planet as the nursery of the seed-royal, whose nature is shared by his Son for ever.

In his Ascension our Lord showed that He had acquired as man the power to overthrow and cast out the devil. As a matter of fact, it is probable that he was cast out from the presence-chamber of God, where he had accused Job, and the high priest Joshua, and others of the saints. He was cast out into the heavenly places, where he is still prince of the power of the air, until Christ descends thither with his Church. He shall then be cast out into the earth with great wrath, knowing that his hour has come; and he shall afterwards be cast down into the bottomless pit, and finally into the lake of fire. The Lord's death and ascension did potentially that which he has been realizing actually ever since.

This is a fertile subject for holy meditation and for practical help; because if the Lord has cast Satan out of his strongholds, He will be able to cast him out also from every soul of man that offers itself to Him, appealing for deliverance.

Take heart, O child of God, tempted and tried; your Lord is more than a match for all the power of evil! "Greater is He that is in you than he that is in the world." Let Him effect your emancipation, and chase your foe from all his strongholds within, until he be utterly cast out, and you entirely delivered.

36

THE TRUE LIGHT OF GOD'S CHILDREN

"Walk while ye have the light, lest darkness come upon you: for he that walketh in darkness knoweth not whither he goeth. While ye have light, believe in the light, that ye may be the children of light."

JOHN xii. 35, 36.

THE LIFE of the Lord Jesus was bathed through and through with the Light of God. He was Light, because God is Light; and God filled Him as the light fills the pure transparent air. It was enough for Him that God should shine through his being, as through a transparent medium; nothing being added or subtracted from the intensity and glory of his rays. To believe on Him was to believe on God. To see Him was to see God. To hear Him speak was to hear what the Father had said to Him, and was saying to men through Him (44, 45, 49).

Light is so beautiful, so pure, so gladdening, so gentle in its all-pervasiveness, so mysterious in its sevenfold web of colour! What better could set forth the nature of Him who is the express image of God's Person; and, therefore, the beam of his glory! And in this, as the element of our being, we were meant to spend our lives, having no part dark; but saturated with the radiant inshining of Him who gathers up in Himself, after a spiritual fashion, all those qualities which naturally we ascribe to light. There are, however, three injunctions here to which we must conform, if we would know the blessedness to which our Lord refers as being possible to us.

I. BELIEVE IN THE LIGHT.—There is no moment, no duty, no trial in life, in which the Lord Jesus is not present. You may not see Him; but, nevertheless, He is there. No furnace, but the Son of Man treads upon the glowing embers. No storm, but the Master walks over the turbulent billows. No isle of banishment, but the Lord is near the lonely exile. It may be that we do not see Him, or hear his voice; but we must believe. We must dare to believe on the strength of his own assurances, and in spite of all appearances to the contrary. Did He not say, "Lo! I am with you alway"?

It is much when men begin to study the acts and promises of Christ as indicating his character. This is what we all do at the outset with every new friendship which comes into our life. We are not quite certain of our new-found acquaintance, and we eagerly question each trait and indication of what he is. But after a while we have formed our mental conception, and are no longer on the alert. We have passed behind the actions to the character, and we rest there. We are not always looking to find him out; sight is exchanged for faith.

So we must not only believe that Christ is in all, but we must go on to believe that He is light; that in all the bitter and painful experiences of life He is always love, joy, peace, long-suffering, gentleness, and goodness; and that He is conducting us surely and safely into the truest, gladdest, and most perfect life. This, surely, is something at least of the meaning contained in the words, "Believe in the light."

II. OBEY THE LIGHT. *Walk in obedience to its laws* (35).—What a true word Mary spoke at Cana, when she said to the servants, "Whatsoever He saith unto you, do it"! She must have learnt that lesson out of those long, quiet, blessed years at Nazareth. Often she had been unable to understand some deep word of his, and had been compelled to content herself with just doing some obvious duty to which He pointed; and as she did it, all became clear. She knew that there was no such way of understanding Him, as by rendering Him literal obedience; and she passed on the results of her experience to us all. And how often has this taken place since! We have eagerly thought and read about the Master, trying to penetrate into the deep mystery of his nature, but baffled and rebuffed; but when we have set ourselves to obey some simple injunction, and to do the duty which lay next to us, all our doubts have dispersed, and being willing to do his will we have known of the doctrine. Men would never know what the forces of Nature can do for them except by setting themselves to obey them. And it is so in relation to Christ and the laws of his spiritual realm.

All over the world men are asking how they may come to know Christ; and there is but one answer: "Believe that He loves you; that He is prompting you by his good Spirit; that He is breathing through every yearning and perception of the better life. Dare to obey all these; follow them whither they point; walk in the light which streams forth from them, and which really has its origin and fount in Him; and you will come to know the Light, and to be changed into its image."

The light of Christ is always distinguishable because it means the next duty, the deepest impression of what is right, the clearest conviction of the will of God. It may be that even now, as you read these lines, there is some duty you shirk; some cross you refuse to lift; some act from which you flinch. You have no doubt about it. And though you may not have directly associated it with Him, yet you cannot doubt that if you did it He would be pleased. It is useless to try to know Him until that nearest act of obedience is wrought; but directly it is, He will become clearer than any words could portray. "Walk while ye have the light"; so you will know the light and become light in the Lord.

How different is this teaching from that of the world around! There we are bidden to know, before we dare to entrust our lives to any leader or commander, whatever be his fair speeches and promises; but Christ bids us obey the first glimmer of light breaking on us through the words of a friend, or the summons of Inspiration, or the promptings of the Spirit; and He undertakes that if we do, we shall not walk in darkness, but shall know whither we go, and shall have the Light of Life.

Disobedience like scales veils Christ from us; whilst obedience leads us into his very presence. The judgment always becomes just, and the vision clear, when we deny ourselves, and set ourselves to follow whatsoever things are true, just, pure, and of good report.

III. BECOME CHILDREN OF LIGHT (36).—It is wonderful how soon we become like what we love and pursue. Love appropriates and fixes the tones and gestures and thoughts of the one that is loved. As the fish resemble the bottom on which they lie, and as the Arctic hares change with the colour of their world, so do hearts and lives take on the complexion of the people and things which predominate and preponderate in their daily experience.

So let it be in your relation to the Lord Jesus, who indeed is the true Light of souls, "lightening every man that cometh into the world." Think of Him. Imitate Him. Ask continually what He would wish. Saturate your mind with his words and teaching. Live up to his will so far as you know it. Obey Him to the uttermost. And there will come a growing resemblance between you and Him. You will be transformed, as you behold, into his likeness. Men, as they come into contact with you, will be constrained to admit that his character has become transfused with yours, and to acknowledge you as a child of the light.

Oh to descend into the world each morning as sunbeams from the fount of day!—bearing with us something of the beauty of the world from which we come; shedding joy and blessedness on dark hearts; and living lives as transparent, as beautiful, as unobtrusive, and as helpful in our measure as his was, from whom we have received all we have and are.

But let us remember that if we refuse the solicitations and promptings of his Spirit, our hearts will become hard, and our eyes blind. There are some mentioned in this paragraph who believed in Him but would not confess Him, and loved the praise of men more than the praise of God. How could such men enter into the fullness of his blessed light? Was it not inevitable that it should become dim?

Live up to all you know, and you will know more and resemble Him more perfectly; and when kings die, and nations rock to ruin,

G

and all nature is out of joint, you will see the King seated on his throne amid the worship of the Seraphim, and you will begin to live with his Life, to reflect his Light, and to love with his Love. And the day of those blessed experiences shall never wane, or be overcast by the gathering twilight, but shall glow with magnificent splendour; suns glimmering far beneath as the flash of fire-flies; the raptures of earth remembered as the pastimes of childish joy; whilst through eternal ages we shall follow the Lamb deeper into the heart of his own ineffable bliss—in Him, with Him, like Him, for ever!

37

The Laver in the life of Jesus

"He poureth water into a bason, and began to wash the disciples' feet, and to wipe them with the towel wherewith He was girded."

JOHN xiii. 5

In the court of the Temple there were two objects that arrested the eye of the entering worshipper—the brazen altar, and the laver. The latter was kept always full of pure, fresh water, for the constant washings enjoined by the Levitical code. Before the priests were consecrated for their holy work, and attired in the robes of the sacred office, they washed there (Ex. xxix. 4). Before they entered the Holy Place in their ordinary ministry, and before Aaron, on the great Day of Atonement, proceeded to the Most Holy Place, with blood, not his own, it was needful to conform to the prescribed ablutions. "He shall bathe his flesh in water" (Lev. xvi. 4).

First, then, the Laver, and then the Holy Place; the order is irreversible, and the teaching of the types is as exact as mathematics. Hence, when the writer of the Epistle to the Hebrews invites us to draw near, and make our abode in the Most Holy Place, he carefully obeys the Divine order, and bids us "draw near with a true heart, in full assurance of faith, having our hearts sprinkled from an evil conscience, and our bodies washed with pure water."

In this scene (John xiii. 1–14), on the eve of our Lord's betrayal, we find the spiritual counterpart of the Laver, and in the following chapters we stand in the Presence-Chamber.

I. The Circumstance that led to this Act of Love.—In order fully to understand this touching incident, it is necessary to remember the circumstances out of which it sprang. On the way from Bethany to the upper room in which the Supper had been prepared, and on entering therein, our Lord must have been deeply absorbed in the momentous events in which He was to be the central figure; but He was not unmindful of a contention which had engaged his disciples, for they had been disputing one with another as to which of them should be the greatest. The proud spirit of the flesh, which so often cursed the little group, broke out in this awful hour with renewed energy; as though the prince of this world would inflict a parting blow on his great Antagonist, through those whom He loved best. It was as if Satan said, "See the results of thy tears and teaching, of thy prayers and pleadings; the love which Thou hast so often inculcated is but a passing sentiment, that has never rooted itself in the soil of these wayward hearts. It is a plant too rare and exotic for the climate of earth. Take it back with Thee to thine own home if Thou wilt, but seek not to achieve the impossible."

It was heartrending that this exhibition of pride should take place just at this juncture. These were the men who had been with Him in his temptations, who had had the benefit of his most careful instructions, who had been exposed to the full influence of his personal character; and yet, notwithstanding all, the rock-bed of pride, that cast the angels down from heaven, that led to the fall of man, obtruded itself. This occasion in which it manifested itself was very inopportune; already the look of Calvary was on the Saviour's face, and the sword entering his heart. Surely, they must have been aware that the shadow of the great eclipse was already passing over the face of their Sun. But even this did not avail to restrain the manifestation of their pride. Heedless of three years of example and teaching; unrestrained by the symptoms of our Lord's sorrow; unchecked by the memory of happy and familiar intercourse, which should have bound them for ever in a united brotherhood, they wrangled with high voices and hot faces, with the flashing eye and clenched fist of the Oriental, as to who should be first.

And if pride thus asserted itself after *such* education, and under *such* circumstances, let us be sure that it is not far away from any one of us. We do not now contend in so many words for the chief places; courtesy, politeness, fear of losing the respect of our fellows, restrain us. But our resentment to the fancied slight, or the assumption by another of work which we thought our own; our sense of hurtness when we are put aside; our jealousy and envy; our detracting speeches, and subtle insinuations of low motive, all show how much of this loveless spirit rankles in our hearts. We have been planted in the soil of this world, and we betray its flavour; we have come of a proud stick, and we betray our heredity.

II. Love's Sensitiveness to Sin on the part of its Beloved.—Consider these epithets of the love of Christ:

It was unusually tender.—When the hour of departure approaches, though slight reference be made to it, love lives with the sound of the departing wheels or the scream of the engine always in its ear; and there are given a tenderness to the tone, a delicacy to the touch, a thoughtfulness for the heartache of those from whom it is to be parted, which are of inexpressible beauty. All that was present with Christ. He was taking that Supper with them before He suffered. He knew that He would soon depart out of this world unto the Father. His ear was specially on the alert, his nature keenly alive, his heart thrilling with unusual tenderness, as the sands slowly ran out from the hour-glass.

It was supreme love.—"Having loved his own that were in the world, He loved them unto the end." These last words have been thought to refer to the end of life, but it surely were superfluous to tell us that the strong waters of death could not quench the love of the Son of Man. When once He loves, He loves always. It is needless to tell us that the Divine heart which has enshrined a soul will not forsake it; that the name of the beloved is never erased from the palms of the hands; that the covenant is not forgotten though eternity elapse. Of course Christ loves to the end, even though that end reaches to endlessness. We do not need to be assured that the Immortal Lover, who has once taken us into union with Himself, can never loose his hold. Therefore it is better to adopt the alternative suggested by the margin of the Revised Version, "He loved them to the uttermost." There was nothing to be desired. Nothing was needed to fill out the ideal of perfect love. Not a stitch was required for the needle-work of wrought gold; not a touch demanded for the perfectly achieved picture; not a throb added to the strong pulse of affection with which He regarded his own.

It is very wonderful that He should have loved such men like this. As we pass them under review at this time of their life, they seem a collection of nobodies—with the exception perhaps of John and Peter. But they were his own, there was a special relationship between Him and them. They had belonged to the Father, and He had given them to the Son as his special perquisite and belonging. "Thine they were, and Thou gavest them Me." May we dare, in this meaning, to apply to Christ that sense of proprietorship, which makes a bit of moorland waste, a few yards of garden-ground, dear to the freeholder?

> *"Breathes there the man with soul so dead,*
> *Who never to himself hath said,*
> *This is my own . . . ?"*

It was because these men were Christ's *own*, that the full passion of his heart set in towards them, and He loved them to the utmost bound; that is, the tides filled the capacity of the ocean-bed of possibility.

It was bathed in the sense of his Divine origin and mission.— The curtain was waxing very thin. It was a moment of vision. There had swept across his soul a realisation of the full meaning of his approaching triumph. He looked back, and was hardly conscious of the manger where the horned oxen fed, of the lowly birth, of the obscure years, in the sublime conception that He had come forth from God. He looked forward, and was hardly conscious of the cross, the

nail, the thorn-crown, and the spear, because of the sublime consciousness that He was stepping back, to go to Him with whom He realised
his identity. He looked on through the coming weeks, and knew that
the Father had given all things into his hands. What the devil had
offered as the price of obeisance to himself, that the Father was about
to give Him—nay, had already given Him—as the price of his self-
emptying. And if for a moment He stooped, as we shall see He did,
to the form of a servant, it was not because of any failure to recognise
his high dignity and mission, but with the sense of Godhead quick
on his soul.

The love which went out towards this little group of men had
Deity in it. It was the love of the Throne, of the glory He had with
the Father before the worlds were, of that which now fills the bosom of
his ascended and glorified nature.

He was aware of the task to which He was abandoning these men.—
He knew that as He was the High Priest over the house of God, they
were its priests. He knew that cleansing was necessary before they
could receive the anointing of the Holy Ghost. He knew that the great
work of carrying forward his Gospel was to be delegated to their hands.
He knew that they were to carry the sacred vessels of the Gospel, which
must not be blurred or fouled by contact with human pride or uncleanness. He knew that the very mysteries of Gethsemane and Calvary
would be inexplicable, and that none might stand on that holy hill,
save those that had clean hands and a pure heart. And because of all
this, He turned to them, by symbol and metaphor, to impress upon
their heart and memory the necessity of participating in the cleansing
of which the Laver is the type.

The highest love is ever quickest to detect the failures and incon-
sistencies of the beloved. Just because of its intensity, it can be content
with nothing less than the best, because the best means the blessedest;
and it longs that the object of its thought should be most blessed for
ever. It is a mistake to think that green-eyed jealousy is quickest to
detect the spots on the sun, the freckles on the face, and the jarring
discords in the music of the life; love is quicker, more microscopic,
more exacting that the ideal should be achieved. Envy is content to
indicate the fault, and leave it; but love detects, and waits and holds
its peace until the fitting opportunity arrives, and then sets itself to
remove, with its own tenderest ministry, the defect which had spoilt
the completeness and beauty of its object.

Perhaps there had never been a moment in the human consciousness
of our Lord, when, side by side with this intense love for his own,
there had been so vivid a sense of oneness with his Father, of his unity
with the source of Infinite Purity and Blessedness. We might have
supposed that this would have alienated Him from his poor friends,
but in this our thoughts are not as his. Just because of his awful

holiness. He was quick to perceive the unholiness of his friends, and could not endure it, and essayed to rid them of it. Just because of his Divine goodness, He could detect the possibilities of goodness in them, and be patient enough to give it culturing care.

The most perfect musician may be most tortured by incompetence; but he will be most likely to detect true merit, and give time to its training. "The powerfullest magnet will pick out, in the powdered dust of the ironstone, fine particles of metal that a second or third rate magnet would fail to draw to itself." Do not dread the awful holiness of Jesus; it is your hope. He will never be content till He has made you like Himself; and side by side with his holiness, never fail to remember his gentle, tender love.

III. THE DIVINE HUMILITY, THAT COPES WITH HUMAN SIN.—"He riseth from supper, and layeth aside his garments; and He took a towel and girded Himself." This is what the Apostle calls taking upon Himself the form of a servant. The charm of the scene is its absolute simplicity. You cannot imagine Christ posturing to the ages. There was no aiming at effect, no thought of the beauty or humility of the act. Christ did not act thus for show or pretence, but with an absolutely single purpose of fulfilling a needed office. And in this He set forth the spirit of our redemption.

This is the key to the Incarnation.—With slight alteration the words will read truly of that supreme act. He rose from the Throne; laid aside the garments of light which He had worn as his vesture; took up the poor towel of humanity, and wrapped it about his glorious Person; poured his own blood into the basin of the cross; and set Himself to wash away the foul stains of human depravity and guilt.

As pride was the source of human sin, Christ must needs provide an antidote in his absolute humility—a humility which could not grow beneath these skies, but must be brought from the world where the lowliest are the greatest, and the most childlike reign as kings.

This is the key to every act of daily cleansing.—We have been washed—once, definitely and irrevocably, we have been bathed in the crimson tide that flows from Calvary; but we need a daily cleansing. Our feet become soiled with the dust of life's highways; our hands grimy, as our linen beneath the rain of filth in a great city; our lips —as the white doorstep of the house—are fouled by the incessant throng of idle, unseemly and fretful words; our hearts cannot keep unsoiled the stainless robes with which we pass from the closet at morning prime. Constantly we need to repair to the Laver to be washed. But do we always realise how much each act of confession on our part involves from Christ on his? Whatever important work He may at that moment have on hand; whatever directions He may be giving to the loftiest angels for the fulfilment of his purposes; however pressing the concerns of the Church or the universe upon his broad shoulders—He must needs turn from all these to do a work He will not delegate. Again He stoops from the Throne, and girds Himself with a towel; and, in all lowliness, endeavours to remove from thee and me the stain which his love dare not pass over. He never loses the print of the nails; He never forgets Calvary and the blood; He never spends one hour without stooping to do the most menial work of cleansing filthy souls. And it is because of this humility He sits on the Throne and wields the sceptre over hearts and worlds.

This is the key to our ministry to each other.—I have often thought that we do not often enough wash one another's feet. We are conscious of the imperfections which mar the characters of those around us. We are content to note, criticise, and learn them. We dare not attempt to remove them. This failure arises partly because we do not love with a love like Christ's—a love which will brave resentment, annoyance, rebuke, in its quest,—and partly because we are not willing to stoop low enough.

None can remove the mote of another, so long as the beam is left in the eye, and the sin unjudged in the life. None can cleanse the stain, who is not willing to take the form of a servant, and go down with bare knees upon the floor. None is able to restore those that are overtaken in a fault, who does not count himself the chief of sinners and the least of saints.

We need more of this lowly, loving spirit: not so sensitive to wrong and evil as they affect us, as anxious for the stain they leave on the offender. It is of comparatively small consequence how much we suffer; it is of much importance that none of Christ's disciples should be allowed to go on for a moment longer, with unconfessed and unjudged wrongs clouding his peace, and hindering the testimony which he might give. Let us therefore watch for each other's souls: let us consider one another to provoke to love and good works; let us in all sincerity do as Christ has done, washing each other's feet in all humility and tender love. But this spirit is impossible save through fellowship with the Lamb of God, and the reception of his holy, humble nature into the inmost heart, by the Holy Ghost.

38

THRICE BIDDEN TO LOVE

*"A new commandment I give unto you, That ye love one another; as I
have loved you, that ye also love one another."*—JOHN xiii. 34.

ANACRÆON complains that when they asked him to sing of heroic deeds,
he can only sing of love. But the love with which he fills his sonnets
will bear as much comparison with that of which Jesus spoke in his
last discourse, as the flaring oil of a country fair with the burning of
the heavenly constellations. Even the love that binds young hearts is
too selfish and exclusive to set forth that pure ray which shone from
the heart of the Son of Man, and shines, and will shine. What word
shall we use to describe it?

Charity?—The disposition denoted by this great word does not fulfil
the measure of the love of Christ. It is cold and severe. It can be organised. It casts its dole to the beggar and turns away, content to have
relieved the sentiment of pity. By being employed for one manifestation
of love, charity is too limited and restricted in its significance to become
an adequate expression of the Divine love which brought Jesus from
the Throne, and should inspire us to lay down our lives for the brethren.

Philanthropy?—This is a great word, "the love of man." And yet
the philanthropist is too often content with the general patronage of
good works, the elaboration of schemes, the management of commit-
tees to do much personal work for the amelioration of the world. The
word is altogether too distant, too deficient in the personal element, too
extensive in its significance. It will not serve to represent the Divine
compassion with which the heart of Christ was, at the moment of
speaking, in tumult.

Complacency?—No; for this is the emotion excited by the contemplation of merit and virtue, which turns away from sin and deformity;
and the sentiment denoted by our Master's words is one that is not
brought into existence by virtue, nor extinguished by demerit and vice.

Since all these words fail, we are driven to speak of love, as Christ
used the word, as being the essence of the Divine nature; for God is
Love. It is the indwelling of God in the soul. It is the transmitting
through our lives of that which we have received in fellowship with the
uncreated glory of the Divine Being. That which was in the beginning
between the Father and the Son; that which constrained our Emmanuel
to sojourn in this world of sin; that which inspired his sacrifice; that
which dwells perennially in his heart, vanquishing time and distance;
which overflows all expressions, and defies definition—is the love of

which these words speak, and which we are commanded to entertain towards each other.

It is a commandment.—"These things I command you." "This is his commandment: that we should believe in the name of his Son Jesus Christ, and love one another even as He gave us commandment." Obviously, then, obedience must be possible. Christ had gauged our nature not only as Creator, but by personal experience. He knew what was in man. The possibilities of our nature were well within his cognisance; therefore it must be possible for us to love one another qualitatively, if not quantitatively, as He has loved us. Do not sit down before this great command and say it is impossible; that were to throw discredit on Him who spake it. Dare to believe that no word of his is vain. He descries eminence of attainment which it is possible for us all to reach: let us surrender ourselves to Him, that He may fulfil in us his ideal, and make us experts in the science of love.

It is a new commandment.—Archbishop Ussher on a memorable occasion called it the eleventh. It is recorded that having heard of the simplicity and beauty of the ordering of Rutherford's home, he resolved to visit it for himself. One Saturday night he arrived alone at the Manse, and asked for entertainment over the next day. A simple but hearty welcome was accorded him; and after partaking of the frugal fare, he was invited to join the household in religious exercises which ushered in the Lord's day.

"How many commandments are there?" the master asked his guest, wholly unaware who he was.

"Eleven," was the astonishing reply; at which the very servants were scandalised, regarding the new comer as a prodigy of ignorance. But the man of God perceived the rare light of character and insight which gleamed beneath the answer, and asked for a private interview. This issued in the invitation to preach on the following day. To the amazement of the household, so scandalised on the previous night, the stranger appeared in the master's pulpit, and announced as his text the words on which we are meditating, adding, "This may be described as the eleventh commandment."

Obedience to this fulfils the rest.—Love is the fulfilling of the law. Do we need to be told to have no other gods but God, to forbear taking his name in vain, and to devote one day in seven to the cultivation of a closer relationship with Him, if we love Him with all our soul and mind and strength? Do we need to be warned against killing our neighbour, stealing his goods, or bearing false witness against his character, if we love him as ourselves? Only let a man be filled with this Divine disposition which is the unique characteristic of God; let him be filled with the spirit of love; let him be perfected in love: and, almost unconsciously, he will not only be kept from infringing the prohibitions of the law of Sinai, but will be inspired to fulfil the requirements of the Mount of Beatitudes. Love, and do as you like. You will like to do only what God would like you to do.

There is a very important purpose to be realised in obeying this command.—"By this shall all men know that ye are my disciples, if ye have love one to another." Every Church claims to be the true representative of Christ—the Eastern, because it occupies the lands where Christianity was cradled; the Roman Catholic, because it professes to be able to trace its orders to the apostles. But, amid the hubbub of rivals claims, the world, unconvinced, still awaits the emergence of the true Bride of the Lamb. The one note of the true Church is Love. When once men of different nationalities and countries behold its manifestation, they do not hesitate to acknowledge the presence of God, and to admit that those who are animated by perfect love to Him and to one another constitute a unique organisation, which cannot have originated in the will or intellect of man, but, like the New Jerusalem, must have come out of heaven from God. So sublime, so transcendent, so unearthly is love, that its presence is significant of the handiwork of God as the fire that burned in the bush indicated that the "I AM" was there.

Love is the supreme test, not only of the Church, but of the individual. It has been the mistake of every age to make faith rather than love the test of Christianity—"Tell me how much a man believes, and I shall know how good a Christian he is!" The whole endeavour of the mediæval Church was to reduce the followers of Christ to a uniformity of belief. And in our own time, a man is permitted by consent to be of a grasping disposition, imperious in temper, uncharitable in speech, without losing position in the Church, so long as he assents to all the clauses of an orthodox creed.

With Christ, however, love is all-important. A man may have faith enough to remove mountains, but if he have not love, he is nothing, and lighter than vanity in the estimation of Heaven. Faith ranks with hope and love, but it is destined to pass as the blossoms of spring before the fruit of autumn, whilst love shall abide for evermore. A man may have a very inadequate creed; like the woman of old, he may think there is virtue in a garment; like Thomas, he may find it impossible to attain the exuberant confidence of his brethren; but if he loves Christ enough to be prepared to die for Him, if through the narrow aperture of a very limited faith love enough has entered his soul from the source of love, Christ will entrust him with the tending of his sheep and lambs, and call him into the secret place. Of course, the more full-orbed and intelligent our faith, the quicker and intenser will be our love. But faith, after all, is but the hand that takes, whilst love is the fellowship of kindred hearts that flash each on the other the enkindling gleam.

If you do not love, though you count yourself illumined with the light of perfect knowledge, you are in the dark. "He that hateth his brother is in the darkness, even until now."

If you do not love, you are dead. "He that loveth not, abideth in death." The light sparkle of intellectual or emotional life may illumine your words and fascinate your immediate circle of friends, but there will be no life towards God. *Love* is the perfect tense of *live*. Whoso does not love does not live, in the deepest sense. There are capacities for richer existence that never unfold until love stands at the portal and sounds his challenge, and summons the sleeper to awake and arise.

If you do not love, you are under the thrall of the devil, into whose dark nature love never comes. "In this the children of God are manifest and the children of the devil. Cain was of that wicked one, and slew his brother."

"As I have loved you." Life is one long education to know the love of God. "We have known and believed the love that God hath to us," is the reflection of an old man reviewing the past. Each stage of life, each phase of experience, is intended to give us a deeper insight into the love wherewith we are loved; and as each discovery breaks upon our glad vision, we are bidden to exemplify it to others. Does Jesus forgive to the seventy-seventh time? We must forgive in the same measure. Does Jesus forget as well as forgive? We, too, must forget after the same fashion. Does Jesus seek after the erring, and endeavour to induce the temper of mind that will crave forgiveness? We also must seek the man who has transgressed against us, endeavouring to lead him to a better mind. The Christian knows no law or limit but that imposed by these significant words, spoken on the eve of Christ's sacrifice: "As I have loved you."

Thus all life gives opportunities for the practice of this celestial temper and disposition. It has been said that talent develops in solitude, whilst character is made in the strain of life. Be it so. Then the character of loving may be made stronger by every association we have with our fellows. Each contact with men, women, and children may give us an opportunity of loving with a little more of the strength, purity, and sweetness of the love of Christ. The busiest life can find time for the cultivation of this spirit. That which is spent in a crowd will even have greater opportunities than the one which is limited to solitude. The distractions and engagements that threaten to break up our lives into a number of inconsiderable fragments may thus conduce to a higher unity than could be gained by following one occupation, or concentrating ourselves on one object.

Let us gird up the loins of our minds, and resolve to seek a baptism of love from the Holy Ghost, that we may be perfected in love; that we may love God first, and all else in Him; ascending from our failures to a more complete conformity to the love wherewith He has loved us; embracing the sinful and erring in the compass of our compassion, as we embrace the Divine and Eternal in the compass of our adoration and devotion.

39

HEAVEN DELAYED BUT GUARANTEED

*"Simon Peter said unto Him, Lord, whither goest Thou? Jesus
answered him, Whither I go, thou canst not follow Me now; but thou
shalt follow Me afterwards."*—JOHN xiii. 36.

THESE chapters are holy ground. The last words of our dearest,
spoken in the seclusion of the death-chamber to the tear-stained
group gathered around, are not for all the world, and are recorded
only for those whose love makes them able to appreciate. And what
are these words that now begin to flow from the Master's lips, but his
last to his own. They were held back so long as Judas was there.
There was a repression caused by his presence which hindered the
interchange of confidence; but, when he was gone, Love hastened to
her secret stores, and drew forth her choicest, rarest viands to share
them, that they might be in after days a strength and solace.

This marvellous discourse, which begins in chapter xiii. 31, con-
tinues through chapters xiv., xv., xvi., and closes in the sublime
prayer of chapter xvii. Better that all the literature of the world should
have shared the fate of the Alexandrian library, than that these
precious words should have been lost amid the fret of the ages.

The Lord commences his discourse by speaking of his speedy departure. "Little children," He said, using a term which indicated that
He felt towards them a parental tenderness, and spoke as a dying
father might have done to the helpless babes that gathered around his
bed, "I am to be with you for a very little time longer; the sand has
nearly run out in the hour-glass. I know you will seek Me; your love
will make you yearn to be with Me where I am, to continue the
blessed intimacy, the ties which within the last few weeks have been
drawn so much closer; but it will not be possible. As I said to the
Jews, so I must say to you, Whither I go, ye cannot come." He then
proceeds to give them a new commandment of love, as though He
said: "The *cannot* which prevents you following Me now is due to a
lack of perfect love on your part, as well as for other reasons; it is
necessary, therefore, that you wait to acquire it, ere you can be with
Me where I am."

Simon Peter hardly hears Him uttering these last words; he is
pondering too deeply what he has just heard, and calls the Master
back to that announcement, as though He had passed it with too light
a tread: "Going away! Lord, whither goest Thou?" To that question

our Lord might have given a direct answer: "Heaven! The Father's bosom! The New Jerusalem! The City of God!" Any of these would have been sufficient; but instead, He says in effect: "It is a matter of comparative indifference whither I go; I have no wish to feed curiosity with descriptions of things in the heavens, which you could not understand. The main point for you, in this brief life, is to become assimilated to Me in humility, devotion, likeness, and character, that you may be able to be my companion and friend in those new paths on which I am entering, as you have been in those which I am now leaving. 'Whither I go, thou canst not follow Me now; but thou shalt follow Me afterwards.'"

The words staggered Peter; he could not understand what Christ meant; he could not see how much had to be done before he could share in Christ's coming glory. He made the same mistake as James and John had made before, and wanted the throne, without perceiving that it was conditioned on fellowship in the cup and the baptism into death. With deep emotion he persisted in his inquiries: "Why cannot I follow Thee now? There is no place on earth to which I would not go with Thee. Have I not already left all to follow Thee? Have I not been with Thee on the Transfiguration Mount, as well as in thy journeyings? There is but one experience through which I have not passed with Thee, and that is death; but if that stands next in thy life-plan, I will lay down my life for thy sake. Anything to be with Thee."

How little Peter knew himself! How much better did Christ know him. "What! dost thou profess thyself willing to die with Me? Verily, verily, I say unto thee, thou shalt deny Me thrice, between now and cock-crow to-morrow morning." These words silenced Peter for all the evening afterwards. He does not appear to have made another remark, but was absorbed in heart-breaking grief; though all the while there rang in his heart those blessed words of hope: "Whither I go, thou canst not follow Me now; but thou shalt follow Me afterwards"—words which our Lord caught up and expanded for the comfort of them all; for now for the first time they realised that they were about to be parted from Jesus, and were almost beside themselves with grief: "Let not your heart be troubled . . ."

I. THE DESIRE TO BE WITH CHRIST.—This was paramount. These simple men had little thought of heaven as such. If Christ had begun to speak of golden pavement, gates of pearl, and walls of chrysolite, they would have turned from his glowing words with the one inquiry, "Wilt Thou be there?" If that question had been answered uncertainly, they would have turned away heart-sick, saying: "If Thou art not there, we have no desire for it; but if Thou wert in the darkest, dreariest spot in the universe, it would be heaven to us."

There were three desires, the strands of which were woven in this one yearning desire and prayer to be with Christ. They wanted his love, his teaching, his leading into full, richer life. And is not this our position also? We want Christ, not hereafter only, but here and now, for these three self-same reasons.

We want his love.—There is no love like his—so pure and constant and satisfying. What the sun is to a star, and the ocean to a pool left by the retiring tide, such is the love of Jesus compared with all other love. To have it is superlative blessedness; to miss it is to thirst for ever.

We want his light.—He speaks words that cast light on the mysteries of existence, on the dark problems of life, on the perplexing questions which are perpetually knocking at our doors.

We want his life.—Fuller and more abundant life is what we crave. It is of life that our veins are scant. We desire to have the mighty tides of Divine life always beating strongly within us, to know the energy, vigour, vitality of God's life in the soul. And we are conscious that this is to be found only in Him.

Therefore we desire to be with Him, to drink deeper into his fellowship, to know Him and the power of his resurrection, to be brought into an abidingness from which we shall never recede. We have known Christ after the flesh; we desire to know Him after the Spirit. We have known Him in humiliation; we want to know Him in his glory. We have known Him as the Lamb of the Cross; we want to know Him as the Divine Man on the throne.

II. The Fatal Obstacle to the Immediate Granting of these Desires.—"Thou canst not follow Me *now*." There is thus a difference in his words to his disciples, and those to the Jews. These also were told that they could not follow Him, but the word *now* was omitted. There was no hope held out to them of that great gulf being bridged. This was the *cannot* of moral incompatibility (John vii. 34; viii. 21); that, of temporary unfitness, which by the grace of God would finally pass away, and the whole of their aspirations be realised.

It is easy to see why Peter was unfit for the deeper realisation of Christ in his resurrection. Our Lord had just spoken of being glorified through death. It was as Judas left the chamber, intent on his betrayal, that Jesus said, "Now is the Son of Man glorified!" He saw that the hidden properties of his being could only be unfolded and uttered through death and resurrection. But Peter had little sympathy with this; he might avow his determination to die, but he had never really entered into the meaning of death, and all it might involve.

He could not detect evil. The traitor was beside him; but he had to ask the beloved disciple to elicit from Jesus who it might be by whom the Master would be betrayed.

He was out of sympathy with the Lord's humiliation, so that he reproved Him for stooping to wash his feet; and if he could not understand the significance and necessity of this lowly deed of love, how could he enter into the spirit of that life which was planted in death, and which bore even in resurrection the print of the nails?

He strove with the rest for the primacy. Who should be the greatest, was the question that agitated them, as the other evangelists tell us, in that solemn hour. And none that was possessed with that spirit of pride and emulation could be in harmony with that blessed world where the greatest are the lowliest, the highest the least, and the King set on the right hand of power, because more capable of humbling Himself than any beside.

But, besides all this, Peter was animated by the strong spirit of self-assertion and determination. On the lake shore he had always been able to get to the front by his stronger voice, and broader shoulders, and more vehement manner. Why should he not do the same now? Why could he not keep pace with Christ even through the dark valley, and accompany Him through unknown worlds?

It cannot be, said Christ; you are too strong in your carnal strength, too self-reliant, too confident. It is not possible for you to be with Me in the life that springs from death, and to which death is the door, till you have deeply drunk into the spirit of my death. You are too strong to follow Me when I descend to the lowest on my way to the highest; I must take for my companion now a forgiven malefactor; but I will some day come for you, and receive you to Myself.

So Peter had to be broken on the wheel of a servant-girl's question, and humbled to the dust. In those bitter hours he was thoroughly emptied of his old proud, self-reliant, vain-glorious spirit, and became as a little child.

This must be our path also. We must descend with Christ, if we would ascend to sit at his side. We must submit to the laying of our pride in the very dust. We must accept humiliations and mortifications, the humblings of perpetual failure and shortcoming, the friction and fret of infirmity and pain; and when we have come to an end of ourselves, we shall begin to know Christ in a new and deeper fashion. He will pass by and say, "Live!" The spirit of his life will enter into us; the valley of Achor will become a door of hope, and we shall sing God's glad new song of hope. The ideal which had long haunted us— in our blood, but unable to express itself—will burst into a perfect flower of exquisite scent and hue.

III. The Certainty of the Ultimate Gratification of every Desire God has Implanted.—This is an absolute certainty, that God inserts no desire or craving in our nature, for which there is no appropriate gratification. The birds do not seek for food which is not ready for them. The young lions do not ask for prey that is not awaiting them somewhere in the forest glade. Hence the absoluteness of that *shalt*—"Thou *shalt* follow Me afterwards." It is as if Jesus said, "I have taught you to love Me, and long after Me; and I will certainly gratify the appetite which I have created."

Pentecost was the Divine fulfilment of all those conditions of which we have been speaking. It was not enough that Peter should be an emptied and broken man; he must become also a God-possessed, a Spirit-filled man. Thus only could he be fitted to know Christ after a spiritual sort, and to participate in his Resurrection Life. It was surely to the Advent of the Holy Ghost that our Lord referred in that significant *afterwards*.

We too must seek our share in Pentecost. Do not be content with "Not I"; go on to say, "but Christ." Do not be satisfied with the emptying of the proud self-life; seek the infilling of the Holy Spirit. Do not stop at the cross, or the grave; hasten to the upper room, where the disciples are baptized in fire and glory. The Holy Spirit will enable you to abide in Christ, because He will bring Christ to abide in you; and life, through his dear grace, shall be so utterly imbued with fellowship with the Blessed Lord, that, whether present or absent, you will live together with Him. It is the man who is really filled with the Spirit of God who can follow Jesus, as Peter afterwards did, to prison and to death, who can drink of the cup of which He drank, and be baptized with the baptism with which He was baptized.

"Why should I fear?" asked Basil, of the Roman prefect. "Nothing you have spoken of has any effect upon me. He that hath nothing to lose is not afraid of *confiscation*. You cannot banish me, for the earth is the Lord's. As to *torture*, the first stroke would kill me; and *to kill me is to send me to glory*."

40

"MANY MANSIONS"

"I go to prepare a place for you."—JOHN xiv. 2.

THE CURE for heart-trouble, when the future is full of dread, is faith—faith directed to Jesus; and just such faith as we give God, for He is God. He has shown Himself well worthy of that trust; all his paths towards us have been mercy and truth; and we may therefore safely rest upon his disclosures of that blessed life, of which the present is the vestibule. "Let not your heart be troubled," He says; "ye believe in God, believe also in Me." Or it might be rendered, "Believe in God, believe also in Me."

Let us listen to Him, as He discourses of the Father's house, and its many mansions.

Heaven is a home.—"My Father's house." What magic power lies in that word! It will draw the wanderer from the ends of the earth; it will nerve the sailor, the soldier, and the explorer with indomitable endurance; it will bring a mist of tears to the eyes of the hardened criminal, and soften the heart of stone. When the bands played "Home, sweet Home," one night in the trenches of the Crimea, a great sob went right through the army.

But what constitutes *home?* Not the mere locality or building; but the dear ones that lived there once, but are scattered never to be re-united, and only one or two of whom are spared still. It was father's house, though it was only a shepherd's shieling; he dwelt there, and mother, and our brothers and sisters. And where they dwell, or where wife and child dwell, there is home.

Such is Heaven. Think of a large family of noble children, of all ages, from the little child to the young man beginning his business career, returning after long severance to spend a season together in the old ancestral home, situated in its far-reaching grounds, and you can form some idea of what it will be when the whole Family of the Redeemed gather in the Father's house. All reserve, all shyness, all restraint gone for ever. God has given us all the memory of what home was, that we may guess at what awaits us, and be smitten with homesickness. As the German proverb puts it: "Blessed are the homesick, for they shall reach home."

Heaven is very spacious.—There are "*many* mansions." There is no stint in its accommodation. In the olden Temple there were spacious courts, long corridors, and innumerable chambers, in which a vast multitude could find a home day and night. The children trooped about and sang around their favourite teacher. The blind and lame sheltered themselves from heat or storm. The priests and Levites in great numbers lived there. And this probably suggested the Master's words.

Heaven, too, will contain immense throngs, without being crowded. It will teem with innumerable hosts of angels, and multitudes of the redeemed which no man can number. Its children will be as the grains of sand that bar the ocean's waves, or the stars that begem the vault of night. But it can easily hold these, and myriads more. Yet there is room! As age after age has poured in its crowds, still the cry has gone forth, There is abundant room! The many mansions are not all tenanted. The orchestra is not full. The complement of priests is not complete.

Do not believe those little souls, who would make you imagine that Heaven is a little place for a select few. If they come to you with that story, tell them to begone! Tell them that they do not know your Father's heart; tell them that all He does must be worthy of Himself. Jesus shall see of the travail of his soul, and be satisfied.

Heaven is full of variety.—It is not like one great hall; there are myriads of adjacent rooms, "mansions," which will be fitted up, so to speak, differently. One for the sweet singer, another for the little ones and their teachers, another for the student of the deep mysteries of the Kingdom, another for those who may need further instruction in the mysteries of God.

Heaven's life and scenery are as various as the aptitudes and capacities of souls. Its music is not a monotone, but a chorale. It is as a home, where the parents delight to develop the special tastes of their children. This is surely what Jesus meant when He said, "I go to prepare a place for you." He is ever studying our special idiosyncrasies —what we need most, and can do best; and when He has ascertained it, He suits our mansion accordingly.

When a gardener is about to receive some rare exotic, he prepares a place where it will flower and fruit to the best advantage. The naturalist who is notified of the shipment of some new specimen, prepares a habitat as suited as possible to its peculiarities. The mother whose son is returning from sea, prepares a room in which his favourite books and pictures are carefully placed, and all else that her pondering heart can devise to give him pleasure. So, our Lord is anxious to give what is best in us its most suitable nourishment and training. And He will keep our place against our coming. It will not suit another, and will not be given to another.

That all this will be so, is witnessed by the instincts of our hearts; and if it had not been so, He would have told us. That little clause is inimitably beautiful; it seems to teach that where He permits his children to cherish some natural presentiment of the blessed future—its solemn troops and sweet societies; its friendships, recognitions, and fellowships; its holy service and special opportunities—He really assents to our deepest and most cherished thoughts. If it had not been so, He would have told us.

The charm of Heaven will be the Lord's presence.—"Where I am, ye shall be also." We shall see his face, and be for ever with Him. What would not men give, if some old MSS. might turn up with new stories of his wondrous life, new parables as charming as those of the Good Shepherd and the Prodigal Son, new beatitudes, new discourses like that on the Vine. God might have permitted this. But what would it be in comparison with all that lies before! The past has lost much; but the future holds infinitely more. We shall see new Gospels enacted before our eyes, behold Christ as a real visible person in the glory of Divine manhood, hear Him speak to us as his friends, and know what He meant when He promised to gird Himself and come forth to serve his servants.

If you are in doubt as to what Heaven is like, is it not enough to know that it will be in accord with the nature and presence and choice of Jesus Christ?

After his resurrection, He spent forty days among his disciples, that men might see what the risen life was like. As He was, and is, so shall we be. His body is the pattern in accordance with which ours shall be fashioned. What He was to his friends after his resurrection, we shall be to ours, and they to us. We shall hear the familiar voices and the dear old names, shall resume the dear relationships which death severed, and shall speak again of the holy secrets of our hearts with those who were our twin-spirits.

And He will come again, either in our death-hour, or in his Second Advent, "to receive us" to Himself. If we only could believe this, and trust Him who says it, our hearts would not be troubled, though death itself menaced us; for we should realise that, to be received at the moment of dissolution by the hands of Jesus, into the place on which He has lavished time and thought and love, must be "far better" than the best that earth could offer.

The Reality of which Jacob's Dream was the Shadow

"Jesus saith unto him, I am the way, the truth, and the life: no man cometh unto the Father, but by Me."—JOHN xiv. 6.

WE ALL know more truth than we give ourselves credit for. A moment before the Lord had said, "Whither I go ye know, and the way ye know." Thomas the pessimist—always inclined to look at the dark side of things—directly contradicted Him, saying, "master, we are absolutely ignorant of the goal to which thy steps are bending; it is impossible, therefore, for us to know the path that lies through the gloom, and by which Thou art to come to it." This was a strange collision—the Master's "Ye know," and Thomas's "We know not." Which was right?

There is no doubt that Jesus was right, and that they did know. In many a discourse He had given sufficient materials for them to construct a true conception of the Father's house, and the way to it. These materials were lying in some dusty corner of their memory, unused, and Christ knew this. He said, therefore, in effect, "Go back to the teachings I have given you; look carefully through the inventory of your knowledge; let your instincts, illumined by my words, supply the information you need: there are torches in your souls already lighted, that will cast a radiant glow upon the mysteries to the brink of which you have come."

This is true of us all. Christ never conducts to experiences for which He has not previously prepared us. As the great ocean-steamers take in their stores of coal and provisions, day and night, for weeks previous to their sailing; so, by insensible influences, Christ is ever anticipating the strain and stress of coming circumstance, passing in words which are spirit and life, though they may stand in their heavy packing-cases in the hold, until we are driven to unpack, examine, and use their contents. Not seldom sorrow is sent for no other purpose than to compel us to take cognisance of our possessions. Many a fabric of manufacture, many an article of diet, many an ingenious process has been suggested in days of scarcity and famine. So, old words and truths come back in our sore need. Christ often speaks to us, as a teacher to a nervous child, saying, "You know quite well, if you would only think a little." More truth is stored in memory than recollection can readily lay hands upon.

Thomas persisted in his protestations of ignorance, and so the

213

Lord uttered for his further information the royal sentence, which sums up Christianity in the one simple pronoun "I." It was as if He said to his disciples gathered there, and to his Church in all ages, "To have Me, to know Me, to love and obey Me, this is religion; this is the light for every dark hour, the solution for all the mysteries." Christianity is more than a creed, a doctrinal system, a code of rules—it is Christ.

I. CHRIST AS THE WAY.—"I am the Way," said our Lord. The conception of life as a pilgrimage is as old as human speech. On the third page of our Bibles we are told that "Enoch walked with God." The path of the Israelites through the desert was a pilgrim's progress, and the enduring metaphor for our passage from the cross to the Sabbathkeeping. Isaiah anticipated the rearing up of a highway which should be called the way of holiness, which should not be trodden by the unclean; no lion should be there, or ravenous beast go up thereon; but the ransomed of the Lord should walk there, and go with singing to Zion. But in the furthest flights of inspired imagination, the prophet never dreamt that God Himself would stoop to become the trodden path to Himself, and that the way of holiness was no other than that Divine Servant who so often stood before him for portrayal. "*I* am the Way," said Christ.

He fulfils all the conditions of Isaiah's prediction. He saw a highway.

A highway is for all: for kings and commoners; for the nobleman daintily picking his way, and the beggar painfully plodding with bare feet. And Jesus is for every man. "Whosoever will, let him come"; let him step out and walk; let him commit himself to Him who comes to our doors that He may conduct us to the pearly gate.

It was a way of holiness, where no unclean or leprous person was permitted to travel. Neither can we avail ourselves of the gracious help of Christ, so long as we are harbouring what He disapproves, or doing what He forbids.

It was plain and straight, so that wayfaring men though fools could not mistake it. And the Master said, that whilst the wise and prudent might miss his salvation, babes would find it. "Hidden from the wise and prudent, but revealed to babes."

It afforded perfect immunity from harm. The wild beasts of the forest might roar around it, but they were kept off that thoroughfare by an invisible and impassable fence. Who is he that can harm us whilst we follow that which is good? The special Divine permission was necessary before Satan could tempt Job, whose heart was perfect with his God.

It was trodden with song. And who can describe the waves of joy that sometimes roll in on the believing, loving soul! There is always

peace, but sometimes there is joy unspeakable and full of glory. The
hands of Jesus shed the oil of gladness on our heads, whilst the lamen-
tation and regret that haunt the lives of others are abashed, as the
spectres of the night before the roseate touch of morn.

What further thought did Christ mean to convey, when He said, "I
am the Way"? We cannot see the other side of the moon: so the full
import of these words, as they touch his wonderful nature, as it lies
between Him and his Father, is beyond us; but we may at least study
the face they turn towards our lives.

The true value of a way is never realised until we are following it
through an unknown country, or groping along it in almost absolute
darkness. I remember, during a tour in Switzerland, on starting for a
long day's march, the comfort of the assurance that I had to keep to
one road which was clearly defined, and it would inevitably bring me
to my destination. How different this from another experience of
making my way, as I might, across the hill-sides in the direction which
I fancied was the right one! All that had to be done in the first
instance was to follow the roadway, to obey its sinuous windings, to
climb the hills where it climbed, to descend the valleys where it
descended, to cross the rivers and torrents at the precise point with it.
It seemed responsible for me as long as I kept to it. Whenever I
thought to better myself by wandering right or left, I found myself
landed in some difficulty, and when I returned to it, it seemed to say,
"Why did you leave me? I know that sometimes I am rough and
difficult; but I can do better for you than you can for yourself, and
indeed I am the only possible way. Obey me, and I will bring you
home." It is so that Christ speaks to us.

Each day, as we leave our home, we know that the prepared path
lies before us, in the good works which God has prepared for us to
walk in. And when we are ignorant of their direction, and are at a loss
as to where to place our steps, we have only to concern ourselves with
Christ, and almost unconsciously we shall find ourselves making progress in the destined way. Christ is the Way: love Christ, trust
Christ, obey Christ, be concerned with Christ, and all else will be
added. Christ is the Way. When the heart is wrapt up in Him, it is on
the way, and it is making progress, although it never counts the rate
or distance, so occupied is it with Him.

"I fear I make no progress," sighs the timid soul.

"But what is Christ to thee?"

"Everything."

"Then if He be all in all to thee, thou art most certainly on God's
way; and thou art making progress towards thy home, albeit that it is
unconsciously. Be of good cheer, Christ is the Way; remember the
ancient pilgrims, of whom it is written that the way was in their
hearts."

"But God the Father is so little to me!"

"But to deal with Christ is to deal with God: to be wrapt up in the love of Christ is to make ever deeper discoveries into the heart of God. He is the Way to God: to know Him is to come to the Father."

II. CHRIST AS THE TRUTH.—The thought grows deeper as we advance. Obedience to the Way conducts to the vision of the Truth; ethics to spiritual optics. The truth-seeker must first submit himself in all humility and obedience to Christ; and when he is willing to do his will, he is permitted to know.

Christ is more than a teacher. "We know that Thou art a Teacher come from God," said Nicodemus. He is more, He is the Truth of God. All truth is ensphered in Him. All the mysteries of wisdom and knowledge are hidden in Him. We fully know truth only as it is in Jesus. When the Spirit of Truth would lead us into all truth, He can do nothing better than take of the things of Christ, and reveal them to us, because to know Christ is to know the truth in its most complete, most convenient, and most accessible form. If you know Christ intimately and fully, even if you know nothing else, you will know the truth, and the truth will make you free. If you love truth, and are a child of the truth, you will be inevitably attracted to Christ, and recognise the truth that speaks through his glorious nature. "He that is of the truth heareth my voice."

Distinguish between Christ the Truth, and truth about Him. Many true things may be said about Him; but we are not saved by truths about Him, but by Himself, the Truth.

Not the indubitable fact that Jesus died; but the Person of Him who died and lives for evermore.

Not the certain fact that Jesus lay in the grave; but the blessed Man Himself, who lay there for me.

Not the incontestable facts of his resurrection and ascension; but that He has borne my nature to the midst of the Throne, and has achieved a victory which helps me in my daily struggle.

This is the ground basis of all true saving faith. The soul may accept truths about Christ, as it would any well authenticated historical facts; but it is not materially benefited or saved until it has come to rest on the bosom of Him of whom these facts are recorded.

To know Christ as Truth demands truth in heart and life. The insincere man; the trifler; the flippant jester, who takes nothing seriously; the superficial man, who uses the deepest expressions as counters for society talk; the inconsistent man, who is daily doing violence to his convictions by permitting things which his conscience condemns—must stand for ever on the outskirts of the Temple of Truth: they have no right to stand before the King of Truth. If you have never discerned the truth as it is in Jesus, it becomes a serious question whether you are perfectly true, or whether you are not, like Pilate, harbouring insincerity in your heart, which blinds your eyes to His ineffable attributes.

Concern yourself with Christ. Be content to let the world and its wisdom alone. "The wisdom of this world is foolishness with God . . . He taketh the wise in their own craftiness." Give yourself to know Christ, who is made unto us wisdom, as well as sanctification and redemption. To know Him is to be at the fountain-head of all truth; and the soul which has dwelt with Him by day and night will find itself not only inspired by an undying love for the truth, but able to hold fellowship with truth-lovers and truth-seekers everywhere; nay, will be able even to instruct those who have the reputation of great learning and knowledge in the schools of human thought. "I have more understanding than all my teachers; for thy testimonies are my meditation. I understand more than the aged, because I have kept thy precepts." To know and to possess Christ is to have the Word, that is the Wisdom of God, enshrined as a most sacred possession in the heart.

III. CHRIST AS THE LIFE.—It is not enough to know: we need life. Life is, indeed, the gate to knowledge. "This is life eternal, that they should know Thee." It was imperative, therefore, that Jesus should become a source of life to men, that they might know the Truth, and be able to walk in the Way; and more especially since death had infected and exhausted all the springs of the world's vitality.

It was into a world of death that the Son of God came. The spring of life in our first parents had become tainted at its source. At the best Adam was only a living soul. Dead—dead—dead in trespasses and sins; such was the Divine verdict, such the course of this world. Earth resembled the valley in the prophet's vision, full of bones, very many and very dry. All the reservoirs of life were spent; its fountains had died away in wastes of sand.

Then the Son of God brought life from the eternal Throne, from God Himself; and became a Life-giving Spirit. His words were spirit and life: He was Himself the Resurrection and the Life: those that believed in Him became partakers of the Divine Nature. The tree of life was again planted in the earth's soil, when Jesus became incarnate. "I give eternal life unto my sheep," He said, "and they shall never perish." "He that believeth on the Son hath eternal life."

If, then, you are wanting life, and life more abundantly, you must have Christ. Do not seek *it*, but *Him*: not the stream, but the fountain; not the word, but the speaker; not the fruit, but the tree. He is the Life and Light of men.

And if you have Christ, you have life. You may not be competent to define or analyse it; you may not be able to specify the place or time when it first broke into your soul; you may hardly be able to distinguish it from the workings of your own life: but if you have Christ, trust Christ, desire Christ above all, you have the Life. "He that hath the Son hath the Life; he that hath not the Son of God hath not the Life." "We know Him that it true, and we are in Him that is true . . . this is eternal life." "I," said Jesus, "am the Way, the Truth, and the Life."

42

Christ Revealing the Father

*"Philip saith unto Him, Lord, show us the Father and it sufficeth us.
Jesus saith unto him, He that hath seen Me hath seen the Father."*
JOHN xiv. 8, 9.

THE LONGING of the universal heart of man was voiced by Philip,
when he broke in, rather abruptly, on our Lord's discourse with the
challenge that He should answer all questions, dissipate all doubt, by
showing them the Father. Is there a God? How can I be sure that
He is? What does He feel towards us? These are questions which
men persistently ask, and wait for the reply. And the Master gave
the only satisfactory answer that has ever been uttered in the hearing
of mankind, when He said in effect, "The knowledge of God must be
conveyed, not in words or books, in symbols or types, but in a life.
To know Me, to believe in Me, to come into contact with Me, is to
know the deepest heart of God. He that hath seen Me hath seen the
Father; how sayest thou then, 'Show us the Father'?"

I. PHILIP'S INQUIRY.—*It bore witness to the possible growth of the
human soul.* Only three short years before, as we are told in the first
chapter of this Gospel, Christ had found him. At that time he was
probably much as the young men of his age and standing. Not
specially remarkable save for an interest in, and an earnestness about,
the advent of the Messiah; his views, however, of His person and
work were limited and narrow: he looked for his advent as the time
for the re-establishment of the kingdom of David, and deliverance
from the Roman yoke. But three years of fellowship with Jesus had
made a wonderful difference in this young disciple. The deepest
mysteries of life and death and heaven seemed within his reach.
He is not now content with beholding the Messiah; he is eager to
know the Father, and to stand within the inner circle of his presence-
chamber.

The highest watermark ever touched by the great soul of Moses
was when he said, amid the sublimities of Sinai, "I beseech Thee, show
me thy glory." But in this aspiration Philip stands beside him. There
is a close kinship between the mighty lawgiver and the fisherman of
Bethsaida. How little there is to choose between, "Show me thy
glory," and "Show us the Father." Great and marvellous is the
capacity of the soul for growth!

It truly interpreted the need of man.—"It sufficeth us." From nature, with all her voices that speak of God's power and Godhead; from the page of history, indented with the print of God's footprints; from type and ceremony and temple, though instituted by God Himself; even from the unrivalled beauty of our Saviour's earthly life—these men turned unsatisfied, unfilled, and said, "We are not yet content; but if Thou wouldest show us the Father, we should be."

And would it not suffice *us*? Would it not be sufficient to give new zest and reality to *prayer*, if we could realise that it might be as familiar as the talk of home, or like the petitioning of a little child? Would it not suffice to make the most irksome *work* pleasant, if we could look up and discern the Father's good pleasure and smile of approval? Would it not suffice to rob *pain* of its sting, if we could detect the Father's hands adjusting the heat of the furnace? Would it not suffice to shed a light across the dark mystery of *death*, if we felt that the Father was waiting to lead us through the shadows to Himself? How often the cry rises from sad and almost despairing hearts, "Show us the Father, and it sufficeth us."

But surely this request was based on a mistake.—Philip wanted a visible theophany, like that which Moses beheld, when the majestic procession swept down the mountain pass; or as the elders saw, when they beheld the paved sapphire work; or after the fashion of the visions vouchsafed to Elijah, Isaiah, or Ezekiel. He wanted to see the Father. But how can you make wisdom, or love, or purity visible, save in a human life?

Yet this is the mistake we are all liable to make. We feel that there must be an experience, a vision, a burst of light, a sensible manifestation, before we can know the Father. We strain after some unique and extraordinary presentation of the Deity, especially in the aspect of Fatherhood, before we can be completely satisfied, and thus we miss the lesson of the present hour. Philip was so absorbed in his quest for the transcendent and sublime, that he missed the revelations of the Father which for three years had been passing under his eyes. God had been manifesting his tenderest and most characteristic attributes by the beauty of the Master's life, but Philip had failed to discern them; till now the Master bids him go back on the photographs of those years, as fixed in his memory, to see in a thousand tiny illustrations how truly the Father dwelt in Him, and lived through his every word and work.

Are you straining after the vision of God, startled by every footstep, intently listening till the very atmosphere shall become audible, expecting an overwhelming spectacle? In all likelihood you will miss all. The kingdom comes not with outward show. When men expected Christ to come by the front door, He stole in at the back. Whilst Philip was waiting for the Father to be shown in thunder and lightning, in startling splendour, in the stately majesty that might become the Highest, he missed the daily unfolding of the Divine Nature that was being afforded in the Life with which he dwelt in daily contact.

Philip's request emphasised the urgent need of the ministry of the Holy Spirit.—"If ye had known Me . . ." the Saviour said. "Have I been so long time with you, and yet hast thou not known Me?" They failed to know the Father, because they failed to know Christ; and they failed in this because they knew Him only after the flesh. They were so familiar with Him as their Friend, his love was so natural, tender, and human, He had become so closely identified with all their daily existence, that they did not recognise the fire that shone behind the porcelain, the Deity that tabernacled beneath the frail curtains.

Often those who dwell amid the loveliest or grandest scenery miss the beauty which is unveiled to strangers from a distance. Certain lives have to be withdrawn from us before we understand how fair they were, and how much to us. And Jesus had to leave his disciples before they could properly appreciate Him. The Holy Spirit must needs take of the things of Christ, and reveal them, before his followers could realise their true significance, symmetry, and beauty.

Two things are needful, then: first, we must know Christ through the teaching of the Holy Ghost; and next, we must receive Him into our hearts, that we may know Him, as we know the workings of our own hearts. Each knows himself, and could recognise the mint-mark of his own individuality; so when Christ has become resident within us, and has taken the place of our self-life, we know Him as we know ourselves. "What man knoweth the things of man save the spirit of man which is in him?—but we have the mind of Christ."

II. THE LORD'S REPLY.—"He that hath seen Me hath seen the Father."

He did not rebuke the request, as unfit to proffer, or impossible to satisfy. He took it for granted that such a desire would exist in the heart, and that his disciples would always want to be led by Him into the Father's presence. In this his ministry resembled that of the great forerunner, who led his disciples into the presence of the Bridegroom, content to decrease if only He might increase. The Master's answer was, however, widely different from John's. The forerunner pointed to Jesus as He walked, and said, "Behold the Lamb of God"; Jesus pointed to Himself, and said, "I and my Father are One; to have seen Me is to have seen the Father; to have Me is to possess the Father."

It troubled the Lord greatly that He had been so long time with them, and yet they had not known Him; that they had not realised the source of his words and works; that they had concentrated their thought on Him, instead of passing, as He meant them to do, from the stream to the source, from the seal to the die, from the beam of the Divine glory to its Sun. He bade them, therefore, from that moment realise that they knew and had seen the Father in knowing and seeing Himself. Not more surely had the Shekinah dwelt in the tabernacle of old, than it indwelt his nature, though too thickly shrouded to be seen by ordinary and casual eyes.

Let us get help from this. Many complain that they know Christ, pray to Christ, are conscious of Christ, but that the Father is far away and impalpable. They are therefore straining after some new vision or experience of God, and undervaluing the religious life to which they have already attained. It is a profound mistake. To have Jesus is to have God; to know Jesus is to know God; to pray to Jesus is to pray to God. Jesus is God manifest in the flesh. Look up to Him even now from this printed page, and say, "My Lord and my God."

Jesus is not simply an incarnation of God in the sense in which, after the fashion of the Greek mythology, gods might come down in the likeness of men, adopting a disguise which they would afterwards cast aside; Jesus *is* God. All the gentle attributes of his nature are God's; and all the strong and awful attributes of power, justice, purity, which we are wont to associate with God, are his also.

Happy is the moment when we awake to realise that in Jesus we have God manifest and present; to know this is the revelation of the Father by the Son, of which our Saviour spoke in Matt. xi. 27.

III. A GLIMPSE INTO THE LORD'S INNER LIFE.—This Gospel is the most lucid and profound treatise in existence on his inner life. It is the revelation of the principles on which our Saviour lived.

So absolutely had He emptied Himself that He never spake his own words: "The words that I speak unto you, I speak not of Myself." He never did his own works: "My Father worketh hitherto, and I work. . . . The Father abiding in Me doeth his works." This was the result of that marvellous self-emptying of which the Apostle speaks. Our Lord speaks as though, in his human nature, He had a choice and will of his own. "Not my will, but thine be done," was his prayer. Perhaps it was to this holy and divine personality that Satan made appeal in the first temptation, bidding Him use his powers for the satisfaction of his hunger, and in independence of his Father's appointment. But however much of this independence was within our Lord's reach, He deliberately laid it aside. Before He spoke, his spirit opened itself to the Father, that He might speak by his lips; before He acted, He stilled the promptings of his own wisdom, and lifted Himself into the presence of the Father, to ascertain what He was doing, and to receive the inflow of his energy (John v. 19; xii. 44, 49).

These are great mysteries, which will engage our further consideration. In the meanwhile, let us reason that if our Lord was so careful to subordinate Himself to the Father that He might be all in all, it well becomes us to restrain ourselves, to abstain from speaking our own words or doing our own works, that Jesus may pour his energies through our being, and that those searching words may be fulfilled in us also, "Striving according to his working, which worketh in me mightily."

43

THE GREAT DEEDS OF FAITH

"Verily, verily, I say unto you, He that believeth on Me, the works that I do shall he do also; and greater works than these shall he do; because I go unto my Father."—JOHN xiv. 12.

WHENEVER our Lord was about to say something unusually important, He introduced it by the significant expression, *"Verily, verily"*; or, as it is in the original, "Amen, amen, I say unto you." The words well become his lips, who in the Book of Revelation is called "the Amen, the Faithful and True Witness." They are really our Lord's most solemn affirmation of the truth of what He was about to utter, as well as an indication that something of importance was about to be revealed.

Indeed, it was necessary in the present case that the marvellous announcement of the text should receive unusual confirmation, because of its wide extent. If our Lord had ascribed this power of doing greater works than He achieved in his earthly life, to apostle, prophet, or illustrious saint, we should have required no special assurance of its deliberate truth; but to learn that powers so transcendent are within the reach of any ordinary believer, to learn that anyone who believes may outdo the miracles on the outskirts of Nain and at the tomb of Bethany, is as startling as it is comforting. There is no reason why the humblest soul that ponders this page should not become the medium and vehicle through which the Christ of the glory shall not surpass the Christ of Galilee, Jerusalem, and Judea.

The best method of treating these words is to take them clause by clause as they stand.

I. THE FIRST NOTE IS FAITH.—"He that believeth on Me." Three varieties of faith are alluded to in the context. Faith in his works: "Believe the works." Faith in his words: "Believe Me." Faith in Himself, as here. In the Greek the preposition translated *in,* would be better rendered *into,* as though the believer was ever approaching the heart of Christ in deeper, warmer, closer fellowship; perpetual motion *towards,* combined with unbroken rest *in.* Each of these three forms of faith plays an important part in the Christian life.

Arrested by the works of Christ—his irresistible power over nature, his tender pity for those who sought his aid, the blessed and far-reaching results of his miracles—we cry with Nicodemus, "Verily, this is a Teacher come from God; for none can do such miracles, except God be with Him." The Master perpetually appealed to the witness borne by his works to his Divine mission; as when He said, "If I had not done among them the works which none other did, they had not had sin; but now have they both seen and hated both Me and my Father." And again, "The very works that I do bear witness of Me." But at the best the works of Christ are only like the great bell ringing in the church-tower calling attention to the life being unfolded within, and are not calculated to induce the faith to which the greater works are possible.

Next we come to the words of Christ. They are spirit and life: they greatly feed the soul. He speaks as none other has ever spoken of the mysteries of life, death, God, and eternity. It is through the words that we come to the Speaker. By feeding on them we are led into vital union with Himself. But his words, as such, and apart from Him, will not produce works that shall surpass those He wrought in his earthly ministry.

Therefore from works and words we come to the Lord Himself with a trust which passes up beyond the lower ranges of faith; which does not simply receive what He waits to give, or reckon upon his faithfulness, but which unites us in indissoluble union with Himself. This is the highest function of faith; it is *unitive*: it welds us in living union with our Lord, so that we are one with Him, as He is one with God.

We are in Him in the Divine purpose which chose us in Him before the foundation of the world; grafted into Him in his cross; partaking of a common life with Him through the regeneration of the Holy Ghost. But all these become operative in the union wrought by a living faith; so that the strongest assertions which Jesus made of the close relationship between his Father and Himself become the current coin of holy speech, as they precisely describe the union which subsists between us and Jesus. The living Saviour has sent us, and we live by the Saviour. The words we speak are not from ourselves; but the Saviour within us, He doeth his works. We are in Him, and He in us; all ours are his, and his ours.

Stay, reader, and ask thyself whether thou hast this faith which incorporates thee with the Man who died for thee on the cross, and now occupies the Throne—the last Adam who has become a life-giving Spirit.

II. A TRUE FAITH ALWAYS WORKS.—"He that believeth on Me, the works that I do shall he do also."

There are many counterfeits of faith in the world. Electroplate! veneer! They will inevitably fail in the supreme test, if not before. The Apostle James especially calls attention to the distinction between a living and a dead faith. It becomes us to be on our guard.

H

The test of genuine faith is twofold. In the *first* place, a genuine, living faith has Christ for its object. The hand may tremble, but it touches his garment's hem; the eye may be dimmed by doubt, but it is directed towards his face; the feet may stumble, but as the fainting pilgrim staggers onward this is his repeated cry, "Thou, O Christ, art all I want."

In the *second* place, a true faith works. Its works approve its nature, and show that it has reached the heart of Christ, and has become the channel through which his life-forces pour into the soul. Jacob knew that Joseph was alive and that his sons had opened communications with him, because of the waggons that he sent; and we may know that Jesus lives beyond the mist of time, and that our faith has genuinely connected us with Him, because we feel the pulse of his glorious nature within our own. And when this is so, we cannot but work out what He is working within.

Do you ask me why a true faith must work? Ask why the branch can do no other than bear clusters of juicy grapes; its difficulty would be to abstain from bearing; the vitality of the root accounts for its life and productiveness. Blame the lark, whose nature vibrates in the sunshine, for pouring from its small throat volumes of sound; blame the child, full of bounding health, for laughing, singing, and leaping; blame the musician, whose soul has caught some fragments of the music of eternity, for pouring it forth in song—before you wonder why it is that the true faith which has opened the way from the believer to his Lord produces those greater works.

III. THERE ARE TWO KINDS OF WORK INDICATED.—(I) "*The works that I do shall he do also.*"—What a blessing Christ's ministry must have been to thousands of sufferers! He passed through Galilee as a river of water of life. In front of Him were deserts of fever blasted by the sirocco, and malarious swamps of ague and palsy, and the mirage of the sufferer's deferred hope; but after He had passed, the parched ground became a pool and the thirsty land springs of water, the eyes of the blind were opened and the ears of the deaf unstopped, the lame man leapt as a hart and the tongue of the dumb sang.

How glad the sick of any district must have been when it was rumoured that He was on his way to it! What eager consultations must have been held as to the best means of conveying them into his presence! What sleepless nights must have been spent in speculation as to whether, and how, He would heal!

Such results followed the labours of the apostles. The lame man at the beautiful gate of the Temple; the palsied Æneas; the dead Dorcas; the crowds in the streets overshadowed by Peter's passing figure; the miracles wrought by Paul at Paphos, Lystra, Philippi, and Malta—all attested the truth of the Master's words, "The works that I do shall he do also." There is no doubt that, if it were necessary, such miracles might be repeated, if only the Church exercised the same faith as in those early days of her ministry to the world. But there are greater works than these.

(2) *"Greater works than these shall he do."*—The soul is greater than the body, as the jewel than the casket. All work, therefore, which produces as great an effect on the soul-life as miracles, on the physical life, must be proportionately greater, as the tenant is greater than the house, as the immortal than the mortal. It is a greater work to give sight to the blind soul than to the blind body; to raise the soul from its grave than Lazarus from his four days' sleep.

Again, eternity is also greater than time, as the ocean is greater than a creek. The ills from which the miracles of Christ delivered the suppliant crowds were at the most limited by years. The flesh of the leper became wrinkled with old age; Jairus' daughter fell again on sleep; the generation which had been benefited by the mighty works passed away without handing on a legacy of health to succeeding time! But if a sinner is turned from the error of his ways, if salvation comes to a nature destined for immortality, and lifts it from the slough of sin to the light of God, the results must be greater because more permanent and far-reaching.

Moreover, the pain from which the word of the Gospel may save is infinitely greater than that which disease could inflict. Men have been known to brave any physical torture rather than endure the insupportable anguish of a sin-laden conscience. The worm that never dies is more intolerable than cancer; the fire that is never quenched keener than that of fever. To save a soul from these is, therefore, a greater work.

Christ hinted at this distinction in one of his earliest miracles, when He proposed to forgive the sick of the palsy his sins, before bidding him walk; and bade the seventy rejoice more that their names were written in heaven than that the devils were subject to them. The apostles bear witness to a growing appreciation of this distinction, by the small space given in the Acts of the Apostles to their miracles, compared with the greater attention concentrated on their discourses; and surely the history of Christendom bears witness to the great and permanent character of spiritual work. The Church could not have influenced the world as she has done, had she been nothing more than a healer of diseases and an exorciser of demons.

IV. The Source of these greater Works.—"Because I go to the Father." Clearly the Church has had an argument to present to men which even her Master could not use. He could not point, except indefinitely, to the cross, its flowing blood, its testimony to a love which the cold waters of death could not stanch. Through the ages this has been the master-motive, the supreme argument.

Then, again, the Master could not count as we can upon the co-operation of the Spirit in his convicting power. "When He is come, He will convict the world of sin"; but He did not come till after that brief career of public ministry had closed. Speaking reverently, we may say that the Church has an Ally that even her Master had not.

But the main reason is yet to come. Perhaps an illustration will best explain it. Supposing the great painter, Raphael, were to infuse his transcendent power, as he possessed it during his mortal life, into some young brain, there is no reason why the genius of the immortal painter should not effect, through a mere tyro in art, results in form and colour as marvellous as those which he bequeathed to coming time. But suppose, further, that after having been three hundred years amid the tones, forms, and colours of the heavenly world, he could return, and express his thoughts and conceptions through some human medium, would not these later productions be greater works than those which men cherish as a priceless legacy? So if the Lord were to work in us such works only as He did before He ascended to his glory, they would be inferior to those which He can produce, now that He has entered into his glorified state, and has reassumed the power of which He emptied Himself when He stooped to become incarnate. This is what He meant when He said, "Because I go unto the Father."

Open your hearts to the living, risen, glorified Saviour. Let Him live freely in your life, and work unhindered through your faith; expect Him to pour through you as a channel some of those greater works which must characterize the closing years of the present age. Remember how the discourses and miracles of his earthly life ever increased in importance and meaning; for such must be the law of his ministry in the heavenlies. According to our faith it will be unto us. The results which we see around us are no measure of what Christ would or could do; they indicate the straitening effect of our unbelief. Lift up your heads, O ye gates, and be ye lifted up, ye low-browed doors of unbelief; and the King of Glory shall come in with his bright and mighty retinue, and shall go out through human lives to do greater works by the instrumentality of his people than ever He wrought in the course of his earthly ministry.

44

How to Secure More and Better Prayer

*"And I will pray the Father, and He shall give you another Comforter,
that He may abide with you for ever."*—John xiv. 16.

The great lack of our life is that we do not pray more. And there is
no failure so disastrous or criminal as this. It is very difficult to account
for it. If in all times of discouragement and vicissitude we could have
access to one of the wisest and noblest of our fellow-creatures, or to
some venerated departed saint, or to the guardian angel deputed to
attend our steps, or to the archangel that presides as viceregent over
this system of worlds, how strong and brave we should become! Whatever our need, we would at once seek his august presence, and obtain
his counsel and assistance. How extraordinary is our behaviour then
with respect to prayer, and that we make so little of our opportunities
of access into the presence of our Father, in whom wisdom, power, and
love blend perfectly, and who is always willing to hear us—nay, is
perpetually urging us to come!

The reason may lie in the very commonness of our opportunities.
The swing-door of prayer stands always waiting for the least touch of
faith to press it back. If our Father's presence-chamber were opened
to us only once a year, with how much greater reverence would we
enter it, how much more store would we set on it! We should anticipate for the whole year the honour and privilege of that interview, and
eagerly avail ourselves of it. Alas, that familiarity with prayer does
not always increase our appreciation of its magnificence!

The cause of our apathy is probably also to be sought in the effort
which is required to bring our sensuous and earth-bound natures into
true union with the Spirit of God. True prayer is labour. Epaphras
laboured in his intercessions. Our feet shrink from the steep pathway
that climbs those heights; our lungs do not readily accustom themselves
to the rare air that breathes around the summit of the Mount of
Communion.

But there is a deeper reason yet: we have not fully learnt or obeyed
the laws and conditions of prayer. Until they are apprehended and
complied with, it is not possible for us to pray as we might. They are
not, however, very recondite. The least advanced in the Divine school
may read them on this page, where Christ unbares the deepest philosophy of devotion in the simplest phrases.

It is evident that He expected that the age which Pentecost was to
inaugurate, and to which He so frequently refers as "in that day,"

would in a special sense be the age of prayer. Mark how frequently in this last discourse He refers to it (xiv. 13, 14; xv. 7, 16; xvi. 24, 26). Clearly the infilling of the Holy Spirit has a special bearing on the prayerfulness of the individual and the Church. But this will unfold as we proceed.

I. THE PRAYING CHRIST.—"I will pray the Father." It is true that He sat down at the right hand of the Majesty on high, because He had completed the work for which He became man. That session indicated a finished atonement. As the Father rested from the work of creation, so the Son entered into his rest, having ceased from the work of redemption, so far as it could be effected in his death, resurrection, and ascension. But as the Father in his rest worked in providence, sustaining that which He had created, so did the Saviour continue to work after He had entered into his Sabbath-keeping.

We have already dealt with one branch of his twofold activity, in *his work through those who believe.* The greater works which the risen Saviour has been, and is, achieving through his people bear witness to the perpetual energy streaming from his life in the azure depths. "The apostles," Mark tells us, "went forth and preached everywhere, the Lord working with them, and confirming the word with signs following."

The other branch of his twofold ministry is *his intercession on our behalf.* He says, "I will pray the Father" for you.

(1) What a contrast to the assertions which we have already pondered of his oneness with the Father, and to his assurance in almost the same breath that He would Himself answer his people's prayers! It is inexplicable, save on the hypothesis that He has a dual nature, by virtue of which, on the one hand, He is God, who answers prayer, and on the other the Son of Man, who pleads as the Head and Representative of a redeemed race.

(2) It is, however, in harmony with Old Testament symbolism. The High Priest often entered the presence of God with the names of the people on his breast, the seat of love, and on his shoulder, the seat of power; and once a year, with a bowl of blood and sprig of thyme in his hands, pleaded for the entire nation. What more vivid portrayal could there be of the ceaseless intercession of that High Priest who was once manifested to bear the sin of many, and who now appears in the presence of God for us!

(3) In the days of his flesh, He pleaded for his *Church,* as in the sublime intercessory prayer of chapter xvii; for *individuals,* as when He said, "Simon, Simon, Satan hath desired to have you, that he may sift you as wheat; but I have prayed for thee"; and for *the world,* as when He first assumed his High-priestly functions, saying from his cross, "Father, forgive them; they know not what they do." Thus He

pleads still. For Zion's sake He does not hold his peace, and for Jerusalem's sake He does not rest. For his Chuch, for individual believers, for thee and me, He says in heaven, as on earth, "Father, I pray for them." Perennially from his lips pours out a stream of tender supplication and entreaty. This is the river that makes glad the city of God. Anticipating coming trial; interposing when the cobra-coil is beginning to encircle us; pitying us when the sky is overcast and lowering; not tiring or ceasing, though we are heedless and unthankful—He pleads on the mountain brow through the dark hours, whilst we sleep.

(4) These intercessions are further stimulated by our love and obedience. "If ye love Me, keep my commandments, *and* I will pray the Father." He looks on us; and where love is yearning to love more fully, and obedience falters in its high endeavours, He prays yet more eagerly that grace may be given us to be what we long to be. He prays for those who do not pray for themselves; but He is even more intent on the perfecting of those who, because of their loyalty and love, are the objects of his special interest—"I pray for them; I pray not for the world."

(5) His special petition is that we may receive the gift of Pentecost. "I will pray the Father, and He shall give you another Comforter." It would almost seem as though He spent the mysterious ten days between his ascension and Pentecost in special intercession that his Church might be endued with power from on high. The pleading Church on earth and the pleading Saviour in heaven were at one. The two voices agreed in perfect symphony, and Pentecost was the Father's answer. The Saviour prayed to the Father, and He gave another Comforter. Nor has He ceased in this sublime quest. It is not improbable that every revival of religion, every fresh and deeper baptism of the Spirit, every new infilling of individual souls, has been due to our Saviour's strong cryings on our behalf. It may be that at this hour He is engaged in asking the Father that He would dower the universal Church with another Pentecost; and if so, let us join Him in the prayer.

II. THE PRAYING CHURCH.—"Whatsoever ye shall ask in my name."

(1) Prayer must be addressed to the Father. As soon as we utter that sacred name, the Divine nature responds; and, to put it vividly, is on the alert to hear what we desire. A little child cannot utter a sigh however slight, a sob however smothered, without awakening the quick attention of its mother; and at the first whisper of our Father's name, He is at hand to hear and bless. Alas! we have too often grieved his Holy Spirit by a string of selfish petitions, or a number of formal platitudes. To the wonderment of angels, we thus fritter away the most precious and sacred opportunities. Be still, then, before you pray, to consider what to ask; order your prayers for presentation: and be

sure to begin the blessed interview with words of sincere and loving appreciation and devotion.

(2) The conditions of successful prayer are clearly defined in these words. There must be love to Christ and to all men; obedience to his will, so far as it is revealed; recognition of his mediation and intercession, as alone giving us the right to draw nigh; identification with Him, so as to be able to use his name; passionate desires for the Father's glory. Where these five conditions exist, there can be no doubt as to our receiving the petitions which we offer. Prayer that complies with these conditions cannot fail, since it is only the return tide of an impulse which has emanated from the heart of God.

(3) Note how the Saviour lives for the promotion of his Father's glory. How often, during his earthly ministry, He declared that He was desiring and seeking this beyond all else! Though his prayer could only be granted by his falling into the ground to die, He never flinched from saying, "Father, glorify thy Name." But here He tells us that through the ages as they pass He will still be set on the same quest. By all means He must glorify his Father; and if, in any prayer of ours, we can show that what we ask will augment the Father's glory, we are certain to obtain his concurrence and glad acquiescence. "That," He says, "will I do."

(4) We must pray "in his Name." As the ambassador speaks in the name of queen and country; as the tax-collector appeals in the name of the authorities; both deriving from their identification with their superiors an authority they could not otherwise exercise—so our words become weighted with a great importance when we can say to our Father, "We are so one with Jesus that He is asking in and through us; these words are his; these desires his; these objects those on which his heart is set. We have his sanction and authority to use his name." When we ask a favour in the name of another, that other is the petitioner, through us; so when we approach God in the Name of Jesus, it is not enough to append his sacred name as a formula, but we must see to it that Jesus is pleading in us, asking through our lips, as He is asking through his own in the heart of the sapphire Throne.

III. THE LINK BETWEEN THESE TWO.—"He shall give you another Comforter." The word "Comforter" might be rendered "Advocate." We have two Advocates: one with the Father, Jesus Christ the Righteous, the other with us. As the one ascended, the other descended. As the one sat down at the right hand of God, the other rested on the heads and hearts of the company in the upper room. As the one has compassion on our infirmities, so the other helps our infirmities. As the one ever liveth to intercede for us in heaven, so the other maketh intercession in us for the saints with groanings that cannot be uttered.

This is the clue to the mystery of prayer. It is all-important that the

Church on earth should be in accord with its Head in his petitions before the Throne. Of what avail is it for a client and advocate to enter an earthly court of justice unless they are in agreement? Of what use is it to have two instruments in an orchestra which are not perfectly in tune? And how can we expect that God will hear us unless we ask what is according to his will, and, therefore, what is in the heart and thought of Jesus?

This, then, is the problem that confronts us. How can we ascertain what Jesus is pleading for? We may guess it generally, but how be assured of it particularly? Who will tell us the direction in which the current of his mighty pleadings is setting, that we may take the same direction? These inquiries are answered in the ministry of the Holy Spirit. On the one hand, He fills and moves the Head, and on the other, his members. There is one Spirit of life between Jesus in the glory and his believing people everywhere. One ocean washes the shores of all natures in which the life of God is found.

Be still, therefore, and listen carefully to the voice of the Spirit of God speaking in thine heart, as thou turnest from all other sounds towards his still small whisper, and He will tell thee all. Coming, as He does, from the heart of Jesus, He will tell thee his latest thought. In Him we have the mind of Christ. Then, sure that we are one with Him, and therefore with the Father, we shall ask what is according to his will to give. Prayer goes in an eternal circle. It begins in the heart of God, comes to us through the Saviour and by the Spirit, and returns through us again to its source. It is the teaching of the rain-drops, of the tides, of the procession of the year; but wrought out and exemplified in the practice of holy hearts.

45

THE OTHER PARACLETE

"He shall give you another Comforter."—JOHN xiv. 16.

THERE was no doubt in our Lord's mind that his asking would be at once followed by the Father's giving. Indeed, the two actions seemed, in his judgment, indissolubly connected—"I will ask, and He shall give." From which we learn that prayer is a necessary link in the order of the Divine government. Though we are assured that what we ask is in God's purpose to communicate—that it lies in the heart of a promise, or in the line of the Divine procedure—yet we must nevertheless make request. "Ye have not," said the Apostle James, "because ye ask not." "Ask," said the Master, his eye being open to the laws of the spiritual world, "and it shall be given you."

The prayer of the Head of the Church was heard, and He received the Holy Spirit to bestow Him again. "Having received of the Father the promise of the Holy Spirit," said the Apostle Peter, "He hath shed forth this, which ye now see and hear." Thus the Holy Spirit is the gift of the Father, through the Son; though He is equal with each of the blessed Persons in the Trinity, and is with them to be worshipped and glorified.

I. THE PERSONALITY OF THE HOLY GHOST.—That word, "another" —"He shall give you *another* Comforter"—is in itself sufficient to prove the Divinity and Personality of the Holy Ghost. If a man promises to send another as his substitute, we naturally expect to see a man like unto himself, occupying his place, and doing his work. And when Jesus foreannounced another Comforter, He must have intended a Person as distinct and helpful as He had been. A breath, an afflatus, an impersonal influence, could not have stood in the same category with Himself.

There are those who think that the Holy Spirit is to the Lord Jesus what a man's spirit is to his body; and imagine that our Lord simply intended that the spirit of his life-teaching and self-sacrifice would brood over and inspire his followers; but this could not have fulfilled the promise of "the other Comforter." It would simply have been Himself over again—though no longer as a living Person; rather as the momentum and energy of a receding force which gets weaker and ever weaker as the ages pass. Thus the spirit of Napoleon or of Cæsar is becoming little more than a dim faint echo of footsteps that once shook the world.

Jesus knew how real and helpful He had been to his followers—the centre around which they had rallied; their Teacher, Brother, Master; and He would not have tantalised them by promising another Paraclete, unless He had intended to announce the advent of One who would adjust Himself to their needs with that quickness of perception, and sufficiency of resource, which characterize a personal Leader and Administrator. There were times approaching when the little band would need counsel, direction, sympathy, the interposition of a strong wise Hand—qualities which could not be furnished by the remembrance of the past, fading like the colours on clouds when the sun has set; but which could only be secured by the presence of a strong, wise, ever-present Personality. "I have been one Paraclete," said the Lord in effect; "but I am now going to plead your cause with the Father, that another Paraclete may take my place, to be my other self, and to abide with you for ever."

There is no adequate translation for the word *Paraclete*. It may be rendered Comforter, Helper, Advocate, Interpreter; but no one word suffices. The Greek simply means one whom you call to your side, in a battle, or a law-court, to assist you by word or act. Such a One is Christ; such a One is the Holy Spirit. He is a definite Person whom you can call to, and lean on, and work with. If a man were drowning, he would not call to the wandering breath of the wind; but to any person who might be on the bank. The Spirit is One whom you can summon to your side; and it is therefore quite in keeping with Scripture to pray to the Holy Spirit. On the whole we are taught to direct prayer to the Father, through the Son, and as prompted by the Holy Spirit; but as a matter of practice and habit, it is indifferent which Person in the Holy Trinity we address, for each is equally God. As the Father is God, so also is the Son, and so the Holy Spirit. In her hymns and liturgies the Church has never hesitated to summon the Holy Spirit to her help.

It is in recognition of the Personality of the Holy Spirit that the historian of the Acts of the Apostles quotes his solemn words, "Separate *Me* Barnabas and Saul"; tells us that Ananias and Sapphira lied to Him; and records that the Church at Jerusalem commenced its encyclical letter with the words, "It seemed good to the Holy Ghost and to us." Happy that body of Christians which has come to realize that the Holy Ghost is as certainly, literally, and personally present in its midst, as Jesus Christ was present when in the days of his flesh He tarried among men!

II. A SEVENFOLD PARALLEL BETWEEN THE ADVENTS OF THE TWO PARACLETES.—(1) *Each was in the world before his specific advent.*— Long before his Incarnation the delights of the Son of God were with men. In Angel-form, He visited their tents, spoke with them face to face, calmed their fears, and fought on their behalf. He trod the holy fields of Palestine with noiseless footfall that left no impress on the lightest sands, long before He learned to walk with baby-feet, or bore his cross up Calvary.

So with the Holy Spirit. He brooded over chaos, strove with men before the Deluge, moved holy men to write the Scriptures, foreshadowed the advent of the Messiah, equipped prophets and kings for their special mission. In restraining evil, urging to good, preparing the way for Christ, the Holy Spirit found abundant scope for his energies. But his influence was rather external than internal; savoured rather of gift than grace; and dealt more often with the few than with the many—with the great souls that reared themselves to heaven like Alpine summits touched with the fires of dawn, rather than with the generality of men, who dwelt in the valley of daily commonplace, enwrapt in the mists of ignorance and unbelief. It was to be the special prerogative of this age, that He should be poured out on *all* flesh, so that sons and daughters should prophesy, whilst servants and handmaidens participated in his gracious influences.

(2) *The advent of each was previously announced.*—From the Fall, the coming of the great Deliverer was foretold in type and sign, in speech and act, in history and prophecy. Indeed, as the time of the Incarnation drew nigh, as Milton tells us in his sublime ode on the Incarnation, surrounding nations had caught from the chosen people the spirit of expectancy, and the world was in feverish anticipation of the coming of its Redeemer. He was the Desire of all nations. All the ages, and all the family of man, accompanied Mary to Bethlehem, and worshipped with the Magi.

So with the Holy Spirit. Joel distinctly foretold that in the last days of that dispensation, God would pour out his Spirit—and his message is echoed by Isaiah, Zechariah, Ezekiel, and others—till Jesus came, who more specifically and circumstantially led the thoughts of his disciples forward to the new age then dawning, which should be introduced and signalised by the coming and ministry of the Spirit.

(3) *Each was manifested in a body.*—The Lord Jesus in that which was prepared for Him by the Father, and born of a Virgin. We are told that He took on Him the form of a servant, and was made in the likeness of man. Similarly, the Holy Spirit became, so to speak, incorporate in that mystical Body, the Church, of which Jesus is the Head.

On the day of Pentecost, the hundred and twenty who were gathered in the upper room, and who, up to that time, had had no corporate existence, were suddenly constituted a Church, the habitation and home of the Divine Spirit. What the human body of Jesus was to the second Person of the Holy Trinity, that the infant Church was to the third; though it did not represent the whole body, since we must add to those gathered in the upper room many more in heaven and on earth, who by virtue of their union with the risen Christ constituted with them the Holy Catholic Church, which is his body, the fullness of Him who filleth all in all. "This," said the blessed Spirit, "is my rest for ever; here will I dwell, for I have desired it."

(4) *Each was named before his advent.*—"Thou shalt call his name Emmanuel." "His name shall be called Wonderful, Counsellor, the Mighty God, the Everlasting Father, the Prince of Peace." Thus was the Lord Jesus designated to loving hearts before his birth.

So also with the Holy Spirit. The last discourses of Jesus are full of appellatives, each setting forth some new phase of the Holy Spirit's ministry; some freshly-cut facet of his character. The Spirit of Truth; the Holy Spirit; the Paraclete; the Spirit of Conviction—such are some of the names by which He was to be known.

(5) *Each was dependent on another.*—Our Lord said distinctly, "The Son can do nothing of Himself, but what He seeth the Father do"; and He said of the Holy Spirit, using the same preposition, "He shall not speak of Himself, but whatsoever He shall hear, that shall He speak."

What a conception is here! It is as though the Holy Spirit were ever listening to the Divine colloquy and communion between the Father and the Son, and communicating to receptive hearts disclosures of the secrets of the Deity. The things which eye hath not seen, nor ear heard, God hath revealed unto us by his Spirit; "for the Spirit searcheth all things, yea, the deep things of God."

(6) *Each received witness.*—The Father bore witness to his Son on three separate occasions. On the first, at his baptism, He said, "This is my beloved Son, in whom I am well pleased"; on the second, when the three apostles were with Him on the holy mount, and He received from the Father glory and honour; and on the third, when the inquiry of the Greeks reminded Him of his approaching death, and the voice from heaven assured Him that glory would accrue to the Father through his falling into the ground to die.

So in regard to the Holy Spirit. Seven times from the Throne the ascended Lord summons those that have ears to hear what the Spirit saith to the churches; as though to emphasise the urgent importance of his message, and the necessity of giving it our most earnest heed, lest we should drift past it.

(7) *The presence of each is guaranteed during the present age.*—"I am with you," said the Lord, and they were among the closing words of his posthumous ministry, "all the days, even unto the end of the age"; and here it is foretold that the Comforter would abide *during the age,* for so the phrase might more accurately be rendered.

This is specially the age of the Holy Spirit. He may be grieved, ignored, and rejected; but He will not cease his blessed ministry to the bride, till the Bridegroom comes to claim her for Himself. Oh, let us avail ourselves of his gracious presence to the utmost of our opportunity, that He may realise in us the full purpose of his ministry. Let us not pray for Him, as if in any degree He had been withdrawn, but as believing that He is as much with the Church of to-day as on the day of Pentecost; as near us as when awestruck eyes beheld Him settling in flame on each meekly-bowed head.

The Lord said, "He shall remain with you to the end of the age." The age is not closed, therefore He must be with us here and now. There can be no waning of his grace or power. The pot of oil is in the Church, only she has ceased to bring her empty vessels. The mine is beneath our feet, but we do not work it as of yore. The electric current is vibrating around, but we have lost the art of switching ourselves on to its flow. It is not necessary then for us to pray the Father that He should give the Holy Paraclete in the sense in which He bestowed Him on the day of Pentecost in answer to the request of our Lord. That prayer has been answered: the Paraclete is here; but we need to have the eyes of our heart opened to perceive, and the hand of our faith strengthened that we may receive, Him.

The work of the Holy Spirit in and through us is conditioned by certain great laws, which call for our definite and accurate obedience. Not on emotion, nor on hysteric appeals, nor on excitement, but on obedience, does the power of God's Spirit pass into human hearts and lives. Therefore, let us walk in the Paracletism of the Paraclete, continually in the current of his gracious influences, which will bear us on their bosom ever nearer to our Lord. Oh to glorify Him; to know and love Him; to become passionately eager that all hearts should enthrone Him regardless of the personal cost it may involve!

46

THE THREE DISPENSATIONS

"The Spirit of truth; whom the world cannot receive, because it seeth Him not, neither knoweth Him: but ye know Him; for He dwelleth with you, and shall be in you."—JOHN xiv. 17.

THEY ARE lofty themes which we have been discussing in the foregoing pages; and just because they touch the highest matters of the spiritual life, they involve us in profound responsibility. It was because Capernaum had been exalted to heaven in privilege, that she should be cast down to hell. Of those to whom much is given, much is required. Better not to have known these truths of the inner life, if we are content to know them only by an intellectual apprehension, and make no effort to incorporate them into the texture of our character. Few things harden more certainly than to delight in the presentation of the mysteries of the kingdom, without becoming a child of the kingdom.

The object therefore which now engages us is less one of elucidation than of self-examination. Let us discern ourselves. Let us see whether we be in the faith. Let us expose soul and spirit to the discrimination of the Word of God, which is a discerner of the thoughts and intents of the heart.

I. THERE ARE TWO AVENUES OF KNOWLEDGE: *Perception and Reception.*—"Whom the world cannot receive, because it seeth Him not, neither knoweth Him." Three things are specified as beyond the range of the world's power: it does not receive, it does not know, it does not see, the things of the unseen and eternal world. It cannot see them, therefore it does not know them, and therefore does not receive them; and this is especially true of its attitude towards the Holy Ghost.

When the world hears of the Holy Spirit, it brings to bear upon Him those organs of cognition which it has been accustomed to apply to the objects of the natural world, and even to the human life of Christ. But, as might have been expected, these are altogether useless. It is as absurd to endeavour to detect the presence of the spiritual and eternal by the faculties with which we discern what is seen and temporal, as it would be to attempt to receive the impression of a noble painting by the sense of taste, or to deal with the problems of astronomy by the tests that are employed in chemical analysis. The world, however, does not realise its mistake. It persists in applying tests to the Spirit of God which may be well enough in other regions of discovery, but which are worse than useless here. "The natural man receiveth not the things of the Spirit of God, neither can he know them, because they are spiritually discerned." "Whom the world cannot receive, for it beholdeth Him not, neither knoweth Him."

There was a touch of this worldly spirit even in Thomas, when he said, "Except I see in his hand the print of the nails, and thrust my hand into his side, I will not believe"; and in so far as the world-spirit is permitted to hold sway within us, our powers of spiritual perception will be blunted, and become infected with the tendency to make our intellect or imagination our sole means of apprehending divine truth.

There is a better way than this; and our Lord indicates it when He says, "Ye know Him, for He abideth with you, and shall be in you." Pascal said, "The world knows in order to love: the Christian loves in order to know." The same thought underlies these words of Christ. The world attempts to see the Spirit, that it may know and receive Him; the child of God receives Him by an act of faith, that he may know Him.

An illustration of this habit is given in the story of Naaman. The spirit of the world whispered to him of the desirability of *knowing* that the waters of Israel possessed curative properties, before he committed himself absolutely to the prophet's directions; and if he had waited to know before bathing, he would have remained a helpless leper to the end of his days. His servants, however, had a clearer perception of the way of faith, and persuaded him to dip· seven times in the Jordan. He acted on the suggestion, dipped seven times, and his flesh became as that of a little child. Similarly we are called to act upon grounds which the world would hold to be inadequate. We hear the testimony of another; we recognise a suitability in the promises of the Scripture to meet the deep yearnings of our soul; we feel that the words and works of Jesus Christ constitute a unique claim for Him, and we open our hearts towards Him. In absolute humility and perfect obedience we yield to Him our whole nature. Though the night be yet dark, we fling wide our windows to the warm south-west wind coming over the sea. The result is that we begin to know, with an intuitive knowledge that cannot be shaken by the pronouncements of the higher criticism. We have received the Spirit, and our after-life is too short to unfold all that is involved in that unspeakable gift. We know Him because He abideth with us, and is in us. No man knoweth the things of a man, save the spirit of man which is in him; and we can only know the Spirit of God when He has taken up his residence within us, and witnesses with our spirit, as One who is interwoven with the very texture of the inner life.

Consecration is therefore the key to this higher knowledge; and if any who read this page are yearning after a discernment of the things of God on which they may build the house of their faith amid the swirl of the storm and the beat of the wave of modern doubt, let them open their entire nature, humbly to receive and diligently to obey that Spirit whom Christ waits to give to all who seek.

II. The Characteristic of this Dispensation.—"He shall be *in* you." It has been repeatedly said that creation is the work of the Father; redemption, of the Son; and regeneration, of the Holy Spirit. It may also be said that there are three dispensations: that of the Father, in the earlier history of mankind; that of the Son, culminating in our Lord's ascension; and that of the Holy Spirit, in which we are now living. In the history of the world these were successive; in the history of souls they may be contemporaneous. In the same house one member may be in the dispensation of the Father, another in that of the Son, and a third in that of the Holy Spirit. It is highly necessary, says the saintly Fletcher, that every good steward of the mysteries of God should be well acquainted with this fact, otherwise he will not rightly divide the word of life. There is peril lest we should give the truth of one order of dispensation to those who are living on another level of experience.

There is a remarkable illustration of this in the life of John the Baptist, who clearly realised the distinction on which we are dwelling, and used it with remarkable nicety when approached by various classes of character. When Gentile soldiers came to him, in Roman regimentals, he merely bade them do violence to no man, and be content with their wages. When Jews came, he said, "Behold the Lamb of God!" To his eagle eye a further dispensation was unveiled to which he alluded when he said, "He shall baptize you with the Holy Ghost, and with fire." Similarly they to whom inquirers address themselves should diagnose their spiritual standing, that they may lovingly and wisely administer the truth suitable to their condition.

The dispensation of the Father includes those who hope that He has accepted and forgiven them, but have no clear perception of the atoning work of Christ; who are governed rather by fear than love; who tremble beneath the thunders of Sinai more often than they rejoice at the spectacle of Calvary; who are tossed to and fro between hope and despair; who desire the favour of God, but hesitate to speak confidently of having attained it. Such are to be found in churches where the Gospel is veiled beneath heavy curtains of misconception and formalism. In the same class we might put men, like Cornelius, who in every nation fear God and work righteousness.

The dispensation of the Son includes those who clearly perceive his divine nature, and rejoice in his finished propitiation; they know that they are accepted in the Beloved; they receive his teachings about the Father; they submit to the rule of life which He has laid down; but they know comparatively little of the inner life, or of their oneness with Christ in resurrection and ascension; they understand little of what the apostle meant by speaking of Christ being formed in the soul; and, like the disciples at Ephesus, they know but little of the mission and infilling of the Holy Spirit.

The dispensation of the Holy Spirit includes those who have claimed their share in Pentecost. In their hearts the Paraclete dwells in sanctifying grace, on their heads He rests in mighty anointing. Those of the dispensation of the Son resemble Ruth the gleaner; those of the dispensation of the Spirit, Ruth the bride. Those dwell in Romans vii. and Hebrews iii.; these in Romans viii. and Hebrews iv. For those the water has to be drawn from the well; in these it springs up to everlasting life. Oh to know the "in-ness" of the Holy Spirit. Know ye not that Jesus Christ is in you by the Spirit—unless ye be reprobate!

III. THE TOKENS OF THE INDWELLING.—We must distinguish here, as Dr. Steele suggests, between what are variable, and what are constant.

These vary—(1) The joy of realisation, which is sometimes overpowering in its intensity, at other times like the ebbing tide.

(2) Agony for souls, which would be insupportable if it were permanent. Christ only asks us to watch in Gethsemane for one hour.

(3) Access in prayer. Sometimes the vision is face to face; at others, though we grasp as in Jacob's night-wrestle, we cannot behold. Like Esther, we seem to wait in the ante-chamber. As the lark of which Jeremy Taylor speaks, we rise against the east wind.

(4) The openings of Scripture. The Bible does not seem to be always equally interesting. At times it is like the scented letter paper, smelling of aloes and cassia, bearing the handwriting we love; at others it resembles the reading book of the blind man, the characters in which, by constant use, have become almost obliterated, so as hardly to awake answering thought.

(5) The pressure of temptation. We sometimes think that we are getting out of the zone of temptation. The pressure is so reduced that we think we shall never suffer again as we have done. Then, all suddenly, it bursts upon us—as the fury of the storm, when, after an hour's cessation, it takes the mariner unawares.

All these symptoms are too variable to be relied upon for a diagnosis of our spiritual condition, or an evidence of the dispensation to which we belong.

These are constant—(1) The consciousness of being God's. This is to be distinguished from the outgoing of our faith and love towards God. At the beginning of our experience we hold Him; but as the Holy

Spirit dwells more fully we realise that we are held by Him. It is not our love to God, but his love to us; not our faith, but his faithfulness; not the sheep keeping near the Shepherd, but the Shepherd keeping the sheep near to Himself. A happy sense steals over the heart, as over the spouse—"I am my Beloved's, and his desire is toward me."

(2) The supremacy of Jesus in the heart. There is no longer a double empire of self and Christ—as in the poor Indian who said to the missionary, "I am two Indians, good and bad"; but there is the undivided reign of Christ, who has put down all rule and authority and power—as in the case of Martin Luther, who said, "If any one should ask of my heart, Who dwells here? I should reply, Not Martin Luther, but Christ."

(3) Peace, which looks out upon the future without alarm, because so sure that Christ will do his very best in every day that lies hidden beneath the haze of the future; which forbears to press its will too vehemently, or proffer its request too eagerly, because absolutely certain that Jesus will secure the highest happiness possible, consistently with his glory and our usefulness to men.

(4) Love. When the Spirit of God really dwells within, there is a baptism of love which evinces itself not only in the household and to those naturally lovable, but goes out to all the world, and embraces in its tenderness such as have no natural traits of beauty. Thus the soft waters of the Southern Ocean lap against unsightly rocks and stretches of bare shingle.

Where love reigns in the inner chamber of the soul, doors do not slam; bells are not jerked violently; soft tones modulate the speech; gentle steps tread the highways of the world, bent on the beautiful work of the messengers of peace; and the very atmosphere of the life is warm and sunny as an aureole. There is no doubt of the indwelling Spirit where there is this out-going love.

(5) Deliverance from the love and power of sin, so that it becomes growingly distasteful, and the soul turns with loathing from the carrion on which it once fed contentedly. This begets a sense of purity, robed in which the soul claims kinship to the white-robed saints of the presence-chamber, and reaches out towards the blessedness of the pure in heart who see God. There is still a positive rain of smut and filth in the world around; there is a recognition of the evil tendencies of the self-life, which will assert themselves unless graciously restrained; but triumphing above all is the purity of the indwelling Lord, who Himself becomes in us the quality for which holy souls eagerly long.

47

Three Paradoxes

"I will not leave you comfortless: I will come to you."
"The world seeth Me no more; but ye see Me."
"Because I live, ye shall live also."

JOHN xiv. 18, 19.

THE BIBLE and the Christian life are full of paradoxes. Paul loved to enumerate them; they abound also in the discourses of our Lord. Here are three.

The Master had declared his purpose of leaving his apostles and friends and returning to his Father: but in the same breath He says, "I will not leave you desolate; I will come to you."

Again, He had forewarned them that He would be hidden from them; yet now He tells them that they would still behold Him.

Further, with growing emphasis and clearness, He had unfolded his approaching death by the cruel Roman method of the cross; yet He claims the timeless life of an ever-present tense, and insists that their life will depend on his.

Absent, yet present; hidden, yet visible; dying, yet living and life-giving—such are the paradoxes of this paragraph in his marvellous farewell discourse; and they reveal three facts of which we may live in perpetual cognisance.

I. WE MAY ENJOY THE PERPETUAL RECOGNITION OF THE ADVENT OF CHRIST.—"I will not leave you orphans [or desolate]: I come unto you" (R.V.). Note the majesty of those last words; they are worthy of Deity; He speaks as though He were always drawing nigh to those He loves: "I come unto you."

Christ is always present, yet He comes.—The Creator had been always immanent in his universe, but He came in each creative act; the Lawgiver had been ever-present in the Church in the wilderness, but He came down on Sinai, and his glory lit up the peaks of sandstone rock; the Deliverer was never for a moment absent from the side of the shepherd-king, but in answer to his cry for help He came down riding upon a cherub, flying on the wings of wind; the Holy Spirit had been in the world from the earliest days of prayer and inspired speech, but He came down from the Throne to sit on each bowed head in lambent flame. So Christ is with us all the days, yet He comes. He will come at last to receive his own to Himself, and to judge the world; but He comes in dark and lonely hours that we may not be desolate.

244

> *"For warm, sweet, tender, even yet*
> *A present help is He;*
> *And faith has still its Olivet,*
> *And love its Galilee.*
> *The healing of his seamless dress*
> *Is by our beds of pain;*
> *We touch Him in life's throng and press,*
> *And we are whole again."*

He comes when we need Him most.—When the storm is high, and the water is pouring into the boat; when the house is empty because the life that made it home has fled; when Jericho has to be attacked on the morrow, and the Jordan crossed; when lover and friend stand aloof; when light is fading before dimming eyes, and names and faces elude the grasp of the aged mind; when the last coal is turning to grey ash; when the rush of the river is heard in the valley below—Jesus says, I come. It is in the hour of desolation, when Lazarus has been in the grave four days already, that the glad tidings are whispered in the ear of the mourner, "The Master is come." "I will not leave you orphans," He said: "I come unto you." Oh, blessed orphanhood, it were well to be bereaved, to have such comforting!

He pays surprise visits.—He does not always wait to be invited; but sometimes, when we lie sleeping with wakeful hearts, we hear his gentle voice calling to us, "Arise, my love, and come away." Then as we lift the door-latch, we are refreshed with the sweet-smelling myrrh which betrays his presence. How often when we have been losing ground, getting lukewarm and worldly, we have suddenly been made aware of his reviving presence, and He has said, I come. He comes, as the wood-anemones and snowdrops (the most fragile and tender flowerets of spring) penetrate the hard ground to announce that the winter is over and gone, and that the time of the singing of birds is come.

It is well to put ourselves in his way.—There are certain beaten tracks well-worn by his feet, and if we would meet Him we must frequent their neighbourhood. Olivet, where He used to pray; Calvary, where He died; Joseph's garden, where He rose, are dear to Him yet. When we pray or meditate; when we commemorate his dying love at the memorial feast; when we realise our union with Him in death and resurrection; when we open our hearts to the breathing of the Holy Spirit—we put ourselves in his way, and are more likely to encounter Him when He comes. "To them that look for Him shall He appear." "Behold, the Bridegroom cometh: go ye out to meet Him" —but take the path by which He is sure to travel. Be in the upper room, with the rest of the disciples, so that you may not, like Thomas, miss Him when He comes.

His footsteps are noiseless.—It is said of old, "Thy footsteps are not known"; therefore we need not be surprised if He steal in upon us as a thief in the night, or as spring over the wolds. There is no blare of trumpet or voice of herald; we cannot say, Lo here, or Lo there; when the King comes there is no outward show. "He does not strive, nor cry, nor cause his voice to be heard in the street."

"He entered not by the eyes," says St. Bernard, "for his presence was not marked by colour; nor by the ears, for there was no sound; nor by the touch, for He was impalpable. How then did I know that He was present? Because He was a quickening power. As soon as He entered, He awoke my slumbering soul. He moved and pierced my heart, which before was stony, hard, and sick. He began also to pluck up and destroy, to build and plant, to freshen the inner drought, to enlighten the darkness, to open the prison-house, to make the crooked straight and the rough smooth; so that my heart could bless the Lord with all that was within me."

Oh, lonely, desolate soul, open thy door to Him; wait not on the alert to detect his entrance, only believe that He is there: and presently, and before ever thou art aware, thou wilt find a new fragrance distilling through the heart-chamber, a new power throbbing in thy pulse.

II. WE MAY ENJOY THE PERPETUAL RECOGNITION OF THE PRESENCE OF CHRIST.—"The world beholdeth Me no more; but ye behold Me." Nothing makes men so humble and yet so strong as the vision of Christ.

It induces humility.—When Isaiah beheld his glory more resplendent than the sheen of the sapphire Throne, he cried that he was undone; when Peter caught the first flash of his miraculous power gleaming across the waves of Galilee, just when the fish were struggling in the full net, he besought Him to depart, because he felt himself a sinful man; and when John saw Him on the Isle of Patmos, he fell at his feet as dead—though, surely, if any of the apostles could have faced Him unabashed, it had been he.

This is specially noticeable in the Book of Job. Few books are so misunderstood. It is supposed to contain the description of the victory of Job's patience; in reality it delineates its testing and failure. It shows how he who was perfect, according to the measure of his light, broke down in the fiery ordeal to which he was exposed, and finally was forced to cry, "I have heard of Thee by the hearing of the ear, but now mine eye seeth Thee; wherefore I abhor myself, and repent in dust and ashes."

Wouldst thou be humble? wouldst thou know thyself a worm and no man? wouldst thou see that thou art verily undone, defiled, and helpless? Then ask the blessed Spirit to reveal Jesus in all his matchless beauty and holiness, eliciting the confession that thou art the least of saints and the chief of sinners. This is no forced estimate, when we take into account the opportunities we have missed, the gifts we have misused, the time we have wasted, the light we have resisted, the love we have requited with neglect.

It produces strength.—See that man of God prone on the floor of his chamber, shedding bitter tears of godly sorrow, not forgiving himself, albeit that he knows himself forgiven; bowing his head as a bulrush, crying that he is helpless, broken, and at the end of himself— will he be able to stand as a rock against the beat of temptation, and the assault of the foe? Yes, verily; for the same presence which is to him a source of humility in private, will inspire to great deeds of faith and heroism when he is called to stand in the breach or lead the assault.

It is this vision of the present Lord that, in every age of the Church, has made sufferers strong. "The Lord is on my right hand, I shall not be moved," said one. "The Lord stood by me, and strengthened me," said another. In many a dark day of suffering and persecution; in the catacombs; in the dens and caves where Waldenses hid; on the hillsides where the Covenanters met to pray; in the beleaguered cities of the Netherlands; in prison and at the stake—God's saints have looked to Him, and been lightened, and their faces have not been ashamed. "Behold," said the first martyr, "I see the heavens opened, and the Son of Man standing on the right hand of God."

Oh for more of the open vision of Jesus, ministered to us by the gracious Spirit! Would that his words, "Ye behold Me," were oftener verified in our experience! He is always with us; and if only our eyes were not holden, we should behold Him with the quick perception of the heart. Indeed, the race can only be rightly run by those who have learnt the blessed secret of looking off unto Him. "We see Jesus."

It is a most salutary habit to say often, when one is alone, "Thou art near, O Lord"; "Behold, the Lord is in this place." We may not at first realise the truth of what we are saying. His presence may be veiled, as the forms of mountains swathed in morning cloud. But as we persist in our quest, putting away from us all that would grieve Him, and cultivating the attitude of pure devotion, we shall become aware of a divine presence which shall be more to us than a voice speaking from out the Infinite.

III. WE MAY ENJOY THE PERPETUAL RECOGNITION OF THE LIVING CHRIST.—"Because I live, ye shall live also." There are many life-verses in this Gospel which shine like stars in the firmament of Scripture. For example—in the first chapter, that in the Word, as manifested to men, was *life*; and in the fifth chapter, that "as the Father had life in Himself, He gave to the Son to have life also in Himself." The Father is the fountain of life. Eternal life is ever rising up in his infinite Being with perennial vigour; and all things living, from the tiny humming-birds in the tropical forest to the strongest archangel beside the sapphire Throne, derive their being from Him. Thus we have seen ferns around a fountain, nourishing their fronds on its spray. All things owe their existence and continued being to the unmeasured life which has been from all eternity treasured up in God, and is ever flowing out from God.

This life was Christ's, in the mystery of the eternal Trinity, before the worlds were made; but it was necessary that He should receive it into his human nature, so as to become the reservoir and storehouse from which all who were one with Him might receive grace on grace. "I am come," He said, "that they might have life, and that they might have it more abundantly." This life dwelt in Him during his earthly ministry, though comparatively few availed themselves of it; his death set it abroach for all the world; the smitten rock yielded streams of living water; the last Adam became a life-giving Spirit; from his throne He proclaimed Himself as He that liveth, though He became dead, and is alive for evermore.

We live by his life.—Our life is as dependent upon Him as a babe's on its mother. Could aught happen to Him, we should instantly feel the effect. We have no independent, self-derived, or self-sustained life. Apart from Him we wither.

We live in his life.—The tiny streamlet of our being has joined his, is merged in it, and flows on together with it, to the great ocean of eternity. To us to live is Christ, both here and hereafter. Our aims and purposes are merged in his; we are enriched in all that enriches Him; gladdened by all that promotes his happiness and glory; made more than conquerors through our oneness with Him, in the victory that has overcome the world.

We live because He lives in us.—At the moment of regeneration He came to indwell. He that hath the Son hath life; he that hath life hath the Son. It has pleased God to reveal his Son in us. We have found Him of whom Moses in the law and the prophets did write, and we have found Him in our hearts. Where dwellest Thou? we asked Him; and He replied, Come and see: and He manifested Himself as having become to us the inward principle of an endless life. Christ dwells deep in our heart, and we are beginning to comprehend the immensity of the Divine love of which He is the exponent.

Let us draw on this life more confidently, availing ourselves of it perpetually in all our time of need—in all time of our sickness and of our wealth, in adversity and prosperity, in the hour of mortal anguish and the day of judgment; and finding what we could not do or bear or encounter, Jesus can do and bear and meet in and through us, to the Father's eternal glory.

> *"Lord Jesus Christ, grow Thou in me,*
> *And all things else recede."*

48

MANY MANSIONS FOR GOD

"If a man love Me, he will keep my words: and my Father will love him; and we will come unto him, and make our abode with him."

JOHN xiv. 23.

THE IMMANENCE of God! That God should be willing to make his home *with* man is much; but that He should be willing to come in—to indwell, occupy, and possess our nature—this is incomprehensible to the intellect, though it may be received and rejoiced in by the heart. This is no subject for light and thoughtless speech. We touch on the profoundest mysteries of the Being of the Infinite, and the capacity of human nature. Be reverent, O my soul, in the consideration of such a theme; and take the shoes from off thy feet, for the Bush burns with fire!

It was owing to the question of Jude that the universal application of our Master's words is so clear. A day or two before, our Lord had entered Jerusalem amid the enthusiasm of the crowds, and the disciples fondly thought the long-expected time had arrived when He would manifest Himself to the world as the Messiah. "This is the beginning of the Messianic reign," said each apostle in his secret heart, as the great procession passed over the shoulder of Olivet; and each began to wonder what special post would be allotted to him in the new empire that seemed so close at hand. These nascent hopes, however, had been rudely dissipated by our Lord's declaration that the world was to see Him no more, qualified nevertheless by the promise, "But ye see Me."

The apostles therefore were inclined to think that in some special form the manifestations of his grace and glory would be confined to them. Hence Jude's question, "What is come to pass, Master, that Thou wilt manifest Thyself unto us, and not unto the world?" Jesus answered in effect, "Think not that thou and thy fellows are to have the exclusive rights of beholding and communing with Me. What I offer to you is open to all who believe, love, and obey. The gate which I throw open shall stand wide for all who choose to enter. The vail shall be rent, that any who fulfil the spiritual conditions may see the light, and hear the voice, and stand in the inner court. If a *man* love Me ...." Note those emphatic words, "a man"—any man; thou and I.

I. THE DIVINE IMMANENCE.—"We will make our abode." The word "abode" is here a translation of the Greek word which is rendered "mansions" in a former part of this chapter. "We will make our *mansion* with him." God is willing to become the mansion of the soul that believes in Christ; but asks in return that such a one should prepare a guest-chamber, and become a mansion in which He may dwell. As He steals with noiseless tread into the loving, believing heart, I hear Him say, "This is my rest for ever; here will I dwell, for I have desired it."

(1) *It is the Immanence of the Father.*—Who is this of whom the Saviour speaks? The infinite God! Time with all its ages is but the flash of a moment in his eternity! Space, "beyond the soar of angel wings," is but a corner in his dwelling-place! Matter, with its ponderous mass, is but the light dust that will not affect the level of the scale! The mighty sun, which is the centre of all worlds, is but a mote floating in the beam of his being! All the gathered wisdom of man, stored in the libraries of the world, is but as a glow-worm's spark compared with the meridian light of his wisdom! O souls of men, consider how marvellous that such a One, whom the heavens cannot contain, who overflows their limits, will yet become the resident of our nature!

Its motive is Love—"The Father will love him." This is wonderful —the more so as we are told that his love toward us is identical with that which He has toward our Lord. Speaking of those who shall believe through his apostles' word, Jesus said, "That the world may know that Thou lovedst them even as Thou lovedst Me." That God should condescend to think about our planet, which is as a leaf in the forest of being; that He should deign to regard mankind, who, in comparison with the material universe, are as a colony of ants compared with the Himalaya, at the foot of which they may have built their home; that He should pity our race—this were much. But that He should *love* the world, that He should *love* individuals belonging to our race, that He should love them with the love He has toward the Only-begotten—we could not have believed this unless we had been assured by the lips of infallible Truth. But the supreme revelation which towers above the rest, like some great banyan tree amid the slender growth of the Indian forest, is that the Creator should indwell and find a mansion in the heart of his creatures.

It is dual, yet one—"We will come." We! Then, are there more than one? Who is this who dares class Himself with the supreme God within the limits of a common pronoun; that challenges the love and trust and obedience of man; that poses as King? The meekest and humblest of men. The One who, above all others of the human family, seems to have least to disturb or darken the incidence of the rays of truth upon his soul; who has cast a light on all the dark problems of human life, and could not possibly have been deceived in respect to his own nature. His conceptions of the holiness, greatness, and purity of

God have stood out in unrivalled magnificence from all others whatsoever; yet it is He who in one small word couples his humanity with
Deity, his meekness with the Infinite Majesty, his personality with
God's. Is not this proof enough that He was conscious of his divine
nature? Is not the fact of his not counting it robbery to be equal with
God evidence that He was God? What can they make of this *We*, who
hold that He was only a good man and a great teacher? Good men are
humble men; great teachers know best their own limitations.

It is in, and with, and through the Son, and by the Spirit, that the
Father comes to indwell.

(2) *It is the Immanence of the Son. To be loved by Him were much!*
—"I will love him." His love is of the rarest quality. True and tender,
strong and sweet, inexorable in its demands upon Himself, inexhaustible in its outflow towards the objects of his affectionate regard.
Such love as He gave to John, who grew like Him beneath the magic
power of that environment; as He gave to Mary, who perhaps most
deeply understood Him; as He gave to Peter, winning him back from
his waywardness—brings with it a heaven of bliss, for which a man
may well be prepared to count all things but loss. But there is a bliss
beyond all this. The Lover of men would indwell them!

It were much that He should seek our love—"He that loveth Me."
We might have supposed that He would have been satisfied with the
vastness of his dominion, and the myriad bright spirits that wait on his
word! But no; the thirst for love cannot be satisfied with gold, or
bright angelic servants. As Isaac could not find a companion among
those who tended the flocks that browsed over the wolds of Canaan, or
among the troops of slaves that gathered round his father's tents, but
Eliezer must bring a bride from across the desert; so the Son of God
must needs come as a suitor to our world to find his Bride, who can
share his inner thoughts and purposes. Here is a marvel indeed. As
the village becomes famous which provides the emperor's bride, so
earth, though it be least among her sister-spheres, shall have the
proud pre-eminence of having furnished from her population the
Spouse of the Lamb. But, great as this marvel is, it is followed by
the greater, that the Immortal Lover is willing to tenant the poor
hearts whose love at the best is so faint and cold.

It were much that He should give us manifestation of his love—"I
will manifest Myself unto him." Have you not sometimes taken up a
daisy, and looked into its little upturned eye, and thought and thought
again, till through the gate of the flower you have passed into an
infinite world of life, beauty, and mystery? There are moments when
even a flower is transfigured before us, and manifests itself to us as a
thought of God, a ray of his glory, the frail product of his infinite
mind, the wick around which trembles the fire of the Shekinah! Have
you not sometimes stood alone amid mountains, glaciers, wooded

valleys, and rushing streamlets, till Nature has dropped her vail, and revealed herself in a phase of beauty and a depth of meaning which struck you as altogether unique and singular? So there are moments in the life of the believer, when Christ, who is ever with us, manifests Himself as He does not to the world. There is borne in upon the spirit a consciousness that He is near; there is a waft of his breath, a savour of his fragrant dress, fresh from the ivory palaces.

All this is much: but how much more to be told that this glorious Christ, the Fellow of Jehovah, who with the Father and the Spirit is God; the Organ of creation; the Mouthpiece of the Godhead; the Mediator of Redemption; the Monarch of all worlds; the Supreme Teacher, Guide, and Saviour of men—is prepared to repeat the experiences of Bethlehem, and make his abode in man! *"We* will come unto him, and make our abode with him."

(3) *Learn to revere the work of God in the souls of others.*—"For thy meat," said the Apostle, "destroy not the soul for whom Christ died." He might have added, "and in whom Christ lives." Weak and erring, trying and vexatious, that fellow-believer may be, yet there is a chamber in his nature in which God has already taken up his abode. The conflict between the light and darkness, the Christ-spirit and the self-spirit, may be long and arduous, but the issue is certain. Help, but do not hinder, the process. Be reverent, careful, mindful of the presence of God.

Be hopeful for thyself.—When an art-student asked Mr. Ruskin whether he would ever be able to paint like Turner, the great critic replied, "It is more likely that you will become Emperor of all the Russias!" But God never daunts a soul with such discouragement. He first sets before it a great ideal—the faith of Abraham, the meekness of Moses, the prayer of Elijah, the love of John—and then, as the source of all perfection, He enters the soul, to be in it all that He has taught it to desire.

Count on the indwelling of his power.—The merchant of to-day has facilities granted to no previous age. The cablegram, telegram, and telephone, put him in communication with the markets of the world; steam and electricity are his willing slaves in manufacture; machinery with its unwearying iron fingers toils for him. A single human brain, which knows how to avail itself of these resources, can multiply its conceptions indefinitely. How vast the space between the untutored savage, doing everything with his hands, and the merchant prince, who has but to press the ivory-plated pushes fixed upon the walls of his room! But not less is the difference between the work we can accomplish by our natural resources, and that which we achieve when we recognise that what is impossible to us is possible to Him who has come in to abide. I cannot; but God is within me, and He can.

II. The Conditions of the Divine Immanence.—(1) *Love to Christ.*—"He that loveth Me shall . . ." We would love Him, but how? Do not think of your love, but of his. "Love is of God." Open the shutters of your being towards the love of God; we love because He first loved. Love is the reflection from us of what we have first received from God.

Love is shed abroad in the heart by the Holy Spirit. The fruit of the Spirit is love. Seek the infilling and inworking of the Spirit; be careful to obey his promptings to love; avoid grieving Him by bitterness, wrath, or evil-speaking; sit as his willing pupil in the school of love; cast on Him the responsibility of securing in your nature obedience to the primal law, which is fulfilled in the one word, "Thou shalt love."

Beneath the nurturing grace of the Spirit, we shall be led to meditate much on the love of Jesus to us, especially as manifested in the death of the cross; and as we muse, the fire will burn, love will glow, and afford the condition of soul which is infinitely attractive to the divine Lover, who requires our love, and produces the love which He requires.

(2) *Obedience to Christ.*—Where there is true love, there will be obedience. This rather than emotion. Many a sincere soul, who questions its love because its emotions are low or fluctuating, would rather die than disobey the least jot or tittle of his commandments. Such a one loves. "He that hath my commandments" (treasured in memory and heart), "he it is that loveth Me." Why do ye call Him, Lord, Lord, and do not the things that He says? There may be the luscious language of the lip, but it does not deceive Him. He looks under the leaves for fruit.

Disobedience robs the soul of the sweet sense of Christ's indwelling. Nothing can compensate for failure to obey. Whatever the protestations, there is no real love to Christ where his commands are knowingly disregarded and set at nought. But each time we dare to step out in simple obedience to his will, it seems as though the inner light shines deeper down into the hidden places of our being, and the residence of Christ extends to new chambers of the heart.

49

Christ's Legacy and Gift of Peace

"Peace I leave with you, my peace I give unto you: not as the world giveth, give I unto you. Let not your heart be troubled, neither let it be afraid."—JOHN xiv. 27.

IT SEEMS a little anomalous to talk of peace at a time when the war-clouds are being swiftly blown up from the horizon, the sea roaring, and men's hearts failing them for fear: and yet, in the deepest aspects, this is of all times the most suitable. It is when the storm rattles on the window-panes that the family draws closer round the fire, and the mother clasps her babe to her breast.

The word Peace is the Eastern salutation and benediction. When one stranger encounters another, as they meet and part they wish each other peace. It was befitting, therefore, that at Christ's entrance into our world the first salutation to men, as conveyed by the angels, should be "Peace on earth"; and that his parting words should be "Peace be unto you." But with what a wealth of meaning does the Lord invest familiar words when they issue from his lips! Let us draw nigh, and allow his sweet and soothing consolations to have their full effect.

I. LET US DISTINGUISH BETWEEN "PEACE" AND "MY PEACE."— "Peace I leave with you, my peace I give unto you." There is a distinction between these two. The former refers to the result of his work for us on the cross: "Being justified by faith, we have peace with God through our Lord Jesus Christ"; the latter refers to *his* indwelling, who is our Peace. The one He has bequeathed as a *legacy* to all men: the Testator died. and left in his will a perfect reconciliation between God and man, which is for all who are willing to avail themselves of it; the other is *a gift*, which must be appropriated and used, or it will be ineffectual.

The order of these two varieties of peace is invariable.—We must have peace *with* God before we can enjoy the peace *of* God. We must receive the atonement, with all its blessed comfort, before we can enter upon our heritage in Christ Jesus. A believer, whose feet were dipping in the chill waters of the river, said to me recently, when speaking of her enjoyment of some of the deeper aspects of Christian experience, "I am afraid I have been building from the top. I see now, as I come near eternity, that one's foundations must be strong and sure before one can build on them. I need now more than ever the blood of Christ." This, perhaps, is one of the perils of the present day. The Church is arraying herself in her beautiful garments. The gold pieces of Christian thought and life are becoming current coin; they are being taken from the coffers, where they have too long lain, and distributed broadcast. Treatises and tractlets on the innermost aspects of the blessed life are plentiful as flowers in May. There is a danger, therefore, of young converts and others occupying themselves with such themes, and not paying sufficient attention to the divine order.

Christ dying *for* us on the cross must precede Christ living *in* us by his Spirit; justification with its evidence must be well apprehended before sanctification with its fruits; the peace *with* God must shed its benediction over the soul before it can enter upon the peace *of* God. Ah, soul! thou hast experienced the former; dost thou know the latter? Dost thou know what it is for Christ to enter into the closed doors of the inner chamber of the heart, and say, "Peace be unto thee"? Dost thou know what it is to hear his voice speaking above the tumult of the inland lake of thy soul, and making a great calm? Dost thou know what it is for Him to deal with the springs of the inner life, which lie deeper than emotion or fancy, and pour in his infinite serenity, so that the outflow may be pellucid and tranquil?

Christ lays stress on *his* peace. He must mean the very peace that filled his own heart; not something like it, but the same, always keeping the heart with the affections, and the mind with its thoughts. This being so, we infer—

That his peace is consistent with a perfect knowledge of coming sorrow.—He knew all things that awaited Him (John xviii. 4): the treachery of Judas, the denial by Peter, the forsaking by all, the shame and spitting, the cross and the grave; and yet He spoke serenely of his peace. It is therefore consistent with the certain outlook towards darkness and the shadow of death. You may know from certain symptoms that cancer has struck its fangs into your flesh, and that paralysis has begun to creep along your spine; that your dearest is barked by the Woodsman for felling; that your means of subsistence will inevitably dry up: but, facing all these, as Jesus faced the cross, you may still be conscious of a peace that passeth understanding.

That it is consistent with energetic action.—Men are disposed to think that peace is one of the last fruits of the tree of life which drop into the hand of the aged. A man says to himself, I shall have to relinquish this active life, to settle in some quiet country home in the midst of nature, and then perhaps I shall know what peace means. A snug home and a competence, the culture of flowers, the slow march of the seasons, tender home-love far away from the hustling throng of the world—these are the conditions of peace. Not so, says Christ: "Arise, let us go hence." Let us leave this quiet harbour, and launch out into the stormy deep. Let us leave this still chamber, around the windows of which the vines cling, and go forth into the garden where the cedars fight with the tempest; and amidst it all we shall find it possible to enjoy the peace that passeth knowledge. Let men and women immersed in the throng of daily toil, young men, busy men, understand that Christ's peace is for those who hear the bugle note of duty summoning them to arise and go hence.

That the chief evidence of this peace is in the leisureliness of the heart.—Christ's possession of peace was very evident through all the stormy scenes that followed. With perfect composure He could heal the ear of Malchus, and stay the impetuosity of Peter; could reason quietly with the slave that smote Him, and bid the daughters of Jerusalem cease their weeping; could open Paradise to the dying thief, and the door of John's home to the reception of His mother. Few things betray the presence of his peace more than the absence of irritability, fretfulness, and feverish haste, which expend the tissues of life.

Oh that you may now receive from Christ this blessed gift! Let the peace of Christ rule in your heart; it is your high privilege, be not backward in availing yourself of it. It will be as oil to the machinery of life.

II. The Sources of Christ's Peace.—(1) *The vision of the Father—* "If ye loved Me, ye would rejoice because I said, I go unto the Father."

Throughout these closing chapters He seems able to speak of nothing else. His mind ranges from the disciples whom He was leaving to the Father to whom He was going. Almost unconsciously He gives us a glimpse of his self-repression in staying so long away from his Father's manifested presence, when He says that if we loved Him we would be glad to lose his bodily presence because He had gone to be with the Father. He gives us to understand how real and near the Father was to Him, and how He longed to be again in his bosom! He was so occupied with this thought, that He reckoned little of what lay between. Hail! ye stormy waters of death, stormy winds, and boisterous waves: ye do but waft my soul nearer its haven in the Father's love!

It is the thought of the Father that gives peace, because it robs life of its terrors and death of its sting. Why fear what life may bring, when the Father has arranged each successive step of its pathway! Why dread Judas or Caiaphas, Herod or Pilate, since the Father lies between them and the soul as a rampart of rock! Why lose heart amid the perplexities and discouragements whose dark shadows lie heavily on the hills, when in the green pastures of the valley the Father's love tends the sheep! Ask Christ to reveal the Father to you. Live in his everlasting love, and learn what He can be amid the storm and tumult as a very present help.

(2) *Disentanglement from the world*—"The prince of this world cometh, and hath nothing in Me." He came first at the beginning of the Saviour's life, with temptations to his ambition; he came again at its close, with temptations to that natural shrinking from pain which is characteristic of a highly organised nature. "Back, Son of Man! Thou canst not bear the cross and spear, the nail and thorn! Thy tender flesh will ill sustain Thee when the sorrows of death and the pains of hell get hold upon Thee!" So Satan came; but there was no response in the heart of Christ, no answering voice from the depths of his soul, no traitor within to join hands with the tempter without. There was no square inch of territory in all Christ's nature which the devil could claim, or from which he could operate.

This is a clue to Christ's peace, which we do well to follow till it lead us out into the open. As long as we are entangled with this world, peace evades us—just as sleep, which comes easily to the labouring man who has nothing beyond his daily wage, vanishes from the pillow of the merchant, who on stormy nights thinks uneasily of the vessels which carry his wealth far out at sea. We must stand clear of the ambitions of the world, of the fear or favour of man, of the avaricious craving for wealth, or of the fear of poverty. We must put the cross of Christ between us and the world, which was judged at Calvary. We must be able to say truly that our treasure is in heaven, and our heart also; and that we seek the things where Christ sitteth at the right hand of God. Then the stock-market may fluctuate; riches go or come; men praise or hate—nought will affect our peace, any more than the tumults of a Continental city, in which we are spending a night in transit, can cause us serious disturbance.

(3) *Supreme love*—"I love the Father." I have often noticed how a supreme love in a young girl's life seems to calm and quiet her, because it draws the whole of her nature in one strong flow towards the man of her choice. Before that, there was a waywardness, a vacillation, a nervous excitement, which passed away as soon as love dawned upon her soul. So long as the heart is subject to every influence, it quivers and wavers as the magnetic needle, when swept by streams of electricity. A strong uniting love does for us what the strong attraction of the pole does for the needle. Christ loved the Father. There was no difficulty in bearing what He sent, or doing what He bade. There were no rival claimants, no questionings or debate within the palace of his heart. Every passion and emotion was quieted and stilled in the set of his whole being towards the Father. If you too would have peace, you must love; you must love supremely Him who alone is worthy, who can never disappoint or fail. And in proportion as you love God, you will find pleasure in all beautiful things, in all lovely persons, in all the fair gifts of nature and life. Oh, love the Lord, O my soul, and all that is within me, love his holy name!

(4) *A supreme source of authority*—"As the Father gave Me commandment, even so I do." Every soul must have a supreme source of authority in its life, if it is to have peace. Its own whim, the suggestion of passion, the vagrant impulse of the moment, are inconsistent with tranquillity. There must be for each of us one voice which is imperative, one command which is indisputable, one authority which admits of no gainsaying. If you will search your heart you will see that this is so. Compare the restlessness of the times of the Judges with the tranquillity of the reign of Solomon, and you will have an apt illustration of your own experience before consecration put Christ on his throne, and afterwards. When the true Melchisedec established his reign within you, at once your heart became Salem, the city of peace. When you put the government upon his shoulder, He set up his reign within you as the Prince of Peace. Happily for you, if of the increase of his government there is no end; for of the increase of your peace there will be no end either.

Combine these four—the sense of God's presence and providence in the details of life; detachment from the world; a supreme love to God; the recognition in everything that you are his bond-servant—and you will comply with the conditions of participating in the peace of Christ which He offers. Some persons have a marvellous faculty of imparting their own tranquillity in an accident, a storm, an illness; their aspect, tones, manner, are like the repose of a summer's evening after a sultry day: so shall Christ be to you, and you to others.

III. CHRIST'S GIVING CONTRASTED WITH THE WORLD'S—"Not as the world giveth, give I unto you."

The world wishes peace, but lightly speaks the word; frequently wishing it when there is least warrant for it; wishing it without doing anything to produce it; wishing it whilst glorying over a wrong, healing slightly a wound, covering with the turf the crater of a volcano. Christ, on the other hand, lays the foundations of peace in suitable conditions of a holy and healthy life.

With the world, peace is a passing emotion; with Christ, a settled principle of action—the perfect balance and equilibrium of the soul, out of which comes all that is fair, strong, wholesome.

The world's peace consists in the absence of untoward circumstances; Christ's is altogether independent of circumstances, and consists in the state of the heart. It matters nothing that in the world we have tribulation; He bids us be of good cheer, because in Him we shall have peace. The wildest conjunction of outward things cannot break the perfect peace of the soul which nestles to his heart, as Noah's dove to the hand which plucked it in from the weltering waters.

"Let not your heart be troubled," the Master says again. You may be troubled on every side; but be not troubled! Do not let the trouble come inside. Watch carefully against its intrusion, as you would against that of any other form of temptation. Let my peace, like a sentinel, keep you; and as you look forward to the unknown future, out of which spectral figures emerge, do not be afraid. There is a part for you to do, as well as for Me. I can give you my peace; but you must avoid any and every thing that will militate against its possession and growth.

The Story of the Vine

"I am the true Vine, and my Father is the Husbandman."
JOHN xv. i.

WE HAVE now a story to tell which, in the eye of heaven, will make our world for ever memorable and wonderful among her sister spheres. It is the story of the Vine, and how it was the divine purpose that our earth should be its fruitful soil, and our race intimately associated with its growth and history.

"I am the *true* Vine," said our Lord. Not improbably, as He was passing forth with his disciples into the moonlit air, He perceived a vine clustering around the window or door; and with an eye ever awake to each touch of natural beauty, and a heart always alert for spiritual lessons, He turned to them and said, What that vine is in the world of nature, I am in relation to all true and faithful souls. I am the *true* Vine—true, not as opposed to false, but true in the sense of real, substantial, and enduring: the essential, as distinguished from the circumstantial; the eternal, as distinct from the temporary and transient.

Nature is a parable of God. In each of her forms we have a revelation of God—not so complete as that given through the mind of prophets, or the life of Jesus Christ; but still a revelation of the Divine. Each natural object, as it stood in Eden's untainted beauty, displayed some aspect of Him whom no man can see and live. The apple-tree among the trees of the wood; the rose of Sharon; the lily of the vale; the cedar, with its dark green foliage; the rock with its strength; the sea with its vast expanse; the heaven with its limpid blue, like the divine compassion, over-arching all—these are some of the forth-shadowings in the natural world of spiritual qualities in the nature of God.

I. THE VINE AND ITS BRANCHES.—*The unity of the vine.*—The vine and its branches constitute one plant. Some branches may be trailed along the trellis-work outside the cottage door, others conducted through hothouse after hothouse; yet one life, one stream of sap, one essential quality and character, pervades them all—from the dark root, buried in the soil, to the farthest twig or leaf. Yonder branch, waving its fronds high up against the hothouse glass, cannot say to that long leafless branch hidden beneath the shelf, You do not belong to me, nor I to you. No twig is independent of another twig. However different the functions, root and branches, leaves and cluster, all together make one composite but organic whole. So is it with Christ. All who are one with Him are one with each other. The branches that were nearest the root in the days of Pentecost are incomplete without the last converts that shall be added in the old age of the world. Those without these will not be made perfect.

This is the underlying truth of the holy Catholic Church. Men have tried to show that it must be an outward and visible organisation, consisting of those who had received, through a long line of apostolical succession, some mystic power of administering rites and conferring absolution upon those who came beneath the touch of their priestly hands. That theory has notoriously broken down. But the truth of which it is a grotesque travesty is presented in our Lord's conception of the vine, deeply planted in the dark grave of Joseph's garden, which has reached down its branches through the ages, and in which every believing soul has a part. Touch Christ; become one with Him in living union; abide in Him—and you are one with the glorious company of the apostles, the goodly fellowship of the prophets, the noble army of martyrs, and the Church of the Firstborn, whose names are written in heaven.

The pliancy of the vine.—More than most plants it needs a husband-man. It cannot stand upright like other fruit-trees; but requires a skilful hand to guide its pliant branches along the espaliers, or to entwine them in the trellis-work. It suggests a true thought of the appearance presented to the world by Christ and his Church.

Mrs. Hamilton King, in her description of the sermon preached in the hospital by Ugo Bassi, on the eve of the great movement which, by the expulsion of the Austrians, gave Italy to the Italians, specially dwells on this. Down five wards the prisoners are living on the hospital-beds from which they will never rise again. To them the deep voice of the hero-preacher tells the story of the vine : how "it is tied to a stake, and if its arms stretch out, it is but crosswise; they are also forced and bound."

Thus it was with Christ. Never following his own way, always bound to the imperative *must* of the Father's will, He yielded to the cross as a willing Sufferer. And so it has been with his followers. Not strong to stand alone, but always yielded to the Father's will, that He should lead them whither He would—to a cross, if needs be; to persecution and shame, if this would better serve his purpose; to a Gethsemane, if that were the only gate to life.

Yield thyself to those loving hands. They may lead thee afar from thy original purpose—twisting thee in and out with many a contortion;

fixing thee with nail and fastening; trailing thee over the wall, to droop thy clusters to the hands of strangers. Nevertheless, be sure to let Him have his way with thee; this is necessary for the accomplishment of his purpose.

The suffering of the vine.—When, in the spring, "the grace of the green vine makes all the land lovely, and the shoots begin to wind and wave in the blue air," the husbandman comes in with pruning-hook and shears, and strips it bare of all its innocent pride. Nor is this all. Even in the vintage it is not allowed to glory in the results of the year; "the bunches are torn down and trodden in the wine-press, while the vine stands stripped and desolate."

So it has always been. The Church has always, but at an infinite cost to herself, been instrumental in promoting the well-being of the world. Christ's people have always been a suffering people; and it is in exact proportion to their anguish that they have enriched mankind. They have saved others, but not themselves. The red stream of blood that has vitalised the world has flowed from broken hearts.

> "Measure thy life by loss instead of gain;
> Not by the wine drunk, but by the wine poured forth:
> For Love's strength standeth in Love's sacrifice,
> And whoso suffers most hath most to give."

The interdependence of vine and branches.—In God from eternity dwelt a wealth of love, pity, and yearning over the souls of men, that could not find direct expression. There was no language for the infinite passion of the divine heart. Hence the gift of the Son, through whom, when He had become flesh, the Infinite might express Himself. But even this was not sufficient. The vine-root is not enough in itself; it must have branches to carry its rich juices to the clusters, so that these may hang free of each other in the sun and air. Christ must have branches—long lines of saved souls extending down the centuries —through which to communicate Himself to men.

We have seen how necessary the Vine is to the branches. Only from it can our fruit be found. But let us humbly, yet gladly, believe that we are also necessary to Christ. He cannot do without us. The Son wants sons; angels will not suffice. Through redeemed men alone can He achieve his eternal purpose. I hear the Vine pleading for more and yet more branch-life, that it may cover the world with goodly shadow and fruit.

II. FRUIT OR NO FRUIT?—From all that has been said, it is clear that the one purpose in the vine is fruit-bearing. See here how the divine Teacher accentuates it. "Fruit," "much fruit," "more fruit." Nothing less will content Him in any one of us. For this, we were taken out of the wild vine in which we were by nature, and grafted into Him; for this, the regeneration of the Holy Ghost, and the discipline of life; for this, the sunshine of his love, and the dew of the Holy Ghost. It becomes each seriously to ask, "Am I bringing forth fruit unto God?" There may be orthodoxy of doctrine, correctness in life, and even heartiness of service; but is there fruit, much fruit, more fruit?

Fruit!—This is the only condition of being retained in living union with the Vine.

Much fruit!—Only thus will the Father be glorified.

More fruit!—Otherwise there must be the repeated use of the knife.

Nowhere does the Lord contemplate a *little fruit*. A berry here and there! A thin bunch of sour, unripened grapes! Yet it is too true that many believers yield no more than this. He comes to us hungry for grapes; but behold, a few mildewed bunches, not fit to eat!

Where there is *no fruit*, there has been no real union with the Vine. Probably you are a professor, but not a possessor; a nominal Christian, an attendant at church or chapel, but not really one with Christ. True union with Him produces a temper, a disposition, a ripe and mellow experience, which certainly indicate that Christ is within. You cannot simulate the holy joy, the thoughtful love, the tranquil serenity, the strong self-control, which mark the soul that is in real union with Jesus; but where there is real abiding, these things will be in us and abound, and we shall be neither barren nor unfruitful in the knowledge of our Lord Jesus Christ.

III. THE KNIFE AND THE FIRE.—"Every branch in Me that beareth fruit," the Father, who is the Husbandman, "purgeth it, that it may bring forth more fruit." Too many children of God, when passing through great physical and other suffering, account it punishment. Nay, it is not punitive, but purgative. This is the pruning-knife, cutting away the shoots of the self-life, that the whole energy of the soul may be directed to the manifesting of the life of the Lord Jesus. It may seem a grievous waste to see the floor of the hothouse or vineyard littered with fronds and shoots and leaves, but there need be no lament: the branches of the autumn will well repay each stroke of that keen edge with fuller, richer fruit. So we gain by loss; we live as we die; the inward man is renewed as the outward decays.

The knife is in the Father's hand; let us never forget that. He will not entrust this delicate and difficult work to man or angel. Shall we not be in subjection to the Father of our spirits and live? Blessed be the Father of our Lord Jesus, and our Father in Him. He that spared not Christ may be trusted to do the best for us.

Employing the same word, the Master said, Now ye have been pruned through the word that I have spoken to you. Perhaps if we were more often to yield ourselves to the pruning of the Word, we should escape the pruning of sore pain and trial. If the work were done by the golden edge of Scripture, it might make the iron edge of chastisement needless. Therefore, when we take the Word of God in hand, let us ask the great Husbandman to use it for the pruning away of all that is carnal or evil, so that his life may have unhindered sway.

But if we will not bear fruit, we must be taken away. We shall lose our sphere of Christian service, and be exposed as hollow and lifeless professors. The vine-branch that has no wealth of purple clusters is good for nothing. Salt which is savourless is fit neither for the land nor the dunghill. Vine-branches that bear no fruit are cast into the fire. Professors that lack the grace of a holy temper, and the beauty of a consistent life, are taken away. "Men cast them into the fire, and they are burned."

These three years the divine Husbandman has come hungrily seeking fruit of thee, yet in vain. Nevertheless, He will spare thee for this year also, that thou mayest mend thy ways. This is the reason of thy multiplied anxieties; He is pruning thee. If thou bearest fruit, it will be well, eternally well; but if not, then it is inevitable that thou shalt be cut away as dead and useless wood.

51

"ABIDE IN ME, AND I IN YOU"

*"Abide in Me, and I in you. As the branch cannot bear fruit of itself,
except it abide in the vine; no more can ye, except ye abide in Me."*
JOHN xv. 4.

THESE words are so familiar by constant repetition, that their power to
awaken the soul is greatly lessened. They go and come through ear
and mind—as a lodger who has gone and come with exactly the same
appearance and at precisely the same hours for years, and no one
notices him now, because there is nothing novel about him to awake
notice or remark. How good would it be if we could hear this tender
injunction for the first time! Next to this, let us ask the divine Spirit
to rid it of the familiarity of long use: to re-mint it, and to make it
fresh and vital; that it may seem to us that we have never before
realized how much Jesus meant when He said, *Abide in Me.*

Perhaps it may assist us if we adopt another English word for *abide*;
and one which, in some respects even more closely, especially in sound,
resembles the Greek. It is the word *remain*; so that we may read the
Master's bidding thus: *Remain in Me, and I in you.*

This word is often employed in the New Testament in connection
with house and home. "Mary abode [or remained] with Elisabeth for
three months"; and, "There abide [or remain]," said our Lord, when
giving his disciples directions for their preaching tour, and referring to
some hospitable house which had been opened to welcome them. It is
used three times in that memorable colloquy which introduced John
and Andrew to their future Teacher and Lord: "Master," they said,
"where abidest [or remainest] Thou? He saith unto them, Come, and
ye shall see. They came therefore, and saw where He abode, and they
abode with Him that day." And again: "Zaccheus, make haste and
come down, for to-day I must abide [or remain] in thy house." We are
to remain in Christ as a man stays in his home.

It is inferred, of course, that we are in Christ.—It would be absurd
to bid a man remain in a house unless he were already within its doors.
We must be sure that we are *in* Christ. Naturally we were outside—
"Remember," says the Apostle, "that aforetime ye were separate from
Christ, alienated from the commonwealth of Israel, and strangers from
the covenants of the promise, having no hope and without God in the
world." We were shoots in the wild vine, partaking of its nature, involved in its curse, threatened by the axe which lay at its root. But all

this is altered now. The Father, who is the Husbandman, of his abundant grace and mercy, has taken us out of the wild vine and grafted us into the true. "Of God are ye in Christ Jesus."

It is quite true that we repented of our sins, and turned towards God; that we have believed in Christ, and taken his yoke; that we have found rest under the shelter of his cross, and joy in expecting his advent: but we must never forget that behind all these movements of our will, and choice, and faith, were the willing and doing of God Himself. It is the Lord's doing, and it is marvellous in our eyes. "Blessed be the God and Father of our Lord Jesus Christ, who hath begotten us again unto a living hope." What confidence this gives us! We are in Christ by the act of God's grace and power; and surely He who puts us in can keep us there. Did He not shut Noah into the ark, and keep him there amid all the crash of the pitiless deluge! We have only to consent to remain, and allow God to perfect that which concerneth us. Be confident of this very thing, that He who began a good work in you will perform it until the day of Jesus Christ.

The stress which the Master lays on our abiding in Him.—He appears to summon all his forces to accentuate his parting message. You always reserve your most important injunctions to the last, that they may remain fresh and impressive as the train steams out of the station, as the boat leaves the landing-stage; so Christ left this entreaty to the last, that it might carry with it the emphasis of a parting message for evermore. But note how He drives it home. Its keyword occurs eleven times in eleven consecutive verses. He depicts the terrible result if we do not abide: we shall wither, be taken away, and consigned to the fire. He shows how utterly we shall miss the one end of our existence —the glorification of the Father by fruit-bearing—unless we strenuously and continuously abide. He allures by the thought of the much fruit; by the assurance of success in prayer; by the promise of fullness of joy, of love, and of blessedness. He entreats, commands, exhorts, all in one breath. It is as though He were to say, "Children, I am leaving you: there are many things I desire for you, many commands to utter, many cautions, many lessons; but I am content to leave all unsaid, if only you will remember this one all-inclusive bidding—Abide in Me, remain in Me; stay where God has put you; deepen, emphasize, intensify, the union already existing between you and Me. From Me is your fruit found. Without Me ye can do nothing. Abide in Me, and I in you. Grow up into Me in all things, which am the Head; rooted and built up in Me, and stablished by your faith, even as ye were taught."

There are many analogies to this appeal.—The sun says to the little earth-planet, *Abide in me.* Resist the temptation to fly into space, remain in the solar sphere; and I will abide in the formation of thy rocks, the verdure of thy vegetation, and all living things, baptizing them in my fire.

Abide in me, says the ocean to the alcove, that shows symptoms of division from its waves. Keep thy channel unsilted and open, and twice in every twenty-four hours I will pour my fullness up to thy farthest shore.

Abide in me: the vine says it to the branch, that it may impart supplies of life and fruit; the air says to the lung, that it may administer ozone and oxygen to its cells; the magnet says it to the needle, that it may communicate its own specific quality, and fit it to guide across the ocean the mighty steamer, laden with the freight of human life.

Abide in me: the artist says it to the novice; Edison would say it to some young Faraday; the preacher to the student. Any man who is eager to impart his ideas to coming time is glad when some young life, eager, quick to receive formative impressions, presents itself. Here, says he, is my opportunity of incarnating myself afresh, and still living, speaking, painting, when my life is done. "Stay with me, young soul; share my home; saturate yourself with my ideas and methods of expression; go to no other fields to glean—and I will give my best self in return."

So, also, the mother speaks to the child. If she is wise, she will be chary of handing it over to the nurse, or sending it away to the care of strangers, except for the hours necessary for education. The child will bring companions and games, books and studies, within the influences of her love; and she, in return, will gladly bestow herself to the eager life that waits on her every movement, look, and word.

In all these cases, it is always the stronger that pleads with the weaker to abide, promising the communication of fuller life. Each, in measure, says, in the words of the glorious Christ, "I am stronger, wiser, fuller, better, than you. All is mine that it may be yours: therefore, abide in Me, and I will abide in you."

Notice Christ's consciousness of sufficiency for the needs of men.— It were blasphemous audacity to speak thus, if He were not more than man. He affirms that there can be no life apart from Him; that souls not united with Him wither on the forest floor. He says that fruit-bearing is only possible to those who receive from his fullness grace for grace. He says that to be in union with Him will secure union with all holy souls. He says that if his words are carefully pondered and obeyed, we shall make no petition which his Father will not grant. He says that his love, in quality and quantity, is like the love that God has towards Himself; that his commands take rank with those of Deity. He offers Himself to all mankind in coming ages, as their contemporary, and as the one sufficient source of life and godliness. All these assumptions are made in the range of these verses; and as we ponder them, we feel that the Speaker must be conscious of being other than human, and as possessing those infinite attributes which are the sole property of the Eternal.

Yet who shall say that He has offered more than He can give? Have not we tested Him in each of these particulars, and do not we, who have come to Him by faith, know that in no one item has He been guilty of exaggeration? We were dead; but behold, we live! We spent our energies in profitless work; but now we bear fruit unto God. We were lonely and isolated; but now have come to the heavenly Jerusalem, to the innumerable company of angels, and to the Church of the First-born. Our prayers were aimless and ineffective; but now we have the petitions we desired. New hope and joy have filled our hearts —as the juicy clusters hang full and ripe in the autumn. Prove Him for yourself, and see if this shall not be so for you also. Only give yourself entirely up to Christ. Abide in Him. Remain in Him. Let thought and speech and life be bathed in the influences of his Holy Spirit; let the sap of his life flow where the sap of the self-life was wont to flow; and lo! old things will pass away, and all things will become new.

The law and method of abiding.—There are two currents always flowing within our reach:

The "Not I," and the "I."

The last Adam, and the first.

The Spirit, and the flesh.

God has put us by his grace into the first of these. The Master says, "Stop there." Much as when a father puts his little boy in the railway carriage, *en route* for home, and says, "My boy, stop where you are. Do not get out; no change is necessary." We are in Christ by regeneration and faith. We may not always be thinking about Him; but we remain in Him, unless by unfaithfulness or sin we consciously and voluntarily leave Him. And if we have left Him for a single moment, it is always possible by confession and renewal to regain our old position.

This is confessedly an inadequate figure of speech. There is a sense in which the member cannot be amputated from the body, and the soul cannot be divorced from its union with Christ. But we are not dealing now with our integral oneness with Christ for life, but with our abiding union with Him for fruit-bearing and service. And again we say, for those who are so immersed in daily business as to be unable for long together to keep their minds fixed on Christ, that their abiding in Him does not depend on their perpetual realisation and consciousness of his presence, but on the faith that they have done and said nothing inconsistent with the holy bond of fellowship.

You are in a lift until you step out of it, though you may not be thinking of the lift. You keep on a road until you take a turning right or left, although, engrossed in converse with your friend, you do not think of the road. You are in Christ, amid the pressure of daily care, and the haste of business, so long as your face is towards the Lord, your attitude that of humble submission, and your conscience void of offence. During the day it is therefore possible at any moment to say, "I am in Thee, O blessed Christ. I have not all the rapture and passion of more radiant hours; but I am in Thee, because I would not by a single act leave thy secret place." If at such a moment you are conscious that you are not able to say as much, instantly go back over the past few hours, discover the place where you severed yourself from your Lord, and return.

Study Godet's beautiful definition of abiding: "It is the continuous act by which the Christian lays aside all he might draw from his own wisdom, strength and merit, to desire all from Christ by the inward aspiration of faith."

When, therefore, temptation arises to leave the words of Christ (ver. 7) for the maxims of the world, step back, remain in Him, deny yourself.

Whenever you are tempted to leave the narrow path of his commandments (ver. 10) to follow the impulses of your own nature, reckon yourself dead to these, that you may run in those.

Whenever you are tempted to forsake the holy temper of Christ's love, for jealousy, envy, hatred—step back and say, I will not go out of my hiding-place; I elect to remain in the love of God. The one effort of life is therefore reduced to a persistent resistance of all the suggestions of the world, the flesh, and the devil, that we should step out of that Blessed Man into whom the Father has grafted us. Then He abides in us. He is strong where we are weak; loving and tender where we are thoughtless; holy where we fail. He is in us as wisdom, righteousness, sanctification, and redemption; and as the hope of glory.

52

PRAYER THAT PREVAILS

*"If ye abide in Me, and my words abide in you, ye shall ask what ye
will, and it shall be done unto you."*—JOHN xv. 7.

CHRIST expected answers to his prayers; and in all his teaching leads
us to feel that we shall be able to obtain, through prayer, what otherwise would not come to our hand. He knew all that was to be known
of natural law and the Father's heart; but, notwithstanding his perfect
acquaintance with the mysteries of the Father's government, He said,
"Ask what ye will, and it shall be done unto you."

A careful comparison of the confident assurances of the Master and
the experience of Christians as detailed in their biographies or personal
confessions, discloses a wide difference between his words and the
findings of his disciples. Many have become accustomed to disappointment in prayer. They have asked so many things which they
have never received; have sought so much without finding; have
knocked so repeatedly, but the door has remained closed. We are in
the habit of accounting for our failure by saying that probably our
prayer was not according to the will of God, or that God withheld
the less that He might give us something better. In some cases there
may be even an unspoken misgiving about the harmony of prayer
with our Father's love and wisdom, or with a perfect confidence in
Him as doing the best for us in the world. We forget that if we prayed
as we should, we should ask what was according to his will. We evade
Christ's definite words, *"Whatsoever* ye shall ask in my name, that
will I do."

When we consider the lives of some who have wrought mightily
for God, it is clear that they had learnt a secret which eludes many
of us. Take this, for instance, from the biography of Dr. Burns Thom-
son. "When much together as students," writes his friend, "we agreed
on special petitions, and the Lord encouraged us by giving answers,
so early and so definite, as could only have come from Himself; so
that no room was left for the shadow of a doubt that God was the
Hearer and Answerer of prayer. Once the answer came the same
day, and at another time, whilst we were yet speaking. My friend
often spoke of our agreement, to the glory of Him who fulfilled to
us his promise; and I refer to it to encourage others." This is but one
leaf out of the great library of prayers, intercessions, and supplications
for all saints, which stand recorded before God.

We naturally turn to our Lord's last utterances, in which his instructions about prevailing prayer are fuller than those of the Sermon on the Mount; and than those given in the mid-passage of his earthly life, which depict the importunity of the widow with the unjust judge, and of the friend with his friend at midnight. The words spoken in the chapter we are now considering are particularly pertinent to our purpose, because they deal exclusively with the age to which our Lord frequently referred as "that day"—the day of Pentecost, the age of the Holy Ghost, the day of this dispensation.

I. OUR LORD TEACHES THAT ANY PRAYER WHICH IS TO PREVAIL WITH GOD MUST PASS FIVE TESTS; though these are but different phases of the same attitude.

(1) *The glory of the Father*—"That the Father may be glorified in the Son" (John xiv. 13). The one purpose of Christ on earth was to glorify the Father; and at the close of his life here He was conscious that He had not striven in vain. "Now," said He, "is the Son of Man glorified, and God is glorified in Him." This was the purpose of his earthly career, and it was perfectly consistent with that of his eternal being; for each person of the Holy Trinity is ever intent on unfolding and displaying the moral beauty of the other twain. Having sat down at the right hand of the Majesty on high, Christ still pursues his cherished purpose of making his Father known, loved, and adored. No prayer, therefore, can hope to succeed with Him, or can claim his concurrent intercession, which is out of harmony with this sublime intent.

Whatever petition we offer should be submitted to this standard—can we establish it in the presence of Christ, that our request will promote the glory of the Father? Bring in your evidence—establish your pleas—adduce your strong reasons. If you can make good your claim, your prayer is already granted. But be sure that it is impossible to seek the glory of God consistently with selfish aims. These two can no more co-exist than light and darkness in the same cubic space. The glory of God will ever triumph at our cost. It is equally certain that none of us can truly pray for the glory of God, unless we are living for it. It is only out of the heart that has but one purpose in life and death that those prayers emanate which touch the tenderest chord in the Saviour's nature, and awaken all his energies to their highest activity: "That will I do."

(2) *In Christ's Name*—"Whatsoever ye shall ask in my name" (John xiv. 13). Throughout the Holy Scriptures, *name* stands for *nature*. The Master says, "You must ask in my nature." In other words, when we pray, it must not be as the self-nature, but as the Christian-nature, dictates. We always know when that is paramount. It excludes boasting; it is pure, peaceable, and loving; it is far removed

from the glare and gaud of the world; it is full of Calvary, Olivet, and Pentecost. There are days in our life when we feel borne along on its tidal current. When Christ is in us, the hope of glory; when a power is working within us beyond what we can ask or think; when we live, yet not we, but Christ in us—these are the times most propitious for prayer. Pour out your heart before God. Let the Christ-nature, which is in you by the Holy Spirit, speak to Christ on the Throne. Let the living water, which has descended from the eternal city, return back to its source through the channel of your heart. This is praying in his name, and according to his nature.

Before we can expect our prayers to prosper, let us sit quietly down, and, putting aside all other voices, permit the Christ-nature to speak. It is only in proportion as it countersigns our petitions that they will reach the audience-chamber of eternity. Surely, if this test were properly applied, many of the petitions we now offer so glibly would never leave our lips; and we should be satisfied about the fate of many another prayer which, like some ill-fated barque, has left our shores, and never been heard of again. But again let it be remembered that none can pray in the name of Christ who do not live for that name— like those early evangelists of whom John says that for the sake of the Name they took nothing of the Gentiles. The name of Christ must be predominant in life, if it is to be efficacious in prayer.

(3) *Abide in Christ*—"If ye abide in Me, . . . ask what ye will" (John xv. 7). We are in Christ by the grafting of the great Husbandman, who took us out of the wild vine of nature, and incorporated us with Christ. That union is for ever; but its conscious enjoyment and helpfulness arise only in so far as we keep his commandments. A limb may be in the body, and yet be dislocated and useless. If you are in a train running through to your destination at the terminus, all that is necessary is to resist the temptation to alight at the stations *en route,* and to remain where you are. If, then, God the Father has put you into Christ, and is seeking to establish you in Him, be careful to resist every temptation or suggestion to depart from living fellowship by any act of disobedience or unbelief.

If you abide in Christ in daily fellowship, it will not be difficult to pray aright, for He has promised to abide in those who abide in Him; and the sap of the Holy Ghost, securing for you fellowship with your unseen Lord, will produce in you, as fruit, desires and petitions similar to those which He unceasingly presents to his Father. Throughout the ages Christ has been asking of God. This is the perpetual attitude of the Son to the Father. He cannot ask what the Father may not give. To get, then, into the current of his prayer is to be sure of success. Abide in Him, that He may abide in you; not only in the activities of holy service, but in the intercessions and supplications of the hour of private prayer.

(4) *Submit prayer to the correction of the Word*—"If my words abide in you" . . . (John xv. 7). Christ's words have been compared to a court of solemn and stately personages, sitting to try our prayers before they pass on into the Master's presence.

Here is a prayer which is selfish and earth-born, grasping at the prizes of worldly ambition and greed. But as it enters it encounters that solemn word, "*Seek ye first the kingdom of God and his righteousness,*" and it turns back surprised and ashamed.

Here is another prayer, full of imprecation and unkindness towards someone who has maligned or injured the petitioner. But it is met by that solemn word of the Master, "*Love your enemies, pray for them that despitefully use you,*" and it hastens to retire.

Here is another prayer full of murmuring regret because of the pressure of the cross, the weight of the restraining yoke. But forthwith that notable word of Christ forbids its further progress, saying, "*In the world ye shall have tribulation; but be of good cheer, I have overcome the world.*" In the presence of that reminder and rebuke, the prayer, abashed, turns away its face and departs. Like the accusers of the woman taken in the act of sin, prayers like these are inwardly convicted of unfitness, and go forth.

The words of Christ forbid unsuitable prayer; but they also stir the heart with great desire for the realisation of those good things which Christ has promised to them that love Him. In this sense prayer becomes a dialogue between the Master who says, "Seek ye my face," and the disciple who responds, "Thy face, Lord, will I seek."

(5) *Fruit-bearing.*—"I appointed you that ye should go and bear fruit that . . ." (John xv. 16). In other words, answers to prayer depend very largely on our ministry to others. If we are prompted by desire for our own comfort, peace, or enjoyment, we shall stand but a poor chance of audience in the secret of his presence. If, on the other hand, our prayers are connected with our fruit-bearing—that is, with our ministry to others, with the coming of the kingdom, and the accomplishment of God's purpose of salvation—the golden sceptre will be extended to us, as when Ahasuerus said to Esther, "What is thy request? Even to the half of the kingdom it shall be performed."

Is sun needed to ripen the fruit? Ask for it. The Father waits to give it. Is dew or rain needed that the pitchers may be filled to the brim with water which is to be made wine? Ask for it. God is not unrighteous to forget your work and labour of love. Ask for all but pruning; this the Father will administer, according to the good pleasure of his goodness. The fruit-bearing branches have a right to claim and appropriate all that is needed for the sweetening and ripening of their precious burden.

The temple of prayer is thus guarded from the intrusion of the unprepared footstep by many tests. At the foot of the marble steps we are challenged for the watchword; and if we do not speak in harmony with God's glory our further passage is peremptorily stayed. The key, engraven with the name of Jesus, will only obey the hand in which his nature is throbbing. We must be in Him, if He is to plead in us. His words must prune, direct, and control our aspirations; his service must engage our energies. We must take part in the camp with his soldiers, in the vineyard with his husbandmen, in the temple-building with his artificers. It is as we serve our King that we can reckon absolutely on his answer to our prayers.

II. THREE CONCLUDING THOUGHTS REMAIN.

First. It is clear that our prayers depend very largely on our inner life. Where that is vigorous and healthy, they will be the same. But let deterioration and failure set in, and the effect will be instantly apparent in our prayers. Out of the abundance of the heart the mouth speaks; and when the mouth is opened in prayer and supplication, the heart speaks.

Second. Bespeak the Spirit's indwelling. He is the bond of communion and fellowship between the Father and the Son, and will lift us into the holy circle of that eternal life, so that the current may pass through us with uninterrupted velocity and force. He makes inward intercession for the saints according to the will and mind of God.

Third. Expect that prayer will become ever more engrossing, as the divine impulse is yielded to; so that what now occupies but a comparatively small portion of time and energy will become with us, as with the great Apostle, an exercise which we prosecute with unceasing ardour, an ever-delightful method of promoting the Redeemer's kingdom.

53

The Hatred of the World

"They shall put you out of the synagogues: yea, the time cometh, that whosoever killeth you will think that he doeth God service. And these things will they do unto you, because they have not known the Father, nor Me."—John xvi. 2, 3.

How near love and hate dwell in these words of Jesus! He had been urging his disciples to cultivate perfect love, the love of God; He now turns to describe the inevitable hatred with which they would be assailed in the world that knew neither the Father nor Himself. And if an additional motive were needed to induce that love, it would surely be given by the consideration of that hate.

This is no unimportant theme. It touches very nearly the lives of thousands of believers amongst us. Though they have not to face the thumbscrew and the stake, they discover painfully enough that the offence of the cross has not ceased. There are amongst us many who daily quiver under the venomous gibe of neighbour and fellow-workman, and find that their acceptance of Jesus Christ as Saviour and Master has suddenly changed their family life and their working life from a garden of roses into a bed of thorns. Many a young man in the city counting-house, many a mechanic at the bench, many a traveller in the commercial-room, many a student on the college-benches, is doomed to discover that the world does not love the Church better than in those days when the fires gleamed in Smithfield, and men and women were burned to death for loving God. But how sweet to know that all this verifies the Master's words: "Ye are not of the world, even as I am not of the world. If ye were of the world, the world would love his own; but because ye are not of the world, but I have chosen you out of the world, therefore the world hateth you."

I. What, then, is "the World"?—It consists of those who are destitute of the life and love of God, as contrasted with those who have received and welcomed the unspeakable gift which is offered to all in Jesus Christ. The great mass of the unregenerate and unbelieving, considered as a unity, is "the world," as that term is sometimes distinctively used by Christ and his apostles.

The world has its god; its religion, which was first instituted by Cain at the gates of Eden; its prince, and court, and laws; its maxims and principles; its literature and pleasures. It is dominated by a peculiar spirit which the Apostle calls a lust or fashion, and resembles the German *Zeit-Geist*: an infection, an influence, a pageantry, a witchery; reminding us of the fabled mountain of loadstone which attracted vessels to itself for the iron that was in them, and presently drew the nails from the timbers, so that the whole fabric fell a helpless, shapeless mass into the waves. The votaries of the world attach themselves to the objects of sense, to the things which are seen and temporal. They have the utmost horror of poverty, suffering, and humiliation; these they consider their chief evils, to be avoided at any cost; whilst they regard as the chief good, riches, pleasure, and honour.

The world is thus a great unity and entity; standing together as a mighty kingdom; united and compacted together as Nebuchadnezzar's image; environing the Church, as the great kingdoms of Assyria and Egypt did the chosen people of God in the days of the kings. It resembles a pack of wolves. "Behold," said Christ, "I send you forth as sheep in the midst of wolves." Between such irreconcilable opposites as the Church and the world, there cannot but be antagonism and strife. Each treasures and seeks what the other rejects as worthless. Each is devoted to ends that are inimical to the dearest interests of the other. Each follows a prince, who met the prince of the other in mortal conflict. Let us thank Him who out of this world chose us for Himself.

II. LET US TRACE THE STORY OF THE WORLD'S HATRED.—*It was foretold in Eden.* "I will put enmity," so God spoke to the serpent, "between thee and the woman, and between thy seed and her seed." We are not disposed to treat that ancient record with which our Bible opens as romance or fairy-story; but to regard it as containing a true and authentic record of what actually transpired. That declaration is the key to the Bible. On every page we meet the conflict, the bruising of the Church's heel by the dark powers, and the increasing area of victory covered by our Emmanuel, the Virgin's Child. This hatred is then in the very nature of things, for this is but another name for God. It is, like others of the deepest facts in the experience of man, fundamental and inevitable, the outcome of mysteries which lie beyond the ken of man.

And it has characterised every age.—Abel is slain by Cain, who was of the evil one, and slew his brother. Joseph is put into a pit by his brethren, and into a prison by his master's wife; the Hebrew is smitten by the Egyptian; David is hunted by Saul as a partridge on the mountains; Micaiah is hated by Ahab because he always testifies against him; Jeremiah lives a very suffering stricken life, until he is slain in Egypt for remonstrating against a policy he could not alter; each of the little company then listening to Christ is forecast for a martyr's death, with, perhaps, the exception of John himself, whose life was martyrdom enough; Stephen sheds the blood of his pure and noble nature; and from that day to this the blood of the saints has poured in streams, until the last harrowing records which have come to light of the indescribable tortures and death of Armenian martyrs.

Each age has had its martyr-roll. They have been tortured, not accepting deliverance; have had trial of mockings and scourgings, yea, moreover of bonds and imprisonment; have been stoned, sawn asunder, tempted, and slain with the sword; wandering in deserts and mountains and caves and the holes of the earth: of whom the world was not worthy.

The root or ground of hatred is not due to the evil discovered in the persons who are the objects of the world's hate.—"They hated Me without a cause," our Saviour sorrowfully said. There might have been some cloak for the shamelessness of the world's sin, if He had not spoken words and done works among them such as none other ever said and did; but in the face of the perfect beauty of his character, the grace and truth of his words, and the loveliness of his deeds, it was by their perfidy He was crucified and slain. In vain He challenged them to convince Him of sin, and to bear witness to any evil which might justify their malicious cruelty. They knew it was innocent blood; but this knowledge, so far from mollifying them, only exasperated them the more.

The world hates the Church, not for the evil that is in it, but for the good. It hates without cause. The holier and purer a life is, the more certainly it will attract to itself malignity and dislike. The more Christlike we are, the more we must suffer the relentless hate that drove the nails into his hands, and the spear into his side. Do not be surprised at this. Think it not strange concerning the fiery trial which cometh to prove you, as though a strange thing happened unto you; but doubt and question and be in fear, if you meet only smiles and flattery and such honours as the world can give. You may then ask yourselves whether you are not one of the world's own.

The real origin and fountain of the hatred of the world is due to Satan's antagonism to God.—In his original creation, he was doubtless as fair as any of the firstborn sons of light; but in his pride he substituted himself for God, and love faded out of his being, making way for the unutterable darkness of diabolic hate. Satan hates God with a hatred for which there are no words; and therefore when the Father sent the Son to be the Saviour of the world, Satan gathered up every energy and resource of his nature to dog his steps, and make his course through the world as painful as possible. Do you wonder that the life of Jesus was so full of suffering? It could not have been otherwise. Directly God, in the person of Jesus, stepped down into the time-sphere, and assumed the conditions of earth and death, He came within the range of the utmost that Satan could do to molest and injure Him. Similarly, when the blessed Lord becomes the tenant of the heart, and in proportion as He is so, that heart attracts to itself the hatred with which the devil from the beginning has hated God. "If they have persecuted Me, they will also persecute you. If they have kept my saying, they will keep yours also. And these things will they do unto you, because they have not known the Father, nor Me."

It is natural for the evil to hate the good.—First, the sinner has an uneasy conscience; and it hurts him to come in contact with those whose character reminds him of what he ought to be, and might be, and perhaps once was. The diseased eye dreads the light. The uncanny, slimy things that lurk beneath stones, and in dark caves, squirm in pain when you let in the day. "Everyone that doeth evil hateth the light, neither cometh to the light, lest his deeds should be reproved."

In addition to an uneasy conscience, the sinner has an unbroken will. He stoutly resists the impression of a superior and condemning goodness. He hardens his heart, and strengthens its defences. "Who is the Lord, that I should obey his voice? Double the tale of bricks: summon the choice chariots and veteran soldiers of Egypt, that we may pursue, overtake, and divide the spoil." Such are the successive boasts and challenges of the hardened heart.

Is it to be wondered at, under such conditions, that the wicked plotteth against the just, and gnasheth upon him with his teeth; that he draws his sword and bends his bow, to shoot privily at the upright of heart? "The wicked watcheth the righteous, and seeketh to slay him. The Lord will not leave him in his hand, nor condemn him when he is judged."

The great object of this hatred is to overcome the good.—In this respect the hate of the world is like the love of the Church. The child of God loves, that he may overcome the evil in the world, by converting evil-doers from the error of their ways and assimilating them to holiness; the child of the devil hates, that he may overcome the good of the world, by arresting their goodness, and assimilating them to evil. Ah, how thankful we may be that we are not of the world, but have been chosen out of it; for it lieth in the wicked one, and is infected with the hatred of hell.

It is not difficult, therefore, to go through the world, and escape its hate. We have only to adopt its maxims, speak its language, and conform to its ways. In a well-known picture, the young girl, with pleading, upturned face, seeks to tie the Royalist scarf around the arm of her Huguenot lover. She will secure his safety if she succeeds! Ah, how many pleading glances are cast at us to induce us to spare ourselves and others, by toning down our speech, and covering our regimentals by the disguising cloak of conformity to the world around! "If you do not approve, at least you need not express your disapproval." "If you cannot vote for, at least do not vote against." If you dissent, put your sentiments in courtly phrase, and so pare them down that they may not offend sensitive ears. Such is the advice which is freely proffered. But those who follow it quickly discover that the compromise of principle involves certainly and awfully the loss of influence for good.

III. OUR BEHAVIOUR AMID THE WORLD'S HATRED.—We have fallen on evil days. The world has been coated over with a Christian veneer, whilst the Church has become leavened with the subtle spirit of the world. It is hard to come out and be separate, because in the dim twilight one is apt to mistake friend and foe. The bribes are so rich for those who conform, the dissuasives so strong for those who refuse to bow to the great golden image. But our duty is clear. We must be true to the Spirit of Christ. We must live a holy and unworldly life; we must avoid all that might be construed as an unworthy compromise of the interests of our Master's Kingdom.

And through all the pitiless storm of hate that beats in our faces, we must be glad. "Blessed are ye," said our Lord, "when men shall revile you, and persecute you, and shall say all manner of evil against you falsely, for my sake: rejoice and be exceeding glad." And why rejoice? Because your reward is great in heaven; because you know that you are not of the world; because you are shown to be on the path trodden by the saints before you, every step of which has been trodden amid similar manifestations of the devil's hate.

Moreover, abound in love. Let there be no slackening of the patient, tender, pitying love, which heaps coals of fire on the head of the wrong-doer, and will never rest content until it has subdued the evil of his heart, overcoming it with good. Love must ultimately conquer hate, as surely as to-morrow's sun will conquer the darkness that now veils the landscape.

54

THE WORK OF THE HOLY SPIRIT ON THE WORLD

"He will reprove the world of sin, and of righteousness, and of judgment."—JOHN xvi. 8.

THREE FACTS forced themselves home on the apostles while listening to the Lord's parting words. *First*, that they were to be bereaved of their Master's presence (ver. 5). *Second*, that they were to be left alone, amid the world's hatred—"Whosoever killeth you" (ver. 2). *Third*, that their mission would be witness-bearing to the unseen Lord (xv. 27).

And as they fully realised all that these facts involved, they became too absorbed in their own sorrowful conclusions to inquire what bourn the Master sought as He set sail from these earthly shores. "O Master," they said in effect, "why canst Thou not stay? Our orphaned hearts will never be able to endure the blank which thy absence will cause. Easier could a flock of sheep withstand the onset of a pack of wolves than we the hatred of the world! And as for our witness-bearing, it will be too feeble to avail aught."

And the Master, in effect, answered thus: "I will not leave you without aid. I shall still be with you, though unseen. My presence shall be revealed to your spirits, and made livingly real through the Blessed Comforter. He will be with you, and in you. He will authenticate and corroborate your witness. He shall testify of Me; and when He is come, He will convince the world of sin, of righteousness, and of judgment. You see then that I shall be able to help you better by sending the Holy Spirit than by staying with you Myself. It is expedient for *you* that I go away; for if I go not away the Comforter will not come to you, but if I depart I will send Him unto you."

We may not be able to fathom all the reasons for Christ's withdrawal before the Spirit's advent was possible. But some of them are obvious enough. The full union of the Son of God with our race must be secured through death and resurrection; and his full union with the Father must be indicated in his glorification with the glory He had or ever the worlds were made—before He could be the perfect channel of communicating the divine fullness to our human nature. The Head must be anointed before the Body. There must be no physical distraction arising from the outward life of Jesus to compete with the spiritual impression of his unseen presence. The text must be completed before the sermon can be preached. Christ must die, or there can be no witness to his atonement; must rise, or there can be no testimony to his resurrection; must ascend, or there can be no declaration as to his finished work and eternal intercession. Since the Spirit reveals Christ, all that was appointed unto Christ to do must be completed ere the Spirit can commence his ministry.

The work of the Spirit on the world is through the Church, and is described by our Lord as threefold. By his revelation of Christ He creates three convictions. Each of these is necessary to the regeneration of man. There must be the sense of sin, or he will not seek the Saviour. There must be a belief that righteousness is possible, or the convicted sinner will die of despair. There must be the assurance that sin is doomed, and shall be finally vanquished, or the baffled warrior will give up the long conflict as hopeless.

I. THE CONVICTION OF SIN.—We are constantly meeting people who are perfectly indifferent to Christianity, because they say they do not feel their need of it. Why should they trouble about it, when they suppose themselves able to do perfectly well without it?

In dealing with these, it is a great mistake to entice them towards the Gospel by describing the moral grandeur of Christ's character and teaching. We should at once seek to arouse them to a sense of their great sinfulness. When a man realises that his life is being eaten out by some insidious disease, he will need no further urging to go to a physician. This is the weakness of modern preaching—that we expatiate on the value of the remedy to men who have never realised their dire necessity.

But what is the truth most appropriate for producing the conviction of sin in the human breast? "Preach the Ten Commandments in all their stern and uncompromising 'shalts' and 'shalt-nots,'" cries one. "Read out the descriptions given in Scripture of the evil things that lurk in the heart of man as filthy things in darksome caves," says another. "Show men the results of sin, take them to the edge of the bottomless pit," insists a third. But not one of these is the chosen weapon of the Holy Spirit. He convicts men of the sin of refusing to believe in Jesus Christ.

There stands the cross, the evidence and symbol of God's love; and there stands the risen Christ, offering Himself to men. There is nothing which more certainly proves the innate evil of the human heart than its refusal of that mystery of grace. Disbelief is the creature, not of the intellect, but of the will. It is not the result of inability to understand, but of stubborn obstinacy and stiffneckedness. Here is the supreme manifestation of moral beauty; but man has no eyes for it. Here is the highest revelation of God's desire for man to be reconciled to Him, and be at one with Him, as his happy child; but man either despises or spurns his overtures. Here is the offer of pardon for all the past, of heirship of all the promises, of blessedness in all the future;

but man owns that he is indifferent to the existence and claims of God, and is quite willing to accept the sleeping retribution of bygone years, and to risk a future irradiated by no star of hope. Here is God in Christ beseeching him to be reconciled, declaring how much the reconciliation has cost; but the frail child of yesterday absolutely refuses to be at peace. No trace of tears in his voice, no shame on his face, no response to God's love in his heart.

This is sin at its worst. Not in a Nero drenched with the blood of relatives and saints; nor in an Alva expert to invent new methods of torture; nor in the brutalised expression of the felon; nor in the degradation of the heathen: but in those beside you, who have heard of the love of Jesus from their earliest childhood, and who know that He died for them, and waits to bless them, but who deliberately and persistently refuse Him—you will find the most terrible revelation of what man is capable of. "This is the condemnation, that light is come into the world, and men loved darkness rather than light, because their deeds were evil."

Conviction in itself is not enough. Many have been convicted who have never gone on to conversion, resembling untimely fruit, which, blighted before its maturity, has dropped to the ground.

Conviction of sin does not come to all in the same manner or to the same extent. Indeed, those who have come to Christ in early life are in a degree exempt from drinking this bitter cup, though they have much tenderness of conscience afterwards.

Do not wait for more conviction; but come to Jesus as you are, and tell Him that the saddest symptom in your case is your inability to feel as you know you should. Do not tarry to be convinced of sin. Do not stay away till you feel more deeply. Do not suppose that strongly roused emotions purchase his favour. His command is absolute—*Believe!* But whenever that true repentance is wrought which needs not to be repented of, or those tears of penitence fall from the eyes of the suppliant, the means will always be the person and work and love of Jesus Christ. This is the burning-glass through which the Spirit focuses the rays of God's love on ice-bound hearts.

II. THE CONVICTION OF RIGHTEOUSNESS.—The aggravation of sin of which the Spirit convicts the sinner seems to present a gloom too dark for any ray to penetrate. He cannot forget. The dead past will not bury its dead. The wind of eternity blows away the leaves with which he tries to hide the corpses of murdered opportunities, broken hearts, and dissipated years. He cannot forget. He may close his eyes, but still the memories of the past will haunt him—the deeds he would undo, the words he would recall, the dark ingratitude towards the love of Jesus. Conscience is a flaming terror till a man finds Christ as his Saviour. Her brow is girt with fire, her voice peals with doom.

"Can I ever be cleansed?" cries the convicted soul. "Can these awful gnawings be ended, and these terrors laid? Can I rise from this ruin and become a new, righteous, God-like man?" These questions are answered by the Spirit who induced them. "There is righteousness," He says, "because Christ is gone to the Father, and ye see Him no more."

He is gone to the Father; and the seal of Divine authenticity has therefore been placed on all He said and did in the Father's name.

He is gone to the Father; and it is clear, therefore, that He has been accepted as the Saviour and Redeemer of men.

He is gone to the Father in the likeness and nature of men; evidently, then, man is an object of God's love, is reconciled to God, and is admitted to the rights and privileges of a son and heir.

The work of Jesus on man's behalf, finished at the cross, accepted by the Father—of which the resurrection is witness—presented by our Great High Priest within the vail, is the momentous truth which the Holy Spirit brings home to the convinced sinner. And inasmuch as we are unable to see within the vail and discern the divine marks of approval and acceptance, the Holy Spirit descends, and in his advent proves that Jesus has gone whither He said, and has done what He promised.

How do we know that the work of Jesus Christ has been accepted in the courts of eternity? On this wise. Before He died the Master said that He was going to the Father, and that when He was glorified He would ask and receive the Spirit in his fullness. After days had elapsed and the second week from his ascension was already passing, the Spirit in pentecostal fullness fell upon the waiting Church, giving it an altogether new power with which to combat the world. What the waggons were to Jacob, proving that Joseph lived and thought of him still, and was indeed supreme in Egypt, that the day of Pentecost was in declaring that Christ's personal righteousness had been vindicated, and that the righteousness He had wrought out for man had received the hall-mark of the divine assay. Therefore the Apostle says, "The Holy Ghost also is a witness to us that He hath perfected for ever by one offering them that are sanctified." And again, "Him hath God exalted with his right hand to be a Prince and a Saviour; and the Holy Ghost, whom God hath given to them that obey Him, is witness of these things."

III. THE CONVICTION OF JUDGMENT.—When we have been freed *from* sin, and made righteous in Christ, we are left face to face with a tremendous struggle *against* sin. The sin of the past is indeed forgiven, the voice of conscience has been hushed, the sinner rejoices to know that he is accepted on the ground of righteousness; but the old temptations still crop up. Passion prompts us to live for present gratification;

the flesh deadens the burning aspirations of the spirit. We ask in sad earnestness, How shall we be able to survive the terrible struggle and to come off victorious? It appears a vain hope that we should ever rise to perfect and victorious purity.

At such a time the Comforter convinces us of judgment. Not, as the words are so often misquoted, of judgment *to come*; but in the sense in which our Lord spoke of judgment to the inquiring Greeks: "Now is the judgment of this world; now shall the prince of this world be cast out." Our Lord's references to the existence and power of Satan are always distinct and unhesitating. It is impossible to accept Him as our supreme Teacher without accepting his statements concerning his great antagonist, to undo whose work brought the Son of God to earth.

The whole Gospel is a story of the duel in which our Lord for ever worsted and mastered Satan. The conflict began with the lonely struggle of the temptation in the wilderness; it pervaded Christ's earthly career; it culminated in the cross. Its first note was, "If Thou be the Son of God, command that these stones be made bread"; its last note was, "If Thou be the son of God, come down from the cross." But when our Lord cried, "It is finished!" with the shout of a conqueror He proclaimed to the universe that, though tempted to the uttermost, He had not yielded in one particular, that evil was not an eternal power, that wrong was not omnipotent. The cross was the crisis of this world's history: the prince of this world measured himself for one final wrestle with the Son of God. Had he succeeded, evil would have reigned; but since he failed, he fell as lightning from heaven.

On this fact the Holy Spirit loves to dwell. He unfolds its full meaning. "See," He says, "Christ has conquered for you, and in your nature. You meet a foe who is not invincible. Christ conquered, not for Himself, but for all who believe. The prince of this world has been judged and found wanting. He is condemned for evermore. Only abide in the last Adam, the Lord from heaven, and let Him abide in you, and He will repeat through you his olden victories."

What a majestic thought is here! The world comes to us first with her fascinations and delights. She comes to us next with her frowns and tortures. Behind her is her prince. But since he has been cast out by a Stronger than himself, and exists only on sufferance, his most potent bribes and lures, his most violent onsets, his most unscrupulous suggestions, must collapse. Believer, meet him as a discredited and fallen foe. He can have no power at all over thee. The cross bruised his head. Thou hast no need to fear judgment. It awaits those only who are still in the devil's power. But thou mayest rejoice that for thee a victory waits, the measure of which will only be realised when thou seest the devil cast into the bottomless pit, and thence into the lake of fire.

55

CHRIST'S RETICENCE SUPPLEMENTED BY THE SPIRIT'S ADVENT

"I have yet many things to say unto you; but ye cannot bear them now."—JOHN xvi. 12–15.

How CONFIDENTLY our Lord speaks of the Spirit's advent; not more so did the prophets foretell his own. Repeatedly He returns to the phrase, *When He is come.* The advent of the Spirit to the heart of the Church on the day of Pentecost was as distinct and marked an event as the advent of the Son of God Himself to the manger-bed of Bethlehem. Let every reader of these words be sure of having taken full advantage of the presence of the Spirit, just as we would wish to have availed ourselves to the uttermost of the physical presence of Christ, had our lot so befallen.

I. THE THEME OF THIS PARAGRAPH IS THE INCOMPLETENESS OF OUR LORD'S TEACHING.—For three and a half years He was perpetually pouring forth his wonderful words; in many *different* places—the market-place, the home at Bethany, the hillside, the Temple cloister; to many *different audiences*—now in thronging crowds, and again to the secret disciple whose footfall startled the night, or the lone woman drawing water from the well; on many *different themes*—to mention all of which would be impossible, though He never spoke on any subject, common as a wayside flower, without associating with it thoughts that can never die. We have but a small portion of his words recorded in the Gospels; it is therefore the more remarkable that He left anything unsaid, and that at the close of his ministry He should have to say, *I have yet many things to say unto you.* Many parables, fair as his tenderest, woven in the productive loom of his imagination, remained unuttered; many discourses, inimitable as the Sermon on the Mount, or as this in the upper room, unspoken; many heavenly mysteries unrevealed.

A comparison between the Gospels and the Epistles will indicate how much our Lord had left unsaid. The relation of the law of Moses to his finished work was left to the Epistle to the Romans: the relation between his Church and the usages of the heathen world, for the Epistle to Corinth: the effect of his resurrection on the sleeping saints, for the Epistle to the Thessalonians. He said nothing about the union of Jew and Gentile on terms of equality in his Church; this mystery, hidden from ages and from generations, was only fully unveiled in the

Epistle to the Ephesians. It was left for the Epistle to the Hebrews to disclose the superseding of the Temple and its ritual by the realities of the Christian dispensation. The practical precepts for the right order-ing of the churches were left for the pastoral Epistles; and the course of the Church through the ages of the world's history, for the Apoca-lypse of the beloved Apostle. When we perceive the many things, taught in the Epistles, which were not unfolded by the Lord, we dis-cern a fresh meaning in his assurance that He left much unsaid.

We are perpetually assailed by the cry, "Back to Christ," which is significant of men's weariness of theological system and organised ecclesiasticism, and of a desire to get away from the accretions of the Middle Ages and the dead hand of Church Tradition, into the pure, serene, and holy presence of Jesus of Nazareth. It always seems to us as if the cry should be *Up* to Christ, rather than *Back* to Him. To put it as men generally do, suggests the inference that Christ lies far in the wake of human progress, and behind the haze of eighteen centuries; that He was, but is no longer, a potent factor in the world's life: where-as He is here, now, with us, in us, leading us as of old through rugged passes, and to mountains of transfiguration.

If the endeavour to get back to Christ means the reception of the Synoptic Gospels to the exclusion of the Fourth, or the Epistles; or the Sermon on the Mount to the exclusion of the Epistle to the Romans; or Jesus to the exclusion of his apostles—we feel it is but half the truth. Our Lord Himself protested that his teachings were incomplete; that there was much left unsaid which would be said by the Comforter, as even He could not—because the Spirit of God speaks in the inner shrine of the soul, uttering to the inner ear truths which no voice could speak or ear receive. Let us always remember therefore that the Gospels must be completed by the Epistles; and that the Spirit who spake in the Son spake also in those whom the Son had prepared to be his mouthpieces to men.

II. THE PARTIAL MEASURE OF HUMAN ABILITY TO KNOW.—"Ye cannot bear them now." Our Lord's reticence did not arise from ignorance—all things were naked and open to his eye; but He had a tender regard for these men whom He loved.

Their bodies could not bear more. When the mind is strongly wrought upon, the delicate organism of the body is deeply affected. On the banks of the River Hiddekel, words of such wondrous impor-tance were uttered to Daniel, that the lonely exile fainted, and was sick many days. "When I saw Him," said John, "I fell at his feet as dead." Flavel, on more than one occasion, asked that the excessive revelation might be stayed. Our Lord, therefore, feared that in their weakened state, torn by anxiety and sorrow, his followers would collapse if fur-ther strain were imposed upon their powers of spiritual apprehension.

Their minds could not bear more. The mind cannot receive more than a certain amount. After awhile its eye gets weary, it ceases to receive, and even to remember. There are multitudes of cases in which, when too great a weight has been crowded on the delicate organism through which thoughts move, its balance has been upset, and it has drivelled into idiocy. Against this danger, also, our Lord guarded, for his disciples were already excited and overstrained. Their brains were so exhausted that in a few moments they would be sleeping on the cold ground of Gethsemane. Had He poured the light of the other world in full measure upon them, the tide of glory had submerged them, like spent swimmers.

Their affections could not bear more. Because He had spoken to them, sorrow had filled their heart; and He forbore to describe the valley of the shadow through which they were still to pass, lest their hearts should break. They had hardly commenced to drink its cup: what would its dregs be? The footmen had wearied them: how would they contend with the horses? The brink had terrified them: how would they do in the swellings of Jordan?

It is thus that He deals with us still. He knows our frame, and proportions our trials to our strength. He carefully feels our pulse before commencing the operation through which He would lead us to perfect health. He tempers his discipline to our spiritual capacity. We desire to know many things: the reason why sin has been permitted; the fate of the impenitent; the state of the great masses of men who have passed into eternity without a true knowledge of God. Peter asks for John, "What shall this man do?" Each wants to know the secret plans, whether for himself, or his beloved, which are lying in the mind and purpose of the Eternal. What will the end be? Where does that path lead by which I am going, and which descends steeply into the ravine? Will the fight between evil and good be much prolonged? What are hell, and the bottomless pit, and the meaning of Christ's references to the undying worm and unquenchable flame? And Christ says, "My child, you cannot bear it; you could not sleep at night, you could not play with the merry children by day, you could not perform your slender tasks, if you knew all that I know, and see as I see. Be at rest. Trust Me. I will tell you as soon as you are strong enough. Nothing shall be kept back from you, all shall be revealed." And surely the sufferings and limitations of this present time will not be worthy to be compared with the exceeding weight of glory, when in the presence of our Lord we shall see eye to eye, and know even as we are known.

In the light of these words we may get comfort. When some crushing trouble befalls us, He who only spoke as they were able to bear will not permit the flame to be hotter, the tide stronger, or the task more trying, than we have strength for. We often do not know our strength nor the power of his grace. Sorrow may be sent to reveal us to ourselves, and show how much spiritual energy we have been silently acquiring. Do not therefore run to and fro and say, "It is too much, I cannot bear it." But know and be sure that Christ has ascertained your resources, and is sure of your ability, before He permits the extreme ordeal to overtake you. Dare to say with the Apostle, "I can do all things through Christ who strengtheneth me."

III. The Teaching of the Divine Spirit.—His *personality* is unmistakable; though the Greek word for Spirit is neuter, a masculine pronoun is used in conjunction with it when Jesus says, "He, the Spirit of Truth." The personal Christ sent as a substitute for Himself no mere breath or influence, but the personal Spirit. The Advocate before the Throne is well represented by the Advocate in the heart of the Church; and these two agree in one—distinct as different Persons, but one in the mystical unity of the Holy Trinity.

Note the *method* of the Holy Spirit. He teaches truth by taking of the things of Christ and revealing them. There are two methods of teaching children—by precept, and by example. I go into a schoolroom one summer afternoon, and remark the hot cheeks and tired eyes of the little ones. Outside the open window the bees are droning past, the butterflies flit from flower to flower, and Nature seems to cry to the little hearts, "Come and play with me." Does a garden ever look so beautiful as to children shut up to their studies? "What are you learning, little ones?" I say. "Botany," is the sad answer. "We've got to learn all these hard names, and copy these diagrams." "Well," I say, "shut up your books, and come with me." And presently I teach them more botany by contact with the flowers themselves, than they would have learned by hours of poring over lesson-books. It is so the Spirit teaches. Is gentleness or purity, self-sacrifice or prayer, the lesson that we are set to acquire? There is no need for Him to make a new revelation to us. It is enough if He but bring us face to face with Jesus, and show these qualities shining through his words and deeds. The truth certainly, but the truth as it is in Jesus.

The condition of proficiency in the Spirit's school is *obedience*. "He will *guide* you into all truth." This word is very significant. Literally it means, *Show the way*. Ordinarily, men ask to know the truth before they obey. The Spirit demands that they should obey before they know. Let me know the outcome of this act—its philosophy, its reasonableness, its result—then I will obey. But the Spirit answers, "It is enough for thee, O child of man, to know Me. Canst thou not trust? Wilt thou not obey? And as thou obeyest thou shalt know. Take this path, plod along its difficult way, climb where it climbs; so shalt thou ascend the steep of obedience, and at each step a further horizon of the truth will open outspread beneath thee."

Let us be more sensitive to the guidance of the Spirit, following whithersoever He clearly indicates—as when the Spirit said to Philip, "Go, join thyself to this chariot." We shall know when we follow on to know the Lord. His going forth is prepared for those who are prepared to obey whatsoever He may appoint.

The *purpose* of the Spirit is to glorify our Lord. "He shall glorify Me, for He shall receive of mine." The Spirit's presence, as such, should not be a subject of our close scrutiny, lest we conflict with his holy purpose of being hidden, that Jesus may be all in all before the gaze of saint and sinner. He is so anxious that nothing should divert the soul's gaze from the Lord whom He would reveal, that He carefully withdraws Himself from view. "There must be nothing, not even God Himself, to distract the heart from Jesus, through whom we come to God. But remember that when you have the most precious views of your dear Lord, it is because the Holy Spirit, all unseen, is witnessing and working within you."

The *authority* of the Holy Spirit appears in the words, "He shall not speak of Himself; but whatsoever He shall hear, that shall He speak." Where does He hear the truths He utters? Where? There is only one place. In the depths of the eternal Throne, in the heart of Deity itself, in the secret place of the Most High. Oh, marvel! surpassing thought, yet true—that things which pass between the Father and the Son, in the depths which no angel can penetrate, may be disclosed and made known to those humble and contrite hearts who are willing to make a space and pause for the divine Spirit to speak the deep things of God.

May it be ours to be patient and willing pupils in this heavenly school, in which the Holy Spirit is Teacher, and Jesus the Text-Book, and obedience the essential condition of knowledge.

K

56

THE CONQUEROR OF THE WORLD

"In the world ye shall have tribulation: but be of good cheer; I have overcome the world."—JOHN xvi. 33.

IT WAS the road between Jerusalem and the Gate of the Garden. Behind, lay the city bathed in slumber; before, the Mount of Olives with its terraced gardens; above, the Passover moon, pouring down floods of silver light that dropped to the ground through the waving branches of the trees. The Lord was on his way to betrayal and death, along that path flecked by chequered moonlight.

The farewell talk had been prolonged until the disciples had grasped something of the Master's meaning. With many a comforting assurance it had borne them forward to the magnificent but simple declaration, *"I came forth from the Father, and am come into the world; again, I leave the world, and go to the Father"* (ver. 28). At that announcement light seems to have broken in upon their hearts, and they said unto Him, *"Lo, now speakest Thou plainly: . . . by this we believe that Thou camest forth from God."* Jesus replied—not as translators render it, *"Do ye now believe?"* but as it should be rendered —*"At last ye believe"*: and He proceeded to formulate three paradoxes:

First, That within an hour or so He would be alone, yet not alone.

Secondly, That they would have tribulation, and yet be in peace.

Thirdly, That though He was going to his death, He was certainly a Conqueror, and had overcome the world, whose princes were about to crucify Him.

The word *overcome* occurs but twice in the recorded sayings of our Lord; in the present instance it made a lasting impression on the Apostle John, who constantly makes use of it in his Epistles. We meet with it *six* times in his First Epistle, and *sixteen* times in the Book of Revelation. Who can forget the sevenfold promise spoken by the risen Lord to those who overcome; or the sublime affirmation concerning the martyrs, that they overcame by the blood of the Lamb and by the word of their testimony?

I. CHRIST AND HIS DISCIPLES HAVE A COMMON FOE—"The world." —And what is the world? *It is well to take the inspired definition given in 1 John ii. 16.* After enumerating her three daughters—the lust of the flesh, the lust of the eyes, and the pride of life—the Apostle goes on to say: "All that is in the world . . . is not of the Father," *i.e.* does not originate or proceed from Him, but has its source in the world itself. We might reverse this proposition and say: "All that does not emanate from the Father, which you cannot trace back to his purpose in creation, is that mysterious indefinable influence or spirit which makes the world." The world, in this sense, is not primarily a thing, or a collection of people, but a spiritual influence poured out into the very atmosphere of our lives.

The spirit of the world insinuates itself everywhere. It is what we call society; the consensus of fashionable opinion; the spirit which finds its satisfaction in the seen and transient; the ambition that is encircled by the rim of an earthly horizon; the aims, plans, and activities, which are comprehended, as the Preacher says, "under the sun." You meet it in the country town, where strict lines are drawn between the professional or wholesale man and the retailer; in gatherings of well-dressed people, stiff with decorum and the punctilious observance of etiquette.

The world has formulated its *Beatitudes*, thus:

"Blessed are the rich: for they shall inherit the earth."

"Blessed are the light-hearted: for they shall have many friends."

"Blessed are the respectable: for they shall be respected."

"Blessed are they who are not troubled by a sensitive conscience: for they shall succeed in life."

"Blessed are they who can indulge their appetites to the full: for they shall be filled."

"Blessed are they who have no need to conciliate their rivals: for they will be saved from anxiety."

"Blessed are they who have no poor relations: for they shall be delivered from annoyance."

"Blessed are they of whom all men speak well."

The world's code says, "Do as others do; don't be singular; never offend against good taste; have a tinge of religiousness, but remember that too much is impracticable for daily life; whatever you do, don't be poor; never yield an inch, unless you are going to make something by the concession; take every advantage of bettering your position, it matters not at what cost to others—they must look after themselves, as you to yourself."

But it was reserved for John Bunyan to draw Madame Bubble's portrait: "This woman is a witch. 'I am mistress of the world,' she says, 'and men are made happy by me.' She wears a great purse at her side; and her hand is often in her purse fingering her money. Yea, she has bought off many a man from a pilgrim's life after he had fairly begun it. She is a bold and impudent slut also, for she will talk to any man. If there be one cunning to make money, she will speak well of him from house to house. None can tell of the mischief she does. She makes variance betwixt rulers and subjects, 'twixt parents and children, 'twixt a man and his wife, 'twixt the flesh and the heart. 'Had she stood by all this while,' said Standfast, whose eyes were still full of her, 'you could not have set Madame Bubble more amply before me, nor have better described her features.' 'He that drew her picture was a good limner,' said Mr. Honest, 'and he that so wrote of her said true.' 'Oh,' said Standfast, 'what a mercy it is that I did resist her! for to what might she not have drawn me!'"

II. CHRIST AND HIS DISCIPLES HAVE A COMMON CONFLICT.—It is inevitable that there should be collision, and therefore conflict, and as a result tribulation. The world-spirit will not brook our disagreement with its plans and aims; and therefore they who persist in living godly lives in this present evil world must suffer persecution.

Conflict about the use of power and prerogative.—At his baptism our Lord was proclaimed to be the Son of the Highest, and anointed with the Holy Ghost and with power. Instantly the prince of this world came to Him with the suggestion that He should use it for the purposes of his own comfort and display. "Make these stones bread for thine hunger; cast Thyself down and attract the attention of the crowds." Here were the lust of the flesh, and the lust of the eyes. But our Lord refused to use for Himself the power which was entrusted to Him for the benediction and help of men.

Conflict as to the way of helping and saving men.—The world's way was to leap into the seat of power at any cost, and from the height of universal authority administer the affairs of the world. But Christ knew better. He saw that He must take the form of a servant, and humble Himself to the lowest. If He would save men, He cannot save Himself: if He would bring forth much fruit, He must fall into the ground to die: if He would ascend far above all heavens, bearing us with Him to the realms of eternal day, He must descend first into the lower parts of the earth.

Conflict in the estimate of poverty and suffering.—The world looked on these as the most terrible disasters that could befall. Christ, on the other hand, taught that blessedness lay most within reach of the poor in spirit, the mourners, the merciful, the forgiving, and the persecuted. But the Pharisees, who were lovers of money, when they heard all these things, scoffed at Him.

Conflict in their diverse notions of royalty.—The Jews looked for a Messiah who should revive the glories of the days of David and Solomon, driving the Gentiles from the land, and receiving the homage of the surrounding nations, whilst every son of Abraham enjoyed opulence and ease. Referring to this expectation, the Master said, "My kingdom is not of this world: if my kingdom were of this world, then would my servants fight." His conception of royalty was founded on service, which would wash the disciples' feet; on humility, which meekly bore the heavy yoke; on patience, which would not quench the smoking flax; on suffering, which flinched not from the cross; on the nobility and dignity of the inner life, which shone through the most humble circumstances, as the transfiguration glory through his robes. For this He died. The chief priests and scribes hunted Him to death, because He persisted in asserting that He was the true King of men. "And Pilate wrote a title also, and put it on the cross, *Jesus of Nazareth, the King of the Jews.*"

Conflict in regard to religion.—The people of Christ's day were very religious. The world likes a flavour of religion. It makes a good background and screen; it serves to hide much that is unbecoming and questionable; it is respectable, and satisfies an instinctive longing of the soul. The world, however, manages its religion in such a way as not to interfere with its self-aggrandisement, but, in fact, to promote it. Christ, on the other hand, taught that religion was for the Father in secret; and consisted, not in the rigorous observance of outward rite, but in pity, mercy, forgiveness, solitary prayer, and purity of heart.

Thus the Lord's life was the reversal of everything that the world prized. Wherever He touched it there was conflict and collision, strong antagonism was evoked, and profound irritation on the part of the poor hollow appearance-loving world. So it must be with his followers. "These pilgrims must needs go through the fair. Well, so they did; but behold, even as they entered into the fair, all the people in the fair were moved, and the town itself as it were in a hubbub about them. They were clothed with such kind of raiment as was diverse from the raiment of any who traded in that fair; few could understand what they said; and the pilgrims set very light by all their wares. And they did not believe them to be any other than bedlams and mad. Therefore they took them and beat them, and besmeared them with dirt, and then put them in the cage, that they might be made a spectacle to all the men at the fair."

Child of God, your conflict may be altogether *hidden* from the eyes of those around you, *lonely* with the awful loneliness of one in a crowd of unsympathising strangers, *painful* with the tribulation that Christ foretold. You have been ridiculed, sneered at, maligned; your tools hidden, your goods injured, violence threatened or executed. You have been as a speckled bird, pecked at by the birds around. But this is the way the Master went. By these marks you may be sure that you are in the way of his steps.

III. THE COMMON VICTORY.—"Be of good cheer; I have overcome the world."

In the midst of a battle, when the soldiers are weary with fatigue, galled with fire, and grimed with smoke, if the general rides into the midst to cheer them with a few hearty words, and tells them that the key to the position is in their hands, they cheer him enthusiastically, and take up new hope. So down the line our Leader and Commander sends the encouragement of these inspiring words. Let us drink their comfort and encouragement to the full, that, amid our tribulation, in Him we may have peace.

He conquered for Himself.—The Lord has shown that a great and blessed life is possible on conditions which the world pronounces simply unendurable. He would not accept the world's maxims, would not be ruled by the world's principles, did despite to the world's most favourite plans. He even tasted the dregs of reprobation that the world metes out to those who oppose her, enduring the cross, and despising the shame. But his life was blessed while it lasted; his name is the dearest and fairest treasure of our race; and He holds an empire such as none of the world's most favoured conquerors ever won. Does not this show that the world is a lying temptress; that there is another and a better policy of life than hers; that the real sweets and prizes of this brief existence are, after all, not in her gift? Christ has overcome the world. Her prince came to Him, but found no response to any of his proposals. He disregarded her flatteries and threatenings; He would not have her help and despised her hate; He prosecuted his path in defiance of her, and has left an imperishable glory behind. Thus He overcame the world.

And He conquered as our Representative and Head,—What He did for Himself He is prepared to repeat in the life-story of his followers. Ah! lonely soul, thou shalt not be left unaided to withstand the seductions of the temptress world; Jesus is with thee, thy Great-heart and Champion. As the Father was with Him, so He is with thee; so thus thou mayest boldly say, "The Lord is my helper: I will not fear what man can do unto me."

He does more. Behind the light of this world's glory, Jesus reveals another; and it is as when the sun rises, while the yellow moon still lingers in the sky. She comes to have no glory by reason of that glory which excelleth. We are content with this world until He reveals the glory of the unseen and eternal; then a holy discontent arises within us, such as the patriarchs felt towards Canaan, when by faith they beheld the city which hath foundations. I only say to you, get that vision, and it becomes as easy for you to refuse the passing and worthless attractions of the world as for an angel to ignore a wanton's beauty, or a child to make light of diamonds in the rough.

In Jesus you may have peace. It is not certainly ours, unless we follow the two conditions He lays down. First, of abiding in Him; and, secondly, of meditating on his words. But if these be observed, we shall have peace in the midst of strife, just as there is an oratory in the heart of the castle keep; a hollow cone in the midst of the candle flame; and a centre of safety in the midst of the sweeping whirlwind. Oh, abide there, child of God!

And, in addition to peace, there shall one day be victory. We also shall overcome, and shall sit with Christ on his throne, as He overcame, and sits with the Father upon his. Then the fruit of the tree of life, immunity from the second death, the hidden manna, the white stone, the morning star, the confession before the angels of God, and the pillar in the temple of Eternity!

57

CONSECRATED TO CONSECRATE

"For their sakes I sanctify Myself, that they themselves also may be sanctified in truth."—JOHN xvii. 19 (R.V.).

"THE MOST precious fragment of the past," is the unstinted eulogium which a thoughtful man has passed on this transcendent prayer; transcending in its scope of view, its expressions, its tender pathos, all other prayers of which we have record.

Its primary characteristic is *timelessness*. Though uttered within a few hours of Calvary, it contains thoughts and expressions which must have been familiar to our Lord at any moment during the centuries which have followed. As we study it, therefore, we are listening to words which have been uttered many times on our behalf, and will be uttered until we are with Him, where He is, beholding the glory of the divine Son, superadded to that of the Perfect Servant.

The R.V. margin substitutes the word *consecrate* for *sanctify*; and it probably conveys a better meaning, because devotion to the will of God is prominent, rather than the holiness of personal character. Devotion to God's will is the primary thought suggested by the word; but of course it involves a blameless and spotless character. Thus we might read the words, "For their sakes I consecrate Myself, that they also may be consecrated in truth." Through the dim twilight the Lord clearly foresaw what was awaiting Him—the agony and bloody sweat, the cross and passion, the foresakenness and travail of his soul. The cross with outstretched arms waited to receive Him; the midnight darkness to engulf Him; the murderous band to wreak their hate on the unresisting Lamb—and yet He flinched not, but went right forward, consecrating Himself.

> *"'Twas thus He suffered, though a Son,*
> *Foreknowing, choosing, tasting all;*
> *Until the dreadful work was done,*
> *And drank the bitter cup of gall."*

1. THE SUBJECTS OF CHRIST'S SOLICITUDE.—In the earlier verses the Lord speaks of Himself, of his finished work, of the glory which He had left, of that to which He went; asking only that He might be able to glorify the Father in every movement of his coming sorrow (1–5).

Then He launches Himself on the full current of intercession, and pleads for those who had been given to Him, as distinguished from the world of men out of which they had come. Evidently the same thought was in his mind as inspired his words in John x., when He spoke of the sheep whom the Father had given to Him, that He might give them eternal life (27-29). And it may be that each of these two utterances was inspired by older words yet, that Zechariah had addressed to the poor of the flock when he cut asunder his two staves, Beauty and Bands (Zech. xi. 7-14).

The underlying conception in all these passages seems to be that the Father has entrusted to the special keeping of Jesus certain elect spirits having an affinity to his nature, and who should stand in the inner circle to Him because associated with Him from high redemptive purpose. All souls are God's by right of creation, and all are included in the redemption wrought on the cross; but not all had been included in the divine gift of which Jesus speaks, "Thine they were, and Thou gavest them Me." We conclude that in the eternity of the past, as the Father beheld all future things as though they were present, and surveyed the vast multitudes of the human family, He discerned those who would be attracted by indissoluble union with his Son manifest in the flesh; and whom He did foreknow, these also He did predestinate to be his flock, his brethren and sisters, his chosen band of associates in his redemptive purpose. These were the subjects of his powerful solicitude, "I make request, not for the world, but for those whom Thou hast given Me."

What then? Did not God care for the world? Certainly. He so loved the world that He gave his only begotten Son.

How then can we reconcile the love of God to the world with the selection of some as the flock of the Lamb, whilst the great world seems expressly excluded from his prayer? That question is fitly put. The emphasis is on the word *seems*. It is only to the superficial view that the world is excluded. Are the planets excluded from the law of gravitation because suns are filled with fire and light? Are the lower orders of creation excluded from the circle of enjoyment because man with his high organisation is more richly endowed than they? Are sufferers excluded from the healing virtues of nature because a comparative few are specially qualified as surgeons and physicians? Can a missionary be charged with neglecting a dark continent because he concentrates thought and care on a few elect spirits gathered around him? For instance, could Columba be held guilty of neglecting the Picts and Scots when on Iona's lone isle he focused his care upon the handful of followers who assembled around the ancient pile, whose ruins are his lasting memorial? There is but one answer to these questions. Election is not exclusive, but inclusive. Its purpose is not primarily the salvation or delectation of the few; but their equipment to become the apostles to the many. And if Jesus thought, cared, and prayed so much for those whom the Father had given Him, his ulterior thought was that the world might believe that the Father had sent Him (ver. 21). If, then, it should be proved that you, my reader, are not included in the band of the given ones, that would not necessarily involve you in the eternal condemnation and loss of the future; though it would exclude you from sharing with Christ in his lofty mission to the sons of men.

What are the marks, then, that we belong to the inner circle of the given ones? They are these—

1. That we have come to Him (John vi. 37).
2. That we hear his voice, listening for the slightest indication of his will (John x. 27).
3. That we follow his steps through the world.
4. That we receive his words and believe that the Father sent the Son to be our Saviour.
5. That the world hates us (ver. 14).

Wheresoever these marks are present, they indicate the hand of the Great Shepherd and Bishop of souls; and though we be amongst the most timid and worthless of the flock, He is pledged to keep us so that none shall snatch us from his hand, and to conduct us through the valley of the shadow to those dewy upland lawns over which He will lead us for evermore.

II. WHAT HE SOUGHT FOR THEM.—"That they might be consecrated in truth."

Christ does not ask that his own should be forgiven, comforted, supplied with the good things of life—all thought for these pales in the presence of his intense desire that they should be consecrated, *i.e.* inspired by the same consuming passion as was burning in his heart. He knew that He was no more in the world. High business connected with its interests summoned Him to the far country, whither He went to receive the kingdom and return. But He desired that the passion which filled his soul, his tears, his prayers, and, to some degree, his sufferings, might always be represented amongst the sons of men, might be embodied in human lives, might find utterance through human lips. He could not Himself perpetuate his corporeal, visible ministry among men; and therefore desired with a great desire that those whom the Father had given Him should evermore "show the Lord's death till He come"—not simply by gathering at his table, but by going forth to live his life, and to fill up that which is behind of his sufferings.

Is this your life? We have sometimes heard consecration stated as though it were a matter of choice whether believers should bind themselves by its obligations or not. When a student enters the university there are certain subjects in which he must matriculate, but there are special ones which he may graduate in or not, as he pleases. Should he refuse them, he is not blamed. The matter is within his option. Now, let it be clearly understood from these words of Christ that consecration is not in the same sense optional, but obligatory. For all those whom the Father had given Him He pleaded with his dying breath that they should be consecrated; and if you are not consecrated—if there are extensive reserves in your life, if you are holding back part of the price, if you are saying of aught that you have, It is my own, I shall do as I choose—then understand that you are in direct conflict with Christ's purpose and prayer. He asked that you might be consecrated; and you have chosen to regard consecration as the craze of the fervid enthusiast.

III. Christ's Method of Securing the Consecration of his Servants.—"For their sakes I consecrate Myself."

(1) *There is the potency of example.*—"Leaving us an example, that ye should follow his steps." "He that saith he abideth in Him ought himself also so to walk, even as He walked." Once when He was praying in a certain place his disciples said, "Lord, teach us to pray." They had come within the powerful attraction of his Spirit. Like a swift current it had caught them, and they were eager to emulate Him. It is impossible for the saint to gaze long on the *stigmata* without becoming branded with the marks of Jesus: impossible to see Him hastening to the cross without being stirred to follow Him; impossible to behold the intensity of his purpose for a world's redemption without becoming imbued with it; impossible to see Him in love with the cross without feeling a similar infatuation. And it is impossible to behold Him plunging into the dark floods of death that He might emerge in the sunlit ocean, without the consciousness of the uprising of an insatiable desire to be like Him, to drink of his cup, and be baptized with his baptism, to fall into the ground to die that He may not bide alone, to know the fellowship of his sufferings and conformity to his death, that He may appoint unto us a kingdom, as the Father hath appointed to Him.

(2) *There is our implication in his mediatorial work.*—"I have been crucified with Christ," the Apostle said. And, again, "Ye died with Christ from the rudiments of the world." Of course, Christ died *for* us, presenting to the claims of a broken law a perfect satisfaction and oblation. It is also true that we died *with* Him, were *in* Him as our Representative, wrought *through* Him as our Forerunner; the first-fruit sheaf contained the promise of all its companions.

Consider for a moment a remarkable expression that casts light on this whole subject. In that memorable discussion with the Jews in Solomon's porch, which practically closed our Lord's public ministry,

He said that the Father had sanctified and consecrated Him and sent Him into the world (John x. 36). In these sublime words He undoubtedly refers to a moment which preceded the Incarnation, when the Godhead designated the Second Person to redeem men. Was it the same moment, think you, as that in which Jesus said, "Sacrifice and offering Thou wouldest not, but a body Thou hast prepared Me (or, mine ears hast Thou pierced). I delight to do thy will, O my God"? If so, what an august scene that must have been when, in the presence of the assembled hierarchies of heaven, the Father solemnly set apart the Son for his redemption work; consecrating Him to bring in everlasting salvation, to destroy the works of the devil, and to bring together in one the children of God that are scattered abroad!

In that solemn consecration of the Head all the members were included. The King stood for his kingdom; the Shepherd for his flock. Any who refuse to be consecrated contravene and contradict that momentous decision.

When Christ approached his death in these words, He renewed his act of consecration, and again implicated those who belong to Him; bearing us with Him, He went to the cross; involving us by his actions, He yielded Himself up to death. In his holy purpose we were quickened together with Him, and raised up together, and made to sit together in the heavenly places; and by the same emphasis with which we declare ourselves to be his, we confess that we are amongst those who are bound to a life of consecration. We are pledged to it by union with our Lord. We cannot draw back from the doorpost to which He was nailed without proving that we are deficient in appreciating the purpose which brought Him to our world, the surrender that withheld not his face from spitting, his soul from the shadow of death.

IV. OUR DUTY.—"Yield yourselves unto God." When Abraham Lincoln dedicated, for the purposes of a graveyard, the field of Gettysburg, where so many brave soldiers had lost their lives, he said: "We cannot dedicate, we cannot consecrate, we cannot hallow this ground. The brave men who struggled here have consecrated it far beyond our power to add or detract. It is for us, the living, rather to be dedicated to the unfinished work which they who fought here have thus far so nobly advanced. It is rather for us to be here dedicated to the great task remaining before us, that from these honoured dead we take increased devotion to that cause for which they gave the last full measure of devotion; and that we here highly resolve that these dead shall not have died in vain."

These noble words, when we have made the needful alterations and adaptations, are most applicable to our present point. Let us dedicate ourselves to the great task before us, and to which Jesus has pledged us. Let us devote ourselves to the great cause for which Jesus died. Let us highly resolve that He shall not have died in vain. Let us offer and present ourselves, our souls and bodies, to be a reasonable, holy, and living sacrifice unto God, that his will might be done through us, as it is done in heaven.

> *"My Master, lead me to thy door;*
> *Pierce this now willing ear once more;*
> *Thy bonds are freedom, let me stay*
> *With Thee, to toil, endure, obey.*
>
> *"Yes; ear and hand, and thought and will!*
> *Use all in thy dear slavery still!*
> *Self's weary liberties I cast*
> *Beneath thy feet; there keep them fast."*

58

THE LORD'S PRAYER FOR HIS PEOPLE'S ONENESS

*"That they all may be one. . . One in us. . . That they may be one,
even as we are one. . . . Perfect in one."*—JOHN xvii. 21-23.

THUS OUR High Priest pleaded, and thus He pleads. In all the power
of his endless life He ever liveth to bear this great petition on his
heart: and as the weight of the jewelled breastplate lay heavy on the
heart of the high priest of old, so does it press on Him, as the ages
slowly pass by in their never-ceasing progress towards the consum-
mation of all things. Listen to that voice, sweet and full as the distant
rush of many waters, as it pleads in the midst of eternity that those
who believe in Him may be one.

Nor is it true that this prayer awaits an answer indefinitely future.
There seems good reason to believe, as we shall see, that in these
words our Lord was making a request which began to be fulfilled on
the day of Pentecost, and is being fulfilled continually—although the
oneness which is being realised is still, like his kingdom, in mystery,
and is waiting for the manifestation of the sons of God. Then, as the
gauzy mists of time part before the breath of God, the accomplished
oneness of the Church shall stand revealed.

I. THE ONENESS OF BELIEVERS IS A SPIRITUAL ONENESS.—Can
there be any reasonable doubt of this when our Master asks so clearly
that we may be one, *as the Father and He are one*? The model for
Christian unity is evidently the unity between the Father and Son by the
Holy Spirit; and since that unity, the unity of the blessed God, is not
corporeal, nor physical, nor substantial to the eye of the flesh, may we
not infer—nay, are we not compelled to infer—that the oneness of
believers is to be after the same fashion; and to consist in so close
an identity of nature, so absolute an interfusion of spirit, as that they
shall be one in aim, and thought, and life, and spirit—spiritually one
with each other, because spiritually one with Him?

The Church of Rome, which has ever travestied in gross material
forms the most spiritual conceptions of God, sought to prove herself
the true Church by achieving a oneness of her own. It was an outward
and visible oneness. In the apostate church everyone must utter the
same formularies, worship in the same postures, and belong to the
same ecclesiastical system. And her leaders did their best to realise
their dream. They endeavoured to exterminate heresy by fire, and

sword, and torture. They spread their network through the world. And just before the dawn of the Reformation they seemed to have succeeded. At the beginning of the sixteenth century, Europe reposed in the monotony of almost universal uniformity, beneath the almost universal supremacy of the Papacy. Rome might indeed have adopted the insolent language of the Assyrian of prophecy: "As one gathereth eggs that are left, have I gathe d all the earth; and there was none that moved the wing, or opened the mouth, or peeped." And what was the result? *What but the deep sleep of spiritual death?* And herein lay the most crushing condemnation of the Roman Catholic conception of the unity of the Church.

Many modern notions of Christian unity seem to proceed on the same line. The assent to a certain credal basis, the meeting in great catholic conventions, the exchange of pulpits—these seem to exhaust the conceptions of large numbers, and to satisfy their ideal. But surely there is a bond of union—deeper, holier, more vital and more blessed than any of these—which shyly reveals itself, now and again, in one or more of them, but is independent of all, and when all of them are wanting, still constitutes us *one*. And what is that bond of union but the possession of a common spiritual life, like that which unites the Father and the Son; and which pervades us also, making us one with each other, because we are already one with God?

You may not care to admit it; you may even be ignorant of the full meaning of this marvellous fact; you may live an exclusive life, never going beyond the walls of some small conventicle, or the barriers of some strict ecclesiastical system; you may bear yourself impatiently and brusquely towards those who differ from you; you may even brand them with your anathema: but if they are one with God, by his gracious indwelling Spirit of Life, and if you are also one with Him, you positively cannot help being one with them. Your creed may differ, or your mode of worship, or your views about the Church; but you cannot be otherwise than one with those who are one with God, in a union which is not material but spiritual.

II. This Oneness also admits of Great Variety.—"One, as Thou, Father, art in Me, and I in Thee." Now, of course, we all admit the unity of the Godhead. The first article of the Jew is also the first article of the Christian, that the Lord our God is one God, one in essence, one in purpose, one in action. The Son does nothing of Himself; the Father does nothing apart from the Son; the Holy Ghost proceedeth from the Father and the Son. We cannot, as yet, understand this mystery; but with reverence we accept it as the primary basis of our faith.

But though God is One, there is evidently a variety of function in the ever-blessed Trinity. The Father decrees, the Son executes. The

Father sends, the Son is sent. The Father works in Creation, the Son in Redemption and Judgment. And the functions of both Father and Son differ from those of the Holy Spirit.

Since then, according to our Lord's request, the unity of the Church is to resemble the unity of the Godhead, we may expect that it will not be physical, nor mechanical, nor a uniformity; but that it will be variety in unity—a unity of spirit and purpose, and yet a unity which admits of very diverse functions and operations. Diversities of gifts, but the same Spirit; differences of administrations, but the same Lord; diversities of operations, but the same God who worketh all in all.

(1) *The very conception of unity involves variety.*—You take me out into a piece of waste land, and pointing to a heap of bricks, say, "There is a unity." I at once rebut your assertion; there is uniformity undoubtedly, but not unity. Unity requires that a variety of *different* things should be combined to form one structure and carry out one idea. A collection of bricks is not a unity, but a house is. A pole is not a unity, but a hop-plant is. A snow atom is not a unity, but a snow crystal is. And when our Lord spoke of his disciples as one, He not only expected that there would be varieties amongst them, in character, mind, and ecclesiastical preference; but by the very choice of his words He meant us to infer that it would be so. The unity on which He set his heart was not a uniformity.

(2) *But with variety there may be the truest unity.*—There is variety in the human body—from eyelash to foot, from heart to blood-disc, from brain to quivering nerve-fibre; yet, in all this variety, each one is conscious of an indivisible unity. There is variety in the tree: the giant arms that wrestle with the storm, the far-spreading roots that moor it to the soil, the myriad leaves in which the wind makes music, the cones or nuts which it flings upon the forest floor; yet for all this it is one. There is variety in the Bible: variety of authorship—king, prophet, priest, herdman, fisherman, scholar, sage, and saint; variety of style—prose, poetry, psalmody, argument, appeal; variety of age— from the days of Moses to those of John, the beloved apostle, writing amid the persecutions of the empire. Yet for all this there is a oneness in the Bible which no mere binding could give. So with the Church of Christ: there may be, there must be, infinite varieties and shades of thought and work. Some will prefer the methods of Wesley, others the freedom of Congregationalism. Some will pray most naturally through the venerable words of a liturgy, others in the deep silence of a Friends' Meeting; some will thrive best beneath the crozier of the Bishop, others in the plain barracks of the Salvation Army. But, notwithstanding all this variety, there may be a deep spiritual unity— many folds, but one flock; many regiments, but one army; many stones, but one breastplate. "There is one body, and one Spirit, even

as ye are called in one hope of your calling; one Lord, one faith, one baptism; one God and Father of all, who is above all, and through all, and in you all."

III. THE BASIS OF CHRISTIAN UNITY IS THE UNION OF EACH BELIEVER TO CHRIST.—"I in them, that they may be made perfect in one." However much true believers in Christ differ, there are two points in which they agree.

(1) *Each believer is in Christ*—in Christ's heart, loved with an everlasting love, the beloved name engraven on its secret tables; in Christ's book, enrolled on those pages which are sealed so fast that He alone can break the sevenfold seal; in Christ's hand, which holds the ocean as a drop upon its palm, and which was pierced on Calvary, from which no power shall ever pluck the trembling soul; in Christ's grace, rooted as a tree in luxuriant soil, or a house in a foundation of rock; but above all in Christ's Person, for He is the Head, "from whom the whole body is fitly framed and knit together by that which every joint supplieth." There are innumerable texts which speak of the Church as the Body of Christ (Eph. i. 23; Col. i. 24); and directly a man believes in Christ, he becomes a member of that mystical body. "We are members of his body, of his flesh, and of his bones." You may be a very obscure member, or even a paralysed member; but be sure of this, if you are a Christian you are in Christ, as the eye is in the eye-socket, the arm in the shoulder-joint, and the finger in the hand.

(2) *Christ is in each believer.*—The texts that teach Christ's real presence in the believer are as numerous as spring flowers. "Christ liveth in me." "Know ye not that Jesus Christ is in you, except ye be reprobate?" "Ye shall know that I am in my Father, and ye in Me, and I in you." The Lord Jesus is in the heart which makes Him welcome—as the steam is in the piston, as the sap is in the branch, as the blood is in the heart, as the life is in the body. It would be impossible for words to describe a more intense spiritual Oneness than that which is here presented to us. The Saviour is in each of us; as the Father is in Him and we are in Him, and He in God. "Our life is hid with Christ in God." Therefore we are not only one with Jesus Christ, but through Him we are one with God. "I in them, Thou in Me." The very life of God is pouring its glorious tides through us, and would do so more largely if only we were more receptive and obedient. He pours water out of the mouth of the Congo at the rate of a million tons per second; and is willing to do marvels as mighty through each believer. And as this life permeates us all alike, it makes us one, not only with the blessed God, but with all who believe—as the blood makes all the members of the body one, and the sap the branches of the tree.

IV. THE MEANS OF THIS SPIRITUAL UNITY ARE THE INFLUENCES OF THE HOLY SPIRIT.—Influence means *inflow*. It was by the Holy Spirit that our Lord's human nature was made one with his Father's. And this same Holy Spirit He has bequeathed to us, that He may be the same bond of spiritual life between us and our Lord as He was between our Lord and his Father. May not this be the meaning of his words: "The glory which Thou gavest Me I have given them; that they may be one, even as we are one"? May not that glory have consisted in the oneness of his human nature with God the Father, by the Holy Spirit? And if so, it may be shared by us. The more believers receive the indwelling of the Holy Spirit, the more clearly will they appreciate this great mystery, and the more closely will they be drawn to all other believers; hushing jealous thoughts and uncharitable words, and "endeavouring to keep the unity of the Spirit in the bond of peace."

It is abundantly clear, then, that this unity cannot be broken unless we break away from Christ. Men have used the word *schism* with terrible effect. If a man has broken away from some visible church, they have pointed to him as a schismatic. But what is schism? It is breaking away from the Body of Christ. But what is the Body of Christ? The Body of Christ, as Scripture plainly teaches, is that great multitude which no man can number, of all nations, and kindreds, and peoples, and tongues, and sects, and eras, who are united by faith with the Saviour. The Church of Christ is not conterminous with any earthly or visible organisation; it is long as the ages, wide as the poles, broad as the charity of God; it includes all in heaven and on earth who hold the Head. The only condition of membership in that Church is simple faith in Christ. And the only method of severance from that Church is through the severance of the soul's trust in Christ. He only is a schismatic who ceases to be Christ's.

The papal legate told Savonarola that he cut him off from the Church Militant and from the Church Triumphant. "From the Church Militant you may," was the martyr's reply; "but from the Church Triumphant, never!" It was well spoken; but Savonarola might have gone further, and defied the scarlet-coated functionary even to cut him off from the Church Militant—nothing could do that but apostasy. A man may be excommunicated from our church systems, or he may never have belonged to one of them; but so long as he believes in Christ, he is a member of the Holy Catholic Church. And schism is more likely to be charged against those who violate the spirit of Christian charity in making harsh and false statements against their fellow-members in the Body of Christ. Let us not retaliate, lest we also commit that sin. We can afford to wait. *Five minutes in heaven, or less, will settle it all.*

The object for which Christ prayed is already being partially accomplished. The world may not be as yet surrendering to the claims of Jesus Christ, but it is becoming increasingly impressed with his divine mission: "that the world may believe that Thou hast sent Me." And in proportion as the Holy Spirit pervades and fills the hearts of the children of God, the manifestation of the life of God in them and through them will have an ever-increasing effect, and will do what church systems and even the preachings of her thousand pulpits cannot effect in convincing and saving men.

Let us remember that Christ's own conception of the unity of his Church is that which is the result of the indwelling of the one Spirit. Such unity is already a fact in the eye of God, though undiscerned as yet in all its fullness by men. Let us thank God that this marvellous request has been already so largely realised; and let us dare to hold fellowship as Christians with all those who are indwelt by the Spirit of Life which is also in Christ Jesus.

59

The Love that Bound Christ to the Cross

"Jesus therefore, knowing all things that should come upon Him, went forth, and said unto them, Whom seek ye?"—JOHN xviii. 4.

THE CEDRON was never more than a mountain brook, and it is now dry. Its stony bed alone shows where it used to flow through the valley that separated Mount Zion from the Mount of Olives. The main road which led from the city gate, over the Mount of Olives to Bethany and Jericho, crossed it by an ancient bridge, from which, on this especial night, a fair scene must have presented itself.

Above, the Passover moon was shining in full-orbed splendour, turning night into day. Beneath, the little stream was rippling down the valley, catching the moonlight on its wavelets. On the one slope dark, thick woods, above which rose the ancient walls and gates of the city; on the other, the swelling slopes of Olivet. Presently the Lord emerged out of the shadow, engaged in earnest converse with the apostles; crossed the bridge, but, instead of pursuing the path as it wound upward towards Bethany and Bethphage, they all turned into a large enclosure, well known as the garden of the oil-press, and which we know best as Gethsemane. Somewhere, no doubt, within its enclosure stood the rock-hewn trough in which the rich juicy olives were trodden by naked feet. "When Jesus had spoken these words, He went forth with his disciples over the brook Cedron, where was a garden, into the which He entered, and his disciples."

The sequel was so fully narrated by the other evangelists that there was no need for the writer of this narrative to tell of the awful anguish, the broken cries, the bloody sweat, the running to and fro of the disciples, the sleep of the chosen three, the strengthening angel. He confines himself almost entirely to the circumstances of the Lord's arrest.

Two hours only had passed since Judas left the Supper-table; but that had given him all the time needed for the completion of his plan. Hastening to the authorities, he had told them that the favourable moment had arrived for his Master's arrest; that he knew the lonely spot to which He was wont to resort for meditation and prayer; and that he had need of an armed band to overpower all possible resistance on the part of Himself or his followers. This they were able to supply from the guards and custodians of the Temple. They were going against One who was deserted and defenceless; yet the soldiers were armed with sticks and staves. They were about to arrest One who would make no attempt at flight or concealment, and the moon was full; yet, lest he should make his escape to some limestone grotto, or amid the deep shadows, they carried torches and lanterns.

The Lord had just awoke his disciples for the third and last time, when probably his ear detected the tread of hurrying feet, the muffled clank of swords, the stifled murmur of an advancing crowd; perhaps He saw also the glancing lights, as they advanced through the garden shrubs, and began to encircle the place where He had prayed. By such signs, and especially by the inner intimation of the Holy Spirit, He knew all things that should come upon Him; and without waiting for his enemies to reach Him, with calm and dignified composure He went forth to meet the rabble band, stepping out into the moonlight and saluting them with the inquiry, "*Whom seek ye?*"

There are some deep and memorable suggestions here as to the voluntariness of Christ's death. In order to his death having any value it must be free. If it could be shown that He had no choice but to die, because his own purpose was overmastered by the irresistible force of circumstances, his death could not have met the claims of a broken law, or inaugurated a new code of morals to his Church. But there are several points in this narrative which make it clear that He laid down his life of Himself—that none took it from Him; that He had power to lay it down, and power to take it again.

(1) When Jesus asked them the question, "Whom seek ye?" there were, no doubt, many in the band who knew Him well enough, and that He was the object of their midnight raid; but not one of them had the courage to answer, "Thee." A paralysing awe had already commenced to cast its spell over their spirits. Those who knew Him shrank from identifying Him, and were content to answer generally, "Jesus of Nazareth." But when He answered, "I am He," what was it that so suddenly affected them? Did some stray beams of concealed glory burst forth from their confinement to indicate his majesty? Did they dread the putting-forth of that power which had been so often exerted to save and bless? Or was there a direct miracle of Divine power, which secured their discomfiture? We cannot tell. But, whatever the cause, the crowd suddenly fell back in confusion, and were flung to the ground.

Here, for a moment, the would-be captors lay, as though pinioned to the dust by some unseen hand. The spell was soon withdrawn, and they were again on their feet, cursing themselves for their needless panic. But—and this is the point—the power that sent that rough hireling band reeling backwards to the ground could easily have held them there, or plunged them as Korah, Dathan, and Abiram into living graves. "One flash came forth to tell of the sleeping lightning which He would not use"; and then, having revealed the might which could have delivered Him from their puny arms, He returned to his attitude of willing self-surrender. Who, then, shall say that our Saviour's death was not his own act and deed?

(2) When that rabble crew were again on their feet, confronting Jesus, He asked them a second time, *"Whom seek ye?"* Again they replied, "Jesus of Nazareth." Jesus answered, "I have told you that I am He; if, therefore, ye seek Me, let these go their way." And, forthwith, He put forth such a power over his own as secured their freedom from arrest.

It is evident that it was no part of his foes' purpose beforehand to let them go; for on their way back they arrested a young man, probably Mark himself, whom curiosity had drawn from his bed, and whom they took for one of his disciples. He escaped with great difficulty from their hands. It is hardly doubtful that if some special power had not been exerted over them, they would have treated the whole of the followers of Jesus as they sought to treat Him. Is it not evident, then, that the power which secured the safety of his disciples could have secured that of the Master Himself; or that He might have passed away through the midst of them, as He did through the infuriated crowd which proposed to cast Him headlong over the precipice near Nazareth at the commencement of his ministry? Every arm might have been struck nerveless, every foot paralysed with lameness. Who, then, shall deny that Christ's death was his own act?

(3) But again, when Jesus had spoken thus there seemed some wavering among his captors—perhaps a hesitation as to who should first lay hand on Him. At this juncture, when the whole enterprise threatened to miscarry, Judas felt that he must, at all hazards, show how safe it was to touch the person of his Master; so, though the bold challenge of Jesus had made the preconcerted signal needless, he resolved still to give it, that the spell of that presence might be broken. The traitor, therefore, stepped up and kissed the Lord.

Encouraged by this sacrilegious act, his myrmidons now laid hands on Jesus, grasping his sacred person as they might have done Barabbas, or some other member of his gang. They then proceeded to bind Him after the merciless Roman fashion. Peter could not bear to see this. He sprang forth from the covert of the shadow, drew his sword, and cut at the nearest assailant's head. But the blade, glancing off the helmet, cut off the ear.

It was an unwelcome interference with the behaviour of the meek and gentle Lord, whose hand was already bound. It could not be permitted. "Suffer ye thus far," He said to the rude soldier who was binding Him; and with his own finger touched the ear, stanched the flowing blood, and healed it. It has been remarked that this was the only act of healing wrought on one for whom it was not asked of Him, and who had no faith in his beneficent power. But, surely, the hand that could work that miracle could have broken from the bonds that held it as easily as Samson from the two new cords which burnt as flax in the flame. The power with which Jesus saved others might have saved Himself. Who, then, shall say that his death was not his own free act? Listen, moreover, to his own words. Then said Jesus unto Peter, "Put up thy sword into the sheath; the cup which my Father hath given Me, shall I not drink it?" "Thinkest thou that I cannot now pray to my Father, and He shall presently give Me more than twelve legions of angels; but how then shall the Scripture be fulfilled that thus it must be?"

As, then, we view the death of the cross we must ever remember the voluntariness of that supreme act, which is all the more conspicuous as the agony of the garden reminds us how greatly the Lord's spirit dreaded the awful pressure of the world's sin, which made Him cry: "My God, my God, why hast Thou forsaken Me?" How greatly He must have loved us! It was love, and only love, that kept Him standing at the bar of Pilate, bending beneath the scourge of the soldiers, hanging in apparent helplessness on the cross. Not the iron hand of relentless fate; not the overpowering numbers or closely-woven plots of his foes; not the nails that pierced his quivering flesh. No, it was none of these. It was not even the compulsion of the Divine purpose. It was his own choice, because of a love that would bear all things if only it might achieve redemption for those whom He loved more than Himself. "He loved me, and gave Himself for me."

Surely we may trust that love. If it moved Him to endure the cross and despise the shame, is there anything that it will withhold, anything that it will not do? His love is stronger than death, and mightier than the grave. Strong waters cannot quench it, floods cannot drown it. It silences all praise, and beggars all recompense. To believe and accept it is eternal life. To dwell within its embrace is the foretaste of everlasting joy. To be filled by it is to be transfigured into the image of God Himself.

60

DRINKING THE CUP

"The cup which my Father hath given Me, shall I not drink it?"—
JOHN xviii. 1–14.

IN OUR Master's arrest the one feature which stands out in unique
splendour is its voluntariness. He went into the garden "knowing all
things that should come upon Him." Even at the last moment He
might have evaded the kiss of the traitor, and the binding thong with
which Malchus sought to manacle his gracious hands. The spell of his
intrinsic nobleness and glory, which had flung his captors to the
ground, might have held them there; the power that could heal the
wounded ear might have destroyed with equal ease the entire band.

The reason for all this hardly needs explaining. His life and death
were not merely a sacrifice, but a self-sacrifice. He freely gave Himself
up for us all. Each believer may dare to appropriate the words of
the Apostle: "He loved me, and gave Himself for me." It was through
the Eternal Spirit that He offered Himself without spot to God. It was
from his own invincible love that He gave Himself for the Church,
his Bride. "From beginning to end the moving spring of all his actions
was deliberate self-devotedness to the good of men, and the fulfilment
of God's will, for these are equivalents. And his death as the crowning
act of this career was to be conspicuously a death embodying and
exhibiting the spirit of self-sacrifice." Let us learn:

I. THE SUPREME NOBILITY OF SURRENDER TO THE EVITABLE.—
It is, of course, most noble, when the martyr goes to his death without
a murmur of complaint; allowing his enemies to wreak their vengeance
without recrimination or threatening; bowing the meek head to the
block; extending the hand to the hungry flame. He has no alternative
but to die; there are no legions waiting under arms to obey his summons; no John of Gaunt to stand beside him, as beside Wycliffe, to
see him fairly tried and insist on his acquittal. Then, there is nothing
for it but to evince the patience and gentleness of Christ in being led
as a lamb to the slaughter.

But though this spectacle stirs the hearts of men, there is one still
more illustrious—when the sufferer bends to a fate which he might
easily avoid, but confronts for the sake of others. The former is submission to the inevitable, this to the evitable. That is bearing a yoke
which is imposed by superior authority; this taking a yoke which might

be evaded without blame, as judged by the tribunal of public opinion. And this is the sublimest spectacle on which the eye of man or angel can rest; for thus the sacrifice of Christ finds its noblest counterpart and fulfilment.

When a missionary, with ample means and loving friends, deliberately spends among squalid and repulsive conditions the precious years which might have been passed among congenial society and luxurious comfort in the homeland; chooses a lot from which nature inevitably shrinks instead of that to which every conclusion but one points; and stays at his post, though his return, so far from being resented, would actually be favoured by all whose opinion is of weight—this is a voluntary submission to the evitable.

When a home pastor stays by his poor flock because they need him so sorely, and sets his face towards grinding poverty and irksome toil when the city church invites him to a larger stipend and wealthier surroundings—this again is a voluntary surrender to the evitable.

When a wealthy bachelor is willing to forgo the ease and quiet of his beautiful home to welcome the orphans of his deceased brother, who might have been sent to some charitable institution or cast on strangers, that they may be beneath his personal supervision, and have a better chance in life—this again is voluntary submission to the evitable.

In each such case, it is not inevitable that the cross should be borne, and the hands yielded to the binding thong. The tongue of scandal could hardly find cause for criticism if the easier path were chosen. Perhaps the soul hardly realises the kindredness of its resolve with the loftiest that this world has seen—but it is superlatively beautiful, nevertheless. And let it never be forgotten, that nothing short of this will satisfy the standard of Christ. No Christian has a right to use all his rights. None can claim immunity from the duty of seeking the supreme good of others, though it involve the supreme cost to himself.

II. THE RECOGNITION OF GOD'S WILL IN HIS PERMISSIONS.—In the bitter anguish which had immediately preceded the arrest, our Lord had repeatedly referred to his cup. "If this cup," He said, "may not pass from Me, except I drink it, thy will be done." The "cup" evidently referred to all the anguish caused to his holy nature in being numbered among the transgressors, and having to bear the sin of the world. Whether it was the anguish of the body, beneath which He feared He would succumb, as some think; or the dread of being made a sin-offering, a scapegoat laden with sins, as others; or the chill of the approaching eclipse, which extorted the cry of forsakenness, as seems to me the more likely—is not pertinent to our present consideration. It is enough to know that, whilst there was much that cried, "Back!" there was more that cried, "On!"—and that He chose from the profoundest depths of his nature, to do the Father's will, to execute his part in the compact into which they had entered before the worlds were made, and to drink to the dregs the cup which his Father had placed in his hands.

But here we note that to all appearances the cup was mingled, prepared, and presented by the malignity and hate of man. The high priests had long resolved to put Him to death, because his success with the people, his fresh and living comments on the law, his opposition to their hypocrisies and pretensions had exasperated them to madness. Judas also seemed to have had a conspicuous share in his discovery and arrest. Had we been left to our unaided reasonings we might have supposed that the most bitter ingredients of his cup had been supplied by the ingratitude of his own, the implacable rancour of the priests, and the treachery of Judas; but, see, He recognises none but the Father —it is always *the Father*, always the cup which the Father had given.

There have been times in our lives when we may have been tempted to distinguish between God's appointments and permissions, and to speak of the former as being manifestly his will for us, whilst we suspended our judgment about the latter, and questioned if we were authorised in accounting them as being equally from Heaven. But such distinctions are fatal to peace. Our souls were kept in constant perturbation, as we accounted ourselves the shuttlecock of rival powers, now God's, now man's. And we ended in ruling God out of more than half our life, and regarding ourselves as the hapless prey of strong and malicious forces to which we were sold, as Joseph to the Ishmaelites.

A deeper reading of Scripture has led us to a truer conclusion. There is no such distinction there. What God permits is as equally his will as what He appoints. Joseph tells his brethren that it was not they who sent him to Egypt, but God. David listens meekly to Shimei's shameful words, because he feels that God allowed them to be spoken. And here Jesus refuses to see the hand of his foes in his sufferings, but passes beyond the hand which bore the cup to his lips to the Father who was permitting it to be presented, and reposed absolutely in the choice for Him of One who loved Him with a love that was before the foundation of the world.

O sufferer! whether by those strokes, which, like sickness or bereavement, seem to come direct from Heaven, or by those which, like malicious speeches or oppressive acts, seem to emanate from man, look up into the face of God, and say, "My Father, this is thy will for me; thine angels would have delivered me, had it been best. But since they have not interposed, I read thy choice for thy child, and I am satisfied. It is sweet to drink the cup which thy hands have prepared."

III. THE DEEP LAW OF SUBSTITUTION.—Some of the rabble crowd had probably shown signs of a disposition to arrest some of Christ's followers. He, therefore, interfered, and reminded them of their own admission, that *He* was the object of their midnight raid, and bade them allow *these* to go their way. Is it surprising that the evangelist generalises this act, finding in it an illustration of his Master's ceaseless interposition on behalf of his own—that of those whom the Father had given Him He should lose none?

In brief, this scene affords a conspicuous and striking illustration of the great doctrine of substitution. As the Good Shepherd steps to the front and sheathes the swords of his foes in his own breast, while He demands the release of the cowering flock, He is doing on a small scale what He did once and for ever on Calvary; when, exposing Himself to the penalty due to sin, and braving the concentrated antagonism of a broken law, the drawn sword of inviolable justice, the sharpness of death, the shame of the cross, and the humiliation of the grave, He said, "If ye seek Me, let these go their way."

Christ sheltered us without reckoning the cost to Himself. He stood to the front, and bore the extreme brunt of all that was to be borne. He substituted his suffering for ours, his wounds for our pain, his death for our sins. If you are fearing the just recompense of your sins, like a band of arresting soldiers lurking in the dark shadows and threatening to drag you forth to pay the uttermost farthing, take heart; Jesus has met, and will meet, them for you. Listen to his majestic voice, saying, "Take Me; but let this soul, who clings to the skirts of my robe, go his way." He is arrested, and led away; thou art free—that in thy freedom thou shouldest give thyself to be his very slave.

61

The Hall of Annas

"They led Him away to Annas first, for he was father-in-law to Caiaphas, which was the high priest that same year."—John xviii. 13.

THE BAND that had arrested Jesus led Him back across the Cedron bridge, up the steep ascent, and through the ancient gateway, which at this season of the year stood always open, even at night.

The passage of the armed men through the quiet streets must have aroused from their slumbers many sleepers, who hurried to the windows to see them pass below in the clear moonlight. But no one guessed who was being taken into custody; and most of them probably thought that the soldiers had captured some more of the Barabbas gang, who, at that season of the year, would make a rare harvest by plundering pilgrims to the feast.

Their destination, in the first place, was the mansion of Annas, the head of the reigning priestly family, who was father-in-law of the actual high priest. He was now an old man—wealthy, aristocratic, and laden with all the honours his nation could give. For many years he had worn the high priest's robes, and though he had now nominally retired from that exalted office, he still kept his hand upon the reins of government. Caiaphas, at the time of which we speak, had held the priesthood for seventeen years under his tutelage; and he retained it for five years after. It is easy therefore to understand why Annas is described as the high priest. He was still the most powerful living bearer of that title. The whole family partook of his character, and was notorious for unwearied plotting. The gliding, deadly, snake-like smoothness with which Annas and his sons seized their prey is said to have won them the name of "hissing vipers."

Annas and Caiaphas probably shared the same cluster of buildings, which was presumably the official residence of the high-priestly family. In the East the houses of the great are frequently a group of buildings of unequal height standing near each other and surrounded by the same court, but with passages between, independent entrances, and separate roofs. Sometimes they would form a square or quadrangle with porticos and corridors around it, plants and fountains in the midst, and a slight awning overhead to protect the open courtyard from the sun or rain, the communication with the street being through a smaller courtyard and archway, called in the Gospels "a porch." In some such cluster of splendid buildings Annas and Caiaphas and others of their family would live, and the whole would be called the high priest's palace.

In one of the large reception halls Annas waited, impatient and feverish, to know the result of the midnight expedition. He had a nervous dread of what Jesus might do when driven to bay; and feared lest the secret should leak out, and the Galilean pilgrims rise in defence of their favourite Prophet, whom four days before they had escorted into the city with shouts. What if Judas should not prove true? All these disquieting thoughts chased each other like pursuing phantoms through his mind; and it was an immense relief when the clank of weapons in the court assured him of the safe return of Malchus' party, and answering voices told him that Jesus was at last safe within his power.

The prisoner was at once brought before the old man, who eagerly scrutinized his features in the flickering light of lanterns and flambeaux, casting shadows which a Rembrandt would have loved to paint. One or two intimates may have stood around him; but the main inquiry was left to himself, as he put the Master through a preliminary and informal examination, in the hope of extracting from his replies materials on which the Court, which was hastily summoned for an early hour in the morning, might proceed.

On the surface the inquiry seemed fair and innocent enough. The high priest, we learn from verse 19, asked Jesus of his disciples and his doctrine. But the lamb-skin hid a wolf. For the questions were so worded as to entangle, and to provide material on which to found the subsequent charge, which was even then being framed, that Jesus was a disturber of the public peace, and a teacher of revolutionary doctrine.

First, then, about his disciples.—Annas would like to be informed what this association of men meant. Why were they formed into a society? By what bond were they united? What secret instructions had they received? What hidden objects had they in view? If Jesus refused to answer these questions, might it not be made to appear that an attempt was on foot to organize a confederation throughout the entire country? If so, it would be easy to awaken the jealousy of the Roman authorities, and lead them to feel that they must take immediate steps to stamp out the plot by executing the ringleader.

And, next, as to his doctrine.—Had not Jesus repeatedly spoken about the Kingdom of Heaven? What did this mean? Was He contemplating the setting-up of a kingdom? Did He intend it to be understood that He was the expected Messiah, and that He meditated revolt against Rome? Was the manifestation of force, which had accompanied his recent entrance into the city, at his instigation?

Our Lord at once penetrated the design of his crafty interrogator. And in his answer He took care not to mention his disciples, speaking only of Himself. He affirmed that He had nothing to say which He had not already said a hundred times in the synagogues and the Temple, before friends and foes. He had no secret doctrines for the initiated, but had declared all that was in his heart. Between his disciples and Himself there had been no connection other than was obvious on the surface. No meetings under cover of night; no discussions of revolutionary topics; nothing that could not bear the fullest scrutiny. "I spake openly to the world; I ever taught in the synagogue, and in the temple, whither the Jews always resort; and in secret [that is, in the sense in which you use the word] have I said nothing. Why askest thou Me? Ask them which heard Me, what I said unto them: behold, they know what I said."

Our Lord's reference to those who had heard Him is probably an allusion to the armies of spies whom Annas had set on his track, watching his actions, reporting his words. Was not this examination of the prisoner a confession that the close scrutiny to which He had been subjected for so long had failed to elicit aught on which a criminal charge could be based? Jesus knew that his most secret words had been tortured in vain to yield an accusation against Him. How great, then, was the hypocrisy which could feign ignorance! How evident it was that Annas was only intent on inveigling his prisoner to say something on which to base his after-accusation.

All this was implied in our Lord's noble and transparent words. We shall see that He adopted another tone when He was properly arraigned before the assembled Sanhedrim; but in this more private, injudicial, inquisitorial interview, with one scathing rebuke He tore away the cloak of assumed ignorance with which this crafty man veiled his sinister purpose, and laid his secret thoughts open to the gaze of all.

For the time Annas was silenced. He had made small headway in the informal examination of his prisoner, and he now gave it up. Whatever resentment he may have felt at our Lord's answer he carefully concealed, biding the hour when he might vent the vials of his hate without stint.

We must not suppose there was any anger in that long-suffering heart towards this judge. He was even then about to die for *him*, and to bear the guilt of the very sin He so pitilessly exposed. But surely it was the part of love to show Annas what he was, and to utter words of rebuke in which, as in a mirror, his secret thoughts might be revealed. But if, in the moment of his humiliation, Jesus could thus search and reveal a man, what will He not do when He is no longer prisoner, but Judge? Oh those awful eyes, which are as a flame of fire! Oh those awful words, which pierce to the dividing asunder of the joints and marrow, and discern the thoughts and intents of the heart! What wonder that men shall at last call on the rocks to hide them from the wrath of the Lamb! Kiss the Son, less ye perish from his presence, when his wrath is kindled but a little! Blessed are they who can stand before Him without blame!

Then followed one of the grossest indignities to which our Lord was at this time subjected. On speaking thus, one of the officers, in the spirit of that despicable flunkeyism which will sacrifice all nobility and self-respect to curry the favour of a superior, smote our Lord with a rod, saying, "Answerest Thou the high priest so?"

When afterwards they came around Him to mock and smite, He answered nothing; but when this first stroke was inflicted the Master said quietly, "If I have spoken what is false or unbecoming, prove that I have done so; but if you cannot, why do you strike Me? No one has the right to take the law into his own hands, much less a servant of the Court."

It is impossible not to recall the mighty utterances against the resistance of wrong, spoken from the Mount, in the Messiah's manifesto: "I say unto you that ye resist not evil; but whosoever shall smite thee on thy right cheek, turn to him the other also." Clearly our Lord did not literally do so in this instance, because He saw an opportunity of revealing to this man his true condition, and of bringing him to a better mind. Our bearing of wrong must always be determined by the state of mind of those who ill-use us. In the case of some we may best arrest them by the dignity of an unutterable patience, which will bear to the utmost without retaliation—this is to turn the other cheek. In the case of others we may best serve them by leading them calmly and quietly to take the true measure of their crime. In all cases our prime consideration should be, not what we may be suffering, nor the utter injustice which is meted out to us; but how best to save the evil-doer, who is injuring his own soul more fatally than he can possibly injure us, and who is sowing seeds of harvest of incredible torture to his own conscience, in the long future which lies behind the veil of sense.

If only we could drink into the pure love of Jesus, and view all wrong and wrong-doers, not in the light of *our* personal interest, but of *their* awful condition and certain penalty; if only we could grieve over the infinite horror of a warped and devil-possessed soul, drifting like a ship on fire before the breeze, straight to the rocks; if only we could see the wrong done to our Father God and his sorrow, we should understand Chrysostom's beautiful comment on this scene: "Think on Him who said these words; on him to whom they were said; and on the reason why they were said: and, with Divine power, they will cast down all wrath that may arise within thy soul."

62

How it fared with Peter

"Peter stood at the door without. Then went out that other disciple, which was known unto the high priest, and spake unto her that kept the door, and brought in Peter."—John xviii. 16.

REMEMBER that this very circumstantial account was given by one who was an eye-witness of the whole scene; and who, withal, was then and in after years the warm friend and companion of Peter. But his love did not lead him to conceal his brother's sins. Peter himself would not have wished him to do so, because where sin had abounded, grace had had the greater opportunity to super-abound.

At the moment of the Lord's arrest, all the disciples forsook Him and fled. "The Shepherd was smitten and the flock scattered." Two of them, however, speedily recovered their self-possession, and followed at a distance, eager to see what would befall. When the procession reached the palace gate John seems to have entered with the rest of the crowd, and the ponderous massive doors closed behind him. On looking round for Peter he missed him, and concluding that he had been shut out and was still standing without, he went to the maid that kept the wicket-gate, opening in the main entrance doors for the admission of individuals, and asked her to admit his friend. She recognised him as being well known to the high priest, and readily assented to his request.

A fire of wood had been hastily lighted in the open courtyard, and cast its rays on the chilly April night; so that whilst Jesus was being examined by Annas the men who had taken part in the night adventure were grouped around the fire, discussing the exciting incident, with its moment of panic, the case of the arrest, the hurt and healing of the ear of Malchus, the seizure of the rich Eastern dress from the young man whom they had encountered on their homeward march. Peter did not wish to be recognized, and thought that the best way of preserving his incognito was to put on a bold face and take his place among the rest as though he, too, had been one of the capturing band, and had as much right to be there as any other of that mixed company. So he stood with them, and warmed himself.

Meanwhile, the doorkeeper, leaving her post, came to the fire, and in its kindling ray her eye fell upon Peter's face. She was surprised to see him there, feigning to be one of themselves. If, like John, he had gone quietly into some recess of the court, and waited unobtrusively in the shadow, she could have said nothing. In her kind-heartedness she would have respected them both; for she knew that they sympathized with the arrested Nazarene. But to find him there talking and acting as though he had no personal interest in the matter was so unseemly and unfit that she was provoked to expose him. She looked at him earnestly—as another evangelist tells us—to be quite sure that she was not mistaken; and feeling quite certain in her identification, said abruptly, "Art *thou* not one of this man's disciples?"

Peter was taken off his guard. If he had been arrested, and taken for trial, he would no doubt have played the hero—he had braced himself up for that; but he had not expected that the supreme trial of his life could come in the question of a servant-maid. It is so often thus. We lock and bolt the main door, and the thief breaks in at a tiny window which we had not thought of. We would burn at the stake; but in an hour of social intercourse with our friends, or a trivial business transaction, we say the word which fills our life with regret. Confused at the sudden pause in the conversation, and the turning of all eyes towards himself, Peter's first impulse was to allay suspicion, and he said bluntly, "I am not." Such was his *first* denial.

After this, as Matthew and Mark tell us, he went out into the outer porch or gateway, perhaps to avoid the glare of the light and the scrutiny of those prying eyes. He remembered afterwards that, at the same moment, a cock was heralding the dawn—the dawn of the blackest, saddest day that ever broke upon Jerusalem, or the world. But its warning notes were just then lost on him; for there another maid, speaking to some male acquaintances, pointed him out as one of the Nazarene's friends. "This man also was with Jesus the Nazarene." Probably no harm was meant; but the words alarmed Peter greatly, and he denied, as Matthew says, with an oath, "I know not the man." This was the *second* denial.

An hour passed; Peter, as we learn from the twenty-fifth verse, was again at the fire, and it was hardly possible for him to talk in a large company without unconsciously, and by force of character, coming to the front and taking the lead. His perturbed spirit was perhaps the more vehement to drown conscience. But now he is challenged by many at once. They say unto him, "Art not thou also one of his disciples?" And another saith, "Of a truth, thou wast with Him"; and another, a kinsman to Malchus, and therefore specially likely to remember his relative's assailant, saith, "Did I not see thee in the garden with Him?" Beset and badgered thus, Peter begins to curse and to swear, saying, "I know not the man of whom ye speak." When men lose their temper, they drop naturally into their native speech; and so, as Peter's fear and passion vented themselves in the guttural *patois* of Galilee, he gave a final clue to his identification. "Thou art a Galilean: thy speech betrayeth thee." And again he denied with an oath, "I know not the man." This was his *third* denial. And immediately the cock crew.

It may have happened that, at this moment, Jesus was passing from Annas to Caiaphas, and cast on Peter that marvellous look of mingled sorrow and pity, of suffering more for his sake than his own, and of tender allusion to the scene and words of the previous evening, which broke Peter's heart, and sent him forth to weep bitterly.

The light was breaking over the hills of Moab, flushing with roseate hues the marble pinnacles of the Temple, whilst the city and surrounding valleys were still shrouded in the grey gloom, as Peter went forth alone from the high priest's palace. Only those whose last words to the beloved dead were rude and thoughtless—not expecting that there would be no opportunity to unsay them and ask forgiveness, but that, ere they met again, death would have sealed in silence the only lips that could speak words of relief and peace—can realise just what Peter felt. Did he know Him? Of course he did, and ever since that memorable hour, when Andrew first brought him into his presence, he had been growing to a more perfect knowledge. Did he love Him? Of course he did; and Jesus, who knew all things, knew it too. But why had he acted thus? Ah, the reasons were not far to seek. He had boasted of his superiority to all his brethren; had relied on his own braggart resolutions; had counted himself strong because he could speak strongly and loudly when danger was not near; had thought that he could cope with Satan, though arrayed in no stronger armour than that which his red-hot impulse forged. He thought his resolutions wheat and his Master's cautions light as chaff; he had to learn his weakness and see his confidence winnowed away as clouds of chaff while Satan sifted him.

The resolutions of the evening are not strong enough to carry us victoriously through the morning conflict. We must learn to watch and pray, to lie low in humility and self-distrust, and to be strong in the grace which awaits all tempted ones in God.

And where could Peter go to weep his bitter tears but to Gethsemane! He would surely seek out the spot where his Master's form was still outlined in the crushed grass, and his tears would fall where the bloody sweat had fallen but a few hours before. But how different the cause of sorrow! The anguish of the blessed Lord had none of the ingredients that filled the cup of Peter to the brim! And all the while the memory of that sorrow, of those broken cries, of that coming and going for sympathy, of those remonstrances against his senseless sleep, and of that last tender, yearning, pitiful look of love, came back on him to arouse successive surges of grief. Contrast Christ's love with your ingratitude, Christ's constancy with your fickle devotion, Christ's meekness to take the yoke of his Father's will, and your unwillingness to bear the shame of his cross —and ask if you, too, have no cause for tears like those that Peter shed.

It is remarkable that Peter should have fallen here. His open, ingenuous nature was not given to lying, his impetuous character was not prone to cowardice. Accustomed from boyhood to meet death in the wrestle with nature for daily sustenance, he was not subject to the apprehensions of a nervous dread. None of his fellow-disciples would have expected the rock-man to show that he was clay or sand after all. But this was permitted that he and we might learn that our noblest natural qualities as much need to be dealt with by the grace of God as our vices and defects. Many a fortress has been taken from a side which was deemed impregnable. No one expected that Wolfe would assail Quebec from the Heights of Abraham.

How often we have fallen into the same trap! We have, perhaps, been thrown into a company where it was fashionable to sneer at evangelical religion, and we have held our peace; where the ready sneer was passed on those who dared still to believe in miracle and inspiration, and we have been silent; where condemnation has been freely passed on some man of God whom we owned as friend, and knew to be innocent, and we have not tried to vindicate him; where some great religious movement in which we were interested was being discussed and condemned, whilst we have coolly joined in the conversation as if we had not made up our minds, or were totally indifferent. We have been unwilling to be unpopular, to stand alone, to bear the brunt of opposition, to seem eccentric and peculiar. Let those who are without sin cast their stones at Peter; but the most of us will take our place beside him, and realise that we, too, have given grief to Christ, and grave cause to his enemies to blaspheme.

But, be it remembered, the true quality of the soul is shown, not in the way in which it yields to temptation in some moment of weakness and unpreparedness, but in the way in which it repents afterwards. Do we weep, not for the penalty we dread, but because we have sinned against Christ? Are we broken down before Him, waiting till He shall restore? Do we dare still to believe in his forgiving and renewing grace? Then this is a godly repentance, which needs not to be repented of. These are tears which his love shall transform to pearls. How different this to the attitude of a Judas! Each fell; but in their demeanour afterwards the one was shown to be gold, silver, precious stones; the other wood, hay, and stubble.

How may we be kept from falling again?

(1) Let us not sleep through the precious moments which Heaven affords before each hour of trial; but use them for putting on the whole armour of God, that we may be able to stand in the evil day.

(2) Let us not cast ourselves needlessly into situations where our most cherished convictions are likely to be assailed by wanton men;

63

The Trial before Caiaphas

"Annas had sent Him bound unto Caiaphas the high priest."
JOHN xviii. 24.

It was as yet but two or three o'clock in the morning. Jerusalem was still asleep, and well it was for the foes of Jesus that no suspicion of what was on foot had breathed into the minds of the crowds of pilgrims; for, had the Galileans only known what was being done to their favourite prophet, they would have risen, and the plot must have miscarried before Jesus was handed over to the Romans. But, as the Lord said, "It was their hour and the power of darkness." The darkest hour before the dawn!

When Annas had completed his preliminary inquiry he gave orders that He should again be bound with the thongs of which He had been relieved, and led to that part of the palace specially used by Caiaphas, who was high priest, but a mere puppet in the hands of the wily Annas. By this time the leading Pharisees, Sadducees, and priests had been got together, summoned by special messengers; and though the formal meeting of the Council was probably not held till a little later (compare Matt. xxvi. 57 with xxvii. 1, 2), the trial was really conducted at that untimely hour, and the evidence procured on which final action was taken.

They awaited the prisoner in one of the larger halls of the palace, sitting in Oriental fashion on cushions and pillows, in a half-circle, with turbaned heads, crossed legs, and bare feet; the high priest in the centre, the others on either side, according to age.

All the rules of justice were violated. The judge was chief inquisitor; witnesses against the prisoner were alone summoned; and the Court set itself from the first to get evidence to put the accused to death.

Ever since Jesus had commenced his ministry it had been certain that He would have to face some such tribunal as this. His soul was aflame for Righteousness and Truth; it was inevitable that He should come into conflict with these representatives of a traditional and external religiousness, which consisted in a number of formal rules and rites from which the life had long since fled.

This Gospel specially narrates the progress of the quarrel in the holy city. As far back as ch. ii. 18 we are told that there had been an altercation on the Lord's right to cleanse the Temple.

Ch. iv. 1-3.—He left Judæa because of the irritation of the Pharisees at the numerous baptisms which were taking place under his ministry.

325

Ch. v. 18.—He was only at the beginning of the second year of his ministry, and had just healed the impotent man at the pool of Bethesda; and we find the Jews consulting how they might kill Him, and He was compelled again to retire from Judæa.

Ch. vii. 19.—Such was the spirit of vindictiveness excited against our Lord that when twelve months afterwards He came to Jerusalem at the Feast of Tabernacles, one of his first words was, "Why go ye about to kill Me?" The people were well acquainted with the designs of the rulers (vers. 25, 26); and ultimately officers were sent to arrest Him (vers. 30, 32).

Ch. viii. 59.—They were so exasperated with his words that they took up stones to stone Him.

Ch. ix. 34.—They excommunicated the blind man because their hated foe had cured him, and he in his favour had dared to protest.

Ch. x. 31.—The Jews (and the Apostle always uses that word of the Sanhedrim and their allies) took up stones to cast at Him; and in verse 39 we read that they sought again to take Him; but He escaped out of their hand to Perea, where He remained until the message of the sisters called Him from his retreat.

Ch. xi. 47.—The raising of Lazarus produced such an effect that a special Council was called to consider what should be done, with the result that from that day they took counsel to put Him to death.

Ch. xii. 10.—Their malignity was so great that they consulted whether they should not put Lazarus to death also; because by reason of him many of the Jews went away and believed in Jesus.

It was all this that made them fall in so eagerly with the proposal of Judas that he should betray Him unto them.

Now at last they had Him in their power, and their object was to convict Him of some crime which would justify the infliction of the severest sentence of the law. To preserve the appearance of justice, witnesses were called to testify to some action or speech which would involve blasphemy against their law, and, if possible, against the Roman law as well; and it was necessary that two of them should agree in some specific charge. The chief priests, and elders, and all the Council, Matthew tells us, sought for witness against Jesus to put Him to death. They brought forward many, but either their charges did not reach the required degree of criminality, or the clumsy witnesses, brought hastily forward, undrilled beforehand, broke down so grossly in their story that for shame's sake they had to be dismissed.

At last two witnesses appeared who seemed likely to agree on a very momentous charge. They said they had heard Him utter, more than two years ago, words which seemed to threaten the very existence of the Temple. But, when more closely questioned, their witness also broke down utterly. It seemed as though Jesus was not to die, except on his own testimony to his own supreme claims. All lesser counts failed.

All this time, as witness after witness was brought in, our Lord maintained an unbroken silence. He seemed as though He heard not, but was absorbed in some other scenes from those transpiring around. What need was there for Him to interpose, when all the charges proved abortive? He was, moreover, waiting till the Father gave Him the signal to open his lips.

At last Caiaphas could restrain his impatience no longer; he sprang to his feet, and with unconcealed fury fixed his eyes on Jesus and said: "Answerest Thou nothing? Hast Thou nothing to say, no question to put, no explanation to offer as to what these witnesses say?" Jesus quietly returned the look, but held his peace. There are times when it is treason to hold our peace; when God demands of us to raise our voice and cry like a trumpet. But when it is clear that high-handed wrong is bent on securing the condemnation of the innocent, and that the case is prejudged, it is the highest wisdom to be as a lamb dumb before its shearers, and not open the mouth.

There was a last alternative. Caiaphas might put Jesus on his oath, and extort from his own lips the charge on which to condemn Him; but he was evidently reluctant to do it, and only availed himself of this process as a last resource. It was well known to this astute and cunning priest that Jesus on more than one occasion had claimed, not only to be the long-expected Messiah, but to stand to God in the unique relationship of Son. Nearly two years before, He had called God his own Father, making Himself equal with God (John v. 18); and again, comparatively recently, at the Feast of Dedication, He had claimed that He and the Father were one; in consequence of which the bystanders threatened to take his life because that, being a man, He made Himself God (x. 31-33). Gathering, therefore, the two claims in one, and in the most solemn form, putting Jesus on his oath, the high priest said unto Him, "I adjure Thee by the Living God, that Thou tell us whether Thou be the Christ, the Son of the Blessed?" (Matt. xxvi. 63; Mark xiv. 61). There was no need for further hesitation. Charged in this way, in the highest court of his nation, and by the representative of his people, He could not hold his peace without inconsistency with the whole tenor of his life and teaching. John, representing his disciples and friends, must be assured that his Master did not vacillate by a hairbreadth at that supreme moment. Those high officials must understand, beyond the smallest possibility of doubt, that if they put Him to death He would die on the supreme count of his Messianic and Divine claims; and, therefore, amid the breathless silence of the Court, without a falter in the calm, clear voice, Jesus said, "I AM." The Father that sent Him was with Him; He had not left Him in that awful moment *alone*: and it was a great pleasure to the Saviour to be able publicly to avow the relationship, which was shedding its radiance through his soul. Then, with evident allusion to the sublime vision of Daniel, He added, "Ye shall see the Son of Man sitting at the right hand of power, and coming with the clouds of heaven." Though Son of God, He was not less the Son of Man; and though one with the Father before the worlds were made, was yet prepared to exercise the functions of the expected Prince of the House of Israel. This is the force of *nevertheless* in Matt. xxvi. 64—I am the Son of God: *nevertheless*, ye shall see the Son of Man sitting on the right hand of power.

The words were very grateful to the ears of Caiaphas and his confederates, as they afforded ground for the double charge they needed. For a man to claim to be Son of God would make him guilty of blasphemy, and he must be put to death according to Jewish law; whilst if there was a prospect of his setting up a kingdom, the Romans' suspicions would at once be aroused. But in their glee at having entrapped their victim they must not forget to show a decorous horror of his crime. In well-assumed dismay the high priest rent his clothes, saying, "He hath spoken blasphemy: what further need have we of witnesses? Behold, now ye have heard the blasphemy." And then came the decisive question which the judge was wont to put to his co-assessors, "What think ye? And they all condemned Him to be guilty of death."

Then ensued a brief interval, until the early formal session of the Sanhedrim could be held: and during this recess the disgraceful scenes were repeated which had already taken place in the hall of Annas. Luke tells us that the men that held Jesus mocked Him, beat Him, and asked Him to prophesy who it was that smote Him. Matthew adds that they spat in his face. But Mark lets in still more light on the horror of the scene, when he appears to distinguish between *some* who began to spit on Him, and to cover his face, and *the officers* who received Him with blows of their hands. And the expression *some* occurs so immediately after the record of their condemning Him, that the suggestion seems irresistible that several of these reverend dignitaries did not hesitate to disgrace their grey hairs in personally insulting the meek and holy Sufferer; venting their spleen on one who gave no show of retaliation, though one word from those pale compressed lips would have laid them low in death, or withdrawn the veil of eternity, behind which legions of angels were waiting impatient to burst upon the impious scene. But do not condemn them as though they were sinners beyond all others; remember that we have all the same evil human heart.

At last the morning broke, and as soon as it was day the assembly of the elders of the people was gathered together, both chief priests and scribes; and they led Jesus away into their Council (Luke xxii. 66). This scene had already been so well rehearsed that it probably did not take many minutes to run through the necessary stages, according to the precise formulæ of Jewish procedure. The method that had already proved so valuable was quickly repeated. Questioning Him first as to his Messiahship, Caiaphas, as spokesman to the rest, said formally, "If Thou art Christ, tell us."

It was a sorry figure that stood before them. Dishevelled and in disarray, with disordered garments, the spittle still hanging about his face, and the marks of the awful storm and mental anguish stamped on every feature, the innate dignity and glory of Jesus shone out in his every movement, and notably in his majestic answer, "Why do you ask Me? You have no real desire to know! If I tell you, ye are in no mood to-believe! And if I ask you your warrant for refusing to believe, if I argue with you, if I adduce Scripture to support my claims, ye will not answer; but though I read the motive of your inquiry, I will give you all the evidence you desire. From henceforth shall the Son of Man be seated at the right hand of God."

As to the other charge, involving his divine nature, the admission of which involved the crime of blasphemy, they were too eager to wait for Caiaphas; but with swollen faces, excited gestures, and loud cries, rising from their seats, and gesticulating with the fury of religious frenzy, they *all* said, "Art Thou then the Son of God?" And He said unto them, solemnly and emphatically, "Ye say that which I am."

Then they turned to one another and said, "What further need have we of witness? for we have heard from his own mouth." The inquiry was at an end so far as Jesus was concerned. But they held a further Council against Him, how to construct the indictment which would compel Pilate to inflict death; for the execution of the sentence of death was kept resolutely by the Roman Procurator in his own hands.

Finally, as soon as they dared disturb him, they led Jesus from Caiaphas into the Prætorium, the place of the Roman governor, who, in accordance with his custom, had come up from his usual residence at Cæsarea to the Jewish capital, partly to keep order amid the vast crowds that gathered there at the feast, seething with religious fanaticism, and partly to try the cases which awaited his decision. The Jewish authorities anticipated no great difficulty in securing from him the necessary ratification of the death-sentence. It surely would not matter to him to add another to the long tale of robbers and revolutionaries which were awaiting the cross; the more especially as they were able to prefer a charge of treason against the Roman power substantiated by the prisoner's own admissions made recently in their presence.

It is an awful spectacle, and one over which we would fain draw a veil; but let us dare to stay to watch the evolution of the diabolical plot to the end. This, at least, will become manifest—that Jesus died, because He claimed to be the Son of God, in the unique sense of oneness with the Father; that made Him equal with God, and constituted blasphemy in the eye of the Jewish law. And He who has taught the world Truth could neither have been a deceiver, nor deceived, in this high claim.

64

"Judas, which Betrayed Him"

"Judas, which betrayed Him."—John xviii. 2.

On the Wednesday evening before our Lord died, He supped with his disciples in Bethany at the house of Simon. Lazarus was there, and his sisters—Martha, who served, and Mary, who anointed Him beforehand for his burying. The Master's reception of this act of love, and his rebuke of the parsimony which sought to check all such manifestations of devotion, exasperated Judas beyond all bounds; so, after supper, when Jesus and the rest had retired to their humble lodging, he crossed the intervening valleys and returned by the moonlight to Jerusalem.

At that untimely hour the Sanhedrin may have been still in session, plotting to destroy Jesus. At any rate, the chief priests and captains were quickly summoned. Judas may have been in communication with some of them before; but, in any case, he met with a glad welcome. They were glad, and covenanted to give him money.

In the word, *communed* with them, used by the evangelist Luke, it is suggested that there was a certain amount of bargaining and haggling before the sum was fixed. Perhaps he wanted more, and they offered him less, and at last he was induced to take less than he had hoped, but more than they had offered; and the price of betrayal was fixed at thirty pieces of silver, about £8, the price of a slave. From that moment he sought opportunity to betray Him unto them.

At the Passover Supper provided on the next day by Peter and John in the upper room, Judas must have reclined on the Lord's left, and John upon his right, so that the beloved disciple could lean back his head on the bosom of his Friend. When all were settled, Jesus exclaimed, with a sigh of innermost satisfaction, "With desire I have desired to eat this Passover with you before I suffer"; and as He uttered the words, Judas must have felt a thrill passing through his nature, as he realised more clearly than any around that table what was approaching. Evidently, then, the Master had guessed what was being prepared for Him! Did He also know the share that he had in preparing it? In any case, it was clear that, so far from resisting, He was prepared to suffer. Apparently, He would not take the opportunity of asserting his claims; but would allow events to take their course, yielding Himself to the will of his foes!

When He had given thanks, the Lord passed round the first cup; then followed the washing of the disciples' feet, in the midst of which He looked sorrowfully towards Judas, exclaiming, "Ye are clean, but not all"; for He knew from the first who would betray Him. It was with a strange blending of awe and wonder that the little group saw the dark cloud of anguish gather and rest on the beloved face when, on resuming his place, He was troubled in the spirit, and testified, and said, "Verily, verily, I say unto you, that one of you shall betray Me." The disciples looked at one another, doubting of whom He spoke, and Peter beckoned to John to ask. But Judas knew. And when He went on to say, "The Son of Man goeth even as it is written of him; but woe unto that man through whom the Son of Man is betrayed! good were it for that man if he had not been born"—again Judas' heart smote him. It may be that he asked himself whether he might not even now draw back.

For three years he had played his part so well that, in spite of his constant pilfering from the bag which held the slender resources of the little band, no one suspected him. His fellow-disciples might contend for the first places at the table, but all felt that Judas, at any-rate, had a prescriptive right to sit near Jesus. All round, in sorrowful tones, the question passed, "Lord, is it I?" Each, conscious of the unfathomed evil of his own nature, thought himself more likely to be the traitor than that the admirable Judas should do the deed. It was terrible to know that the Shepherd should be smitten, and the flock scattered; but more, that the Master would be betrayed by the inner circle of his friends! But there seemed no reason for challenging his announcement, backed as it was by a quotation from a familiar Psalm, "He that dippeth his hand with Me in the dish, the same shall betray Me." From these words also it was evident that the traitor must be one of two or three; for only these could reach the common dish in which Jesus dipped his food.

It became, therefore, more and more clear to Judas, that the Master knew perfectly well all that had transpired, and he said to himself, "If He knows so much, it is almost certain that He knows all." There-fore, partly to disarm any suspicions that might be suggested to the others if he did not take up their question, partly because he felt that probably there was nothing to be gained by maintaining his disguise before Jesus, and being withal feverishly anxious to know how much of his plan was discovered, he asked, adopting the colder title Rabbi, rather than that of Lord, as employed by the others, "Rabbi, is it I?" Probably the question was asked under his breath, and that Jesus replied in the same tone, "Thou hast said."

Immediately the thoughts of Judas sprang back to the foot-washing, and all the other marks of extraordinary tenderness with which Jesus had treated him. At the time he had thought, "He would not act like this if He knew all." Now, however, he realised that Jesus had acted in the full knowledge of all that had passed, and was passing in his heart. It must have struck him as extraordinary that the Master should continue to treat him thus when He had read the whole dark secret. Why did He not unmask and expose him? Why not banish him from his company? Why count him still on speaking terms? Not till afterwards was he aware of Jesus' motive, nor did he detect the loving purpose which was laying siege to his stony heart as though to turn him from his evil purpose before it was too late.

Once more the Lord made an effort to prove to him that though He knew all He loved him still—even to the end. It was the Jewish custom for one to dip a morsel in the common dish and pass it to another in token of special affection, so when He had dipped the sop, Jesus took and gave it to Judas, the son of Simon. He had previously answered John's whispered question, "Lord, who is it?" which had been suggested by a sign from Peter, by saying, "He it is to whom I shall give a sop when I have dipped it." But He did not give the token of love merely as a sign to John and Peter, but because He desired to assure Judas that, notwithstanding His perfect knowledge, His heart was full of tender affection.

When the sun strikes on a fœtid pond, its rays, beneath which all creation rejoices, bring out the repulsive odours that otherwise had slept undiscovered; so the love of God is ever a savour of life unto life or of death unto death, and the very fervour of Christ's love seems to have driven Judas almost to madness. Shutting his heart against the Saviour, he opened it to Satan, who was waiting his opportunity. "After the sop, then Satan entered into him." Instantly the Master saw the change, and knew that He could do nothing more to save his disciple from the pit which he had digged for himself. Nothing could be gained by further delay. Jesus therefore said unto him, "That thou doest, do quickly."

So carefully had the Lord concealed his knowledge of Judas' real character that none of those who sat at table guessed the real significance and purport of his words. For some thought, because Judas had the bag, that Jesus said unto him, "Buy what things we have need of for the feast"; or that he should give something to the poor. Only John, and perhaps Peter, had the slightest suspicion of his possible errand. The sacred narrative adds significantly, "He then having received the sop, went out straightway, and it was night"; as though the black pall of darkness were a befitting symbol of the blackness of darkness that was enveloping his soul—a night broken only by one star, when Jesus once more in the garden sought to arrest him with the words, "Friend, to what a deed thou art come! Betrayest thou the Son of Man with a kiss?" But that lone star was soon obscured. The cloud-wreath hastened to conceal it. Headlong and precipitate over every obstacle, he rushed to his doom, until his career was consummated in the despairing act which the evangelist so solemnly records.

The specified fee was no doubt paid to Judas, on his delivery of Jesus into the hands of the high priest. As soon as the great doors closed behind the arresting band, Judas went to some inner pay-office, claimed his money, and then waited in the shadow to see what befell. Perhaps he met John; and if so, avoided him. Perhaps he heard Peter deny the Lord with oaths, and congratulated himself that there was not much to choose between them. But for the most part his mind was absorbed in what was transpiring. He beheld the shameful injustice and inhumanity of the trial. Though he had kissed his Master's face, his soul winced from the blows and spittle that befell it. Perhaps he had entertained some lingering hope and expectation that when the worst came to the worst the Master would use on his own behalf the power He had so often used for others. But if that thought had lodged in his mind, the dream was terribly dissipated. "He saw that He was condemned."

Then the full significance of his sin burst upon him. The veil fell from his eyes, and he stood face to face with his crime in all its naked horror—his ingratitude, his treachery, his petty pilfering, his resistance of a love which the strong waters of death could not extinguish. And the money scorched his hand. A wild and haggard man, he made his way into the presence of the chief priests and scribes, as they were congratulating themselves on the success of their plot. There was despair on his face, a piercing note in his voice, anguish in his soul; the flames of hell were already consuming him, the thirst of the bottomless pit already parching his lips; his hand convulsively clutched the thirty pieces of silver.

"I have sinned," he cried. "I have sinned. He whom you have condemned is innocent; take back your money, only let Him go free; and oh, relieve me, ye priests, accustomed to deal with burdened hearts, relieve me of this intolerable pain."

But they said, with a gleam as of cold steel, "What is that to us? That is your business. You made your bargain, and you must stand to it: see thou to it."

He knew that it was useless to parley with them. That icy sarcasm, that haughty indifference, told him how man must ever regard his miserable act. He had already refused the love of God, and dared not expect anything more from it. He foresaw how coming ages would spurn and abhor him. There seemed, therefore, nothing better than to leap into the awful abyss of suicide. It could bring nothing worse than he was suffering. Oh, if he had only dared to believe in the love of God, and had fallen even then at the feet of Jesus, he might have become a pillar in his temple, and an apostle of the Church. But he dared not think that there could be mercy for such as he was. He passes out into the morning air, the most wretched of men, shrinks away into some lonely spot, puts a rope around his neck, and dies.

We have been accustomed to think of Judas as one whose crime has put him far in front of all others in the enormity of his guilt. Dante draws an awful picture of him as alone even in hell, shunned by all other sinners, as Turkish prisoners will shun Christians, though sharing the same cell. But let us remember that he did not come to such a pitch of evil at a single bound. There was a time, no doubt, when, amid the cornfields, vineyards, and pastoral villages of his native Kerioth, he was regarded as a promising youth, quick at figures, the comfort of his parents, the pride of his instructors, the leader of his comrades.

During the early years of his manhood, Jesus came through that same country on a preaching tour, and there must have been a wonderful fascination in Him for young men, so many of whom left their friends and callings to join and follow Him. Judas felt the charm and joined himself to the Lord; perhaps Jesus even called him. At that time his life must have been fair, or the Master would never have committed Himself to him. He was practical, prompt, and business-like, the very man to keep the bag. But the continual handling of the money at last awoke within him an appetite of the presence of which he had not been previously aware. He did not banish it, but dwelt on it, allowing it to lodge and expand within him, till, like a fungus in congenial soil, it ate out his heart and absorbed into itself all the qualities of his nobler nature, transmuting them into rank and noisome products. All love for Christ, all care for the poor, all thought of his fellow-disciples, were quenched before that remorseless passion; and at last he began to pilfer from those scant treasures, which were now and again replenished by those that loved to minister to the Master's comfort. At first, he must have been stung by keen remorse; but each time he sinned his conscience became more seared, until he finally reached the point when he could sell his Master for a trifle, and betray Him with a kiss.

Alas! Judas is not the only man of whom these particulars have been true. Change the name and you have an exact description of too many. Many a fair craft has come within the reach of the circling eddies of the same boiling whirlpool, and, after a struggle, has succumbed. The young man hails from his native village home, earnest and ingenuous. At first he stands firm against the worldly influences around; but gradually he becomes careless in his watch, and as money flows in he realises the fascination of the idea of being a wealthy man. He becomes increasingly absorbed, until he begins to drift towards a goal from which in other days he would have shrunk in horror. If any reader of these words is conscious of such a passion beginning to lay hold of him, let him beware, lest, like Judas, he be lost in the divers hurtful lusts which drown men in perdition.

And if already you have been betrayed into sins which would bear comparison with that of Judas, do not despair—true, you have sinned against light and love, the eager, tender pleadings of God's love; but do not give up hope. Cast yourself on a love which wants to abound over sin, and glories in being able to save to the uttermost.

65

The First Trial before Pilate

"Then led they Jesus from Caiaphas unto the hall of judgment: and it was early; and they themselves went not into the judgment hall, lest they should be defiled; but that they might eat the passover."

JOHN xviii. 28.

THERE is no doubt that had Pilate been absent from Jerusalem at the time of our Lord's trial before the Sanhedrin, they would have rushed Him to death, as afterwards Stephen, and have risked the anger of the governor. But they dared not attempt such a thing beneath the eyes of the dreaded Roman eagles. They must needs obtain Pilate's countersign to their death-sentence, and, indeed, consign their victim to him for execution. The Lord was to die, not the Jewish death by stoning, but the terrible Roman death of crucifixion.

why?

The day then breaking was that before the Passover. If the order for execution were not obtained that morning, the case could not come on for seven days, and it would have been highly impolitic, from their point of view, to keep Jesus so long in bonds. The national sentiment might have awoke and refused to sanction their treachery. For the same reason it was necessary to carry the sentence into effect with as little delay as possible, or the whole plot might miscarry. Then led they Jesus from Caiaphas to the official residence of Pilate, which had been the palace of the magnificent Herod—*and it was early.*

In the palace there was a hall where trials were usually conducted; but the Jewish dignitaries who had not scrupled shamelessly to condemn Jesus were too scrupulous to enter the house of a Gentile on the eve of the feast, for fear there might be a single grain of leaven there, and the mere suspicion of such a thing would have disqualified them from participating in the feast. Remember that these men had just broken every principle of justice in their treatment of Jesus, and now they haggle over minute points of Rabbinical casuistry. So Philip of Spain abetted the massacres of Alva, but rigorously performed all the rites of the Church; and the Italian bandit will carefully honour priest, and host, and church. How well our Lord's sharp sword cut to the dividing of soul and spirit, in such cases as these: "Ye pay tithe of mint, and cummin, and anise, and have omitted the weightier matters of the law." It is an evil day when religion and morality are divorced.

Pilate knew too well the character of the men with whom he had to do, to attempt to force their scruples, and went out to them; so that for most of the time his intercourse with Jesus was apart from their interference and scrutiny. Without much interchange of formalities, the governor asked, "What accusation bring ye against this man?"

It was not a little disappointing to their pride to be obliged to adduce and substantiate capital charges against Jesus, so they replied in general terms, and with the air of injured innocence, "If He were not a malefactor, we would not have delivered Him unto thee." It was as though they said, "There is no need for thee to enter into the details of this case; we have thoroughly investigated it, and are satisfied with the conclusive evidence of our prisoner's guilt; you may be sure that men like ourselves would never come to thee at such an hour, on such an errand, unless there were ample grounds for it."

But Pilate was in no mood to be talked with thus. He saw their eagerness to ward off inquiry, and this was quite enough to arouse his proud spirit to thwart and disappoint them. He knew well enough that they wanted him to pronounce the death-sentence; but he pretended not to, and said, in effect, "If your judgment, and yours only, is to settle the case, take ye Him and judge Him according to your law, inflicting such penalty as it directs."

The Jewish notables at once saw that they must adopt a more conciliatory tone, or they would lose their case; they therefore explained that they wanted a severer sentence than they had the right to inflict. "It is not lawful," they said, "for us to put any man to death."

Pilate again asked for a statement of the crime of which Jesus was accused.

Now mark the baseness of their reply. The only crime on which they had condemned Jesus to death was his claim to Deity; but it would never have done to tell Pilate that. He would simply have laughed at them. They must find some charge which would bring Him within the range of the common law, and be of such a nature that Pilate must take cognisance of it, and award death. It was not easy to find ground for such a charge in the life of one who had so studiously threaded his way through the snares they had often laid for Him; who had bade them render Cæsar's things to Cæsar; and protested that He was neither a ruler nor judge. Their only hope was to rest their charge on his claim to be the Messiah; construing it as the Jews were wont to do, but as Jesus never did, into a claim to an outward and visible royalty. They said, therefore, as Luke informs us, "We found this man perverting the nation and forbidding to give tribute to Cæsar, saying that He Himself is Christ a King."

This was quite enough to compel Pilate to institute further inquiry. There were thousands of Jews who questioned Cæsar's right to tax them, and were willing to revolt under the lead of any man who showed himself capable. It was certainly suspicious that such a charge should be made by men who themselves abhorred the yoke of Rome. However, Pilate saw that he had no alternative but to investigate the case further. He therefore went within the palace to the inner judgment hall, summoned Jesus before him, and said, not without a touch of sarcasm in his tones, "Art Thou the King of the Jews?" Thou poor, worn, tear-stained outcast, forsaken by every friend in this thy hour of need, so great a contrast to him who built these halls and aspired to the same title—art thou a king?

He probably expected that Jesus would at once disclaim any such title. But instead of doing so, instead of answering directly, our Lord answered his question by propounding another—"Sayest thou this thing of thyself, or did others tell it thee concerning Me?" The purport of this question seems to have been to probe Pilate's conscience, and make him aware of his own growing consciousness that this prisoner was too royal in mien to be an ordinary Jewish visionary. It was as though He said: "Dost thou use the term in the common sense, or as a soul confronted by a greater than thyself? Do you speak by hearsay or by conviction? Is it because the Jews have so taught thee, or because thou recognisest Me as able to bring order and peace into troubled hearts like thine?"

Whatever thoughts had instinctively made themselves felt were instantly beaten back by his strong Roman pride. Never before had he been catechised thus. And he answered haughtily, "Am I a Jew? Thine own nation and the chief priests have delivered Thee unto me: what hast Thou done?"

Our Lord did not answer that question by enumerating deeds which had filled Palestine with wonder; but contented Himself by saying that He had committed no political offence, and had no idea of setting Himself up as king, in the sense in which Pilate and the Jews used the word: "My kingdom is not of this world: if my kingdom were of this world, then would my servants fight, that I should not be delivered to the Jews: but now is my kingdom not from hence."

Never in the history of this world did the lips of man speak or his ears listen to a more pregnant or remarkable utterance. But it has been shamefully misunderstood. Men have misread the words, and said, See, the religion of Jesus is quite unworldly, has nothing to do with the institutions and arrangements of human life. It deals with the spiritual, and not with the secular. It treats of our spirits, not our hands or pockets. So long as we recognise Christ's authority in the Church, we may do as we like in the home, the counting-house, the factory, and the shop.

It was in no such sense that Jesus uttered these words, and the mistake has largely arisen through the misunderstanding of the word *of* as used by our translators. It has not the force of belonging to, or being the property of; but is the translation of a Greek preposition, meaning out of, springing from, originating in. We might freely translate the Master's words thus: "My kingdom does not originate from this world; it has come down from another, to bring the principles, methods, and inspirations of heaven to bear on all the provinces of human thought and activity." The Son of Man claims the whole of man and all that he does as a subject of his realm. He cannot spare one relationship of human life, one art, one industry, one interest, one joy, one hope, from the domain of his empire. He has a word about the weight in the pedlar's bag, the dealings of the merchant on 'Change, the justice and injustice of wars that desolate continents.

The one conspicuous proof of the absolutely foreign origin of this heavenly kingdom is its refusal to employ force. Its servants do not fight. In the garden the King had repudiated the use of force, bidding his servant sheath his sword. Whenever you encounter a system that cannot stand without the use of force, that appeals to the law court or bayonet, you are sure that, whatever else it is, it is not the Kingdom of Christ. Christ's kingdom distinctly and for ever refuses to allow its subjects to fight. They who would surround Christianity with prestige, endow it with wealth, and guard it with the sword, expel its divine Spirit, and leave only its semblance dead upon the field. But if the aid which might be deemed essential is withheld, whether of funds or force, it thrives and spreads until the hills are covered with its goodly shadow, and its products fill the earth with harvests of benediction. All the Gospel asks for is freedom—freedom to do what Jesus did, in the way He did it; freedom because of its belief that the power of truth is greater than all the power of the Adversary. Oh for a second Pentecost! Oh for the holy days of apostolic trust and simplicity! Oh for one of the days of the Son of Man, who came to our world armed with no authority save that of truth, clothed with no power but that of love.

In Pilate's next question there seems a touch of awe and respect: "Art Thou a king then?" That moral nature which is in all men, however debased, seemed for a moment to assert itself, and a strange spell lay on his spirit.

With wondrous dignity our Lord immediately answered, "Thou sayest that I am—a king." But He hastens to show that it was a kingship not based upon material force like that of the Cæsars, nor confined to one race of men: "To this end was I born, and for this cause came I into the world, that I should bear witness unto the truth. Every one that is of the truth heareth my voice." There is no soul of man, in any clime or age, devoted to the truth, which does not recognise the royalty and supremacy of Jesus Christ. There is an accent in his words which all the children of the truth instantly recognise. The idea here given of Jesus gazing ever into the depths of eternal truth, and bearing witness of what He saw, not in his words alone, but in his life and death; and of the assent given to his witness by all who have looked upon the sublime outlines of truth, is one of those majestic conceptions which cannot be accounted for on any hypothesis than that the speaker was divine.

When Pilate heard these words, he probably thought of the Epicureans, and Stoics, and other philosophers, who were perpetually wrangling about the truth, and demanding men's allegiance. "Oh," said he to himself, "here is another enthusiast, touched with the same madness, though He does seem nobler than many of his craft. One thing is clear, that my lord has nothing to fear from his pretensions. He may sit as long as he likes on his ideal throne without detriment to the empire of the Cæsars." With mingled bitterness and cynicism, he answered, "What is truth?" and, without waiting for an answer, went out to the group of Jewish rabbis waiting in the opening daylight, and threw them into convulsions of excitement by saying, "I find in Him no fault at all."

They were the more urgent, saying, "He stirreth up the people, teaching throughout all Judæa, and beginning from Galilee even unto this place."

The mention of Galilee came as a gleam of light to Pilate. He was sincerely desirous not to be an accomplice in the death of Jesus, by falling into the plot which he had been astute enough to detect. But not daring to take the only honourable and safe way of declaring his innocence, and summoning a cohort of soldiers to clear the court, he endeavoured to exculpate himself by throwing the responsibility on Herod. He congratulated himself on the ingenuity of a plan which should relieve him of the necessity of grieving his conscience on the one hand, or of irritating the Jews on the other, and which would conciliate Herod, with whom he was at this time on unfriendly terms. When he knew therefore that He was of Herod's jurisdiction he sent Him unto Herod, who himself was at Jerusalem in those days.

Herod was glad to see the wonderful miracle-worker of whom he had heard so much, and hoped that He might do some wonder in his presence; and, in the hope of extorting it, set Him at nought, and mocked Him, with his mighty men. But the Lord remained absolutely silent in his presence, as though the love of God could say nothing to the murderer of the Baptist, who had not repented of his deed. Finally, therefore, disappointed and chagrined, Herod sent Jesus back to Pilate, admitting that he had found in Him no cause of death.

66

THE SECOND TRIAL BEFORE PILATE

"Ye have a custom, that I should release unto you one at the Passover:
will ye therefore that I release unto you the King of the Jews?"
JOHN xviii. 39.

PILATE must have felt mortified when he heard that Herod had sent
Jesus back to his tribunal. He had hoped that the Jewish monarch
would so settle the matter that there would be no need for him to choose
between his conscience and his fear of the Jewish leaders. But it was
not to be. It was decreed that he should pronounce the judicial sentence on our Lord, and so on himself.

Now was the time for him to act decisively, and to say clearly that
he would be no party to the unrighteous deed to which these priests
were urging him. To have done so firmly and decisively, and before
they could further inflame popular passion, the whole matter would
have come to an end. Alas! he let the golden moment slip past him
unused, and every succeeding moment made it more impossible for
him to retrieve it.

Pilate is one of the most notable instances in history of the fatal
error of preferring expediency to principle. He wished to do right,
but not to do it avowedly because it was right. He wished to do right
without seeming to do it, or making a positive stand for it. And in
consequence he was finally entrapped into doing the very deed which
he had taken the greatest trouble to avoid. Therefore, on the plains of
time he stands as a beacon and warning; and to all who do not dare to
oppose the stream of public passion and practice with the single
affirmation of inflexible adherence to righteousness, the voice of inspiration cries aloud, "Remember Pilate!" However promising a tortuous
course may look, it will certainly end in disaster. However discour-
aging a righteous one may appear, it will at last lead out into the
open. And in doing the right thing, be sure to speak out firmly at
once. It may be harder for the moment, but it will be always easier
afterwards. One brave word will put you into a position of moral
advantage, from which no power shall avail to shake or dislodge
you.

Such a word, however, Pilate failed to speak; and when Jesus was
again brought before him, he began to think of some way by which
he might do as conscience prompted, without running counter to the
Jewish leaders. He, therefore, summoned around him the chief priests

and rulers of the people. The latter are particularly mentioned, as though Pilate thought that his best method of saving Jesus would be by appealing over the heads of the priests to the humanity of the common people. When all were again assembled he made, as Luke tells us, a short speech to them, reiterating his conviction of His innocence, corroborating his own opinion by Herod's, and closing by a proposal which he hoped would meet the whole case. "I will therefore chastise Him and release Him." Was there ever such a compromise? A little before he had solemnly affirmed that he could find in Him no fault at all, but if that were the case, why chastise Him? And if He were guilty of the charges brought against Him, as chastisement might seem to suggest, surely He should not be released. Pilate meant to do the best. The chastisement was intended as a sop to the priests, and to win their acquiescence to their victim's release. But it was not straightforward, or strong, or right. And, like all compromises, it miserably failed.

Those keen Jewish eyes saw in a moment that Pilate had left the ground of simple justice. He had shifted from the principle on which Roman law was generally administered, and they saw that it was only a question of bringing sufficient pressure to bear on him, and they could make him a tool for the accomplishment of the fell purpose on which their heart was set. The proposal, therefore, was swept ignominiously away, and Pilate could never regain the position he had renounced.

Pilate then resorted to another expedient for saving Jesus. It was the custom to carry out capital sentences at feast times, which were the occasions of great popular convocations; but it was also customary for the governor to release any one prisoner, condemned to death, whom the multitude, on the Passover week, might agree to name. Pilate recollected this, and also that there was a notorious criminal awaiting execution, who for sedition and murder had been arrested and condemned to die. It occurred to him that, instead of asking the people generally whom they wished him to release, he should narrow the choice and present the alternative between Barabbas and Jesus. They would hardly fail, he thought, to choose the release of this pale Prisoner, who was innocent of crime, and, indeed, had lived a life notable for its benevolence.

Pilate took care to announce his proposal with the greatest effect. The vast space before his palace was rapidly filling with excited crowds, who guessed that something unusual was astir, and were pouring in surging volumes into the piazza, although it was still early. That he might be the better seen and heard he ascended a movable rostrum, or judgment-seat, which was placed on the tessellated pavement that ran from end to end of the palace. "Whom will ye," he asked, "that I release unto you—Barabbas, or Jesus which is called the Christ?" And then he suggested the answer: "Will ye that I release unto you the King of the Jews?"

At this moment, and perhaps whilst waiting for their answer, a messenger hurried to speak to him from his wife. It must have been most unusual for her to interfere with his judicial acts; but she had been so impressed by a dream about her husband's connection with Jesus, the unwonted Prisoner who stood before him, that she was impelled to urge him to have nothing to do with Him. It was a remarkable episode, and must have made Pilate more than ever anxious to extricate himself from his dilemma.

It was still not absolutely too late to set himself free by the resolute expression of his will. But his temporising policy was making it immensely difficult, and he was becoming every moment more entangled in the meshes of the merciless priests.

He had hoped much from his last proposal, but was destined to be bitterly disappointed. The chief priests and elders had been busy amongst the crowds, persuading and moving them. We do not know the arguments they would employ; but we all know how inflammable a mob is, and presently the name of Barabbas began to sound ominously from amid the hubbub and murmur of that sea of human beings. Presently the isolated cries spread into a tumultuous clamour, which rang out in the morning air, "Not this man, but Barabbas!"

Pilate seems to have been dumbfounded at this unexpected demand; and said, almost pitifully, "What then shall I do with Jesus which is called Christ?" As though he had said, "You surely cannot mean that He should suffer the fate prepared for a murderer!" Then they cried out for the first time, To the cross, to the cross! "Crucify Him! crucify Him!"

Pilate had failed twice; he felt that he was being swept away by a current which already he could not stem, and which was becoming at every moment deeper and swifter. But he was very anxious to release Jesus; and so he tried to reason with them, and said, "Why, what evil hath He done?" But he might as hopefully have tried to argue with an angry sea, or with a pack of wolves. He felt this, and, mustering a little show of authority, said: "I have found no cause of death in Him; I will, therefore, chastise Him, and release Him." But this announcement was met by an infuriated shout of disapproval. "They were instant with loud voices, requiring that He might be crucified." "They cried out the more exceedingly, Crucify Him." A little before this Pilate had been besieged for six days in his palace at Cæsarea by similar crowds, whose persistent fury at last compelled him to give in to them. He dared not provoke similar scenes, lest they should result in a revolution. When he saw that he could prevail nothing, but that rather a tumult was made, he called for water. He said to himself, "I am very sorry; this Man is innocent, and I should like to save Him. But I have done my best, and can do no more. I will, at least, relieve myself of the responsibility of his blood. Slave, bring me water!"

As he washed his hands he said, "I am innocent of the blood of this righteous Man; see ye to it." "Yes, yes," cried those bloodthirsty voices; "his blood be on us, and on our children." See how God sometimes takes men at their word. The blood of Jesus was required of that generation at the sack of Jerusalem, forty years after; and it has been required of their children through all the ages. Why that wandering foot, found in every land, yet homeless in all? Why the hideous tortures, plunderings, and massacres of the Middle Ages? Why the modern Jew-hate, disguised under the more refined term *anti-Semitism?* Why the banishment from their holy places for eighteen centuries? All is attributable to that terrible imprecation which attracted to the race the blood of an innocent Victim. It does not exculpate them to say that they did not realize who Jesus was, and that they would not have crucified Him if they had realized his divine dignity. They are being punished to-day, not because they crucified the Son of God, knowing Him to be such, but because they crucified One against whom they could allege no crime, and whose life had been full of truth and grace.

After he had washed his hands, "Pilate gave sentence that it should be as they required, and released unto them him that for sedition and murder had been cast into prison, whom they desired; but he delivered Jesus to their will."

Those condemned to die by crucifixion first underwent the hideous torture of the scourge. This, then, was inflicted on Jesus, and it was carried out in the inner courtyard by the Roman soldiery, under Pilate's direction. "Then Pilate therefore took Jesus, and scourged Him." Stripped to the waist, and bound in a stooping posture to a low pillar, He was beaten till the officer in charge gave the signal to stop. The plaited leathern thongs, armed at the ends with lead and sharp-pointed bone, cut the back open in all directions, and inflicted such torture that the sufferers generally fainted, and often died.

But the scourging in this case did not satisfy the soldiers, whom scenes of this nature had brutalized. They had been told by their comrades of the mockery of Herod's palace, and they would not lag behind. Had He been robed in mockery as King of the Jews, then He should pose as mock-emperor. They found a purple robe, wove some tough thorns into a mimic crown, placed a long reed in his hand as sceptre, then bowed the knee, as in the imperial court, and cried "Hail, King of the Jews!" Finally, tiring of their brutal jests, they tore the reed from his hands, smote Him with it on his thorn-girt brow, and struck Him with their fists. We cannot tell how long it lasted, but Jesus bore it all—silent, uncomplaining, noble. There was a majesty about Him which these indignities could not suppress or disturb.

Pilate had never seen such elevation of demeanour, and was greatly struck by it. He was more than ever desirous to save Him, and it suddenly occurred to him that perhaps that spectacle of sorrow and majesty might arrest the fury of the rabble. He therefore led Jesus forth wearing the crown of thorns and the purple robe, and, stationing him where all could see, said, "Behold the Man! Behold Him and admire! Behold Him and pity! Behold Him and be content!" But the priests were obdurate. There is no hate so virulent as religious hate, and they raised again the cry, "Crucify Him! crucify Him!" Pilate was not only annoyed, but provoked. "Take ye Him," he said, in surly tones, "crucify Him as best ye can; my soldiers and I will have nothing to do with the foul deed."

Then it was that the Jewish leaders, in their eagerness not to lose their prey, brought forward a weapon which they had been reluctant to use. "We have a law," they said, "and by our law He ought to die, because He made Himself the Son of God." We hardly know how much those words meant to Pilate, but they awakened a strange awe. "He was the more afraid." He had some knowledge of the old stories of mythology, in which the gods walked the world in the semblance of men. Could this be the explanation of the strange majesty in this wonderful Sufferer, whose presence raised such extraordinary passion and ferment? So he took Jesus apart, and said to Him, "Whence art Thou?" "Art Thou of human birth, or more?" But Jesus gave him no answer. This is the fifth time that He had answered nothing; but we can detect the reason. It would have been useless to explain all to Pilate then. It would not have arrested his action, for he had lost control; but would have increased his condemnation. Yet his silence was itself an answer; for if He had been only of earth, He could never have allowed Pilate to entertain the faintest suspicion that He might be of heaven.

Pilate's pride was touched by that silence. It was at least possible to assert a power over this defenceless Prisoner, which had been defied by those vindictive Jews. "Speakest Thou not unto *me*? Knowest Thou not that I have power to release or to crucify Thee?" And Jesus answered, "Thou couldest have no power against Me, except it were given thee from above; therefore, he that delivered Me unto thee hath the greater sin." In these words our Lord seems to refer to the mystery of evil, and specially the power of the prince of this world, who was now venting on Him all his malice. At this moment the serpent was bruising the heel of the Son of Man, who shortly would bruise his head. It would appear as though our Lord were addressing kind and compassionate words to Pilate. "Great as your sin is, in abusing your prerogative, given to you from above, it is less than the sin of that Evil Spirit who has cast Me into your power, and is urging you to extreme measures against Me. The devil sinneth from the beginning." Even in his sore travail, the Lord was tender and pitiful to this weak and craven soul, and spoke to it as though Pilate and not He were arraigned at the bar.

Pilate was now more than ever set on his deliverance. "He sought to release Him." And then the Jews brought out their last crushing and conclusive argument, "If thou release this Man, thou art not Cæsar's friend; everyone that maketh himself a king, speaketh against Cæsar." Pilate knew what that meant, and that if he did not let them have their way, they would lodge an accusation against him for complicity with treason before his imperial master. Already strong representations had been made in the same quarter against his maladministration of his province, and he positively dared not risk another. "When, therefore, he heard these words, he brought Jesus out, and sat down in the judgment-seat at a place called the Pavement, and it was about the sixth hour."

With ill-concealed irritation, and adopting the recent phraseology of the priests, he said, "Behold your King!" At which they cried, "We have no king but Cæsar. Away with Him; away with Him; crucify Him." It gave Pilate savage pleasure to put the cup of humiliation to their lips, and make them drain it to its dregs. "What!" said he; "shall I crucify your King?" Then they touched the lowest depth of degradation, as, abandoning all their Messianic hopes, and trampling under foot their national pride, they answered, "We have no king but Cæsar."

At last, therefore, he delivered Jesus to them to be crucified, signed the usual documents, gave the customary order, and retired into his palace, as one who had heard his own sentence pronounced, and carried in his soul the presage of his doom.

Long years after, when, stripped of his Procuratorship which he had sacrificed Christ to save, worn out by his misfortunes, and universally execrated, he was an exile in a foreign land, with his faithful wife, how often must they have spoken together of the events of that morning, which had so strangely affected their lives!

67

The Seven Sayings of the Cross

"Then delivered he Him therefore unto them to be crucified. And they took Jesus, and led Him away."—JOHN xix. 16.

DRIVEN from one position after another by the Jewish notables and rabble, Pilate at last, much against his will, gave directions for the Lord's crucifixion. The purple robe flung over his shoulders was replaced by his own simple clothes, though the crown of thorns was not improbably left upon his head.

Two others were led out to suffer with Him—highwaymen lately captured in some red-handed deed. Barabbas, their chief, for whom the central cross had been designed, had escaped it by a miracle; but they were to suffer the just reward of their deeds. A detachment of soldiers was told off under a centurion, to see to the execution of the sentence, and the heavy crosses were placed upon the shoulders of the sufferers, that they might bear them to the place of execution.

It was probably about 10 a.m. when the sad procession started on its way. Two incidents took place as it passed through the crowded streets, which surely had never witnessed such a spectacle: no, not even in the days when David traversed them in flight from Absalom.

The beams laid on our Lord proved too heavy in the steeper ascents for his exhausted strength, and his slow advance so delayed the procession that the guard became impatient. Here comes a foreigner! A Jew of Cyrene! Harmless and inoffensive, gladly would he make way for the crowd. Why should he not bear this burden under which Jesus of Nazareth is falling to the ground? The insolent soldiers, with oath and jest, constrain him, and he dares not resist. Probably Simon had no previous knowledge of Him for whom he bore this load, and loathed the service he was compelled to render; but that compulsory companionship with Jesus carried him to Calvary. He beheld the wondrous tragedy, heard the words which we are to recite; from that day became, with his family, a humble follower of Jesus. We at least infer this from Mark's emphatic mention of the fact that he was father of Alexander and Rufus; whilst the Apostle Paul, in the Epistle to the Romans, tenderly refers to Rufus and his mother. This is not the only instance in the history of Christianity when the compulsion of an apparent accident has led a man to Christ. Many a time has compulsory cross-carrying led men to the Crucified.

Of the vast multitude who followed Jesus, a large contingent consisted of women. From the men, in that moving crowd, He does not appear to have received one word of sympathy. Timidity, or questioning with their own hearts, or inveterate hatred, closed their lips. But the women expressed their sorrow with all the outcry of Oriental grief, rending the air with piercing cries. "Weep not for Me," the Saviour said, ever more thoughtful for others than Himself; "but for yourselves and your children." And He who had been mocked because of his claim to be a King, and who would shortly from the cross begin to minister as a Priest, then as Prophet foretold the approaching fate of that fair city, asking significantly, since the Romans dealt thus with Himself an innocent sufferer, what would they not do when exasperated by the pertinacious resistance of the Jewish people in the protracted siege.

Just outside the city gates, by the side of the main road, was a little conical eminence which, from its likeness to the shape of a skull, was called in the Aramaic *Golgotha*, in the Greek *Cranion*, in the Latin *Calvary*. As we speak of the *brow* of a hill, they called the bald eminence a *skull*. There the procession stayed, and what transpired may be best followed as we touch on the seven sentences our Lord uttered on the cross, collated and set in order from the four Gospels.

I. *"Father, forgive them; for they know not what they do."* Arrived at the place of execution, Jesus would be stripped once more, a linen cloth at most being left about his loins. He would then be laid upon the cross, as it rested on the ground, his arms stretched along the cross-beams, his body resting on a projecting piece of rough wood, misnamed a seat. Huge nails would then be driven through the tender palm of each hand, and the shrinking centre of each foot. The cross would then be lifted up and planted in a hole previously dug to receive it, with a rude shock causing indescribable anguish. "So they crucified Him, and two others with Him, on either side one, and Jesus in the midst."

Pilate had written a title to be nailed to the head-piece of the cross, according to the usual custom, with the name and designation of the crucified, "This is Jesus, the King of the Jews." It was written in Greek, the language of science; Latin, the language of government; and Hebrew, the language of religion. It is this fact that accounts for the differences in the Gospels. One evangelist translates from one language, another from another. The inscription was meant to insult the Jews. It was equivalent to saying, "This nation cannot produce a better monarch than this; and this is the fate which will be meted out to all such pretenders." The authorities were indignant, and did their utmost to induce Pilate to alter it. But in vain. He would be master this time, and dismissed them with the curt reply, "What I have written I have written." Each man is writing his conception of the nature and claims of Christ by the way in which he treats Him, either acknowledging his divine glory as he enthrones Him, or repudiating his claims as he tramples Him under foot, and turns away to his sin.

The criminal's clothes fell as a perquisite to the soldiers specially charged with the execution of the sentence. With our Lord's outer clothes they had no difficulty; they were too poor to be worth keeping entire, so they tore them up into equal pieces. But the inner tunic was of unusual texture; perhaps it had been woven for Him by his mother's hands, or by one of the women who so carefully ministered to Him. In any case it was too good to tear. The dice were ready in the pocket, one of the helmets would serve as dice-box; and so "they parted his raiment among them, and for his vesture they did cast lots. These things therefore the soldiers did."

It was probably during this byplay that our Lord uttered the first cry of the cross, and entered on that work of intercession, which He ever lives to perpetuate and crown. He thinks, not of Himself, but of others; is occupied, not with his own pains, but with their sins. Not a threat, nor a menace; but the purest, tenderest accents of pleading intercession.

When was that prayer answered? Seven weeks after this, on the day of Pentecost, three thousand of these people, whom Peter described as the murderers of Christ, repented and believed; and in the days that followed thousands more, and a great company of the priests. That was the answer to this intercession. When we see our brethren sinning a sin not unto death, without realizing its full significance and enormity, if we ask God, as Jesus did, He will give us life for those that sin not unto death. There is a sin unto death, and concerning that we are not encouraged to pray. "I obtained mercy," said the great Apostle, "because I did it ignorantly in unbelief. "

II. *"Woman, behold thy Son; son, behold thy mother."*—The second saying was about his mother. His cross was the centre of bitter mockery. The chief priests, and scribes, and elders challenged Him to descend from the cross, pledging themselves to believe if He did. The crowd caught their spirit with contemptible servility, and repeated their words, "Son of God, come down from the cross, that we may believe." A passer-by called out derisively, "Where is now the boast that He could raise the temple in three days? Let Him do it if He can." The soldiers even caught up the abuse, and vented their coarse jokes on One whose innocence and gentleness appeared to exasperate them. And the malefactors who were hanged cast the same in his teeth.

Were there no sympathisers in all that crowd to exchange glances of love and faith? Yes, there was one little group. When Peter left the hall of Caiaphas, John probably lingered there still, followed to the bar of Pilate, waited long enough to know how the matter would fall, and then hastened to the humble lodgings where Mary and a few other women, in awful suspense, were awaiting tidings. As soon as the mother knew all, she resolved to see her beloved Son once more. "It is no place for women," John would say. But she answered, "I must see Him yet again." Then said John, "If you will indeed go, I will take you." "I too will go," sadly said Mary, her sister, the wife of Cleophas; "and I also," said Mary of Magdala. What a sight for those loving hearts, when they saw the crosses in the distance, and knew that on one of them was hanging the dearest to them of all on earth! But the love that makes the timid deer turn to fight valiantly for its young made them oblivious to everything except to get near Him. How little had the young mother realised that Simeon meant this, when he told her that a sword would one day pierce her soul!

Jesus knew how much she was suffering, and how lonely she would be when He was gone. He had neither silver nor gold to leave, but would at least provide a home and tender care as long as she required them. Elevated but very little above the ground, He could easily speak to the little group. "Woman," He said, "behold thy son." Then, looking tenderly toward John, He consigned her to his care.

Did He give a further look, which John interpreted to mean that he should lead her away? It may have been so, for from that hour he took her to his home; and so she passes from the page of Scripture, except for the one glimpse we have of her, in the upper room, awaiting the baptism of the Holy Spirit.

III. *"To-day shalt thou be with Me in Paradise."*—We cannot explore all the causes which brought about so great a change in this man, and produced so lofty an ideal of his Fellow-sufferer. We have to deal rather with the response of Jesus. Lost by the first Adam, Paradise was being regained by the last; and it is now not far away. A dying man may see the sun leave the zenith, but ere it set in the western wave he may be in the land of Paradise. Absent from the body, present with the Lord. There is no state of unconsciousness between the two. We close our eyes on the dimming spectacles of this world at one moment, to behold the King in his beauty the next.

Men may strip Jesus of everything, but they cannot touch his power to save. In the moment of his greatest weakness He was able to rescue a man from the very brink of perdition, and take him as a trophy of his power to heaven. What will He not be able to do now that the mortal weakness is passed, and that He is exalted to be a Prince and a Saviour!

IV. *"My God, my God, why hast Thou forsaken Me?"*—It would be between eleven o'clock and noon that these incidents took place; but from noon till three in the afternoon a pall of darkness hung over the cross and city. We know not how it came, but it appears to have silenced all the uproar which had surged around the cross, and to have filled the minds of all with awe. Men might have gazed rudely on his dying agony; Nature refused to behold it. Men had stripped Him, but an unseen hand drew drapery about Him. For three hours it lasted, and was a befitting emblem of the darkness that enveloped his soul, when He who knew no sin was made to be sin for us, "that we might be made the righteousness of God in Him."

Do you wonder that He felt thus, and question how such a forsaking had been possible at such an hour? There is but one explanation. This was not a normal human experience. Only once in the history of the race has all iniquity been laid on one head; only once has the curse of the sin of the world been borne by one heart; only once has it been possible, in drinking the cup of death, to taste death for every man. "He who knew no sin was made sin for us. He was wounded for our transgressions, bruised for our iniquities." On no other hypothesis than that Jesus was the Lamb of God, bearing away the sin of the world, can you account for the darkness of that midday midnight which obscured his soul. I cannot tell what transpired; I have no philosophy of the Atonement to offer; I only believe that the whole nature of God was in Christ, reconciling the world unto Himself; and that, in virtue of what was done there, we may apply for forgiveness to the faithfulness and justice of God.

V. "*I thirst*."—During the hours of spiritual anguish, our Lord was largely oblivious to his physical needs; now, as the long hours passed, these latter began to assert themselves. Inflammation, spreading from hands and feet, had resulted in a fever of thirst. He had refused the medicated drink offered at the beginning of his sufferings, because He had no desire to avoid one throb of anguish which lay in his path; but there was no reason why He should not drink of the sour wine which stood hard by the cross, now that He had drunk the cup which God had placed to his lips.

As He looked through the long line of predictions that bore on his passion, He could see that they had all been fulfilled save one; and, that this Scripture might be fulfilled, He said, "I thirst." Some, who stood near the cross, and, in the growing light, began to regain their confidence, tried to make ridicule of this plaintive ejaculation; but one who noticed his pale and parched lips was touched with pity, and took a stalk of hyssop, which was just long enough to reach the mouth of the Sufferer, and elevating a sponge dipped in vinegar, fulfilled thus unwittingly the ancient prediction, "They gave Me also gall for my meat, and in my thirst they gave Me vinegar to drink."

VI. "*It is finished*."—As we compare the Gospels, we find that these words were spoken with a loud voice. It was, in fact, the shout of a conqueror. Finished, the long list of prophecies, which closed, like gates, behind Him. Finished, the types and shadows of the Jewish ritual. Finished, the work which the Father had given Him to do.

Finished, the matchless beauty of a perfect life. Finished, the work of man's redemption. Through the Eternal Spirit, He had offered Himself without spot to God; and by that one sacrifice for sin, once for all and for ever, He had perfected them that are being sanctified. He had done all that was required to reconcile the world unto God, and to make an end of sin.

Finished! Let the words roll in volumes of melody through all the spheres! There is nothing now left for man to do but enter on the results of Christ's finished work. As the Creator finished on the evening of the sixth day all the work which He had made, so did the Redeemer cease on the sixth day from the work of Atonement; and, lo! it was very good.

VII. *"Father, into thy hands I commend my spirit."*—The words were quoted from the Book of Psalms, which He so dearly loved. He only prefixed the name of Father; for the cloud which had extorted the cry, *My God, my God,* had broken, and under a blue heaven of conscious fellowship He exchanged it for *Father.*

If the words, "It is finished," be taken as our Lord's farewell to the world He was leaving, these words are surely his greeting to that on whose confines He was standing. It seems as though the spirit of Christ were poising itself before it departed to the Father, and saw before it no dismal abyss, no gulf of darkness, no footless chaos, but hands, even the hands of the Father—and to these He committed Himself.

The first martyr, who died after Christ, passed away with words of the same import upon his lips, with a significant alteration, *"Lord Jesus,* receive my spirit." We may use them as they have been used by countless thousands in all ages; and we know Him whom we have believed, and are persuaded that He is able to keep that which we have committed unto Him.

And when Jesus had said these words, He bowed his head upon his breast, and breathed out his spirit. No one took his life from Him: He laid it down of Himself: He had power to lay it down.

So ended that marvellous scene. The expectation of all the ages was more than realised. If it be true that on that day a tidal wave of immense volume swept around the world, and rose high up in all rivers and estuaries, this may be taken as an emblem of the much more abounding grace, which on that day rose high above the mighty obstacles of human sin, and is destined to lift the entire universe nearer God. For by it God will reconcile all things to Himself, whether in heaven or on earth.

Three items remain to be noticed.

At the moment that Jesus died there was a great earthquake, which made the earth tremble and the rocks rend; so that the ancient graves were opened, preparatory to the rising of the bodies of the saints on the Resurrection morning, following the Lord from the power of Death. And when the centurion, and they that were with him, watching Jesus, charged to see the sentence executed, saw the earthquake and the things that were done, they feared exceedingly, saying, "Truly this was the Son of God."

The veil of the Temple, also, was rent in twain from the top to the bottom, at the moment that the Great High Priest Jesus was entering the Temple not made with hands, with the blood of his propitiation. Is it to be wondered at that afterwards many priests, who had been in close contiguity to that marvellous type, became obedient to the faith?

Finally, from the pierced side of Christ came out blood and water, as John solemnly attests. "He knoweth that he saith true." This was a symptom that there had been heart-rupture. It was also a symbol of "the double cure" which Jesus has effected. Blood to atone; water to cleanse. "This is He that came by water and blood, not with the water only."

68

CHRIST'S BURIAL

"Then took they the body of Jesus, and wound it in linen clothes with the spices, as the manner of the Jews is to bury."—JOHN xix. 40.

"AGAINST the day of my burying hath she kept this!" so had Jesus spoken when Mary anointed his feet with the very precious spikenard. I do not suppose that any in the room save herself and her Lord understood his reference; not one of them believed that He would really die, and his body be carried to the tomb; but Mary knew better. She had sat at his feet, and drunk in his very spirit. In the glow of the evening twilight, when Martha was busy in the house, and Lazarus was away in the field, they two had sat together, and Jesus, in words similar to those He had so often used to his apostles, had told her of what was coming upon Him. Mary believed it all. She knew that she would not be present at that scene. She did not think that any would be able to perform the last loving rites for that beloved form. She feared that it might be utterly dishonoured; but she did what she could, she came beforehand to anoint the Lord's body for his burying.

It was a beautiful act of tender foresight. But in the sense of being absolutely necessary, as the only act of care and love bestowed on the Lord's dead body, it was not required; for He who at birth had prepared the body for his Son, took care that in death it should receive due honour. When Jesus expired, Luke tells us that many of His acquaintances, and the women that had followed Him from Galilee were standing afar off, beholding all that was done; John too was there, and others who had loved Him and were the grateful monuments of his healing power: they must have wondered greatly what would be done with that loved form. Yet what could they do?—they were poor and unimportant; they had no influence with the capricious and terrible Pilate; they seemed helpless to do more than wait with choking sobs until some possible chance should allow them to intervene.

Meanwhile God was preparing a solution of the difficulty. Amongst the crowd around the cross there stood a very wealthy man named Joseph. He was a native of the little town of Arimathea, that lay among the fruitful hills of Ephraim; but was resident in Jerusalem, where he had considerable property. Some of this lay in the close neighbourhood of the highway by which the cross of our Lord had

been erected. He was also a member of the Jewish Sanhedrin, but
it is expressly stated that he had not consented to the counsel or deed
of them; if indeed he was summoned to that secret midnight meeting
in the palace of Caiaphas, he certainly did not go; he was therefore
innocent of any complicity in our Lord's condemnation and death.
He was a good man and a just; and like Nathanael, and Simeon, and
many more, he waited for the kingdom of God. More than this, he was
a disciple of Jesus, though secretly.

Whatever our judgment may be about this action during the life-
time of our Lord, we have nothing but admiration for the way in which
he acted when He died. What he had seen had more than decided him.
Christ's meekness and majestic silence under all reproaches and
indignities; the veiled sky and trembling earth; the cry of the Forsaken which ended in the trustful committal of the soul to the Father;
the loud shriek and the sudden death—all these had convinced him and
awed his soul, and lifted him far above the fear of man. He had been
waiting for the kingdom, he would now identify himself with the King.

By his side there would seem to have stood an old friend of ours,
Nicodemus. Our evangelist identifies him as having at the first come
to Jesus by night. The very opening of the Lord's ministry in Jerusalem seems to have made a deep impression on his mind; but he was
very timid. He was an old man, a very rich man, a member of the
Sanhedrin, and he did not like to risk his position or prestige. It was
much therefore for him to come to Jesus at all, and especially to come
to Him in the spirit of deep respect and inquiry. There must have
been something very engaging in him; for our Lord, who did not
commit Himself to men in general, made very clear unfoldings of his
great work to this inquiring Rabbi. From that night, even if not a
real disciple, Nicodemus was strongly prejudiced in favour of Jesus;
and on one occasion, at least, brought on himself reproach for attempting indirectly to shield Him. He had not dared, however, to go beyond
his first nervous question. Then, like Joseph, he was decided by what
he had seen: come what may, he will now avow the thoughts which
have long been in his heart.

The two men exchanged a few hurried sentences. "What will be
done with his body?"

"At least it must not suffer the fate of common malefactors. Yet
how shall it be prevented?"

"Look you," says Joseph, "in my garden close at hand there is a
new tomb, hewn out in the rock, wherein was man never yet laid.
I had prepared it for myself; but I will gladly use it for Him, if I can
but get Pilate to yield me his body. I will go at once and ask for it."

"Well," says Nicodemus, "if you can succeed in getting the body, I
will see to it that there are not wanting the garments and spices of
death."

Without a moment's delay, for the sun is fast sinking towards the west, Joseph hastens to Pilate, and asks that he may take away the body of Jesus; and not unlikely he quickens Pilate's response by an offer of a liberal bribe if he will but accede to his request. Pilate, who had just given orders to the soldiers to hasten the death of the crucified, marvelled that Jesus was really dead; nor was he reassured until he had asked the centurion; and when he knew it of him, he gave to Joseph the necessary leave, with which he hastened back to the cross.

The sun would be very low on the horizon, flinging its last beams upon the scene, as he reached Calvary. The crowds would for the most part have dispersed. The soldiers might be engaged in taking down the bodies of the thieves. The body of Jesus was, however, still on the cross; and not far off would be the little band of attached friends of whom we have already spoken, and who would be the sole remnants of the vast crowds who had now ebbed away to their homes. What wonder, what joy, as they see Joseph reverently and lovingly begin to take Him down; with evident authority from the governor, with manifest preparations for his careful burial; they had never before known him to be interested in their Master. And who is this that waits beneath the cross with the clean linen shroud, and the wealth of spices? Ah! that is Nicodemus; but who would have thought that he would help to perform these last offices!

Oh to be a painter, and depict that scene! The discoloured corpse stained with blood, muscles flaccid, eyes closed, head helpless; Joseph, and Nicodemus, and John, and other strong men busy. The women weeping as if their hearts must break, but ready at any moment to give the needed aid. Between them they carry the body into Joseph's garden, and to the mouth of his new sepulchre. There on some grassy bank they rest it for a moment, that it may be tenderly washed and wrapped in the white linen cloth on which powdered myrrh and aloes had been thickly strewn. A white cloth would then be wrapped about the head and face, after long farewell looks and reverent kisses. Then lifted once again, the precious burden was borne into the sepulchre, and laid in a rocky niche. There was no door; but a great stone, probably circular, prepared for the purpose, was rolled with united and strenuous efforts against the aperture, to prevent the entrance of wild beast and unkindly foe. And then as the chill twilight was flinging its shadows over the world, they reverently withdrew.

Joseph and Nicodemus had done their work and had gone to their homes, and yet there were some who lingered as if unable to leave the spot. There were Mary Magdalene, and the other Mary, sitting over against the sepulchre, gazing through their tears at the place where Jesus was laid. How keen was their mental anguish! There was bereaved love; with all purity the strongest love had grown up around

Christ; and now that He was gone, it seemed as if there was nothing more to live for. The prop had been rudely taken away, and the tendrils of their hearts' affection were torn and wrenched. Then there would come a rush of hot tears, indignant passion with those who had pursued Him, with such unrelenting torture, to his bitter end. Then again, broken-hearted grief at the remembrance of his anguish, and gentle patience, and shame. And, mingling sadly with all these, were disappointed hopes. Was this the end? He who died thus could not have been the Messiah! He had taught them to believe He was! He must have been self-deceived! For this life only they had hope in Christ, and they were of all most miserable! That grave-stone hid not only the body of Christ, but the structure of the brightest, fairest hopes that had ever filled the hearts of mortals!

In spite of all, they love. This is the love of women: the object of their fond attachment may be misrepresented and abused; the life may seem to be an entire failure; they may themselves be suffering greatly from the results of the beloved one's mistakes and follies—yet will they love still! And so through the gathering gloom and evening stillness they lingered on, until the increasing darkness told them that the Sabbath had come. Then they returned and rested the Sabbath day, according to the commandment; but neither they, nor Joseph, nor Nicodemus, nor John, would be able to partake of the Paschal festivities. To take part in a burial at any time would defile them for seven days, and make everything which they touched unclean; to do so at that time involved seclusion through the whole of the Passover week, with all its holy observances and rejoicings.

As we pursue this narrative, many thoughts are suggested.

We see the minute fulfilment of prophetic Scriptures.—It has been written by Isaiah on the page of inspiration, that the Messiah would make his grave with the rich. When Jesus died that prophecy seemed most unlikely of accomplishment; but it was literally fulfilled. There is not a prophecy, however minute, concerning our Lord's life and death, which did not have an actual fulfilment; and does not this show us how we are to treat the prophecies which foretell his future glory and second advent? They too shall have a literal and exact fulfilment.

We learn, too, that there are more friends of Christ in the world than we know.—They sit in our legislatures, in our councils, in our pews; we meet them day after day; they give little or no sign of their discipleship; the most large-hearted friend would be surprised to hear that they were Christians. But they are Christ's. Christ knows and owns them. But if they are secret disciples now, they will not be secret disciples always. A time will come when the fire of their love will burn the bushel that hides it, and they will avow themselves on the Lord's side.

We gather, too, that God can always find instruments to carry out his purposes.—The immediate followers of Christ could not see how to preserve the beloved corpse from defilement, but God had his place and his servants ready; and at the very crisis of need He brought them to the point. So has it been again and again; when influence and money and men have been really required for the work of God, they have been all at once forthcoming. He says to men like Joseph, Go, and he goeth; and to men like Nicodemus, Come, and he cometh; and to his servants, Do this, and it is done. Even the king's heart is in the hand of the Lord; as the rivers of water, He turneth it wheresoever He will.

There is also a very significant meaning contained in verse 41: "In the place where He was crucified there was a garden; and in the garden a new sepulchre." There is something startling in the association—the cross, the garden. The one—the symbol of shame and suffering, the most awful witness to the destructive power of that sin which has laid waste our world; the other—where flowers, Eden's brightest relics, were guarded for man's enjoyment. Flowers, blooming in all the luxuriance of an Oriental spring, shed their fragrance around our Saviour when He died. One loves to dwell upon the thought that Golgotha was part of the garden—that earth's fairest, brightest, gentlest nurslings were there, mingling their smiles and balm with the trampling angry footsteps and the cursings of malignant foes. They had been very dear to Him in his life-course; it was only meet that they should be near Him when He died. Was it not symbolical? In a garden man fell; in a garden he was redeemed! And that death of Christ has sown our world with the flowers of peace and joy and blessedness, so that many a wilderness has begun to rejoice and to blossom as the rose.

Whilst the burial of Christ was proceeding, the chief priests and their party were holding a meeting in all haste before the Sabbath began. The success of their scheme was no doubt the theme of hearty congratulation. But they dreaded Him still; they feared that all might not be over; they could not forget that He had spoken of rising the third day; and at the least, might not the disciples steal away the body, and spread abroad the report that He had risen, and so the last error would be worse than the first? A deputation was therefore appointed to wait on Pilate representing their fears. Tired of them and the whole case, he was in no humour to please them. "Ye have a guard," said he brusquely; "go, make it as sure as you can!" This they did. They passed a strong cord across the stone, and sealed its ends, and then placed soldiers to keep due watch and ward that none should lay hands upon the body that lay within.

So Christ lay entombed; but He was not there. He was in the world of spirits. The place of disembodied spirits was called, by the Jews, Sheol. It had two divisions, Paradise and Gehenna. Christ, we know from his own words, went to the former; and from Peter we gather that He also went through the realms of Gehenna, proclaiming his victory.

The practical conclusion of the whole is, however, contained in Romans vi. Just as the body of Christ after crucifixion was buried in the grave, so our sinful, sensual, selfish selves must be done away in the grave of forgetfulness and oblivion and disuse—buried with Christ, "that like as Christ was raised from the dead, through the glory of the Father, so we also should walk in newness of life."

69

THE DAY OF RESURRECTION

"The first day of the week."—JOHN xx. 1.

IT MAY be helpful if we tabulate, in a brief and concise form, the various appearances of our Lord on the great day when He was declared to be the Son of God with power by the resurrection from the dead.

Mary of Magdala—a squalid Arab village on the south of the plain of Gennesaret still bears that name—with another Mary had remained beside the tomb, till the trumpet of the Passover Sabbath and the gathering darkness had warned them to retire. They rested the Sabbath day, according to the commandment, in the saddest, darkest grief that ever oppressed the human heart; for they had not only lost the dearest object of their affection, under the most harrowing circumstances, but their hopes that this was the Messiah seemed to have been rudely shattered. But how tenacious is human love, especially the love of women! How it will cling around the ruins of the temple, even when some rude shock of earthquake has shattered it to the ground! So, when the Sabbath was over (after sundown on Saturday), they stole out to purchase additional sweet spices, which they prepared that night in order to complete the embalming of the body, which had been left incomplete on the day of crucifixion. They would probably sleep outside the city gates, which only opened at daybreak, because they were resolved to reach the sepulchre while it was yet dark.

But before they could arrive, the sublime event had occurred which has filled the world with light and joy in all succeeding years. For while members of the Temple Guard watched at the sepulchre, suddenly there was a great earthquake, and the angel of the Lord descended from heaven, rolled back the stone and sat upon it. At sight of him the keepers panicked, and forsaking their charge, went into the city to report to the chief priests "all things that were done".

But the opening of the sepulchre had revealed that it was unoccupied, proclaiming to the world that in divine majesty the Lord had already risen from the dead, and become the First-fruits of them that sleep.

The woman, meanwhile, were hurrying to the grave, debating as they did so how they would be able to roll away the stone from its mouth. Probably they had heard nothing of the seals and sentries with which the Sanhedrin had endeavoured to guard against all eventualities; for, had they known, they would hardly have ventured to come at all. They were greatly startled, however, when, on approaching the grave, they saw that the stone was rolled away. Mary of Magdala apparently detected this first; and without staying to see further, and with the conviction that it must have been rifled of its precious contents, started off to apprise Simon Peter and the disciple whom Jesus loved. What a shock, as she broke in on their grief, with the tidings, "They have taken away the Lord out of the sepulchre, and we know not where they have laid Him."

What a series of mistakes was hers! She had gone to anoint the dead while the morning light still lingered over the hills of Moab: she did not realize that He could not be holden by the bands of death, and had passed out into the richer, fuller life, of which death is the portal.

She came with aromatic spices that her means had bought, and her hands prepared: she did not know that all his garments were already smelling of aloes and cassia, of the perfume of heaven with which his Father had made Him glad.

She came to a Victim, so she thought, who had fallen beneath the knife of his foes as a Lamb led to slaughter: she was not aware that He was a Priest on the point of entering the most Holy Place on her behalf.

She came for the Vanquished: but failed to understand that He was a Victor over the principalities and powers of hell; and that the keys of Hades and the grave were hanging at his girdle, whilst the serpent was bruised beneath his feet.

She thought that she had come to put a final touch, such as only a woman can, to a life of sad and irremediable failure: but had no conception that on that morning a career had been inaugurated which was not only endless and indissoluble in itself, but was destined to vitalise uncounted myriads.

She thought that the empty tomb could only be accounted for by the rifling hands that had taken away the precious body: but could not guess that the Rifler of the perquisites of death was none other than the Lord Himself.

We all make mistakes like this. Our treasures, whether of things or people, which had been our pride and joy, pass from us; and we stand beside the grave, gazing in on vacancy and emptiness; we think that we can never be happy again; we suppose that God's mercies are clean gone for ever, and that his mercies have failed for evermore. But, all the while, near at hand, the radiant vision of a transfigured blessing waits to greet us, and to fill us with an ecstasy that shall never pall upon us, but make our after-life one long summer day.

In the meanwhile, the other women had pursued their way to the grave. The guard had already fled in terror, so there was none to intercept or frighten them; and entering the sepulchre they saw a young man, emblem of the immortal youth of God's angels, sitting on the right side, clothed in a long white garment—and they were affrighted. Presently, as they were much perplexed, behold, two men stood by them in shining garments; and as they were afraid and bowed down their faces to the earth, they said unto them, "Be not affrighted: Ye seek Jesus, which was crucified. He is not here; for He is risen, as He said. Remember how He said unto you when He was yet in Galilee, that He would rise again. Come, see the place where they laid Him. And go quickly, tell his disciples, and Peter, that He goeth before you into Galilee; there shall ye see Him, as He said unto you." And they departed quickly from the sepulchre with fear and great joy; and did run to bring his disciples word.

In the meantime, Peter and John were hurrying to the sepulchre by another route, and probably reached it just after the women had left. John, younger than Peter, had outrun him, but was withheld by reverential awe from doing more than peering into the empty grave. The linen clothes, lying orderly disposed, seem to have especially arrested his notice, yet went he not in. Peter, however, went at once into the sepulchre; he also saw the linen clothes, and especially that the cloth which had covered the face of the dead was wrapped together in a place by itself. Then John also went in; he saw and believed. It was evident to them both that the tomb had not been rifled, nor the body stolen by violent hands; for these garments and the spices would have been of more value to thieves than a naked corpse, whilst the same indications proved that friends had not removed the body. The convincing evidence of resurrection was the incontestible fact that the grave clothes were undisturbed, having merely slumped together when they were evacuated by the body of the Risen Lord.

When the disciples had gone back to their own home, Mary stood without at the door of the sepulchre weeping; and as she wept she stooped down, and looked into the sepulchre. What earnest heart is there, that has not at some time stood there with her, looking down into the grave of ordinances, of spent emotions, of old and sacred memories, seeking everywhere for the Redeemer, who had been once the dearest reality, the one object of love and life? The two sentry-angels, who sat, the one at the head and the other at the feet, where the body of Jesus had lain, sought in vain to comfort her. "Woman," they said, in effect, "there is no need for tears; didst thou but know, couldest thou but understand, thy heart would overflow with supreme joy, and thy tears become smiles." "They have taken away my Lord," she said, "and I know not where they have laid Him." What could angel voices do for her, who longed to hear one voice only? What were the griefs of others in comparison with hers? In an especial sense Jesus was hers! *my* Lord! Had He not cast out from her seven devils?

Some slight movement behind—or perhaps, as Chrysostom finely supposes, because of an expression of love and awe which passed over the angel faces—led her to turn herself back, and she saw Jesus standing, but she knew not that it was Jesus. Supposing Him, in her grief and confusion, to be the gardener, she said that if He knew the whereabout of the body she sought, she would gladly have it removed at her expense: nay, she even volunteered to bear it off herself. Then He spoke the old familiar name with the old intonation and emphasis; and she answered in the country tongue they both knew and loved so well, "Rabboni!" In her rapture she sought to embrace Him, but this must not be; and there was need for Christ to work in her love, with his high art, as the artificer may carve the stone, or engrave some legend on the intaglio. He therefore withdrew Himself, saying, "Touch Me not." To Thomas afterwards He said, "Behold my hands and my side; reach hither thy finger": because there was no danger of his abusing the permission, or leaning unduly on the sensuous and physical. But Mary must learn to exchange the outward for the inward, the transient for the eternal, and to pass from the old fellowship with Jesus as friend and companion into a spiritual relationship which would subsist to all eternity. Therefore Jesus spoke of his ascension, and bade her look upward, and see, gleaming on high, diviner things. So she was prepared for the time when, in the upper room, she should continue steadfastly in prayer, and come nearer to Him whom she loved than ever previously.

Did you ever realize that the intonations of the voice of Jesus, which had passed unimpaired through death, suggest that in that new life, which lies on the other side of death, we shall hear the voices speak again which have been familiar to us from childhood? As is the heavenly, so are they who are heavenly; and as we have borne the image of the earthly, we shall bear that of the heavenly, and shall speak again with those whom we have lost awhile, and they with us.

Mary Magdalene went and told them that had been with Him, as they mourned and wept, that she had seen the Lord, and that He had spoken these things to her. But they, when they had heard that He was alive, and had been seen of her, believed not.

In close succession, the Lord appeared to others of the little group. To the women, as they ran to bring his disciples word. To Peter, whom He encountered on his way back, in lonely astonishment and awe, and restored with gracious words of forgiveness. To the two that walked to Emmaus, in the afternoon, and talked of all that had happened. Finally He appeared to the whole company of the apostles, as they sat at meat. They had carefully shut their doors, since there was every reason to fear that the rumours of the events of the morning would arouse against them the strong hate and fear of the Pharisees. It may be that they were startled by every passing footfall, and every movement on the stair, as when the two returned from Emmaus to tell how Jesus had been made known unto them in the breaking of bread. Then, suddenly, without announcement or preparation, the figure of their beloved Master stood in the midst of them, with the familiar greeting of peace! And, as the sacred historian naïvely puts it, they were terrified and affrighted, and supposed that they were gazing on a spirit. But the Lord allayed their fears, first by showing them his hands and his feet; and next, by partaking of a piece of broiled fish and of a honeycomb.

Evidently He was clothed in the resurrection or spiritual body of which the Apostle Paul speaks. He was not subject to all the laws that govern our physical life. He could pass freely through unopened doors, and at will He could manifest Himself, speak, stand, and walk, or subject Himself to physical sense.

His words were very significant. He began by upbraiding them for their reluctance to believe that He had risen. Again He said, "Peace be unto you"; and accompanied his words with the indication of his wounds—"He showed them his hands and his side." This was the peace of forgiveness, which falls on our conscience-stricken hearts—as the dew distils on the parched heritage. "Look at the wounds of Jesus," cried Staupitz to Luther; and there is no other sign that will give rest to the penitent.

After this He opened their understandings, that they might understand the Scriptures, and showed them that a suffering Messiah was the thought which pervaded the entire Hebrew Scriptures. "Thus it is written, and thus it behoved the Messiah to suffer, and to rise from the dead the third day." What would we not give to have some transcript of that wonderful conversation! With what new eyes should we read the Bible, if only we could know what Jesus said on that occasion!

Next He repeated the "Peace be unto you," and told them that He was sending them forth as the Father had sent Him—"Go ye into all the world, and preach the gospel to every creature." And He added, "Behold, I send the promise of my Father upon you; but tarry ye in the city of Jerusalem, until ye be endued with power from on high." "And these signs shall follow them that believe. In my name shall they cast out demons; they shall speak with new tongues; they shall take up serpents; and if they drink any deadly thing, it shall not hurt them; they shall lay hands on the sick, and they shall recover."

Then, to fit them for this time of waiting, and that the Holy Spirit might prepare them to receive his fuller inflow, the Lord breathed on them and said, "Receive ye the Holy Ghost; Whose soever sins ye remit, they are remitted unto them; whose soever sins ye retain, they are retained." By which He surely meant that there was no other way by which sins would be forgiven and put away than by the preaching of the Gospel, which He now committed to their trust. They are therefore parallel with Peter's statement in after days, "Neither is there salvation in any other: for there is none other name under heaven given among men, by which we must be saved." The Church of God

alone can proclaim to men the conditions of evangelical repentance—
and those who refuse her testimony, and disbelieve her Gospel, expose
themselves to unspeakable condemnation and loss. "There remaineth
no other sacrifice for sin; but a certain looking for of judgment, and
fiery indignation." Refuse Christ, and there is no alternative way of
salvation.

Whatever else is contained in these words, it is quite clear that there
was nothing exclusively reserved to the apostles and their successors,
which is not equally the possession of all who believe; for we know that
the Lord's words were spoken not to the apostles only, but to the two
that had come from Emmaus with burning hearts, and to those who
were in the habit of commingling with the immediate followers of
Christ. "Them that were with them" (Luke xxiv. 33, 35, 36). All had
been witnesses of these things, and all were now to proclaim in his
name repentance and remission of sins among all nations, beginning
at Jerusalem.

Thomas was not there on that memorable occasion. He was always
accustomed to look on the dark side of things. When Jesus proposed
to go into Judea to raise Lazarus, he made sure that there was no
alternative but to die with Him; and when the Master spoke of his
impending absence, he said gloomily, "Lord, we know not whither Thou
goest, and how can we know the way?" He was doubtless at this time
wandering alone over the scenes of that awful tragedy, which had so
deeply imprinted itself on his imagination that he could not forget the
print of the nails, and the wound in his side, and the unlikelihood of
any surviving such treatment as He had received.

When he heard the story of the others, he seemed inclined to treat
them as too credulous; and with the air of superior caution said, that
he must not only see the wounds which death had made, but touch
them with his fingers and hand. Yet we may be grateful for this story.
First, because it wears the aspect of truth. What weaver of an imaginary history would ever have dared to suggest that the resurrection was
impugned by some of Christ's close followers? And, next, because it
shows us that the resurrection was subjected to the severest tests, just
those which we would ourselves apply.

Thomas was left for a whole week. Day after day he heard the
repeated story of Christ's appearances; and waited for Him to come
again; and became more and more confirmed in his sad presentiment
that the whole story was a myth. How great must have been his anguish
during those days, as he tossed between hope and fear, saw on other
faces the light which he might not share, and thought that the Master,
if really living, was neglectful of his friend!

At last Jesus came, not to anathematise or exclude him, not to break
the bruised reed or quench the smoking flax, but to restore him, and to
lift on him the light of his countenance.

He suited Himself to his needs. He stooped to comply with the con ditions that his poor faith had laid down. He was willing to give proofs, over and above those which were absolutely necessary, to win faith. So eager was He to win one poor soul to Himself and blessedness, that He said unto Thomas, "Reach hither thy finger, and behold my hands; and reach hither thy hand, and thrust it into my side; and be not faithless but believing."

I do not suppose that Thomas availed himself of the invitation. It was sufficient to see. Such an act of cold scrutiny would hardly have been compatible with his joyous shout, "My Lord and my God!" Christ's voice and form, omniscience and humility, in taking such trouble to win one to Himself—these were sufficient to convince him, and dispel all doubt.

Ah, Thomas, in that glad outburst of thine, thou reachedst a higher level than all the rest; and thou art not the last man who has seemed a hopeless and helpless wreck, unable to exercise the faith that seemed so natural to others, but who, after a time, under the teaching of Jesus, has been enabled to assume a position to which none of his associates could aspire!

Because he saw, he believed. Too many wait for signs and manifestations, for sensible emotion and conviction: but there is a more excellent way—when we do not see, and yet believe. When there is no star on the bosom of night, no chart on the unknown sea, no lover or friend or interpreter of the ways of God; and when, in spite of all, the soul knows Him whom it has believed, and clings to Him though unseen, and reckons that neither life, nor death, nor principalities, nor powers, can shut out the love of God in Christ. "Blessed are they who have not seen, and yet have believed."

70

THE LAKE OF GALILEE

"Jesus showed Himself again to the disciples at the Sea of Tiberias."
                                                    JOHN xxi. 1.

ALL YE shall be offended because of Me this night; for it is written, I will smite the Shepherd, and the sheep shall be scattered. But after I am risen again, I will go before you into *Galilee*." So had the Chief Shepherd spoken to his sad and anxious followers on the night of his betrayal. They little understood his meaning, and would perhaps have even forgotten the appointment of the rendezvous, unless it had been recalled again and yet again to their minds. But they were not allowed to forget. On the resurrection morn, the angel said to the first visitants at the empty grave: "Go your way, tell his disciples, and Peter, that He goeth before you into *Galilee*; there shall ye see Him, as He said unto you." And as they went to execute this bidding, Jesus Himself met them and said: "Be not afraid; go tell my brethren, that they go into *Galilee*; there shall they see Me." The customs of the Passover Feast forbade their instant compliance with this command, and the Master sanctioned their delay by appearing to them twice whilst they yet lingered in the metropolis. But as soon as it was possible they hastened back to the familiar scenes of their early life and of the Master's ministry.

We cannot fathom all the reasons that led our Lord to make such special arrangements for meeting with them in Galilee; but it was natural that He should wish to associate his risen life with scenes in which He had spent so large a part of his earthly ministry; and there the greatest proportion of his followers were gathered, and He would have the quietest and securest opportunity of meeting with the five hundred brethren at once. The disciples little thought that this was a farewell visit to their homes, and that within a few weeks they must return to Jerusalem, to stay there for a time, and then to wander forth to all lands, from the ancient Indus on the east to the far-famed shores of Tarshish on the west.

I. It was in the early part of May when they returned to Galilee. They were in evident bewilderment as to their next step. What should they do? Should they continue to lead the artificial life which they had taken up during the Master's ministry? That seemed impossible and needless. Should they do nothing but wait? That appeared unwise when life was yet strong in them, and their means of livelihood were scant. It was of course possible to go back to fishing-smacks and fishing-tackle; but should they? And they hesitated.

But one evening came; the fragrance of thyme and rosemary and of a hundred flowers filled the air; the lake lay dimpled in the light of the setting sun; the purple hills that stood sentinel around seemed by their very peacefulness to promise that no storm should imperil the lives of those that ventured on the blue depths. There stood the boats, yonder lay the nets, in those waters were the finny tribes; the old instinct of the fisherman arose in their hearts, and found expression on the lips of the one from whom we should have expected it. "*Peter* said unto them, I go a-fishing." I see no harm in it. The Master never forbade it. He cannot mean us to loiter our time away. We cannot be preachers without Him. I shall go back to the life from which He called me three years ago, and if it pleases Him to come again, He can find us now, as He found us once, among the fishing-tackle.

The proposal met with an instant assent: "We also go with thee." And in a few moments Peter with six others had leapt into a boat, and they were preparing for the night's work with all the enthusiasm with which men throw themselves into a craft which for some time they have disused. But their ardour was soon checked. Hour after hour passed. The lights went out in the hamlets and towns. The chill night damps enwrapped them. The grey morning at last began to break, whilst again and again the nets were hauled up and let down, but in vain; not a single fish had entered them. "That night they caught nothing." Why this non-success? The night was the most favourable time! These men knew the lake well, and were experienced in their craft. They did their best, but they caught nothing! Why was this? Was it a chance? No, it was a providence; it was carefully arranged, disappointing and vexing though it was, by One who was too wise to err, too good to be unkind, and who was preparing to teach them a lesson which should enrich them and the whole Church for ever.

The failure put an arrest on their temporal pursuits. Had they been successful that night, it would have been very much harder for them to renounce the craft for ever; but their non-success made them more willing to give it up, and to turn their thoughts to the evangelisation of the world. Then, too, our Lord surely meant to teach them that whilst they were doing his work, whether that work was waiting or active service, it was not necessary for them to be anxious about their maintenance; He Himself would see to that, though He had, for each meal, to light a fire and prepare it Himself. And, deeper than all this, there were surely great spiritual lessons to be gained respecting the conditions of success in catching men in the net of his Gospel.

It is difficult to understand how a man can call himself a Christian, and how he can face the awful possibilities of life, except he believes that all is ruled by One who loves us with a love that is infinite, and who wields all power on earth and in heaven. If, however, that be your fixed belief, you may find it often severely tested. "I have waited this livelong night; can this be Christ's will?" "I have done my best in vain; can this be Christ's will?" "I have laboured without a single gleam of success; can this be Christ's will?" Yes, most certainly it is. It is his love which is arranging all, in order to teach you some of the sweetest, deepest lessons that ever entered your heart. There is not a cross, a loss, a disappointment, a case of failure in your life, which is not arranged and controlled by the loving Saviour, and intended to teach some lesson which else could never be acquired. Fitfully, curiously, without apparent art or fixed design, is the web of our lives woven; thread seems thrown with thread at random, no orderly pattern immediately appears; but yet of all that web there is not a single thread whose place and colour are not arranged with consummate skill and love.

But what good can failure do? It may shut up a path which you were pursuing too eagerly. It may put you out of heart with things seen and temporal, and give you an appetite for things unseen and eternal. It may teach you your own helplessness, and turn you to trust more implicitly in the provision of Christ. It is clear that Christians have often to toil all night in vain, that Christ may have a background black and sombre enough to set forth all the glories of his interposition.

II. In the morning Jesus stood on the shore, but the disciples knew not that it was Jesus. It was customary for fish-dealers to go down to greet fishers on their return from the night's toil, in order to buy up fish. Such a one now seemed waiting on the sand in the grey light, and his question was such as a fish-dealer might put: "Children, have you any food?" It therefore never occurred to the disciples to think that it was Jesus. And indeed, after the miracle was wrought, it was only the keen eye of love that knew Him to be the Lord. How often is the Lord near us, and we know Him not! He is standing there in the midst of scenes of natural beauty though his foot leaves no impression on the untrodden sand, and his form casts no shadow on the flowers or greensward. He is standing there in that dingy counting-house, or amid the whirr of the deafening machinery, though He fills no space, and utters no word audible to human ears. He is standing there in that home, watching the sick, noting unkindness and rudeness, smiling on the little deeds done for his sake, though none ever heard the floors creak beneath his weight, or saw the doors open to admit his person. How much we miss because we fail to discern Him!

By acting thus He not only taught his disciples the reality of his presence, but He prepared them also for that new kind of life which they were henceforth to lead—a life of faith rather than of sense; a life of spiritual communion rather than of physical fellowship. He kept showing them that, though out of sight, He was still in their midst. By easy stepping-stones He joined Calvary and Olivet. By gentle progressive lessons those who had believed because they had seen were taught to walk by faith, not by sight, and to love One whom they did not see. And thus it came about that they trod no shore however desolate, went to no land however distant, dealt with no people however boorish, without carrying ever with them the thought, The Master is here!

But let me say here that if you would see Christ everywhere, you must be like John, the disciple of love. Love will trace Him everywhere—as dear friends detect each other by little touches that are meaningless to others. Love's quick eye penetrates disguises impenetrable to colder scrutiny. Not for the wise, nor for the few, but for the least that love, is the vision possible that can make a desert isle like Patmos gleam with the light of Paradise itself.

III. How great a difference Christ's directions made! Before He spoke they were disconsolately dragging an empty net to shore. The moment after He had spoken, and they had done his bidding, that net was filled with a shoal of fish so heavy that it was no easy matter to drag it behind the ship.

Great lessons await us here! We, like these, have embarked in a great fishing enterprise—we are fishers of men! Our aim is to catch men alive for Christ our Lord. For this we are ready to toil, to pray, to wait. But our success depends wholly upon our Lord. He will not give it us until we can bear it, and have learnt the lesson of the night of fruitless toil. And if we are to succeed it must be in his realised companionship, and in obedience to his word.

There is a right side of the ship, and a wrong one; there is a time to plant, and a time to be still; to everything there is a season, and a time to every purpose under heaven. We do not know these. If we are left to ourselves, we may cast the net on the left side of the ship at the time when we should be casting it on the right, and on the right side of the ship when we should be casting it on the left. Christ alone knows, and He will teach us exactly how and when to act with the very best results.

IV. Christ's provision for the needs of his servants. I should imagine that the disciples were somewhat anxious about their bodily needs and their supply. They did not realise that if they were doing Christ's work, Christ would look after their real needs. Christ let them meet with non-success to show how fruitless their toil was. And in the morning, when He stood on the shore, He filled their nets with fish, and called them to fire and bread and fish, to show how easily He could supply all their need. Of course this does not apply to all promiscuously, but it does apply to those who give up time, and labour, and earthly toil, for the cause of Christ. If they are really called to the work, Christ seems to say to them: "Do the best you can for Me, and do not try in addition to make up for your time and labour by night work—you had better use the night for necessary rest; the longest night spent in unbelieving labour will not profit; but I in a single moment in the morning can more than make up to you for all you have spent." Christ never lets us be in his debt. If we lend him a boat for pulpit, He weighs it down to the gunwale. If we give Him time, He makes up what we have lost. If we seek first the kingdom of God and his righteousness, He sees that all things else are added. It is vain for you to rise up early and to sit up late, to eat the bread of carefulness. He giveth his beloved when they sleep.

What delicate attentions to these men! Christ knew that they were drenched with spray, chilled with the keen air, and so He prepared a fire—so thoughtful is He of the tiniest matters that will alleviate discomfort and increase our pleasure. At the same time He is frugal of the miraculous. He will deal lavishly in miracles so long as needed, but not an inch beyond. He might have created fish enough on that fire to supply them all, but that was needless so long as a hundred and fifty and three great fishes lay within easy reach; so Jesus said, "Bring of the fish which ye have now caught."

When Peter heard John say, "It is the Lord," true to his character he sprang into the sea and swam to shore, leaving the rest to drag the heavy net as best they could. Now he seems to remember his failure to bear his share in the toil; so he goes to the margin of the lake, lands the net, counts its contents, examines the meshes, to find them unbroken, and then returns with fish enough to make a breakfast for them all. It was only when all this was done that Jesus said to them, "Come and dine." Then He came forward and took the bread and fish, and gave to them. All were convinced that it was Jesus, but they were dumb with amazement and awe; they would have liked to ask questions, but they felt that they need not; their senses were convinced almost in spite of themselves. "None of the disciples durst ask Him, Who art Thou? knowing that it was the Lord."

This, says John, was the third time that Jesus had shown Himself; not literally the third time that He had shown Himself to anyone; but the third time that He had shown Himself to the disciples assembled in any considerable number. The first time was in the evening of the resurrection day; the second, when Thomas was there; the third, in the incident here recorded.

We all need our rest times, our times of learning, our times of fellowship with Jesus. Happy are we when Jesus says, "Come and dine."

71

PETER'S LOVE AND WORK

"Thou knowest that I love Thee. . . . Feed my lambs."—JOHN xxi. 15.

THAT miraculous catch of fish on which we have dwelt was a parable to the disciples of the kind of work in which they were thenceforward to be engaged. They were to catch men. But there was one amongst them who must have wondered much how he would fare, and what part he would take when that work was recommenced. Might he have a share in it? He would seem to have forfeited all right. With oaths and curses he had thrice denied that he belonged to Jesus. He had given grievous occasion to the enemy to blaspheme. He had failed in a most important part of an apostle's character.

True, he had repented with bitter tears, and had received a message from the empty tomb; on that Easter morn he had heard his forgiveness spoken by the lips of his Lord, and he would not have exchanged that forgiveness for an imperial crown: but he was not quite at ease. His uneasiness betrayed itself in his plunge into the water to swim to Christ's feet, and in his rush to drag the net to the shore. He wished to be restored to the position in the Apostolate which his sin had forfeited; not because of the honour which it would bring, but because nothing less would assure him of the undiminished confidence and the entire affection of Jesus.

The Lord read his heart; and when the morning meal was done, He singled him out from the rest of his disciples, and asked him three times if he loved Him, and then thrice gave him the injunction to feed his flock. In addressing him our Lord calls him by his old name, Simon Bar Jonas, not by his new name, Peter; as if to remind him that he had been living the life of nature rather than of grace.

In considering this subject, it will be convenient to speak of the question; the answer; the command.

I. OUR LORD'S SEARCHING QUESTION—"Lovest thou Me?"

It is a very remarkable question.—We should have expected the inquiry, Dost thou believe Me? Wilt thou obey Me? Art thou prepared to carry out my plans? But lo! the risen Lord seems not anxious about aught of these, and only asks for love, and this from the rugged, manly, headstrong Peter. Yet as we hear the question asked, we realise it is the true one. He who has asked it has struck the right method of dealing with men; and if He only get the love, He will get easily enough the faith and the obedience as well.

373

In this startling question you have unbared to you the distinctive feature which makes Christianity what it is, and which makes it different from all other religions which have flung their clouds or their rainbows over human spirits. It is the religion of love: and a man may speak with a seraph's burning tongue to defend Christianity; he may give his goods to feed the poor in obedience to the precepts of Christianity; he may even burn at the stake rather than renounce Christianity as his intellectual creed; but if he does not love, he is no Christian. If a man love not the Lord Jesus, he is anathema.

But if only there be love—love to God, love to man—then though there may be many deficiencies in head and heart, there is the one prime evidence of Christianship. It was on such grounds that the Rev. Adam Gibb of Edinburgh once acted. He had once or twice dissuaded a young woman from joining the church, deeming her ill-informed, and unable to answer elementary questions; and on his third refusal she answered, "Weel, weel, sir, I mayna, an' I dinna, ken sae muckle as mony; but when ye preach a sermon aboot my Lord and Saviour, I fin' my heart going out to Him, like linseed out of a bag." Anyone who has observed the process will know how lifelike the illustration was, and will not wonder that Mr. Gibb admitted her, and that she lived to be one of the fairest members of his church.

It is a universal question.—Its universality suggests that in Christ there is something universally lovable, and that everyone has the power of loving Him, if only the rubbish is removed which chokes the springs of affection. There are different shades in love—the love of gratitude, where the rescued spirit sings the praise of Him who took it from the terrible pit and miry clay; the love of complacency, with which the holy soul admires Him who is fairer than the sons of men, and dwells with rapture on his majestic beauty and endearing goodness; the love of friendship, in which by constant intercourse a deep attachment arises between the confiding soul and the all-sufficient Saviour. And there are as many methods of manifestation of love as there are different temperaments. With some, it is silent; with others, it speaks. With some, it sits listening at Christ's feet; with others, it hurries to and fro to serve. With some it is exuberant and enthusiastic; with others, it is still and deep. But whatever be the shade or the evidence, in each Christian heart there must be love to Christ, and the heart must be willing to give up its throne to the reign of Jesus as its Lord.

Often it carries a special emphasis.—Peter had grievously sinned. Jesus could not pass it by in utter silence. For his disciples' sake and his own, it was necessary to allude to, and to probe it. But each was performed as gently as possible. Thrice he had been warned, thrice he had denied, and now thrice shall he be asked if he really loves. And in asking him if he loved Him more than the rest, our Lord surely reminded him of his boast that if all the rest forsook Him, he never would. Christ delicately reminded him that his actions had not been consistent with his professions, at the same time giving him an opportunity of wiping out the record of failure by a new avowal of attachment. Thus He deals with us still. He does not drag our secret sins to light before our brethren and friends, and parade them before the sun; but He asks with deep meaning if we love Him, leaving conscience to apply the question. And is there not good reason for Him to ask it? How you have forgotten Him! You have been occupied with the world, pleasure, or even sin. And there is nothing that breaks us down so quickly as this. Peter was grieved. An old man, eighty years of age, reared in connection with a church, once found his way to the penitent form, crying, "I've come here to be broke." Ah, there is nothing that so breaks us down as this!

The question must be asked as a preliminary to service.—Thrice He asked Peter, as if to be perfectly sure ere He sent him forth on a shepherd's work. All the self-denial, patience, tenderness, and delicacy of love are needed, as the Lord knew well, in dealing with men, who are naturally uninteresting, or perhaps repulsive; and hence our Lord saw the necessity that there should be love. But how could there be love to *them*? It was impossible to expect it; and so Christ introduced Himself, saying, in effect, "Dost thou love Me? Henceforth there will be little opportunity of doing anything for Me; thou canst not now shelter Me in thy home, or let Me use thy fishing-boats, or share my toils; but as thou lovest Me, and desirest to show it, expend it on those whom I love, for whom I died, and whom I long to see brought into my fold. If only thou lovest, thou art fit for this."

You may not be naturally fitted to teach children, or shepherd adults; but if you love Christ, you will do better than those more cultured. It is not science, nor intellect, nor eloquence, that wins souls; but love to Christ overflowing in love to man. Love will give you a delicacy of perception, an ingenuity, a persuasiveness, which no heart shall be able to resist. Love will reconcile the accomplished scholar to a life among savages, and will carry the refined and cultured lady up to the sultry attic, or down to the damp and airless cellar. Love will bear all, believe all, hope all, endure all, if only it may win wild wandering sheep for Christ.

II. THE CONTRITE REPLY.—*It was very humble.*—Peter did not now boast that he excelled the rest, he did not even dare to stand sponsor for his own affection; he threw the matter back on his Lord's omniscience, and without mentioning the degree more or less, he said simply, "Thou knowest all things, Thou knowest that I love Thee." There is a delicate shade of meaning in the Greek. The words translated *love* are not the same. Jesus asks Peter if he cherishes towards

Him love—spiritual, holy, heavenly. Peter declines to use that term, and contents himself with speaking of a simpler, more personal, more human affection. If I do not give Thee that love which is thy due as Son of God, I at least give Thee that which befits Thee as Son of Man.

There are many who could not go even as far as this. Yet here are tests of love! Would you be able to enjoy heaven if Christ were not there? Do you feel drawn out to Him in service? Do you do things which you certainly would not do except for his sake? Are you glad to hear of Him in sermon or talk, so that there is a warm feeling rising to Him at the mention of his name? Does it cost you pain to hear Him evil spoken of? Do you sorrow that you do not love Him more? Then you can challenge Him, saying, "Despite my worldliness, my faithlessness, my sins, Thou knowest all things, Thou knowest that I love Thee."

It was very confident.—"Thou knowest all things." Jesus is omniscient. He can see with microscopic eye the lichen on the grey stone, the enamel on the shell, the modest flower; and He can see the love that is in the disciple's heart, though it be but a tiny seed.

When we sin, we are tempted to believe that we have no love to Christ. But let this incident encourage us. It is impossible for any true lover of Christ to go on in a course of sin, but quite possible for him to be betrayed into a single sin. And if that has been your case, do not shun the Master; He still believes that is is possible for you to love, and He is willing even to reinstate you in his blessed service. Who is there that does not long to speak more confidently of his love to Christ? Cease, then, to think of your love to Christ, dwell much on his love to you—"He loved me, He gave Himself for me." Think of its unwearied patience, its delicacy, its tenderness. Consider the character of Christ as unfolded in the New Testament. Commune with Christ as friend with friend. Above all, put away from your heart all that might grieve Him, and throw it open to the Holy Ghost, with prayer that He would shed Christ's love abroad. Then, almost unconsciously, it will arise; though it may not become palpable till some great crisis calls you to the front, and demands some heroic sacrifice, which you will give, not feeling it great.

III. THE DIVINE COMMAND.—In the miracle Peter had been commissioned to do the work of a fisherman, that is, of an evangelist; here he is commissioned to do the work of a shepherd, that is, of a pastor. Feeding and tending lambs and sheep. It is not everyone that is able to care for the sheep; but there is hardly anyone who loves, that cannot feed or tend the lambs. And even if you shrink from the former, what good reason have you to refuse to comply with the latter?

There are in this land hundreds of young lives whom the morning light awakes to hunger, filth, and wretchedness, and whom the evening shadows limit to rooms in which you would not care to keep your dogs. They are growing up without the least sense of decency, or the slightest reverence for God. Their existence is one long struggle against the constituted guardians of society; or if they do not resist, they are always eluding. In addition to these are the children of our homes and families and schools. *"Feed my lambs!"*

It is worthy of note that two Greek words are used in these injunctions. In the first and last, the Master says simply, Feed. In the middle He adds, Do the work of a shepherd. So that the lover of Christ has not fulfilled all his duty, when he has given his sacred lesson or instruction: he must go further, and be prepared to act as shepherd.

72

THE LIFE-PLAN OF PETER AND JOHN

"What is that to thee? follow thou Me."—JOHN xxi. 22.

WE ARE standing on the eastern shore of the Lake of Galilee. The morning breeze blows fresh in our faces; the tiny wavelets run up with a silvery ripple, and die on the white sand; across the expanse of water the white buildings of Tiberias and Capernaum gleam forth. With gunwale all wet and slippery a fishing-smack is drawn up on the deserted shore; near it the nets unbroken, although they had been heavy with finny spoils; yonder the remnants of a fisherman's breakfast and the dying embers of a fire.

The Master has just reinstated his erring apostle and friend, and proceeded to describe the death by which he was ultimately to glorify God: "Verily, verily, I say unto thee, when thou wast young, thou girdedst thyself, and walkedst whither thou wouldest; but when thou shalt be old, thou shalt stretch forth thy hands, and another shall gird thee, and carry thee whither thou wouldest not."

How different this forecast to what Peter would have chosen for himself! What a contrast between that yielding to the will of another, and that impetuous nature which so constantly betrayed itself! Take, for instance, the occasions that are offered in this chapter. As soon as he hears John's suggestion that the Lord is standing on the beach, he lets go the fish that he had spent all night to catch, the nets which it cost hours to make, the boat which was probably his own property, binds his fisher's coat about him, plunges into the water, and never rests till he has cast himself at his Master's feet. As soon as the Lord expresses his desire to mingle some of the recent haul with his own preparations for breakfast, he springs up, hastens to the margin of the sea, drags the net to land, counts its contents, and brings specimens to the little group gathered about the Master. Every movement so quick and energetic! To wish, is to act! To desire a thing, to do it! He makes us think of young manhood in all its vigorous, nervous life.

The Lord did not damp or repress his fervid disciple. He looked on him, to borrow the thought of another, with tender pity; as a parent, who has passed through many of the world's darkest places, beholds the child who is speaking of what he expects life to bring. Fresh from his own agony, the Lord knew how different a temper that would be which had been induced by prolonged suffering and patience: and He knew how necessary it was that that temper should be induced in his beloved disciple, so that he might become a pillar in his Church, and the tender sympathetic writer of that First Epistle, which is so saturated with a spirit of tender patience and sympathy for all who suffer.

Having uttered these cautionary words our Lord seems to have moved away, bidding Peter follow—a mandate which was intended to carry a deeper meaning. John followed them some few steps in the rear. Hearing footsteps, Peter turned and saw him, and with a touch of unworthy curiosity, hardly compatible with the seriousness of the statement Jesus had just made, said, "Lord, and what shall this man do?"

The question was objectionable. It savoured too much of Peter's old, hasty, forward self. The Lord would not become a mere fortune-teller to gratify his inquisitiveness. He put a check, therefore, on the unbefitting inquiry, and yet, in rebuking, answered it: "If I will that he tarry till I come, what is that to thee? follow thou Me."

It is not easy to explain the import of Christ's reply. Some have interpreted it as meaning Christ's coming in death. But this can hardly be; for He would as certainly come to Peter dying amid the agony of martyrdom, as to John dying in a peaceful old age. Surely the period referred to must have been the fall of Jerusalem, only forty years distant, and to which our Lord so often referred as one phase at least of his coming. Then the old economy would fall and pass away; Christianity assume a world-wide importance; and the cross become one of the mightiest factors of human history.

When those words were repeated to them, some of the disciples interpreted them as meaning that John should not die, but they did not convey that meaning to John himself; he only saw in them a general intimation that his lot was in his Master's hands, and in any case would be a very different one from Peter's.

I. Our Life-Plan is Fashioned by the Will of Christ.—What royalty there is in those words, *If I will!* If Jesus were less than divine, how blasphemous they would appear! What arrogance to suppose that He could regulate the time and manner of life or death! Yet how natural it is to hear Him speak thus. No one starts or is surprised, and in that calm acquiescence there is a testimony to the homogeneousness of Christ's character. It is of one piece throughout. There is a perfect consistency between his acts and words.

The ancients thought of their *lives* as woven on the loom of spiteful fates, whom they endeavoured to humour by calling euphonious names. The materialist supposes that his life is the creature of circumstances, a rudderless ship in a current, mere flotsam and jetsam on the wave. The Christian knows that the path of his life has been *prepared* for him to walk in; and that its sphere, circumstances, and character are due to the thought and care of Him who has adapted it to our temperament and capabilities, to repress the worst, and educate the best within us.

We are ignorant of the place and mode of our *death*. Our grave may be in ocean depths with storm-blasts as our dirge, or the desert-waste with the sands as our winding-sheets. Like that of Moses in a foreign land, unknown and untended; or within the reach of friendly hands, which will keep it freshly decked with evergreens. But wherever it may be, it must befall as Christ has willed. We may die by some lingering agony, or the gentle slackening of life's silver cord. The temple may be shattered by an earthquake, or taken down stone by stone. But whether the one or the other, it will be determined by his will. He who makes the hue of each fading leaf different from that of any other in the forest, has some new trait of godliness, some fresh feature of grace to illustrate and enforce in the dying hour; it is therefore written, "Precious in the sight of the Lord is the death of his saints."

There is no lasting happiness, no comfort, no peace, to be had in this life, apart from the belief that the so-called trifles, as well as the apparently greater incidents of existence, are included in the circumference of Christ's will, either executive or permissive. But in speaking thus, I discriminate between ourselves and our surroundings. I am speaking more particularly of the latter, and urge that even where they are apparently moulded by the carelessness or malignity of others, yet these are, unconsciously indeed, but really, effecting what He predetermined should be done. "If I will."

Bind this to your heart. It may be appointed for you to die in early prime, when the purpose of your life seems unfulfilled; or to live a sequestered life, banished to the Patmos of exile and suffering, dying after long years. But in any case, your Saviour has contrived and adjusted all. And He will send the Angel of his Presence with you, to help you, and to bring you to the place that He has prepared.

II. THE LIFE-COURSE OF ANY IS DETERMINED BY THE PECULIARITIES OF CHARACTER AND SERVICE.—Christ tells us that we are destined to a long future; and in doing so gives us the only satisfactory clue to the mystery of existence. If there be no life beyond death, life is a maze of endless wandering, to which there is no clue. But if there be—and after all there is no *if* in it—we can easily understand that the present needs to be carefully adjusted to our nature and our future niche in the great universe of God, that we may be able, to the farthest limit, to realise our Master's anticipations.

There is a conspicuous illustration of this before us. Peter was to be the apostle of sufferers, and write a letter, which should help, as perhaps no other writing has helped, all sufferers to the end of time; but he could never have penned it apart from the fiery trials through which his character was softened and sanctified. How could he have spoken of the humility, meekness, and patience, of the suffering believer, had he not drunk deeply of the cup of suffering for himself and lived in constant anticipation of the martyr-death of which the Lord spoke?

John's work, on the other hand, was to declare, as he does in the Book of Revelation, that Jesus is the Living One, unchanged and unchanging, the King of earth and heaven. And how could he have produced that marvellous work, and received and reported those sublime visions, if he had not lingered on, in loneliness and exile, till Jerusalem had fallen before Titus and his legions, the Temple been destroyed, and the Jews scattered to every nation under heaven?

Neither of these men understood at the time what he was being prepared for. But as each now from heaven reviews the work he did, and the way in which he was prepared for doing it; as each compares the discipline through which he passed with the peculiarities of the people he was to address, and the testimony he was to deliver, he must be full of glad acknowledgments of the perfect adaptation of means to ends, of instrumentalities to results.

And what is manifestly true of them is equally so of each of us. Not always in this world, but in the next, we shall discern the admirable fitness of the discipline through which we passed, to prepare us for our position and ministry both here and hereafter.

> "Great and marvellous are thy works,
> O Lord God the Almighty;
> Righteous and true are thy ways,
> Thou King of the ages."

III. WHILST GOD IS WORKING OUT OUR LIFE-PLAN, WE MUST GIVE OURSELVES TO PRACTICAL OBEDIENCE.—"Follow thou Me." The Master reiterated this command, both when He told Peter his destiny, and when his apostle was prying into secrets with which he had no immediate concern. Whatever threatens us, looming in the future, we must not be deterred from following our Master; and we are not to waste our time in speculation as to matters which lie beyond our ken, but apply ourselves to the practical duties which lie ready to our hand.

But what is it to follow Christ? It is not to live an oriental life beneath these northern skies, nor wear an eastern garb, nor speak in the Hebrew tongue. A man might do all these, and in addition wander like Him, homeless and outcast, through the land, and yet not follow in his steps. No! Following Jesus means our identification in the principles that underlay his life, in his devotion and prayer, in his absolute compliance with God's will, in his constant service of mankind, in the sweetness and gentleness and strength of his personal character. There is no path of legitimate duty into which we are called to go, in which He does not precede; for when He putteth forth his own sheep, He goeth before them, and his sheep follow. As of old, his disciples saw Him going before them ascending up to Jerusalem, and they followed Him; there is no path of arduous duty and suffering in which He does not still precede.

Following Christ involves almost certain suffering at first. When Peter asked what they would have, who had left all to follow Jesus, the Master did not hesitate to say that the bitter herb of suffering would mingle with all the dishes with which their table might be spread: and when James and John tried to bespeak the right and left seats of the throne, He spoke of the cup and baptism of pain. But afterwards, when the cross and grave are passed, then the fullness of joy and the pleasures which are at God's right hand for evermore!

We may follow Christ, and yet our paths diverge. Peter and John had been close friends. In them, the binary stars of love and zeal, labour and rest, action and contemplation, revolved in a common orbit. Together at the grave, in the boat, in the temple, in prison; but their outward fellowship was not permitted to continue; perhaps if it had, it would have been too absorbing. It is in silence and solitude that spirits attain their complete beauty, and so the Master is sometimes obliged to say to us, "What is that to thee? follow thou Me."

In following Jesus, with the shadow of the cross always on his spirit, Peter learned to sympathise with his Master's anticipation of death, which in earlier years had been incomprehensible to him, and had led him to say, "That be far from Thee, Lord"; and it gave him finally the opportunity of fulfilling his first resolve to go with Him to prison and to death. We often think ourselves strong to do and suffer long before patience has done her perfect work. We rush impetuously forward, and are overwhelmed. Then our Master has to lead us about, to take us round by another and longer route, to train us by toils and tears and teachings, till, hopeless of our own strength and confident in his, in our old age we cry, "I must put off this my tabernacle, even as our Lord Jesus Christ hath showed me."

If the old legend is true, Peter was crucified with his head downwards, because he felt unworthy to be so like his Lord—following Him with humility and reverence. But whatever befalls us, whatever be the nature of our experience in life or death, let it be our one aim to glorify God. "And the God of all grace, who hath called us unto his eternal glory in Christ, after that we have suffered a little while, shall Himself perfect, stablish, strengthen us. To Him be the dominion for ever and ever. Amen."

73

BACK TO THE FATHER

"And there are also many other things which Jesus did."
JOHN xxi. 25.

ONCE MORE, as we learn both from the Gospel according to Matthew and the First Epistle to Corinthians, our Lord met the eleven apostles, together with some five hundred brethren beside, on a mountain in Galilee, chosen partly for retirement and seclusion, and partly that all might see Him. The majority of these were alive when Paul wrote. "And Jesus came and spake unto them, saying, All power is given unto Me in heaven and in earth. Go ye therefore, and teach all nations, baptizing them into the name of the Father, and of the Son, and of the Holy Ghost, teaching them to observe all things whatsoever I have commanded you; and lo, I am with you alway, even unto the end of the age."

Only once or twice beside did the Lord appear. He was seen of James, and this interview seems to have determined this saintly man, who was his own brother, either through a previous marriage of Joseph, or as born after his own birth, of Mary, to become a humble follower of Him with whose existence his own was so mysteriously blended. Then He appeared once more to all the apostles, and being assembled with them commanded them to wait in Jerusalem till the promise of the Father was fulfilled, that He would send them another Comforter, the Holy Ghost. "For John," He said, "truly baptized with water; but ye shall be baptized with the Holy Ghost not many days hence."

There seems to have been an interval at that point, during which the disciples had time to think over what the Lord had said. It had suggested to them the idea of the setting-up of the Messianic kingdom, which had always been viewed as coincident with the bestowal of the Holy Ghost. "Lord," they said when they came together again, "wilt Thou restore at this time the kingdom to Israel?" The Lord would not gratify their curiosity, and at that moment it would have been useless to combat and explain their erroneous views. This must be left to the education of time, and circumstance, and that same Spirit. These things were kept in the Father's secret counsels. It was not for them to know, but they should receive power.

Then, with the tenacity of affection for the scenes of his former life, He led them out as far as Bethany. And when they had reached the beloved spot, associated with so many sacred and tender memories,

He lifted up his hands and blessed them; and while He blessed them, He was parted from them and a cloud became both veil and chariot, parting them and receiving Him out of their sight.

Thence He ascended far above all principality, power, might, and dominion, through all heavens to the right hand of the Father, there to pursue his life of ministry and prayer for men, and specially for those He loved. And angels stood beside the little group of lovers, assuring them of his return in the same manner as they had seen Him go. And they worshipped Him, and went forth, and preached everywhere, the Lord working with them, and confirming their word with signs following.